SALISBURY
1830–1903

HATFIELD HOUSE : EAST WING

The large middle window on the ground floor is that of the Prime Minister's study, in which he did much of his official work. His laboratory was in the basement immediately below it.

[*Frontispiece*

SALISBURY

1830–1903

PORTRAIT OF A STATESMAN

---

by A. L. KENNEDY

M.C., M.A.

★

LONDON

JOHN MURRAY, ALBEMARLE STREET, W.

KRAUS REPRINT CO.

New York

1971

To
S. D. K.

L.C. 53-29789

First published 1953

Reprinted with the permission of the original publisher
KRAUS REPRINT CO.
A U.S. Division of Kraus-Thomson Organization Limited

Printed in U.S.A.

CONTENTS

PART I

APPRENTICESHIP

PART II

ACHIEVEMENT

CONTENTS

ILLUSTRATIONS

The " S " on the cover of this book is a transcript of Lord Salisbury's initialing of official documents submitted to him. He always initialed in red ink.

PREFACE

The shunning of publicity which was characteristic of Lord Salisbury in his lifetime has survived him ; no recent Prime Minister of his calibre has been so neglected by biographers. There is, of course, the authoritative and indispensable Life by his daughter, Lady Gwendolen Cecil ; but she died when she had only reached (in four volumes) the end of his second Ministry, leaving the last ten years of his career still untouched. Several minor works appeared just before or after he died—they are mentioned in the Bibliography ; but apart from the model of concise biography in the *D.N.B.* by his nephew Algernon Cecil there is no up-to-date complete Life. Nor have I tried to write a complete Life ; that would require—as Lady Gwendolen's work proves—at least six volumes, for more material has been made available since she died ; and, as she explained, she herself made very little use of Foreign Office documents, finding most of what she needed in the abundant papers at Hatfield. It has seemed to me—and to my publishers—important to keep my book to one volume ; and if the person of whom one is writing has been Prime Minister three times and Secretary of State for Foreign Affairs four times it is manifestly impossible fully to cover his activities in one volume. The need for selection has therefore been more than ordinarily severe ; and I have aimed to make this book not so much a Life as a Portrait. I try to convey the man, his character and his work—but not the whole of his work. I have chosen those episodes of his private and official life which seem to me to be the most important and to illustrate most clearly his political methods and his philosophy of life. I have therefore had to leave out much that should find a place in the full story of Lord Salisbury's achievements. Especially has it been impossible to deal comprehensively with diplomatic negotiations in which several countries were involved. I have had to confine myself mainly to Lord Salisbury's own part in them. I am appalled when I look at the number of my unused notes.

I have always wished to write a book on Lord Salisbury, and

for that reason have questioned everybody who ever knew him whom I have had the good fortune to meet—beginning with my own father, who served under him in the diplomatic service. Among others who have helped me in this way, and to whom I am profoundly grateful for telling me all they knew, have been Lord Crewe, Lord Newton, Lord Perth, Sir Edward Alderson (his nephew) and Mrs. Edgar Dugdale, who are all now dead ; and among those who are still happily living Lady Milner, Algernon Cecil, J. B. Atkins, and most of all Lord Cecil of Chelwood. To him, indeed, I am unable sufficiently to express my thanks, for in speech and in writing he has given me from his intimate knowledge an unrivalled picture of his father at work and at home.

To Lord Salisbury's grandson, the present Lord Salisbury, I am equally indebted. He most kindly placed at my disposal unpublished memoranda left behind by Lady Gwendolen, and gave me permission to have photographs taken in the private wing of Hatfield where the family now lives and in which the Prime Minister did so much of his work. The present Lord Salisbury, as also Lord Cecil, has seen some of my chapters in typescript ; but no alteration has been either requested or made ; and naturally I am solely responsible for the views expressed in these pages. I am most grateful to Mr. Anthony Eden for allowing two photographs to be taken inside the Foreign Office.

I greatly appreciate the courtesy of Messrs. Hodder and Stoughton in agreeing to let me quote from Lady Gwendolen Cecil's volumes, without which indeed it would be impossible even now to write the story of her father's life.

I have also to express my deep appreciation to the Quai d'Orsay for allowing me to make use of French official documents which are still secret, but which are destined for publication at no distant date. And I have had the advantage of going through the papers which Sir Henry Layard's executors left with John Murray half a century ago, copies of which are also to be found in the British Museum. My thanks are also due to Lady Winifred Gore, Sir Dougal Malcolm, Mr. Edward Salmon and Mr. Mark Barrington-Ward for help given, and to the officials of the London Library and the Public Library at Leeds ; nor least to Mr. Frederick Adam, who very kindly consented to read my proofs.

PREFACE

One word more. I express my complete concurrence with the opinion expressed by Sir Duff Cooper (Lord Norwich) in his *Talleyrand* that asterisks, numerals and footnotes " tease the eye and disfigure the page ". I have therefore limited them to the indispensable minimum. Wherever possible I have made my source appear clearly in the text ; but in addition I have added many pages of notes to every chapter, including references to the source of information ; and a general bibliography is printed at the end of the notes.

PRINCIPAL DATES IN LORD SALISBURY'S LIFE

Aet.

1830	February 3	—	Birth.
1853	August	23	Election to House of Commons.
1857	July 11	27	Marriage to Georgina Alderson.
1860	April 1	30	First of his 32 articles contributed to the *Quarterly Review*.
1865	June 14	35	Became Lord Cranborne on death of his elder brother.
1866	July 6	36	Secretary of State for India and Privy Councillor.
1867	March 4	37	Resignation.
1868	April 12	38	Became Marquess of Salisbury on death of his father.
1874	February 21	44	Secretary of State for India.
1878	April 2	48	Secretary of State for Foreign Affairs.
1880	April	50	Out of Office.
1881	May 9	51	Leader of the Opposition in the House of Lords.
1885	June 23	55	Prime Minister and Secretary of State for Foreign Affairs.
1886	January 28	55	Resignation.
1886	July 26	56	Prime Minister (for second time).
1887	January 14	56	Secretary of State for Foreign Affairs (for third time).
1892	August 12	62	Resignation.
1895	June 29	65	Prime Minister (for third time) and Foreign Secretary (for fourth time).
1900	November	70	General Election and reconstruction of his Ministry. Relinquished the Foreign Office to Lord Lansdowne.
1902	July 11	72	Final resignation.
1903	August 22	73	Death.

LORD SALISBURY'S
PRAYER FOR THE NATION

O God, the God of all righteousness, mercy and love, give us all grace and strength to conceive and execute whatever may be for Thine honour and the welfare of the Nation, that we may become at last, through the merits and intercession of our common Redeemer, a great and a happy, because a wise and understanding people ; to Thy honour and glory.

AMEN.

From *A Chain of Prayer across the Ages*, S. F. Fox (John Murray).

PART I
APPRENTICESHIP

HATFIELD—ETON—AUSTRALIA

There are not many houses in England which have descended from the original builder through three centuries in direct line to the present owner ; fewer which have passed without deviation from father to son or grandson : fewer still there are of which the builder himself, and his father before him, were First Ministers of the Crown in their day, and of which the last four owners, carrying on the tradition of public service, have each held ministerial office. All this is true of Hatfield House in Hertfordshire. It was built by the first Lord Salisbury of the present line, Robert Cecil, himself the son of the great Burghley. Cecil had inherited from his father the great house of Theobald's, in the same county, to which he invited King James I. The monarch took such a liking to it that he insisted on having it for himself. He handed over to Cecil in exchange the old palace of Hatfield, of which the new owner proceeded to demolish all but the one wing which still stands. King James also bestowed on his favourite Minister, who served him well, the Barony of Cecil, the Viscounty of Cranborne and the Earldom of Salisbury ; and Cecil, amassing wealth as well as titles, proceeded to design for himself a better house to live in than the old Palace which he had perhaps rather reluctantly accepted instead of his former home. It took him five years to build the mansion he wanted ; and in the very year in which it was ready to be occupied, 1612, its owner died ; so the second Lord Salisbury was the first to live there. He set a standard of lavish entertainment which remained a tradition of the house till recent years and brought men and women renowned in other lands as well as in England to stay there. Many of them gave valuable presents in return, or presented their portraits ; and as the owners were themselves men of taste the house soon became filled with the arts and graces of life, all that the most gifted painters, sculptors, wood-carvers, furniture-makers and writers could supply. In mid-career the Cecils lost their wealth. Only one differed from his predecessors and descendants in being a roysterer and a squanderer, and he preferred to live in another of the family residences, Quickswood, in north Hertfordshire. But the family fortune was dissipated, and Hatfield remained in a neglected condition until his successors, reverting to type, gradually re-created its glory by plain living, thrifty husbandry and fortunate marriages. By the time the subject of this book, Robert Arthur Talbot Gascoyne-Cecil, was born in 1830 (on February 3) the family had fully re-established its position in the county.

Robert Cecil grew up, then, in a house from the walls of which history looked down on him, and with a background of rather despotic but beneficent landlordism ; for with the exception of the one scapegrace already mentioned his family had maintained the standard of responsibility and public service which had characterized the best county magnates of the eighteenth century. And to Robert in his youth the historical associations of the place made a stronger appeal than its function as the centre of county life. On every side he saw, besides the portraits of earlier Cecils, pictures of European monarchs and foreign ambassadors, which sent his thoughts roaming through the vicissitudes of other lands besides his own. And they taught him to think early of Britain as a whole, as one State among many, as a nation with its part to play in the world. He got a sense of historical perspective and checked the events of the day against those of the past. King Edward VI had lived in the old palace . . . Princess Elizabeth had been a prisoner there . . . James I had planted the mulberry trees which still stand, propped by succouring posts, in the garden on the west side of the house. Above all, the house was full of books and of documents ; and the library became Robert's favourite haunt. He was a studious, delicate boy, but he loved to spend long hours there, reading hard, not browsing ; and deciphering the handwriting of his ancestors, Burghley and the first Lord Salisbury, so many of whose original letters are there preserved.

But if the visions of history which Hatfield evokes appealed to him most, Robert Cecil could not but be affected by the impact of country life which played upon him. His father was the most conscientious of landowners, to whom responsibility and direction and local administration were a right and a duty. He and his like were a recognized ruling class, and their normal activities brought them into contact not only with their dependents, for whose welfare they felt personally responsible, but with men of varied rank and occupation all over the country. These country gentlemen absorbed the art of government in their daily occupations. There is the statesmanship of the land and the statesmanship of the city—theirs was that which gave preference to stability and continuity, to slow and sure rhythm as of the seasons, to variation without violence, to controlling and directing nature but never opposing it. The toil of the factory with its curse of monotony was alien to them ; they knew nothing of turning night into day by artificial device. It did not occur to them to try to alter human nature or push it about like the hands of a clock. Britain has been called a nation of gardeners ; and husbandry and gardening are no bad training for statesmanship. They impart the sense of time and growth, and prove the truth of the French proverb, " Le temps respecte peu ce que l'on fait sans lui."

2

It was in this traditional environment that Robert Cecil grew up, and he may to that extent be said to have been the culmination of an English type. After his death, Winston Churchill wrote that " a definite and recognizable period in English history " had come to an end when he finally resigned office in 1902.* The Prime Ministers of two centuries of British history had been drawn from the same class and much the same environment. Lord Mersey, in his *Prime Ministers of Britain*, shows statistically that the typical Prime Minister between 1700 and 1900 was born in the peerage, brought up in the country, educated at Eton and Oxford (except when he emerged from Harrow and Cambridge), and elected to the House of Commons at the age of 25. Married four years later, he came into office at 32. At 48 he entered the House of Lords and at 50 became the leader of a government. Relinquishing office at 60, he died at about the age of threescore years and ten, leaving a family. Lord Salisbury followed this course with remarkable closeness, though he first attained ministerial rank rather later than the

* *Thoughts and Adventures*, p. 207.

average holder of office, and became head of a government for the first time at the age of 56.

But if in these externals Lord Salisbury resembled his predecessors, he was very far from being the average young man of his day. He was a queer and unusual boy. He was moody, nervous and retiring. He detested games. He was bad-tempered and uncompanionable ; and the schooldays, which most Victorians used nostalgically to call the happiest time of their lives, were to him a nightmare. Of his life at his first school, to which he was sent at the age of six, he said later that it had been " an existence among devils " ; and his experience of Eton was no better. His lack of animal spirits and superior mental development did not commend him to his fellows. He passed into the fifth form when he was only 12 years old. It was a positive outrage on school convention ; and the poor " thin, frail little boy ", as his only Eton friend, Lord Dufferin, afterwards described him, was badly knocked about for his precocity. By the time he was 14 his letters from school to his father made even that stern preceptor relent. " I am obnoxious to them," little Robert wrote, " because I can do (Latin) verses but will not do them for others, not choosing to sacrifice my liberty at the bidding of one lower than myself." And " I am bullied from morning to night without ceasing. . . . I am obliged to hide myself all the evening in some corner to prevent being bullied. . . . When I come in to dinner they kick and shin me and I am obliged to go out of dinner without eating anything." By the time he was fifteen, his father at last acquiesced in his boyish complaint that " really now Eton has become insupportable ", and took him away.

In the interval between his first school and going to Eton young Robert had been sent to a tutor, who was no other than the clergyman who wrote " Abide with me ". The Rev. H. F. Lyte seems to have understood a boy's nature as well as he knew how to stir the emotions of his countrymen by his hymns. Appraising and guiding his peculiarities, and especially his aversion from outdoor exercise, he encouraged him to become interested in botany ; and so he provided him with a hobby which was to serve Lord Salisbury well. Through all his active life this inducement to take long walks undoubtedly helped to maintain him in physical fitness. Mr. Lyte's acute and sympathetic understanding also appears in a letter which he wrote to the boy's father (October 3, 1839) : " I do not think that I have ever met with so promising a boy, and I have no doubt of his distinguishing himself hereafter in life." It may also have been from the same inspiring mind that Robert Cecil drew his first keen interest in theology ; for when he went on to Eton one of his masters wrote that his divinity papers were answered " in a very extraordinary manner for so young a boy ".

His unhappy school experiences left an indelible mark of melancholy on Lord Salisbury. So deep had been his dread of meeting any of his school-fellows that on his holidays, when he was in London, he avoided the main streets, dodging in and out of his house by the passages, alleys and mews in its neighbourhood. And when he himself had become a father, he—unlike Chatham, who, miserable at Eton, refused to send his son William to school at all—sent all his sons to Eton ; but even after that lapse of time the experience of escorting his two eldest boys there was too much for him. He suffered a severe fit of depression ; and Lady Salisbury insisted on going without him when the time came to take their younger sons. The psychological inhibition never entirely lapsed. During his final premiership, when he was invited to be one of the guests of honour at an Eton dinner to three illustrious Old Etonians, Lord Salisbury refused the invitation, and would give no reason that was comprehensible to the eager, but baffled, organizers. Psychologists may also trace something of his life-long terror of Pressmen, and indeed of casual encounters with members of the public, to his youthful frustrations. On certain days of the year the park at Hatfield was traditionally thrown open to the public, and Lord Salisbury maintained the custom, though he knew he was ruining the pleasure of his own daily walk or tricycle ride there, because passing holiday-makers would naturally recognize and even salute him. " A silent black gloom " would then overspread his spirits, in the words of the daughter who often accompanied him * when he was not using his tricycle. With pressmen he relieved the strain by making it a kind of sport to elude them. When he was summoned to Balmoral by Queen Victoria to be offered the premiership for the first time, (in 1885), he travelled from King's Cross by sleeping-car. Learning early next morning that journalists intended to interview him at a Scottish station

* Lady Gwendolen Cecil.

he left his sleeper at the first stop, slipped along the platform, and ensconced himself in an empty third-class carriage. He recounted afterwards with glee that he had heard a reporter passing his window and exclaiming to a colleague, " He's certainly not on the train." He never shirked a necessary public appearance on account of his shyness ; but all his life he preferred his library to the rostrum.

The two years after leaving Eton and before going up to Oxford were relatively happy. Although spent at Hatfield, they were lonely years ; and although lonely—or perhaps because they were lonely—he referred to them later on in life as the only happy days he had spent as a boy. His father was much away from home, his sisters were married, his brothers at school ; and his mother was dead. That gifted lady had been the most sympathetic and encouraging influence of his childhood. She had a keen intelligence, warm enthusiasms and strong views. Politically she was a fervent, but unobtrusive Tory, and a friend of the Duke of Wellington, whom she persuaded to stand as godfather to the boy Robert. So Robert had Hatfield almost to himself ; and, since she could not be there, the unsociable boy was happiest alone. A clerical Fellow of St. John's College, Oxford, was his tutor, but he left his charge to his own resources during out-of-lesson hours. These Robert spent in indulging his newly acquired taste for botany ; he rambled over the countryside often for a whole day with a couple of sandwiches in his pocket, searching for new specimens. Even in flowers his interest was intellectual rather than æsthetic.

When he went up to Christ Church he gave some first signs of political predilections, but kept an unexpectedly open mind as to his future occupation in life. Being only the second (surviving) son of his father, he had no definite prospect of inheriting Hatfield, though his eldest brother was a chronic invalid. He meant to earn money ; but ill-health pursued him, and his stay at Oxford, as at Eton, was cut short—he only had time to take a fourth class in mathematics ! But there, just as at Eton, his spirit had refused to let him be cowed into doing what he did not want to do ; and immediately after leaving Oxford he showed that his courage could triumph over weariness and despondency. He had returned to Christ Church to visit some of his rather studious friends and heard that one of their number was designated to be the butt of a " rag " by some of the more raffish members of the House. He was in fact to be ducked in Mercury.* The men of peace consulted their friend on how to meet the attack. Lord Robert at once proposed counter-attack ; and he offered to organize it. According to his plan the intended victim sat in full view at his lighted window, absorbed in a book. Meanwhile Cecil and his friends concealed themselves round about. The attackers, flushed with wine and over-confident, approached in cheerful disorder. Suddenly a yell on the staircase above them coincided with a tumultuous convergence of well-placed groups who hurled themselves upon the intruders and put them to ignominious flight. Thus early in his career did Robert Cecil show that he possessed that indispensable qualification of a successful politician, readiness at all times to meet a challenge.

His doctor had decided that he must take a long voyage to recover from " the complete breakdown of his nervous system." The sad case of his elder brother must ever have been present to his mind and may have influenced his doctor's recommendation. Lord Cranborne's nervous debility was increasing with every passing month ; the course of his malady was never stayed ; and he was destined to die of premature senility before he had reached the age of fifty. With this example before his eyes, with his own weakness of the nerves, suffering for many years from the nightmarish malady of sleep-walking, Lord Robert Cecil might have become a confirmed neurotic, or a dissolute idler, or a mere degenerate. He was saved from any such disaster by an opportune visit to South Africa and Australasia, by an extrovert habit of mind which even in his most desperate moments turned his thoughts to public and political anxiety rather than to his own troubles ; and above all by his humble but robust trust in God.

3

The first part of the curative process was effected by the three countries which were to become the Union of South Africa, the Commonwealth of Australia and the Dominion of New Zealand. Planning played very little part in Lord Salisbury's life.

* The fountain in the middle of Tom Quadrangle.

Instinct rather than calculation suggested Australia, where the gold rush was in full swing ; and the chance of sea-passage took him to South Africa on the way.   Being also quite devoid either of ambition or of imagination—for which he professed contempt—young Robert Cecil can have had no notion that he was one day to be the first Minister of the British Crown to call those young communities into conference with their Mother country.

He set out in a sailing-ship bound for the Cape in July, 1851. He kept a journal, in accordance with a promise made to his family. We find in it little about his health, and nothing in its earlier entries about politics ; but much about ecclesiastical matters. And when he landed from Table Bay it was clerical society that he mostly frequented. Soon after the two months' sea-journey he had a rare impulse to take exercise, and tried to walk up Table Mountain ; but his strength was not yet restored, and half-way up he had to turn back with a throbbing head and overworked pulses. So he reverted to mental exercise. He became intimate with Bishop Grey of Capetown and seems to have employed the greater part of his time in religious discourse. No ultra-solemn, weary-of-the-world, or hair-splitting kind of discussion ; but keen exchanges of views upon fundamentals. A note has survived written by one of his felllow seekers after truth, Archdeacon Merriman of Capetown, who writes : " He (Robert Cecil) is excessively eccentric and thoroughly free from every conventionality . . . he lets the religion that is uppermost in his mind show itself in every sentence he utters—all tempered by a manliness and heartiness and freedom from all cant." There was nothing, the Archdeacon added, that resembled " the dwarfed, languid, nerveless, emasculate dilettantism " which he professes to have found among other members of the " higher classes ". Cecil's stay in South Africa was prolonged by his not finding a ship bound for Australia ; but at length, in December of that year (1851), one appeared in Table Bay. The young man boarded her eagerly ; and on the voyage eastward his chief reading was still theological—this time about the early Fathers of the Church, heirs and successors of the Apostles.

The tall, thin, lanky youth landed in Adelaide in January, 1852, in a black jacket surmounted by a white top-hat. Lord Robert Cecil not only landed in that garb, but he seems to have worn the jacket and topper all through his visit to the gold-diggings. The white hat provided indeed the only subject of chaff which he encountered from the diggers ; and that was on the score of its marking him out for a toff rather than for its unsuitability.

The journal now becomes much more lively. He liked the diggers, and often commented on their civility and, strangely enough, on their love of order. He had not been led to expect so much respect for the law. He found that they almost always sided with the authorities against a malefactor. Once or twice the diarist, himself a rebel by nature, shows annoyance and almost disgust at this submissiveness in Anglo-Saxons and colonists, especially after all he had heard of their independent and unruly dispositions. The young man's notes however show clearly that the diggers were well aware of the usefulness of the local rules and regulations to themselves, and it may have been from an intelligent sense of self-interest that they supported the defenders of lawful claimants to auriferous plots of land.

In one of his letters, however (to the Rev. Charles Cony-beare), Lord Robert offers another explanation, which sprang from the depths of his youthful philosophy. He had seen reports of the kind of lynch-law government then being applied in some-what similar circumstances in California ; and he contrasts to them the British way. " The government here ", he writes, " is of the Queen, not of the mob ; from above, not from below, holding from a supposed right (whether real or not, no matter) and not from ' the people the source of all legitimate power ', and *therefore* (he underlines) instead of murders, rapes and robberies daily, Lynch law and a Committee of Vigilance, there is less crime than in a large English town. . . ."

The strong religious bent of Robert Cecil's mind is still very discernible in his journal, and in this respect also he found more fellow-feeling in the mining community than he had expected. On his first Sunday in the diggings he observes : " The reverent demeanour of those who attended our service this morning was very noticeable " ; and again later on : " I likewise observed that throughout the diggings the orderly quiet with which the Sabbath was kept was very remarkable and very creditable." Even there Cecil made friends with the clergy. Two " Independent Ministers " were " a delightful pair. . . . Their faces were just what Leech would have delighted of copy and their

conversation would have been a perfect treasure to Dickens."
A Roman Catholic priest did not make so favourable an impression. Cecil calls him Dr. Gagen in his diary ; but his real name
was Dr. Geoghegan, and he afterwards became Catholic Bishop
of Adelaide. Cecil spelt the name as it was pronounced, betraying thus early his notorious propensity to take little account of
names and faces. He described the future bishop : "A fat,
droll, merry little Irish priest, very shallow and superficial, with
a great deal of low cunning and an evident desire to be 'all
things to all men' by a display of liberality and a series of profane
jokes."

But our young puritan never assumed a harsh or censorious
attitude towards the licentious conduct of some of his camp companions. He describes with caustic humour " a woman dressed
in the most exaggerated finery, with a parasol of blue damask silk
that would have seemed gorgeous in Hyde Park. She was a
lady of Adelaide notoriety, known as Lavinia, who had been
graciously condescending enough to be the better half of this
unhappy digger for a few days, in order to rob him of his earnings." And he relates with interest that " a *ci-devant* digger
informed me that when he was at Bendigo a lady had offered
'to be his wife' for the moderate charge of 1/6 ". "These
women ", he adds, " are no rareties [*sic*] at the diggings." Of
male miscreants, of whom there were also plenty in spite of the
prevailing "for-the-law" attitude of the diggers, he records :
" The favourite manœuvre among the thieves seems to be what
they call ' picking-up ', that is treating a successful digger to
grog until he is drunk enough to be plundered with impunity."

By about March, a couple of months after his arrival, his
physical and nervous exhaustion seems to have left him. On
the 25th of that month we read, it is true, " From some cause or
other I hardly slept an hour during the night." But otherwise
he hardly mentions his health ; he is up to some stiff walks and
withstands without complaint all kinds of roughness and discomfort. He made the journey to the goldfields in a " spring-cart ".
The road was execrable. " The holes grew more numerous and
the hills far steeper. The dust was absolutely unbearable. It
hung in a dense cloud about the cart, getting into our eyes, ears,
mouth, and nose, stopping respiration utterly and clinging to
hair, whiskers and beard as if it were flour. The particles were

so small that they penetrated through the thickest clothing and choked up every pore of the skin." The carts often became stuck in pot-holes ; and on most of his journeys we find some such entry as " We had to walk a great part of the way." On the first journey up-country from Melbourne he and his varied fellow-passengers had " 50 miles to do " in a cart or beside it and at the end still had a clear five miles to cover on foot in order to reach the Commissioner's tent, during which part of the journey " a desultory *feu de joie* was kept up from various quarters of the huge encampment " ; but happily " most of the cartridges seemed to be blank ".

The young man from Hatfield sometimes criticizes the fare which was provided in the tents of the camp officials and the rude conditions in which the meals were served ; but the criticism is never directed against the officials themselves, and still less is it made by way of complaint ; it is always provoked by a sense of impropriety. These officials were the local representatives of the law, and of Queen Victoria ; it seemed to Cecil that their authority ought to be supported by a trifle more style and punctilio. This is how he describes one of these camp repasts : " It was a solid meal, consisting of damper, mutton and potatoes —the two latter half-cooked in the embers of the camp-fire. We ate these provisions in a species of widened pannikin, something between a wash-hand basin and a soup plate, ingeniously constructed so as to be inconvenient in either capacity. Such a conventionality as a tablecloth was, of course, not to be expected. But I pitied the poor Commissioner, who, being deprived of his only pair of knives and forks by his guests, was reduced to the tantalizing expedient of carving with his penknife. I was honoured by the only chair in the place. . . . Mr. Cockburn (the Commissioner) sat in a corner upon an inverted bucket . . . our beverage was tea, with a strong lash of stringy bark. Afterwards brandy made its appearance—good fiery stuff and no mistake. We sat up some time drinking grog." After another meal, at which no officials were present, " the playful diggers took to throwing bread at each other, and I came in for my share of the pellets." That same evening the diarist notes that he was " obliged to sit up late in order to mend my cloth which was a good deal torn."

From Australia Cecil proceeded to Tasmania ; and here he

formed one of those convictions to which he held tenaciously throughout his life. When he directed the affairs of the Empire from Whitehall, he became famous for his trust of " the man on the spot ". We see the birth of this principle of his administration in the letters he sent home from Hobart. He writes to the Rev. Charles Conybeare on July 11, 1852 : " There is very strong and general discontent at the government of the Colonial Office, and it seems to me in a great measure just. The clerks in Downing Street interfere in every little local question ; at a distance of nine months and 16,000 miles as to a Post Office detail " ; and again in a letter to another clergyman, the Rev. H. Palmer : " I am not much disposed to yield to popular clamour—but the din of indignation against ' Downing Street policy ' is so bad and so incessant that I cannot help thinking there must be something in it. People are apt to be riled at having their minutest affairs . . . settled for them at a distance of 16,000 miles by a staff of clerks who cannot have the faintest notion of the questions they are handling. From the Cape to New Zealand, from Bishop to potboy, the cry is everywhere the same . . ." and the writer of the letter retained to the end of his career this horror of distant bureaucratic control. His preference for giving a free hand to the local administrator, in spite of the steady growth of telegraphic communication, was later to win him the devoted allegiance of the Colonial Service.

The improvement in health which this Antipodean trip brought is best shown by the contrast between his failure to climb Table Mountain and his enjoyment of exercise when he reached New Zealand, the last Dominion to be visited. On one journey there he covered 240 miles on horseback. " People generally walk, but that's not at all in my line," he comments airily, " and by riding I was able to stop every night except one in some European's cottage. I had only one night to sleep in a native hut." Cecil returned to England via Cape Horn, and so completed a journey round the world. These 22 months spent on the sea and in the three Dominions permanently strengthened his physique, broadened his mental outlook, afforded him close contact with types of humanity he would not otherwise have met, and gave him one or two of the permanent characteristics of his statesmanship, not the least of which was a profound belief in the Empire, by no means common among his contemporaries. Posterity remembers a man in the last stage of his career ; and this picture of Lord Salisbury travelling across country on a horse, or in a spring-cart, or on foot, eating half-cooked mutton and drinking grog, exchanging remarks with diggers, some of whom might be liable to arrest, and with their wives who were wives for a week, mending his own clothes and sleeping in a native hut, will be unfamiliar to most students of the statesman. But it well illustrates the robustness, vigour and directness of his outlook, which was inborn, but which the air of South Africa, Australia and New Zealand assuredly confirmed and augmented. They gave him strength in his youth ; he repaid the debt by becoming the first Prime Minister to think in terms of Empire.

On one of the last days of his travels he wrote : " Generally speaking, the voyage has quite answered its end in giving me health. . . . I am scarcely ever at all unwell, unless I sit up late. It will be some time before I shall be able to stand much of that sort of work." In point of fact he was to the end of his life, in his own phrase, " stewed and bored " by dinners and evening parties, and he used, whenever he could, to drive from the Foreign Office at the end of the day's work to King's Cross, and there catch a train which would enable him to spend the night in the spacious quietude of Hatfield.

RELIGION—PARLIAMENT—MARRIAGE

But of all that was to come to him young Cecil, unlike other great men of whom one has read, seems to have had no glimmering at all. Objective political foresight he possessed in strong measure, but no vision of his own future ; at the age of 22 he was quite uncertain even about the profession he would adopt. In a last long letter from overseas to his father (September 2, 1852) he writes in a most pessimistic mood, in spite of his recovered strength. " Now that I have got my health, what am I to do with it ? " He discusses the question from the premise " In choosing some plan of life, the prospect of the greatest usefulness ought to be the only guiding principle of selection " ; and he then goes on to prove to his own satisfaction that he is fit neither for politics nor the Church nor the Bar ! " My chances of getting into the House of Commons are practically nil." " (Holy) Orders is the profession I should place next to it (politics) in usefulness : but from my uncertain health and my inaptitude for gaining personal influence I am as little fitted for it as any man I ever met." As for the Bar : " It seems to me to unite the evils of the other two. It is more destructive of health than any other profession, and among the hundreds who yearly flock into it, I am about as likely to attain eminence in it as I am to get into Parliament." Robert Cecil was indeed a joyless young man— in the worldly sense. But his character cannot be understood except in the light of his intensely strong religious feelings. To him the psalmist's words are literally applicable : " His delight is in the law of the Lord " ; to which might be added, since the events of his life proved their truth, " And look, whatsoever he doeth, it shall prosper." Religion formed the unshakable foundation of his life and career. So profoundly did it affect his outlook, and therefore his private and political conduct, that it is necessary to study the nature of his belief ; and this may best be undertaken before we go any further. It will not then be necessary to interrupt the narrative later ; and it is the more fitting because his views remained fundamentally unchanged for the rest of his life. Having reached his conclusions, he deliberately refrained from re-entangling his mind in problems which, for better or for worse, he felt he had settled to the best of his ability. He made his intellectual conclusions the starting-point of his actions. He once remarked that it was incomprehensible to him that any man could pass the age of 40 without having finally determined upon his religious denomination. Religion was to him first a problem and then a joy ; while theology, which had been the intellectual passion of his youth, became little more than an academic interest in his later years. It was bracketed with history and science as a congenial subject for recreational reading. Then his only zest was for politics ; and it expressed itself in action.

The world into which Cecil was born, with an instinct that made him a theologian while he was yet a schoolboy, was one in which Christian values provided the determining principles of politics and were the criterion of political behaviour—a place where " sermons were as popular as novels are today ".* And Oxford was the very hub from which the sermons radiated. The greatest preacher in the English language, John Henry Newman, son of a banker sire and Calvinist mother, fellow of Oriel College, had a few years earlier gone over to the Church of Rome ; and his perplexed former associates at Oxford University were struggling bravely and not unsuccessfully to hold together the Tractarian Movement which he had ceased to lead. But they gave it another direction than his. The earliest Tracts had been mainly concerned to assert the authority of the Anglican Church and claim Apostolic descent for the Anglican episcopate, following the emancipation of the Roman Catholics in this country. But after the secession of Newman in 1845, two years before Cecil reached Oxford, his successors, going only so far with him as to agree that there might be something to imitate in the Roman ecclesiasticism, advocated a stricter discipline and more rigid orthodoxy in their own Church. From having been its out-and-out defenders they became its critics and reformers. They insisted on the primary importance of the sacraments and accordingly demanded more ritual. This view was adopted by Cecil. He became an unfailing communicant ; and throughout his long years of office he held strictly to this habit contracted

* D. C. Somervell, *English Thought in the Nineteenth Century*, p. 106.

at the University. When he had time, he attended matins on a Sunday ; but nothing else than illness or physical incapacity kept him away from the Communion table in the early morning of every Sunday throughout his life.

But neither the Oxford Movement nor the sermons of Newman which he read so diligently made as strong an impact on his mind as the teaching of Bishop Butler. This great divine was in those days much more closely studied than he is today, though Mr. Gladstone, who edited and annotated his Works, lamented that he was not known even then as he should be. " Oh ! that this age knew the treasure it possesses in him, and neglects," he wrote in 1873 ; and those who believe, as most of us surely do, in the greatness of either Gladstone or Salisbury or both, may spare a moment to consider some of the tenets of this eighteenth-century teacher, who went into semi-retirement for eight years in order to write his classic, *The Analogy of Religion, Natural and Revealed, to the Constitution and Course of Nature.* His fundamental thesis is, as the full title of his book indicates, that an essential unity exists between religion and nature ; that the apparent rules, the perplexities, the unexpectedness and seeming imperfections of the one are made apparent to us in physical form in the other ; and that the teaching of the Bible is illustrated by familiar scenes which are not matters of conjecture but can be known and felt in the experience of life here below. Religion in fact is not the Utopian system which we might ourselves essay to construct in our own imagination. " Everything is what it is, and not another thing " is Bishop Butler's basis of reasoning. If religion, he argues, comes to us with apparent contradictions, and gives us light only to a certain point, telling us something of the next world, but little compared with what it conceals, that is only what we have been familiar with from our birth and what we see in the laws and realities of Nature. " As we cannot remove from this earth, or change our general business on it, so neither can we alter our real nature."

It is of course impossible to do justice to Bishop Butler in a few pages. His writing is, to modern taste, prolix and over-refined in argumentation, which suffers so much from qualifications that it is sometimes hard to follow. But his outlook is robust, in spite of being occasionally sophistical, and he is a supremely honest searcher after truth. He is never in his long series of sermons tempted to sacrifice exactness to a flourish or an epigram. In his habit of trying to see things as they really are and not as they are talked about or appraised by temporary or accidental opinion, as in many other characteristics, he was closely followed by Cecil. Throughout his career Lord Salisbury was never swayed in his assessment of a political situation by the fashionable or popular view. He examined its origin, its data and its implications ; he took his decision on a balanced and completed examination of all the evidence. As we read Bishop Butler we see how close to his mind was Salisbury's. When late in life, having declined the Primacy, the learned Bishop accepted the rich see of Durham, he communed thus : " Increase of fortune is insignificant to one who thought he had enough before ; and I see many difficulties in the station I am coming into, and no advantage worth thinking of, except some greater power of being serviceable to others." We have seen at the beginning of this chapter that young Cecil made its potential " usefulness " his text in choosing a career ; and the Lord Salisbury of later years reasoned on just the same lines as Bishop Butler about becoming the owner of Hatfield, or accepting the post of Prime Minister, which he more than once vainly tried to persuade somebody else to take instead of him. Again, the Bishop (who declined the Archbishopric of Canterbury) was much concerned in all he did to ensure a quiet and orderly existence for all for whom he had any responsibility. The great churchman had lived in turbulent times, when the Stuarts made two separate attempts to regain the throne they had lost ; and Lord Salisbury, when he made it his purpose as Prime Minister first and foremost to ensure order and good government, may have failed to recognize suffi-ciently the need for change. " Reasonable men ", Bishop Butler declared in a sermon preached to the House of Lords, " will look upon the general plan of our Constitution, transmitted down to us by our ancestors, as sacred ; and content themselves with . . . rectifying the particular things which they think amiss, and supplying the particular things which they think deficient in it, so far as is practicable without endangering the whole." And again : " Licentiousness is such an excess of liberty as is of the same nature with tyranny." These two sentiments strike the keynote of Lord Salisbury's Conservatism. Some submission to authority is an essential condition of true liberty ; liberty presupposes self-command and the habit of self-discipline, with all that they imply in social and industrial relationships ; and in Lord Salisbury's view religion, and religion alone, could create those habits. One more particular of similarity of outlook remains to be mentioned—acceptance of the inexplicable. The Bishop and the future Prime Minister both held that the common things of everyday life are full of what is unexplained. " Why am I here ? " " What is life ? " " What is death ? " and so on. When we have carried our knowledge as far as science and our own intelligence can take us, then begins a vast immeasurable domain of what we do not and probably never shall know. And Cecil, when he was 33 years old, jotted down in a notebook : " The narrowness of our knowledge serves to warn us how we bring our bounded intellects and earthly sight to bear on questions far beyond their reach." The creature is finite, the Creator infinite. Our limited intellects cannot, in his own words, " pigeon-hole the mysteries of faith ". Reasoner that he was, he maintained that logical completeness was impossible in religious matters. Truth is inexhaustible and cannot be entirely apprehended by the imperfect mind of man. The comprehension of the human intellect is enriched by science but remains small by comparison with the omniscience of God. There are, he would argue, instincts, impulses and forces at work in this world which we can observe but cannot explain. Our human faculties are not made to understand all—any more than the animal kingdom can understand the human affairs. Ants, bees and beetles live in the same world as we do ; but what do they know of the human way of life or understand of human affairs ? They presumably know that we exist, and beyond that they have nothing to explain us by.

But man, unlike the animal creation, has received the word of God by revelation ; he has been vouchsafed the gift of faith. Lord Salisbury was so richly endowed with it that it was never shaken by his own keenest questionings. He studied science and practised physics, he read Strauss and Renan, Auguste Comte and Thomas Huxley ; he absorbed their arguments ; but he continued to worship Christ. That was the central point of his religion. He believed in the historic Christ, whom even the agnostics and atheists admitted to have lived and died in Palestine. He accepted his divinity, regarded his doctrine as true and had no doubt that his promise of eternal life would be fulfilled. Salisbury combined the reasoning power of an intellectual giant with the faith of a child.

But the result of this direct approach to God was a very individual form of belief. He insisted upon the practical need of doctrine, but even so " Christian love " was for him greater than all doctrines. Even the New Testament, he argued, was not a " perfect summary of Christian doctrine, a digested code of Christian ethics ". It was, he said (with Butlerian downrightness) " A bunch of letters and memoirs ", written to specified persons and containing information on specific points ; and so, as he declared in his later years, although he had never known what it was to doubt the fundamental truth of Christian doctrine as built up and codified by the Church, he had always found a difficulty in accepting the moral teaching of the Gospels.

Religion, he considered, could not be expected to survive without authoritative doctrinal teaching. " The dream of undogmatic religion is too baseless to impose long upon educated minds. . . . We shall either cling to our articles of faith in spite of rationalist and unsectarian teaching, or we shall learn, by a cruel experience, that men will not be moral without a motive, and that a motive can only be furnished by religious belief." * He saw forces of disintegration at work around him, and believed that Christianity could not co-exist for more than two or three generations with a civilization which it did not inspire. Neither a man or a nation can live on spiritual capital indefinitely. Capital of every kind must be continually replenished. Since in Lord Salisbury's younger days British life was still pervaded by religion, even those who had had little religious instruction (and they were few) lived in an atmosphere of church-going and quiet Sundays. The forms of Christianity were almost universally observed. Exception made for some of the big industrial centres, and for dissenters, the whole country was brought up on the Church's catechism. It still indoctrinated the nation. Its teaching set a common standard of conduct and gave it a fundamental moral unity. It was the dogma of the common man—as it was of Lord Salisbury. " Thy duty towards thy neighbour " carried a clear meaning for all. Even his religious antipathies were shared by the majority of his countrymen. He had no taste for

* *Quarterly Review*, July, 1865.

the Roman Church ; and he disliked asceticism—he once described the teaching of the fifth-century Fathers on this point as
" a terrible and most deadly error ".

His unceasingly active mind was always propounding to himself problems that vex every honest seeker after truth—for instance,
" God is all-powerful and God is all-loving—and the world is
what it is ! How are you going to explain that ? " His own
mental response to such problems was acquiescence in incomprehension ; and his practical answer was to try to make the world
a better place within the range of his influence. But as he
advanced in years he drew right away from metaphysical abstrac-
tions and devoted his energies rather to translating his established
convictions into beneficent action. He never cared for arguing
for the sake of argument, especially on those religious points where
nothing could be proved. Discussion for him was only an
approach to decision, and decision should lead to action. Yet
with this intense urge to see practical results he never lost his
earlier taste for quiet reflection, preferably in the seclusion of his
study. Indifferent though he was to poetry, what was written
of the poet was true of him :

> Ah ! two desires toss about
> The poet's restless blood ;
> One drives him to the world without,
> And one to solitude.

2

Mentally and spiritually so constituted, Lord Salisbury's
whole outlook was dominated by the Christian belief in immor-
tality ; and perhaps the most fundamental cleavage between
men's minds is that which separates those who believe in a future
life and those who do not. For the latter, the joys, benefits,
prizes and conquests of this world are all that they have to strive
for ; humanism and materialism must find their satisfaction
in what this world supplies. For those whose hope is set on
the hereafter worldly advantages are secondary and only to
be enjoyed by the way. This was especially true of Lord Salisbury. By the accident of birth he possessed most of the worldly

advantages which come to others only as a result of life-long endeavour. On worldly calculation alone he was free to enjoy them without exertion ; but his religious principles turned him to the disinterested service of his fellow men. They also rendered him utterly indifferent to rewards, and gave him a certain serene detachment. His job, he considered, was to do what he thought right, without any attention to popularity or unpopularity, and to leave the results to Providence. In private conversation with his family he once made the remarkable statement for a man in his position : " With the result I have nothing to do." The phrase " the burden of responsibility ", which is habitually applied to those in high office, meant nothing to him. The burden of decision, on the other hand, was very real ; and the weight of the load varied according to the data available for making up his mind. If the available data were plentiful and above all if they preponderantly inclined him to one definite course, the burden of decision was light. He happened to be discoursing to his family on this topic one day when he was on the point of going out for a walk. He felt the " burden " of deciding at that moment, he said, whether or not to take a great-coat with him. If it had been a fine day or a wet one, he would have known what to do without a thought ; but it was just typical English autumn weather with threatening clouds in the sky, so the conditions afforded no clear lead.

The belief in the overruling power of God gave him, then, the conviction that the course to choose in politics was that which had the most reason behind it. It might or might not produce an immediately favourable result ; but it would, under God's Providence, benefit posterity even if it did not benefit his own generation. To get the " right reaction " from public opinion, a consideration often uppermost in the minds of our political leaders today, did not come into his calculations at all. In the long run, he felt confident, the right consequences would flow from his decision if it had been taken on an honest and sound estimate of the pre-existing conditions. Lord Salisbury's fore-sight was in the event often more correct on long-term estimates than on immediate results.

Another logical consequence of his religious tenets was his attitude to social questions. He believed in a continuous conflict between right and wrong, between the best and the worst instincts in mankind—between God himself and the devil, settled in heaven but never-ending on earth. He did not believe in the perfectibility of man—man will always be compounded of good and evil. The ideal of human perfection, however, while it could never be reached, could always be approached. It was therefore all the time worth working for. But it depended upon the individual himself far more than upon legislation. Happiness in the long run was a matter of self-control, steady work and honest dealing. He would always try to improve the conditions in which these virtues could be exercised—and it should be noted that, contrary to a widely held view, few Prime Ministers before him had passed so much social legislation as Lord Salisbury did during his three premierships.

"Get back to first principles," cried the Italian prophet of the Risorgimento, Mazzini, "and the people will follow you"; and there can be little doubt that the main reason why Lord Salisbury came to be so implicitly trusted by the mass of his countrymen was that they knew him to be a disinterested man who went back to first principles and whose judgment was based upon well-trained power of reasoning. This talent seems often to be stimulated by a study of theology, with its subtle distinctions and need to define beliefs which are not explainable by logic. An unexpected witness to the efficacy of theological training is Talleyrand, who in the last address he delivered, when an octogenarian, to the Académie des Sciences, alluded to his seminary education as "the best preparation for diplomacy". He said that the "instinctive sagacity which was attributed to him" might have come from the study of theology in his young days; and he cited the examples of great priest-politicians, among them the English Wolsey, who had gained clarity and firmness of thought from education in a seminary. And finally Lord Salisbury never confused cause and effect, or supposed one can get satisfactory results for long by merely trading on accumulated effort. Past prestige was not enough. Exertion must never cease. Fresh capital must be created. The fruits of an age-long civilization can be enjoyed only for a limited space of time unless its moral standard is maintained and its material store-house constantly replenished. "It would be a great saving of trouble," Lord Salisbury wrote in one of his best-known articles in the *Quarterly Review*, "if it were possible to cut down oaks without the tedious necessity of planting them first." Just as the religious life of a community must inevitably decay if it is not renewed at the source so also is it impossible for men habitually to break the moral law and hope to evade the consequence of a decline in the national vitality.

3

When Robert Cecil reached home from New Zealand (May, 1853) his doubts about his future career were quickly resolved for him. He was offered a seat at Stamford. There was no opponent ; and he entered Parliament during the second half

---

TO THE

ELECTORS

OF THE

BOROUGH OF STAMFORD.

GENTLEMEN, Having now completed my Canvass, I take the earliest opportunity of announcing to my friends that the result has been most satisfactory ; I therefore request that you will accept my best thanks for the kind and gratifying manner in which I have been received.

As the Election is fixed for Monday next at 10 o'clock precisely, I earnestly request the attendance of my Friends at the George Hotel, Saint Martin's, on that morning, at Half-past 9 o'clock, to accompany me from thence to the Hustings.

I have the honor to be, Gentlemen,

Your obliged and faithful Servant,

ROBERT G. CECIL.

GEORGE HOTEL, Thursday, 18th August, 1853.

H. JOHNSON, PRINTER, ST. MARY'S-HILL, STAMFORD.

The second handbill issued by Lord Salisbury, when Lord Robert Cecil, asking his supporters to accompany him to the hustings. (The use of hustings was abolished by the Ballot Act of 1872)

of that year. His election address exhibited his readiness to accept a *fait accompli*—in this case the abolition of the Corn Laws. It became one of his rules that once a measure had become the law of the land he would not go back on it. His maiden speech was spoken on April 7, 1854. He protested in it against any interference with the ancient endowments of Oxford University, as proposed by the Liberal Lord John Russell, arguing that such endowments could by right only be applied to the purposes for which they had been bestowed or else they should revert to the donor's heirs. Disraeli heard the speech, and wrote flatteringly about it to the new member's father, who had been his ministerial colleague, as Lord Privy Seal, in the last Conservative Government. " I have no hesitation in saying," he declared, " that if he will work, and he has a working look, I will make a man of him "—encouraging patronage from the Opposition Leader in the House of Commons. Next year he was chosen (July 17, 1855) by the Opposition to be one of the speakers against the notorious motion of censure against a Ministry, Lord Aberdeen's, which had already disappeared from office. Two years later (1857) he had gained sufficient confidence to introduce a Bill of his own, designed to make voting more private by enabling it to be effected through the post. This came to nothing ; and during these earliest years of Parliamentary career his private life affords topics of greater interest than his public.

His relations with his father had never been happy. The second Marquess of Salisbury was one of the many local autocrats by whom country politics were directed in the eighteenth and nineteenth centuries. A vigorous, energetic outdoor man, he had longed to be a soldier ; but his own father had vetoed the project. He was however allowed to join the Militia, and he showed his natural bent in organizing and greatly developing the county corps not only in his own Hertfordshire but in Middlesex as well. He threw himself with equal zeal and with the same military rigidity into the civil administration of the county. He was shrewd, able and obstinate. Altruistic in his aims, he was most autocratic in his methods. He never saw the other man's point of view and if anybody of nearly equal standing differed from him there was no issue except through quarrel. But he was always found on the side of his poorer neighbours if they had any difficulties with officials. They belonged to his kingdom, and he would have nobody but himself dictating to them. And he sought their welfare. He instituted, far ahead of his time in this respect, night classes for boys at Hatfield, and deducted six-pence from the wages of every boy employed on his estates for each school attendance he had missed during the week.

This hale countryman was chagrined to find that his son Robert cared neither for hunting nor shooting nor any other of the manly sports so dear to his own heart. He considered cross-country rambles for wild flowers a poor substitute for hunt-ing ; the talent for writing which the weakly boy was develop-ing inspired no enthusiasm in him, and he sorrowfully reflected that none of the first three sons born to him—besides the eldest, an invalid, there had been a second boy who had died in infancy—seemed to have been qualified to carry on the line of Cecil. He would however give Robert one more chance. In April (1855) the colonelcy of the Middlesex Militia fell vacant ; as Lord-Lieutenant of that county he controlled the appoint-ment ; he would bestow it upon Robert and make a man of him. He wrote to make the proposal to him, in almost enthusiastic terms, never doubting that Robert would gratefully accede. The reply shocked him profoundly. Robert's health, so much im-proved by the Australian trip, had deteriorated under the stress of late hours in the House of Commons, and he was suffering again from nervous debility in head and stomach. The answer-ing letter began with the shattering announcement : " Your proposition gave me a stomach-ache all this morning." It ran on from bad to worse : " I detest all soldiering beyond measure. As far as taste goes I would rather be at the treadmill." How-ever, Robert then writes that he must try to look at the proposal " with as much self-forgetfulness as I can put on " and subordin-ate as far as possible his own inclinations. He continues :

" I understand your wish in putting me into Parliament to be that I should learn to speak if I could, and so prepare myself for future political usefulness. To do this at all effectively I must read. With my wretched health it is hardly enough that I can do this [*sic*] as it is : with any other regular duties it will be impossible and must be abandoned. . . . It is the peculiarity of my complaint, that it lays me up and makes me incapable— sometimes for days—without any sort of warning ; and that House of Commons work exposes me to these nervous attacks."

Later on in the same long letter he calls his unfitness for the militia command " ludicrously glaring ".* This first letter, which was evidently written almost in a state of panic, was followed a few days later by a second firmly and finally declining the post ; and the despairing father had to admit that this son, who shocked his Victorian sense of fitness by openly talking about his " nerve storms ", was no good to him at all.

Father Salisbury really loved his son, and he wrote to his doctor about him. Dr. Acland's reply is instinct with deep commonsense and worth recording in view of later developments. He wrote :

" From what I know of him, I should have simply gathered that he was of a very weakly habit, incapable of great fatigue and prone to excessive nervous exhaustion ; and as a consequence of these things he requires great care lest on the one hand he should be over-fatigued, or on the other, by too much yielding, be led into the habits and health of a hypochondriac. My estimate of him would have been that he could be perfectly trusted to exercise a sound discretion in what he can and what he cannot do." † Robert must have felt that if his family would only leave him alone, or at least show that they understood him, he would feel so much better, as he had when he was in Australia.

Then, in the nick of time, the fretted young man was to find someone who could take the required care of him and supplement his own sound discretion in choosing the work he could properly undertake.

It was the most understandable of his father's mis-judgments to regard Lord Robert as a confirmed celibate. He had seemed incapable of enjoying the society of young women. Awkward in his movements, stooping at the shoulders, learned in his tastes, badly dressed and short-sighted, this tall uncouth young man can in any case have had little attraction for the average girl. But soon after his return to England he met one who was very far from being the average girl. For two years, with growing frequency, he found a congenial companion in Miss Georgina Alderson. She was almost as studious as Robert Cecil himself, and like him took a fervent interest in Church history. But besides being devout she had also a particularly bright, eager

* Lady Gwendolen Cecil, Vol. I, p. 50.
† Lady Gwendolen Cecil, Vol. I, p. 51.

and even gay temperament ; so that the young man soon became aware that in her company he not only found the one form of recreation he really enjoyed, the intellectual discussion of current problems, but that he came away from them refreshed, not fatigued, and feeling quite cheerful. The friendship ripened slowly into mutual love—without the young wooer's father knowing anything about it.

When therefore, after two years' acquaintance, the news was announced to Lord Salisbury in the summer of 1856, the shock was almost as sharp to him as had been the rejection of the Militia offer the year before. A love-match at the age of 26 was the very last thing he had expected. Nor, when it came, did he desire it. The young lady was the undowered daughter of a judge ; * she was not good enough, according to his standards, for the son who might now, after all, be the carrier of the Cecil line. He forbade the marriage. Lord Robert's answer is again typical (November 27, 1856) :

" Your objections to my marriage rested mainly on the ' privations ' it would entail. ' Privation ' means the loss of something I enjoy now. If the privation in question is the want of food, warmth, clothing, I am not prepared to face it. But I cannot lose anything else I now enjoy, for the simple reason that I do not enjoy anything. Amusements I have *none*. . . . The persons who will cut me because I marry Miss Alderson are precisely the persons of whose society I am so anxious to be quit. . . . I have come to the conclusion that I shall probably do Parliament well if I do marry, and that I shall certainly make nothing of it if I do not." †

He consented to his father's request that he should neither see nor correspond with his betrothed for six months, but without having the slightest intention of breaking off the engagement ; and the marriage, when it came, proved the justice of his view that with her he would " do Parliament well ". He himself had nothing of the careerist in his make-up ; she supplied the deficiency. And she had other qualities besides ambition which Robert lacked. She was very sociable ; and had a quick discrimination of character. Being more interested in ideas than in persons he was unable to judge a man's worth until he had

* Sir Edward Hall Alderson.
† Lady Gwendolen Cecil, Vol. I, p. 59.

known or at least closely observed him for a long time. He came to depend on her to prevent him from being imposed upon. Some wives release their husband's energies, others exhaust them. Georgina released his, and he grew in confidence and practical ability. She had the more masterful nature of the two. Perhaps she married him rather than he her. But, if that were true, she did a good job for him and for England. They were married on July 11, 1857, in St. Mary Magdalene's Church in Munster Square, and after the service knelt together in Holy Communion.

But they were not destined altogether to escape the trials that tangle the feet of most young couples. After spending their honeymoon in Switzerland and on an island in the Baltic they enjoyed a halcyon period when they set up their first home together in London. He was not often busy until the moment came to go round to the House of Commons, which was then in the late afternoon ; and she would join him later, sitting in the gallery till after midnight ; then they would meet in the lobby, and if it was a fine night walked home together, sometimes in the first dawning of daylight, across St. James's Park and up Green Park, occasionally all the way to the neighbourhood where they lived for a few months in Lady Alderson's house in Park Crescent and then in their own in Fitzroy Square ; communing by the way on the news and the gossip gathered in the House or the lobbies, or at the evening parties which she still liked to attend, and where he, drawn by the new magnet, also put in an appearance when he could.

Finance was the fly in life's fresh fragrant ointment. The stern paterfamilias, who having married a second wife had by now had ten children, had refused to make any extra allowance to his second (surviving) son on his marriage ; even though, before another year was out, this son had a son of his own, which in those days meant a nursery. Robert, in spite of his cheerful life-companion, began to brood on what would happen if the nursery became more crowded. His hopes of even a minor Cabinet post seemed very dim indeed—and at the best no Government was lasting very long just then. Aberdeen, Palmerston, Russell and Derby were following each other in and out like batsmen on a sticky wicket. Moreover, late hours did not really suit him well. Finance became a problem—which may have been of advantage to Robert Cecil, though probably he did not so consider it. Men in his position often used to reach responsible posts without having ever had to bother their minds with pounds, shillings and pence. Cecil had a lesson on their importance. He quickly understood that they percolate and sustain the activities of the body politic as the circulation of the blood sustains those of the human body. He made up his mind to write systematically for an income. He had an open door into political journalism in the person of Alexander Beresford-Hope, of the *Saturday Review*, who had married his sister. His brother-in-law was a Puseyite ; so Cecil put no strain upon his convictions, either religious or political, in writing regularly for him. Soon he was also contributing articles to a now forgotten periodical, *Bentley's Review* ; and in 1860 he began his long connection with John Murray's *Quarterly*. Between that year and 1873, he contributed thirty-two articles to the *Quarterly Review* ; and although, like all his articles, they were unsigned, the author's name soon became known in political circles.

But even regular contributions to a weekly and a quarterly do not make a man's fortune, and the young husband began to look round for a more substantial livelihood. Lord Derby, a friend of the Cecil family, had just become Prime Minister (1858). Why not apply to him for a minor non-political post which would help him out ? He sent off a letter to 10 Downing Street. Very civil was the reply, but it was negative. In the autumn of the same year (1858) he heard of a vacancy in the Inland Revenue. " A political career," he writes to his unresponsive sire, " may not be consistent with due prudence." Both his wife and his friends dissuaded him from actually making his application for that particular post. But his wish for a fixed income was not to be withstood ; and next year two more possibilities were earnestly discussed in the family circle. Sir Edward Bulwer Lytton, the novelist, and a Hertfordshire neighbour, was at the Colonial Office ; and he offered Cecil the governorship of Queensland. Remembering Australia with affection, Cecil liked the prospect ; but he found that his expenses would swallow up all the Governor's salary ; so he would be rather worse off than before. One more chance of financial security opened before him. After the General Election of the year 1859 his father, whose influence now extended to London, had the disposal of one of the two Clerkships of the Council, which had been relinquished by the diarist, George Greville. Lord Salisbury, who was Lord President of the Council, promptly offered it to Robert, and he this time did not look the gift in the mouth. He was delighted, and accepted it at once. But Fate and the Cabinet stepped in. Some time earlier the Treasury had strongly recommended that the second Clerkship should be abolished. When therefore the appointment came before the Cabinet the impropriety of a member of the Government nominating his own son to a post declared to be redundant was too glaring ; and the decision was taken to appoint no successor to George Greville.

So Robert Cecil had to pull himself together and write very hard. His best articles were in fact produced during these years 1860–5.

CHAPTER III—1860–66

WRITING AND POLITICS

During his early period of literary exertion Robert Cecil sorted out his political ideas and made the same distinct pattern of them as he had of his religious tenets. The whole of his later political outlook is already found in these writings. Read the young politician between the ages of 30 and 36 and you know the statesman. For him career did not begin until the process of preparation was finished.

He said afterwards that thinking out his political articles had greatly helped him to think out the construction and sequence of his speeches ; and if his writing was to help his public speaking, his parliamentary work also helped his writing. He drew on his experience in the House to convey to the public outside its scenes and its atmosphere. Near the beginning of the first article which he wrote for the *Quarterly Review* (" The Budget and the Reform Bill ", April, 1860) he describes the scene on the night of Mr. Gladstone's memorable budget of that year. The Liberal statesman, who was to be Cecil's rival in public favour for over a quarter of a century, and who was 21 years his senior, was something of a hero to the young Opposition member in whose make-up hero-worship had little room. Gladstone had been down with bronchitis, so Budget-day had been postponed a week, to February 10. On that day the benches were full when the sitting was opened with the customary prayers. But Gladstone was not there. Question time came. The occupants of the Treasury Bench were taking their places ; but the Chancellor of the Exchequer was not among them. Members became anxious ; and rumours passed round the House. Mr. Gladstone had caught a fresh cold—it was a bad chill—he might not be able to attend the House after all. Then, a few minutes before he was due to rise, the long-looked-for orator came in, " with his usual stealthy, almost timid, step " and took his place at the despatch box. " His face was pale, and he occasionally leant against the table with an appearance of fatigue, as though standing was an effort ; but his tones were as melodious, his

33

play of features and of gesture was as dramatic as ever.   Throughout the whole four hours of intricate argument neither voice nor
mind faltered for an instant."   This little vignette shows Cecil
as a parliamentary sketch-writer of no mean merit ; and one
regrets that he did not bequeath to posterity more such portraits
of his contemporaries.   But he was far more interested in events
than in personalities, in politics than in politicians ; and having
paid his brief tribute to the man, he criticizes in forty pages all
Mr. Gladstone's projects for raising money and lowering the
franchise.   The combined effect, the writer considers, would be
to bring an ultimate divorce between power and responsibility ;
and, in fact, the time would come " when the rich will pay all
the taxes and the poor will make all the laws ".

But if we wish to gauge aright the opinions he expressed at
this time in his writings and his speeches we must first cast an
eye on the events he himself had been observing since he began
to take an interest in public affairs.   When he was a boy of
18 at Oxford he had seen Europe and his own country convulsed
in revolutionary movements.   In February, 1848 (when he was
18) the " bourgeois " King Louis Philippe of France had been
driven out by the mobs of Paris to seek refuge in the same British
Isles which had offered shelter to his predecessor, Charles X,
and were later to receive his successor, Napoleon III.   A *Commission des Travailleurs* had ousted the Peers from the Luxembourg
and occupied its benches in their stead.   Louis Blanc, advocate
of co-operative State workshops, was the most important member
of the Provisional Government, until he in his turn followed the
deposed monarch into the all-embracing arms of old mother
England.   Behind the improvised barricades of the French
Capital " Communism " became for the first time a political
portent ; and from Paris the revolutionary fever spread to other
capital cities—to Vienna, Budapest, Milan, Venice, Florence and
Rome ; an outbreak in Naples had actually preceded the revolution in France.   Even Frederick William of Prussia was forced
to promise to rule through a National Assembly.   The great
Metternich, conqueror of Napoleon, was himself conquered by
his people, and he too sought refuge in England.   The Minister
was followed from Vienna by his Emperor, who however stopped
at Innsbruck and not long afterwards considered it safe to return
to the capital.

But if Windischgraetz had had to re-take Vienna at the head of an army and General Wrangel had surrounded the Berlin Assembly Hall with troops and chased its members from one secretly arranged meeting-place to another, it has to be noted—and it was particularly noted by young Cecil—that the revolutionary leaders, not only in Vienna and Berlin, but in every European capital where they seized office, had made a sad bungle of the business of administration ; and this had conveyed upon the young English politician the impression, which was to become an axiom confirmed by personal experience, that the art of government is the most difficult of all arts and is best conducted by an educated, and a trained, minority. The tumults of 1848 in his own country supported this view. He had read in *The Times* of the Chartists ransacking the gunshops of Glasgow and " flourishing their weapons like madmen or drunkards ", shouting, " Down with the Queen." And everywhere except in Britain the moderate reformers had been ousted by the extremists. A few much-needed changes had certainly been effected, especially in England—largely as a result of ten years of Chartist agitation. But then reaction had come, bringing into power Napoleon III in France and other masterful champions of authority all over Europe. " If you will have democracy ", Cecil wrote in a later essay, " you must have something like Cæsarism to control it." But the word " democracy " must not mislead us. It was then used in a different sense from that of parliamentary democracy, which in Cecil's lifetime came to be fully accepted with all its implications. A hundred years ago it was as often as not meant to imply " mob-rule ", as any reader of the contemporary Press must know. Some day, perhaps, those whom we now call Communists will modify their outlook, form constitutional parties and come to be regarded as a respectable alternative to the Government of the day. They will have ceased to be the mob of destructive malcontents that " democrats " appeared to be to *The Times* and Lord Robert Cecil in 1848.

In this country the last tremor of Chartist disturbance subsided before the steadiness of the special constables and the fixed bayonets of the troops ; and the popular cry at home was now for peace and tranquillity. In 1851 the Great Exhibition inflamed the hopes of all for a fellowship of trading nations whose growing riches would turn their thoughts away from civil riot and international war. As between nation and nation these hopes were soon to be proved visionary. But at home people became engrossed in the development of the wonderful new inventions which were speeding the course of material progress —the railways, the steam-driven machinery, the first public telegraph offices. And the wide extension of practical benefits brought with it new demands from the beneficiaries. The Trade Unions asserted the right of the manual workers to share in the increase of prosperity ; and the growing wealth of the middle-classes produced a well-founded demand for the extension of the then very limited right to exercise the electoral vote.

Cecil spent much of his youthful energy in opposing such demands. He was over-influenced by the unhappy results of the Continental experiments in democratic rule ; and he attached too much importance to the argument of the thin end of the wedge. He was moreover an Ishmælite by nature ; and too often opposed for the sake of opposition. He was frequently a critic of his own leaders. He voted against his Front Bench on a motion criticizing the conduct of the Crimean War. He voted against the admission of Jews to Parliament. He opposed the abolition of the religious test for entering the universities. He was at that time opposed to competitive examinations. He voted against the project to build the Thames Embankment. Often it was just his rebellious spirit, or objection to a detail, which made him oppose. For instance, in the matter of building the embankment along the north side of the Thames he did not criticize the project itself ; but he objected, and with justice, to the method by which it was proposed to pay for it. The money was to come from the Metropolitan Coal Dues. This meant that people living anywhere within fifteen or sixteen miles from the river, many of them very poor, were to be taxed for advantages which, he pointed out, " are, practically, enjoyed by the wealthy classes only ". " The only thing resembling an *octroi* in our taxation," he exclaimed, " is the coal tax. It is raised from one of the necessaries of life. . . . It appears to me that there is great injustice in such a system." He opposed the building of the South Kensington Museum on similar grounds. He argued that the site was badly chosen. " It is useless to cite the number of visitors to South Kensington as an argument in its favour, because, before such an argument can be accepted as worth anything, it must be shown that the visitors belong to that class for whom these collections were intended. If these collections are to be merely the luxurious resort of the rich, of those who from their wealth and position are able, if they please, to set up galleries and create collections for themselves, we give to the people no adequate return for the taxation which was imposed upon them." And this care for the interests of the poorer classes sometimes led to positive action on his part. In 1861 he denounced the harshness of the London Board of Guardians to the workless poor ; and he was instrumental in passing a measure for creating special refuges for " destitute wayfarers ". The relative poverty which had endangered his own career never ceased to influence a mind which was prone to base its judgment on personal experience. His championship of poverty led him to protest indignantly against Mr. Gladstone's attempt to apply the Income-Tax to endowed charities. " These charities are the heritage of the poor," he declared in the House of Commons in 1863, " secured to them by law, and they are as much entitled to them as the son of a peer is to inherit the property of his ancestors."

In those days children were born not only little Radicals or little Conservatives, but also little members of the Upper Classes or little members of the Lower Classes ; and Cecil was born to the tradition of boys and girls in the well-to-do families that they should show interest in and feel responsibility for the welfare of those who were born in less favourable circumstances. It was not unusual for the richer children to be taught that their duty as good Christians was to give one-tenth of their income to the poor. Cecil held with more than the average fervour the opinion that those born in his position had a definite obligation to think of the wellbeing of the masses, without however coupling with that solicitude the weakening of their own position and authority ; but that position could only be maintained on condition that the duty to the whole community was properly performed. Those born in a position of affluence must exert themselves, or their influence would inevitably decline. . . .

Certain it is that he himself habitually thought in terms of the whole nation. The different classes and professions counted very little with him by comparison with the sum of their interests. Thinking of Britain as one among many nations, his main concern was that she should play her part worthily ; and his mind turned most readily to foreign affairs, and to a study of the great figures of the immediate past who had given to Britain the dominant position in Europe which she was beginning to enjoy. In these early writings his best and most enduring contributions are those in which he studies the policies of Pitt and Castlereagh, the general trend of British foreign policy, and the contemporary problems of Poland and the Danish Duchies. These five essays have been accorded the honour, rare among ephemeral publications, of being reprinted in book form.* It was no doubt a fortunate accident that the authoritative Lives of William Pitt and Castlereagh, written respectively by Lord Stanhope and Sir Archibald Alison, should have been published just at this time. But there is never a lack of biographies among the year's new books, and Cecil chose at once for review those upon Pitt and Castlereagh. He never wrote another biographical study ; he modelled himself upon these two statesmen ; and he was destined to combine in his own person for more than ten years the two offices of the premiership and the foreign secretaryship in which Pitt and Castlereagh earned their fame. The majority of his *Quarterly* articles, it is true, dealt with domestic problems. And they had immediate political effect in the limited circles which then governed the country and in which the *Quarterly* was habitually read. But their effect, though more immediate, was less enduring than the relatively few articles which he wrote on foreign affairs.

And of these the essays on Pitt and Castlereagh reflect the views which were always nearest to his heart. They are the key to his own subsequent greatness. They testify to his principles ; they disclose his political methods ; they forecast his career. Moreover, they rise to the height of literature, and perform the function of historical assessment. The final passage of the second essay on Pitt stands out as a good example of the noblest English prose. The writer relates the famous death-bed scene and sustains the authenticity of the dying statesman's last utterance :

" Oh, my country, how I leave my country ! " ; and he proceeds :

" It [this exclamation] was mournfully in character with a life devoted to his country as few lives have been. Since his

* *Essays by Robert Marquess of Salisbury,* 2 vols. " Biographical " and " Foreign Politics " (John Murray).

first entry into the world he had been absolutely hers. For her he had foregone the enjoyments of youth, the ties of family, the hope of fortune. For three and twenty years his mind had moulded her institutions, and shaped her destiny. It was an agonizing thought for his dying pillow, that he had ruled her almost absolutely, and that she had trusted him without hesitation and without stint, and that this was the end of it all. At his bidding the most appalling sacrifices had been made in vain ; and now he was leaving her in the darkest hour of a terrible reverse, and in the presence of the most fearful foe whom she had ever been called upon to confront. Such thoughts might well wring from him a cry of mental anguish, even in the convulsions of death. It was not given to him to know how much he had contributed to the final triumph. Long after his feeble frame had been laid near his father's grave, his policy continued to animate the councils of English statesmen, and the memory of his lofty and inflexible spirit encouraged them to endure. After eleven more years of suffering, Europe was rescued from her oppression by the measures which Pitt had advised, and the long peace was based upon the foundations which he had laid. But no such consoling vision cheered his death-bed. His fading powers could trace no ray of light across the dark and troubled future. The leaders had not yet arisen, who, through un-exampled constancy and courage, were to attain at last to the glorious deliverance towards which he had pointed the way, but which his eyes were never permitted even in distant prospect to behold."

This passage surely gives Lord Salisbury a claim to be counted among the three, or perhaps four, Prime Ministers who would have been acclaimed as brilliant authors if they had not been great statesmen.

The essay on Castlereagh is historical writing of sustained excellence from the first sentence to the last. And it performs at least one of the proudest services of the historian—that of rescuing from disrepute the character of a statesman who had suffered grievously from the misunderstanding and malice of his own generation. The greater the man the greater the abuse he is likely to get from contemporary opponents ; for how many has politics been the most ungrateful of professions ! Castlereagh was howled into his grave ; he had to rely entirely upon the historian to accord him the justice which his contemporaries denied him. Sir Archibald Alison began the process of reinstatement ; but his labours would hardly have been effective without the additional currency given to them by Cecil's championship. Cecil's sympathy went out to the man who cared nothing for praise or blame by comparison with doing whatever in his own eyes seemed best for the country ; and he took the opportunity to pen some scathing sentences about opportunists, time-servers *et hoc genus omne*. These two essays on Pitt and Castlereagh, in fact, convey what Cecil felt about the personal virtues most to be admired in a statesman. Contrasting the profligacy, extravagance and mutability of Fox to the stern and inflexible moderation of Pitt, the author reflects on the " silent disgust " with which the British public regard the factiousness of scheming politicians who, " living only in and for the House of Commons, moving in an atmosphere of constant intrigue, accustomed to look upon oratory as a mode of angling for political support and upon political professions as only baits of more or less attractiveness, acquire a very peculiar code of ethics, and are liable wholly to lose sight of the fact that there is a stiffer and less corrupted morality out of doors ".

Commenting on Pitt's choice of the moment to intervene against revolutionary France, he finds that " as long as English interests were untouched, he pursued the wise policy of nonintervention " ; and that was the touchstone by which he was always to test his own interventions. On another occasion he expressed the opinion that " England should abstain from a meddling diplomacy ". And Quixotism had no place at all in his ideal of statesmanship.

Many of Cecil's aphorisms are inspiring even now by their applicability ; others may stimulate by their challenge. As an instance of the latter kind, most people today would consider his praise of the coldness of Castlereagh's character excessive : " Enthusiasm was precisely the ingredient," he writes, " which had been omitted in the composition of Castlereagh's character . . . no tinge of that enthusiastic temper which leads men to overhunt a beaten enemy, to drive a good cause to excess, to swear allegiance to a formula, or to pursue an impracticable ideal, ever threw its shadow upon Lord Castlereagh's serene, impassive intelligence. . . . If he had only constructed a few brilliant

40

periods about nationality and freedom, or given a little wordy sympathy to Greece, or Naples, or Spain, or the South American Republics, the world would have heard much less of the horrors of his policy." Enthusiasm was one of Lord Salisbury's taboos ; so it is not surprising that in another essay, written at the time of the Polish struggle for freedom in 1863, he should betray little sympathy for the impetuous revolt of that sorely-tried people. He described them as " an excitable race, little used to restraint ", and particularly prone to "factiousness ", which was another of Lord Salisbury's special dislikes. Even before the partition of the country in the eighteenth century " the hearts of the Poles were already parcelled out ", he wrote in his essay " Foreign Politics " ; and, " an independent Poland is a mere chimera ". But later on he added that " an independent Poland will become a possibility when individual Polish leaders shall have shown that they have acquired the moral capacity for self-renunciation ". In the make-up of statesmanship he put character first. " A character for unselfish honesty ", he wrote in his study of Pitt, " is the only secure passport to the confidence of the English people."

2

Throughout the years '63 and '64 the British Government was in a turmoil over the complicated problem known in diplomatic parlance as " the Danish Duchies ". Lord Palmerston at first treated the matter with his usual cavalier, but in this case misplaced, confidence. One of his many reputed *obiter dicta* was that there was only one man in the Foreign Office who understood it and unfortunately he had just died. Being himself now Prime Minister, he gladly left the conduct of the negotiations in the hands of his well-meaning but less competent Foreign Secretary, Lord Russell, who parodied Pam's language, but did not possess his sense of the proper relation between words and acts. British foreign policy, as C. A. Fyffe wrote in his *History of Modern Europe*, became for the time " a thing of snarls and grievances ". The extraordinary intricacies of the disputed succession to the two Duchies are set out in full by Cecil in his *Quarterly Review* article of January, 1864, and show that one man in England at least had not only grasped its details but also understood its larger implications. He denounced with even more than his usual pungency and at more than his accustomed length the vacillations of the Foreign Secretary. His article occupies 52 pages of the *Quarterly*, which, at 440 words to a page, runs to 23,000 words, the length of a small book. We need not follow him through the rival claims to the Duchies of the Duke of Augustenburg and Prince Christian of Gluecksburg, the different solutions proposed by the resuscitated Federal Diet at Frankfort, by Austria or by Prussia, and the various interpositions of Napoleon III, and the British Government, or explain the rash chauvinism of the Danish people. Cecil ran through the history of the Duchies since 1779 ; and his article, being written at the end of 1863, was published a whole year before the dispute was settled. It is all the more remarkable therefore that at this early stage of its international ramifications Cecil should so clearly have perceived the immense importance of its outcome. At that time Prussia and Austria were the two leading countries in the loose confederation which nominally united all German-speaking States, large and small, with its headquarters at Frankfort. But Cecil knew his history, and knowledge of Prussia's past enabled him to penetrate the future with wonderful accuracy. In the essay on Poland published nine months earlier he had written : " Frederick [the Great] had never been troubled with scruples upon the subject of territorial acquisition, and he was not likely to commence them in the case of Poland. Spoliation was the hereditary tradition of his race. The whole history of the kingdom over which he ruled was a history of lawless annexation " ; and the writer unequivocally asserted that the determination of Prussia was, in this case also, to disintegrate Denmark by filching the two Duchies for herself; that it was again " the fable of the Wolf and the Lamb " ; and he added that if Germany succeeded in getting rid of " the present subdivision which neutralizes her natural resources " she would become " one of the most powerful Empires in the world ". Still more remarkably prophetic was it to foresee, when Kiel was a Danish town and no German State possessed a navy, " the German fleet riding in the harbour of Kiel ".*

* In the full passage Lord Salisbury writes that either Germany would become one of the most powerful Empires in the world, or else " the present enthusiasm will exhaust the energies of a people so unpractical, without leading to any definite result, and Germany will fall back into her old

Having thus penetrated the future he warned Lord Russell above everything else to make his position clear and stand firmly upon it. That is just what the Foreign Secretary entirely failed to do. Cecil writes :

" In this Danish matter, the fickle and trimming character of his policy has won for us little respect . . . when Denmark seemed in earnest, and Germany comparatively lukewarm, Lord Russell was a strong Dane. . . . Shortly afterwards . . . Germany became fearfully in earnest, and there was no doubt that if she was in earnest, Germany was the strongest Power. Lord Russell's views underwent a salutary change. He became a decided German."

At the request of the British Government, Cecil went on, Denmark had withdrawn her army from strong positions. If therefore, having deferred to our counsels, she were afterwards abandoned by us and " crushed in the unequal conflict ", a stain which time could not efface would lie upon England's honour. There is no deeper baseness than " the wordy friendship, which, implying the promise of aid, without formally pledging it, beguiles the weaker combatant into a fatal trust in his ally, and then deserts him ". A final warning on the last page of the article contains a prophecy which was not destined to be fulfilled until long after Lord Salisbury's strong hand had ceded to his successors the tiller of British policy. " If, by timid language and a false love of peace, Germany is encouraged to believe that she can set treaties at defiance with impunity, a Continental war will result, in which it is almost impossible that England should not be forced to take a part."

One by-product of the Schleswig-Holstein imbroglio for Cecil was the study which it afforded him of the new Prussian Premier and Foreign Minister, Otto von Bismarck-Schoenhausen. This burly Pomeranian, born of an ancient soldier-race in a Brandenburg manor house, Prussian to the core, loyal, like his fathers, to the King of Prussia and knowing no other loyalty, a jovial hearty man in his forties, whose favourite drink was champagne mixed with beer, concealed an oriental capacity for

condition, more divided, more stagnant, more impotent than before, and more helplessly the slave of Russia ".

Since this passage was written we have seen both prophecies fulfilled in turn.

dissimulation behind his habitually frank outspokenness. And on this his first appearance in a leading role on the European stage he achieved conjurings of ruse and duplicity which in his long and famous career he never excelled. He backed and fooled in turn Prince Christian of Gluecksburg and the Duke of Augustenburg, championed at one time the German Minor States, at another Austria, then set them at loggerheads one with the other, appeased Napoleon III and treated London with polite disregard. He anticipated every rival's move ; brought Austria into war against Denmark side by side with Prussia ; ousted Austria when she had served his purpose ; defied the rest of the German States, and at the end made war on them and on Austria ; and when they were defeated in the " Seven Weeks War " he annexed the Duchies to Prussia and made Prussia the leading German State.

We may be sure that Cecil minutely noted every move. Bismarck gave him his first lesson in power-politics.

The impressions and information flung upon an eager mind were not so numerous in the last century as they are in this age of wireless, popular digests and evening papers which begin to appear in the middle of the morning ; and they did not therefore crowd each other out. The impacts which Cecil received in these impressionable years before he had reached the age of forty were never effaced from his mind ; and their duration gives them their importance. Most of them are comprehended in the one article he wrote on the conduct of British policy by the Foreign Office (" Foreign Politics ", *Quarterly Review*, April, 1864). He wrote a few others before and after this date on individual foreign problems or events ; but in " Foreign Policy " he summed up much that he had written in the articles we have already noticed and foreshadowed many of the policies we shall see him carrying through in his maturity.

He begins this article by taking up the tragic story of the Danish Duchies where he had left it in his essay three months earlier. The situation had in that short interval lamentably deteriorated. The Prussian forces, followed by the Austrians, had just invaded Schleswig ; Rendsburg, the capital of the southern Duchy of Holstein, had earlier been evacuated by the Danes, as we have seen, on British advice. In the earlier article, believing that England would act up to her brave words if the dispute led to blows, Cecil had written, " Happily in this case, as in most others, the policy of honour is also the policy of peace " —an aphorism which was only to be vindicated at Berlin fourteen years later by Disraeli and himself. Now, in April of this year, 1864, he wrote in bitter dejection : " Peace without honour is not only a disgrace, but, except as a temporary respite, it is a chimera "—(a maxim which applies exactly to the Munich peace of 1938). Cecil relates, at a length which makes it impossible to repeat them here, all the assurances and semi-assurances with which Russell and Palmerston incited the Danes to diplomatic firmness. " Willingness on good cause to go to war is the best possible security for peace," he had written in his study of Castlereagh—and from that conviction he never deviated. His own policy, had he been in office in 1864, would probably have been to make the invasion of the Danish Duchies a *casus belli* and to have let Prussia know that that was the British attitude.* It is an interesting speculation that Lord Salisbury might have prevented or greatly retarded the domination of all Germany from Berlin.

But Russell and Palmerston—Cecil throughout places the major blame on Russell—were as ineffective as they were active. " Their interference is incessant, their language is bolder and far more insolent than it was in better times. But the impulse is gone which gave it force." It had been, he writes, the same sequence of bravado and retreat as in the case of the Polish uprising against Russia in 1863. Then likewise it had not been necessary to assume a hostile attitude ; but " to make a feint of striking and then to run away was a simple proclamation of cowardice ". And he continues mordantly : " A nation may uphold its honour without being Quixotic : but no reputation can survive a display of the Quixotism which falters at the sight of a drawn sword." And, since the writer has been condemned for his lack of sympathy with the Poles, let us have one more quotation referring to the Polish insurrection : " To threaten or to hint an intervention which you had no earnest intention of carrying out was contemptible as regarded the Power whom you

* One of his reasons for firm opposition to Prussia on this issue was that England, as " the greatest of commercial Powers ", should never suffer the Sound, " the highway of nations " passing between Denmark and Sweden, to fall into hands that might close it.

pretended to defy, but it was inhuman towards the people with whose agony you were playing."

The lesson, then, that Cecil took to heart from his study of these two failures of policy was never to undertake more than he was in a position to fulfil. "To mislead a small country to its ruin" remained for him the blackest of crimes against loyalty and honour.

Not quite the blackest—the worst offence of all was to be arrogant to the weak and cringing to the strong; and during this period before he himself took over the Foreign Office several examples occurred of the horrible mixture of boastfulness and escapism. Better far a policy of moderation and of occasional concessions. "A policy of moderation is one to which no Christian man could raise an objection. . . . Courtesy of language, a willingness to concede, a reluctance to take offence, if they are impartially extended to all, will always, even when they are carried to excess, command respect and admiration." But to have a "tariff of insolence" which was applied to foreign States according to their strength was beyond all bounds of decency.

Yet this was the character of British foreign policy during the closing years of the Palmerston regime. In the eight years surveyed by Cecil, between 1856 and 1864, there were six separate cases of weak countries being bullied by Britain and three cases where menacing language had been followed by hasty retreat before the manifest firmness of the more powerful countries—first Russia, then Prussia and then the United States. Among the weaker States, China had been the first sufferer. In 1856 a Chinese vessel flying a British flag was seized by the Chinese authorities for piracy; so we bombarded Canton. In the Malay Peninsula in 1862 we bombarded Tringanu in order to hasten the expulsion of a certain ex-Sultan Mahomet, who was accused of turbulence and hostility to Britain. Next year we burnt Epé, on the west coast of Africa, to punish a local chief who had wrongfully levied duties in British territory. In the same year we dismantled the fortifications of the Ionian Islands, to the great distress of the Greek inhabitants—though it must be added that the dismantling was a condition of Britain's voluntary cession of the Islands to Greece. Far more flagrantly unjust in Cecil's view was the seizure of Brazilian trading-ships off Rio de Janeiro (in 1862) because three rowdy British sailors, who were in plain clothes, were locked up for forty-eight hours in the local guard-house before being restored to their ship ; and even more discreditable was the bombardment of the Japanese port of Kagosima by direct order of Lord Russell in January 1864. A certain Mr. Richardson had been mortally wounded by the armed retainers of a Daimio. The Japanese Government expressed its humble regret, undertook to do its best to punish the culprit or culprits, and erected a series of guard-houses along the route usually taken by the Daimios in order to protect foreign lives. These measures were judged totally inadequate by the British Foreign Secretary, who demanded among other things the payment of indemnities amounting to £125,000 and the capital execution of the chief perpetrators in the presence of one or more of Her Majesty's naval officers. The murderers could not be found ; so the British admiral Commanding-in-Chief in Chinese waters informed the representative of Japan that " The settlement of this matter can no longer be delayed. Kagosima is at my mercy." Then, according to the official British account, the admiral spoke again : " You must remember that we are one of the first nations in the world, who, instead of meeting civilized people, as you think yourselves, in reality encounter barbarians." So the British ships opened fire. And at the conclusion of this warlike feat the British Consul reported : " The operations were attended with complete success. . . . The fire, which is still raging, affords reasonable grounds for believing that the entire town of Kagosima is now a mass of ruins."

Japan was a weak country in those days, without military or naval resources ; as was also Brazil. Russia on the other hand was a Great Power, and Prussia was becoming one. That was also true of the United States, where a Canadian subject, one Mr. Shaver, was treated worse than the British sailors had been by Brazil ; he was illegally imprisoned for three months ; the polite notes of the British ambassador were brusquely answered ; and no retributive action was attempted by Britain.

The policy of a tariff of insolence filled Cecil with a sense of shame ; and also with the conviction that it was the duty of a Foreign Secretary—in an age, be it remembered, when national war was an accepted instrument of policy—to make up his mind as early as possible in every international dispute whether or not its importance was sufficient to make the satisfaction of the British claim a *casus belli*. If honour or vital interests were involved, an iron front must be shown from the first ; if not, suitable concession should be proposed for the sake of agreement.* And, were the State concerned great or small, powerful or weak, the negotiations would be conducted with the same unruffled courtesy.

The dreadful combination, during the 'sixties, of arrogance with feebleness, of warlike language with pacifism—the " policy of loopholes " as Cecil called it—had brought English influence in the Councils of Europe to its lowest possible point.† And worse still, the old taunt of " perfide Albion " had been revived and given a currency which could not but be regarded as valid.

European countries have long memories ; and the abandonment first of the Poles and then of the Danes recalled to their minds the several occasions when Britain had used an alliance just so long as it was useful to her and had then cut out. At the end of the Marlborough wars she had abandoned the Austrians and the Dutch. In the next great Continental war she had deserted her ally Frederick of Prussia and left him to face a European coalition as best he might—England having seized the French oversea territories that she coveted, just as she had secured Gibraltar and Minorca during the Marlburian war. Our two-Party system led to abrupt changes in foreign as well as in domestic policy. On a later occasion Bismarck was to say : " England is one of those dexterous Powers with whom it is not only impossible to form any lasting alliance but who cannot be relied upon with any certainty, because in England the basis of all political relations is more changeable than in any other State ; it is the product of elections and the resulting majorities."

* " The only duty incumbent upon him [Lord Russell] was to make up his mind from the first which course it was that English interests required him to take, and to shape both his language and his acts accordingly. The policy of peace and the policy of war were equally consistent with honour and with public law."

† British policy in regard to the Polish rising and the Danish Duchies had brought us into equal contempt in France and in Germany. " The sole difference ", wrote Cecil, " is that on the last occasion what we have had to bear has not been the sharp and biting sarcasm of France, but only the lumbering gibes which in Germany pass for wit."

Not the least of the services Lord Salisbury was to render to Britain was to lift foreign policy, with the cordial concurrence of his Liberal opposite number, Lord Rosebery, from the partisanship of Party politics to the national plane ; and to instil into it the elements of loyalty, integrity and steadfastness in which it had recently been so wanting.

The list of political lessons which Cecil drew from these studies of foreign problems is now nearly complete. But let us note two further points. In Castlereagh's policy after the fall of Napoleon Cecil approved the resolve " so to establish the balance of power that it should not be easily overthrown "— a policy which he was himself successfully to maintain for a score of years. And in the same essay he observes, perhaps a little cynically—but has not subsequent history borne him out ?— that the only bond of union which endures between States is " the absence of all clashing interests ".

The amount of labour which Cecil put into his own political education was indeed prodigious. These articles in the *Quarterly* are full of facts, figures and research. More than once he wrote four of them in the year, amounting to over 80,000 words—that is, to a good-sized volume. Taken together with his contributions to the *Saturday Review* he wrote the equivalent of a book every year from 1860 to 1866. And in addition, he was an active back-bencher. Unlike so many politicians of a modern democracy, he learned his political lessons before he assumed any political responsibilities. He did not begin to practise the art of government until his training was as complete as he could make it. He reduced to a minimum the margin of mistakes which are made by inexperience in office—at the country's expense.

3

In 1865 his eldest brother died. So Robert Cecil assumed the courtesy title of Lord Cranborne, and his prospects were metamorphosed. In Victorian England to be a younger son was one thing, to be the eldest son was quite another. He became heir to a marquessate, for which he cared little, and to Hatfield, for which he cared only a little more, and to an ample fortune, for which he cared most, because it would mean relief from anxiety on behalf of his wife and growing family. He was not a reader of Robert Burns (Alexander Pope was the only poet he was fond of reading), but the Scot it was who had expressed the feelings which had filled much of his mind in the past few years :

> To make a happy fireside clime
> For weans and wife,
> There's the true pathos and sublime
> Of human life.

Choice and chance, as for most of us, were moulding his life. His choice to accept, rather than to refuse, the offer of Stamford directed him to a political career ; the chance of his elder brother's premature death secured to him the succession to Hatfield ; his choice of Georgina was to put the seal on his success at Westminster and on his happiness at home. Whatever doubts had lately lingered in his mind about the profession he should follow were now completely and for ever dispelled. His health also improved with his prospects. Though when over-fatigued he still became abnormally sensitive to noise and even to touch, there is no further record of his being incapacitated by nervous distemper.

CHAPTER IV—1866–1867

OFFICE AND RESIGNATION

Most ambitious young politicians, even in these non-hero-worshipping days, have a hero and a model, who are not always one and the same. The first may more commonly be a figure of the past, the second a contemporary. For Cranborne, as we have seen, both were statesmen of the recent past—his hero Pitt, his model Castlereagh. His own leader in the House of Commons, Disraeli, was neither a hero nor a model in his eyes. He was not even an object of respect. Though later he came to modify his assessment, Cranborne, during his first few years in the House of Commons, thought of Disraeli as an unprincipled Jew who had no right to be there at all, for he shared the view of his godfather, the Duke of Wellington, that Jews ought not to legislate for a Christian community. In the first article he contributed to the *Quarterly* he had written of Disraeli's attitude towards Reform : " His tactics were so various, so flexible, so shameless . . . he had so admirable a knack of enticing into the same lobby a happy family of proud old Tories and foaming Radicals, martial squires jealous for their country's honour, and manufacturers who had written it off their books as an unmarketable commodity—that so long as his party backed him, no Government was strong enough to hold out against his attacks." And he denounced him just as vigorously in the House of Commons itself. After one of his philippics against him in those early days, before he had come to know his leader with any kind of personal intimacy, he went for the weekend to Hatfield, and on arrival he learned to his horror that the great man was himself weekending there as the guest of his father. His biographer-daughter gives an amusing account of the young critic's consternation. He retired to the garden, to think out in solitude the best way in which to manage his first home meeting with the unexpected guest. Earnestly brooding upon this delicate problem he turned a corner of the shrubbery where he had sought seclusion, and almost ran into Disraeli—who opened his arms to him and exclaimed : " Ah, Robert, Robert, how glad I am to see you ! "

Completely outmanœuvred, the youthful rebel realized with a pang of injured pride that to the victim of his attacks they appeared to be of lighter metal than they did to himself.

Disraeli's broad-mindedness was proved in the most practical manner when the Russell-Gladstone Ministry fell in June, 1866, and, in the new Conservative Cabinet, Cranborne was offered the post of Secretary of State for India. The offer indeed came from Lord Derby ; but the new Prime Minister was so much dependent upon Disraeli that he would certainly not have included Cranborne without his consent ; and in fact Disraeli never wavered, even during the more bitter differences that were to come next year, in seeking to keep in touch with and even consult an able young Conservative whom he admired all the more for his displays of independent spirit.

Derby, when he made the offer, thought it necessary to remind Cranborne that at the India Office he would find a Council which was there to advise him but which he should not allow to control him. The advice was unneeded in the case of Cranborne, because, for all his lack of the social touch, he knew by nature how to hold an exact balance between authoritativeness and readiness to consult. He showed from his first entry into the Office in Whitehall a combination of vigour in administration with courtesy to those working under him to which several of his subordinates paid feeling tributes when he so soon resigned.

But none realized more keenly than he that if he was to exercise his authority effectively he must be master of his subject, and it is typical of his outlook that as soon as he had the time for it he began a thorough study of the Koran. Mahomet's bible was still at that time one of the most widely read—or perhaps it would be more correct to say, most widely heard—books in all the world ; for wherever Mahommedans were gathered together its passages were daily read or recited, and it provided the religious, social, legal, and commercial code by which the entire life of Moslems was governed. Cranborne's innate regard for religion as a motive of action made the study of the holy book of a large part of India and of the Middle East a practical matter. To rule the masses, he must understand their motives.

The Indian Mutiny had come and gone, and he considered that his main duty to the people of India was " to keep peace and to push on the public works ". But he had one specific task to perform, and that was to present the Indian Budget to the House of Commons. It was due on July 19th; and as he had taken over his Ministry only on July 2nd, all else had to be put aside for these first two-and-a-half weeks of office. When on the appointed day he rose from his place on the Front Bench few members supposed that he would do more than give them the barest facts and figures. He astonished them all by his complete familiarity with the matter in hand. Even his parenthetical observations pleased the Indian experts in the House. Disraeli, in the late report which he was already sending nightly to Queen Victoria, noted that " the manner was vigorous, and showed a mastery of his matter which . . . evidently surprised the House. Persons of weight, in private, of both Parties, spoke of the effort with approbation." It was not only that Cranborne showed so much knowledge both of India and of finance that surprised the House, but also, and perhaps particularly, that its leading mutineer had proved himself to be at need a laborious official.

2

And yet his first spell of ministerial office, so successfully begun, was brought to an abrupt end by developments entirely unconnected with India. There is no need to go into all the details of the quarrel over " Reform " which almost shattered Derby's Ministry, unsecured by any certain majority, within a few months of its formation. For the last decade there had been a general conviction that the time was ripe for an extension of the franchise beyond the limits of the first and greatest Reform Bill of 1832. Indeed, since 1849 " Reform of the Franchise " had been mentioned six times in a Speech from the Throne. But Tories and Whigs, Conservatives and Liberals, and the group of Liberals known as the " Adullamites "—combined and counter-combined to defeat on matters of detail every project that was brought forward. Mr. Lowe, Reform's most unbending opponent, called the whole business a " Dutch auction ". The numerous and often insincere proposals, however, culminated in 1866 in a serious Bill introduced by Lord Russell and Mr. Gladstone. But when it was put to the vote, some of their own followers seceded; it was consequently defeated; and its authors resigned.

Lord Derby and Mr. Disraeli took their place, and formed a Tory-Conservative Government, in a predominantly Whig-Liberal House of Commons, in which Cranborne, as we have seen, became responsible for the India Office. He had no idea that his leaders, who had directed the attack on the Liberal Reform Bill, were going to introduce a major measure of their own.

Nor is it by any means certain that Derby and his Chancellor of the Exchequer had any such intention themselves. What exactly passed through the inscrutable mind of Dizzy at that time is beyond definition ; certain it is that he had long believed that some concessions to the reformers were necessary. His speeches in the first session of the year had been studiously vague ; and the Queen's speech of February, 1867, contained only the customary imprecise allusion to the subject. Nevertheless, very early in the year the Chancellor had made up his mind to get a Reform Bill on the statute book. It now seems probable that the influence of Queen Victoria had more to do with his change of mind than most people realized. In her downright and practical way, the Queen was vexed at the prolonged discussions which led to no result, and she offered as early as October, 1866, to act mediatorially between the Conservative and Liberal leaders—a " royal project " which Dizzy at first dismissed as " a mere phantom ". But he was ever willing to please his Royal mistress ; and the Queen was in earnest. She wrote to Lord Derby that " if the question of Reform be not taken up in earnest by her Ministers, with a view to its settlement, very serious consequences may ensue ". The Queen's view was also the view of the people of London, who broke down the railings of Hyde Park near Marble Arch ; and the agitation spread to the big industrial centres, Birmingham, Manchester, Leeds, and Glasgow.

It was Derby, and not Disraeli, who light-heartedly set the ball rolling from the point where his Party stood. " Of all possible hares to start, I do not know a better than the extension to household suffrage, coupled with plurality of voting," he wrote to Disraeli in a letter dated December 22, 1866.* Disraeli did not answer at once ; but by January 1867 he had evidently come to the conclusion that an extension of the franchise, with specific

* Buckle, Vol. IV, p. 484.

safeguards, was a political necessity. Derby gave him the mandate of bringing a Reform Bill before the Commons.

For the sake of judging Cranborne's conduct at this crucial moment of his career it is necessary to state the main points of the Disraelian measure. He laid it before the Cabinet on February 19, when Cranborne was of course present. Its central feature was household suffrage—that is to say, that every householder who resided in and paid the rates for his house should have the right to vote. To counter and modify this " very dangerous experiment ", as Cranborne called it and other supporters thought it, Disraeli offered a second vote to every person who paid one pound a year or more in direct taxes, or who owned £30 in the Savings Bank or had £50 invested in government funds or who " was possessed of a superior education ". The Cabinet was to meet again four days later, on Saturday, February 23 ; and in the meantime Cranborne declared himself satisfied, merely suggesting that any man who paid ten shillings (instead of one pound) a year in direct taxation should have the privilege of casting two votes. The Cabinet duly met on the following Saturday and the scheme (without Cranborne's amendment) was accepted by the Cabinet as a whole, including the Secretary for India, though it was well understood by his colleagues that neither he, nor Lord Carnarvon (Colonial Secretary), nor General Peel (Secretary for War), really liked the measure at all.

Then Cranborne exploded his bomb. He had been much taken up with the business of his Department, and it was only on the following day, Sunday, February 24, that he had time thoroughly to examine the effects of the qualifying figures to which he had agreed the day before. After a long day's close scrutiny, in which he was helped by his wife, he came to the conclusion that they would " throw the small boroughs almost, and many of them entirely, into the hands of the voter whose qualification is lower than £10 [rating franchise] ". " I find ", he continues in his memorandum to Lord Derby, " that those of our friends who sit for boroughs with less than 25,000 inhabitants will be in a much worse condition than they would have been in consequence of Mr. Gladstone's [Reform Bill]. . . . I could not look in the face those whom last year I urged to resist Mr. Gladstone." His conclusion was that he could not now assent to the scheme of reform, and he indicated that Lord Carnarvon concurred with him that resignation was the only course open to them.

It will be observed that the definite reason advanced by Cranborne was one of detail, and of practical disadvantage to Conservative members representing small boroughs ; but everybody who knew him well perfectly understood that in fact he was much more moved to his protest by his fundamental objection to the wide extension of the franchise, and, especially, to the sudden and haphazard manner in which Derby and Disraeli introduced it.

The Prime Minister received Cranborne's memorandum at break of dawn on Monday, and sent it round to Disraeli at once, with the scribbled comment : " The enclosed, just received, is utter ruin. What on earth are we to do ? " Dizzy, more buoyant than his chief, scribbled back : " This is stabbing in the back ! I will come to you as soon as possible, but I am not up, being indisposed ; but I shall rally immediately in such dangers. It seems like treachery."

The House was to meet at half-past four that Monday afternoon. Before that, at 2.30, the Prime Minister had arranged to explain to his followers at the Carlton Club what he proposed to do. At two o'clock, he literally did not know himself. But he got together the members of his Cabinet at that time ; and they had ten minutes' discussion, in which they decided to modify the Bill in the sense of restriction, so as to retain the dissident Ministers —General Peel had now definitely been added to the other two.

Disraeli faced an emergency which tried to the uttermost even his gifts of improvisation. He must introduce, in an entirely unprepared speech, and to an eager, excited and critical House, undefined proposals of the first magnitude. He had to be very cautious, and he hated caution. His speech pleased nobody.

Disraeli turned its failure to quick advantage. The storm of indignation which greeted it was in reality not altogether unwelcome to him ; for it convinced both him and the Prime Minister that the only possible policy was to widen the franchise rather than to restrict it, as compared with their proposals of the week before—even at the cost of having to refashion their Cabinet. Disraeli's change of front was tactical rather than fundamental, for his imagination had long been stirred by his dream of a new

Tory democracy. The electorate of 1832 was a Whig creation ; and the Whigs of 1867 were loth to alter their handiwork. Many, perhaps most of them, were half-hearted about extending the franchise further. Moreover, moderate, or as we should say now, leftist, Tories felt very much the same as the more conservative Whigs. Disraeli was intensely eager to create a wholly independent clear-cut Conservative Party ; and he now saw his chance of placing the two older groups, Whig and Tory, into sharply separated camps, and at the same time creating a new democracy which would look to the new Conservatives, with whom the older Tories would be associated as subordinate partners.

Accordingly, at the end of that exciting week, on Saturday, March 2, the Cabinet reverted to its own first and more generous measure of reform ; and Cranborne, Carnarvon and Peel finally handed in their resignations (Cranborne's place at the India Office being taken by Stafford Northcote). When the revived Bill came before the House it was drastically liberalized by amendments, moved by moderate members on the other side of the House, for which Disraelian Conservatives could vote. The earned privilege of a double vote was rejected, and other " safeguards " abandoned. When it finally became law (August 15, 1867) it was an agreed measure ; and it was actually much more advanced than Mr. Gladstone's proposals which the same House had thrown out only the year before. " The process effecting this wide extension of political power to immense classes hitherto without it, was in every respect extraordinary," writes Lord Morley in his Life of Gladstone. " The great reform was carried by a parliament elected to support Lord Palmerston, and Lord Palmerston detested reform. It was carried by a government in a decided minority. It was carried by a Minister and by a leader of opposition,* neither of whom was at the time in the full confidence of his Party. Finally, it was carried by a House of Commons that the year before had, in effect, rejected a measure for the admission of only 400,000 new voters, while the measure to which it now assented added almost a million voters to the electorate." (The total numbers were 1,352,970 in 1867, and 2,243,259 in 1870.) †

* Disraeli's first position in that House of Commons was Leader of the Opposition.
† Morley, Vol. II, pp. 226–7.

So Cranborne found himself out of office within eight months of having achieved the sudden distinction of Cabinet rank ; and not only out of office, but out of favour ; he was now on the worst possible terms with the leaders of his Party, and therefore unlikely to resume his political career for an indefinite period. The Reform Act of 1867 was a brilliant success for the House of Commons' leader ; whatever may be thought of his turns and twists, Disraeli had performed a stroke of parliamentary genius ; his star was in the ascendant ; within a year Derby had resigned and the Jew succeeded him as Prime Minister.

3

And now Cranborne was out of it all and felt that he could never again be a follower, still less a colleague, of such a man. These two Conservatives were indeed as incongruous as any two members of the same Party could well be. Cranborne, far removed as he was in certain respects from the average Tory, had deep in him the instincts of the English country gentleman ; he was far from being alone in distrusting this flamboyant upstart with his curls and his waistcoats, his roses, his flashing phrases and mysterious silences, his social ambitions, and his novel-writing. Now to his fopperies had been added a parliamentary trickery which profoundly shocked the younger man's political fastidiousness. Cranborne had thought of Disraeli as a pantaloon politician in his earliest days ; now he seemed to be outdoing the Tapers and Tadpoles and Mr. Hoaxems about whom he had written with an only humorous disparagement ; perhaps he did in fact regard politics as just a game and a gamble. The author of *Coningsby* and *Sybil* certainly possessed in full measure the novelist's knack of giving expression to the various and opposing opinions of dissimilar characters ; while Cranborne on his part never wrote or spoke a word that he did not personally mean. Disraeli, too, was an actor, like other statesmen before and after him—like the elder Pitt and Mr. Lloyd George. Cranborne detested any kind of ostentation or pose, either in public or private life. He would never, for instance, even allow his adolescent family to engage in private theatricals at Hatfield. They offended his sense of sincerity.

How could he ever trust Disraeli again ? Had he not written

to him from Hughenden soon after taking office : " I have, throughout, been against [Reform] legislation, and continue so." And now ! The part that personal antipathy played in Cranborne's attitude is shown by his marked leniency to Derby, who was after all the responsible Prime Minister in all these political manœuvres, and who, according to Buckle, was the author of the phrase about " dishing the Whigs " which has so often been attributed to Disraeli. Gathorne-Hardy, a shrewd observer and friend of both men, had noted in his diary in February of this year, " Clearly Cranborne will not long act with Disraeli, that is at the bottom of it."

But personal dislike, deep as it was, was all the same not the main cause of severance. Cranborne's devotion to principle was still at this stage uncompromising, and he felt contempt for the political huckstering of the day. Seven years ago he had sarcastically written that the main object of the Parties in Parliament was " to take office ; that is the paramount aim to which all other objects are to yield, and for which the complicated structure of a party organisation has been created. . . . Bodies of honourable men act like the veriest adventurers ". This kind of doctrine, he continued, " strips the political contest of all that is inspiriting and ennobling, and reduces those who take part in it from the rank of Crusaders for a principle to the level of political caterans foraging for booty ". In the article which he now wrote for the *Quarterly* of October, 1867,* he devoted precisely two pages to the actual Reform Act and the whole of the remaining thirty pages to the degradation of public life which he saw around him. The " rapid and sudden " change of front had been effected by using the votes which had placed the Government in office for a policy which was the exact opposite of that which it had professed. " One or two " of the statesmen on the Government Bench " have shown a freedom from scruple surpassing all former example ; others have shown a feebleness of conviction which it is difficult to understand ". " As the wind blows, so they will point." " They live in an atmosphere of illusion, and can seldom be persuaded that any political principle is worth the sacrifice of their own careers " and so on, with the greater effect because he himself had sacrificed office.

His own view of what should be the methods of Conservatism

* " The Conservative Surrender."

when faced by proposals for drastic change emerges at the end
of this article, the best known of all those that he wrote on home
politics ; and one perceives the same practical and judicious mind
which made him a master in foreign affairs. Conservatives, he
writes, " must make up their minds what is worth struggling for,
and then not be afraid to struggle for it. Let them maturely
decide, before the conflict begins, what is of essential and what is
of secondary importance. Let them do their utmost to meet
fair grievances half-way; and to yield, while it can be done
gracefully, all that can be yielded without prejudice to any vital
principle. Concessions made before a contest are no sign of
weakness."

He foresaw with alarm but with singular clarity the day when
" labour gives law to capital, Trades' Union rules supreme,
democratic Parliaments contrive a graduated income tax, the
poor voting supplies and the rich finding ways and means ". A
step was taken in 1867 which was only the first ; the transfer of
power would be completed some day ; and he did not relish
the idea of " placing a great empire under the absolute control
of the poorest classes. . . . To give the guidance of this intricate
machinery of government to the least instructed class in the community, is to adopt in the management of the empire principles
which would not be entertained for a moment in any other
department of human affairs."

Nevertheless, having fought in vain against the big change
which implied bigger changes to come, he accepted the *fait
accompli*. In a classic passage he writes :

" It is the duty of every Englishman, and of every English
party, to accept a political defeat cordially, and to lend their
best endeavours to secure the success, or to neutralise the evil,
of the principles to which they have been forced to succumb.
England has committed many mistakes as a nation in the course
of her history ; but their mischief has often been more than
corrected by the heartiness with which after each great struggle
victors and vanquished have forgotten their former battles, and
have combined together to lead the new policy to its best results."

Cranborne's proved readiness to sacrifice career for a principle
certainly gained immediate recognition both inside and outside
the two Houses of Parliament. The new voters showed no resentment at his hostile attitude. Predominant power did not reach

the poorest workers until his day was over ; and the electorate now enfranchised in his despite returned him to or retained him in office three times in twenty years. It is a startling paradox that though Disraeli showed the greater trust in the British people, the people came to trust Salisbury in a way they had never trusted Disraeli. Salisbury, or Cranborne as we still must call him, stood for the immanent in British politics, for the element of stability and the high standards that should never be lost. He performed the special and obvious function of Conservatism, that of keeping the strand of continuity running through every change in the texture of national life, and conserving all that is best in the political tradition of the country. Disraeli on the other hand, for all his awareness of the value of historical institutions, realized better than Cranborne that Conservatism will moulder unless it remains a developing organism, adapting itself to the wider spread of education, the diffusion of information, and the people's growing consciousness of political issues. Between them the two men impersonated the whole doctrine of British Conservatism.

Disraeli now found himself the target for the slings and arrows of his former colleague, which were aimed at him from inside and from outside the House. He faced them with serenity. He good-naturedly reminded his wrathful assailant that ever since he had led the Party in the Commons he had favoured some enlargement of the electorate. In finding the right moment he had to be opportunist. The Bill of 1867 was admittedly an improvisation, but only because the opportunity to win the favour of a fidgety and irresolute House was sudden and probably fleeting. Reform Bills had been talked about since 1852. It was time for action. Cranborne had known (so he argued) that the grant of household suffrage was in his leaders' minds before the Queen's speech was composed. Why had he not stated his opposition more clearly beforehand ? " The postponement of action [by Cranborne] to the eleventh hour," writes Disraeli's biographer, " the endeavour to embarrass his colleagues by inducing others to accompany him, and the virulence with which, after resignation, he attacked and denounced his leaders, require a good deal of justification." * Cranborne's answer would no doubt have been that he had wished to avoid embarrassing his

* Buckle, Vol. IV, p. 512.

colleagues at all ; and their progress towards drastic reform was at first so gradual and then so erratic that he had no substantial ground for breaking away from them until they actually produced their unexpected Bill. Cranborne's nephew, the historian Mr. Algernon Cecil, has recorded his view that the decisive moment came for him on that Sunday, February 24, when he first had time fully to examine the data of the original Derby-Disraeli Bill and found that Disraeli had contrived " by a judicious manipulation of statistics, to get the more radical measure for household suffrage provisionally accepted by the whole Cabinet " —a stiff charge to make. Cranborne's son, Lord Robert Cecil (later Lord Cecil of Chelwood), wrote a short appreciation of his father after his death (*Monthly Review*, October, 1903) in which this episode of his father's career is given the most important place : " Political principle was at a discount. Except for the Radicals led by Cobden and Bright, who had a definite pro- gramme, the only real difference between the parties seemed to be that one of them sat on the right hand of the Speaker and the other on the left. . . . To his [Cranborne's] consternation the Government, after some hesitation, resolved to introduce a Reform Bill more democratic than that on which the previous [Whig] Administration had been defeated. Here was a crisis to test the sincerity of the young politician's belief in principle. He was only 37, in office for the first time under leaders of great authority and experience. To resign might well wreck his career and would certainly not prevent the Reform Bill from passing. . . . It may well have seemed that the self-sacrifice of a subordinate Minister would be of no advantage to any one." Nevertheless, his father had resigned, and in doing so " performed the greatest of all the services which he rendered to his country ".

This may be the filial hero-worship of one who was himself an idealist ; but the writer is near the mark when he says later in the same article : " It was the possession of the qualities here displayed that forms Lord Salisbury's chief title to greatness and that eventually secured for him the unbounded confidence of his fellow-countrymen." His own career was indeed to prove the truth of the words already quoted, which he had himself written of Pitt, " unselfish honesty is the only secure passport to the confidence of the English people ". Englishmen recognized in him a man who was capable of genuine self-sacrifice for the sake of his beliefs ; and they came to trust a judgment that was never formed until the matter under discussion had been considered in every detail, uninfluenced by conscious personal bias, and supported by extensive knowledge. We may accept as the just estimate the verdict of his biographer : * " Lord Cranborne undoubtedly owed much of the influence which he ultimately achieved to the conviction of his moral steadfastness which the public acquired at this time. It is probable that to this episode may be traced that note of completeness—of a trust without reserve—which characterised the confidence placed in him by his followers in after years."

Only a footnote need be added to this chapter. Disraeli, as soon as he succeeded Lord Derby as Prime Minister (in February of the following year), showed alike his own magnanimity and lack of understanding of Cranborne's feelings and character. He sent Sir Stafford Northcote, who though he had taken Cranborne's place at the India Office remained his good friend, to enquire whether he would rejoin the Cabinet now that Reform was out of the way. The negative answer was tersely worded.

* Lady Gwendolen Cecil, Vol. I, p. 287.

HOME LIFE AND HOUSE OF LORDS

This future Prime Minister was a man of no expectations ; and at this moment, in the springtime of 1867, his prospects seemed more than usually barren. He and his few staunch associates in the House of Commons were by customary standards adjudged political failures. The Party leaders had no use for them ; and the rebels themselves assumed that the new electorate would be hostile. Never a great believer in his own influence, Cranborne began to think of himself as useless and doomed to a life of impotent obscurity. To public disappointment was added private sorrow when his baby daughter died of pneumonia. In his despondency the old haunting thought of abandoning political life awoke again. He wrote to a Liberal friend, who had urged him to continue to be active in the House of Commons, " my opinions belong to the past, and it is better that the new principles in politics should be worked by those who sympathize with them heartily " ; and to Lord Carnarvon he wrote : " I do not agree that my continued presence in the House of Commons would be of much use. . . . Pure ' squire ' Conservatism is played out."

But once again Providence took a hand in his life-course. His father died on April 12, 1868.*

New responsibilities were thrust upon him ; and responsibility always roused him.

He became a landowner ; and the many new interests which his residence at Hatfield involved extended his contacts in every direction. He was nothing if not conscientious. He was elected Chairman of the local Quarter Sessions. He immersed himself in the management of his large estates, in which, so long as his elder brother and father had been alive, he had taken no interest. But the instinct of ten generations began to tell, and he was soon a keen farmer ; and this interest

---

* The two letters just referred to were actually written a few days after the death of his father, but they were answers to letters written before it, in which he was urged to remain an active politician.

in farming, once acquired, never left him. He gradually accumulated a library of works on agriculture ; his desk was overlaid with statistical returns and government reports ; and when electricity became a practical proposition he was one of the first men in the country to try to apply it to farming. He held weekly meetings with his bailiffs. He visited them regularly on their farms ; and he addressed his tenants annually at the rent-dinners held at Hatfield House. He examined accounts himself. He seems actually to have enjoyed doing accounts, as today men enjoy solving crossword puzzles ; he explained that they occupied his mind without worrying him. And in his farming he was severely practical. He disdained the fine fancies of " model " farms. He concentrated on making his pay their way. " If I succeed in that," he wrote to his friend, Mr. Ralph Palmer, " I may try to obtain initiation into the higher branches of the craft, such as the keeping of pedigree stock. But I do not as yet lift my eyes so high." To every undertaking, whether in farming or in statecraft, he applied the touchstone of financial solvency. However attractive, however desirable, a project of reform might be, he would not embark upon it unless he was satisfied that he himself, in private affairs, or his Government in affairs of State, could afford the experiment.

Lady Salisbury often accompanied him on his rounds and they soon reached a decision that the cottages on his property were not up to standard. Here again he made less rapid progress than he would have liked, owing to his rigid adherence to business-like methods ; but, charging the lowest possible economic rents, he built more than 200 cottages in Hatfield parish alone before he died. His aim was to encourage the self-respect of his tenants by making them feel they were in fact paying a rent which corresponded to the cost of their houses. For that reason, as in the case of his farming, he eschewed beauty in building, preferring to spend every penny on practical requirements. He also showed a studied indifference to the moral behaviour of the tenants. As long as they paid their rents and did not make themselves a nuisance to their neighbours, he considered that it was the parson's duty, not his, to guide them along the difficult path of virtue. His attitude may have been partly prompted by his innate cynicism about human nature, but it was due still more to the deep sense of independent responsibility which he attributed to other men—as also to other nations. What they did was their concern, so long as they did not trespass on the rights of their neighbours.

The electricity which he wanted to introduce into his farms he felt free to install in his own house even if the expense did not at first produce proportionate benefits. A few years after the period we have actually reached in the narrative of his life he became interested in Jablokhoff's invention of the arc light ; so he placed lamps outside the entrance to Hatfield to light his guests on a winter evening. Then he experimented with them inside the house. His daughter-biographer gives a very amusing account of their vibrating glare poised over the dining-room table, much to the discomfiture of female guests. Nor were matters much better for them when he substituted the Edison-Swan electric lamps. The power was provided by the river Lea, about a mile and a half from the house, and was carried along wires which were run through a wood ; and short circuits caused by high winds and swaying branches frequently threw the sitting-rooms into blackness. Sometimes there were " miniature storms of lightning " in the room, " ending in complete collapse ". Lord Salisbury was undismayed, and wrote long technical letters about his difficulties to his electrical adviser, Mr. Herbert McLeod, Professor of Chemistry at Cooper's Hill College. " As the lamps are, when hot, about 40 ohms each and 60 when cold (the line being about two ohms) the machine has to drive through a resistance of from three to five hundred ohms. . . . The line is mainly No. 6 copper wire. I do not think we have much trouble from leakage. I have tested the line we are using and find that it has an insulation resistance of 200,000 ohms a mile in wet weather . . ." and so on. By 1883 the experimental stage was passed ; and this old Elizabethan mansion could claim, through the enterprise of its new tenant, to be the first private house in the kingdom to be equipped with electric lighting.

It was also one of the first to have telephones ; and these too were a primitive affair for a few years, with wires laid loosely about the floors and passages. Some of his guests expressed themselves testily about the new-fangled device, after catching their feet in them at moments when the electric light had suddenly failed. He used to test audibility by making his children

listen in different rooms to a nursery rhyme which he shouted
into the rudimentary mouthpiece.

One of the first needs of Lord Salisbury's pioneering mind
on taking over Hatfield had naturally been to provide himself
with a laboratory ; and there he spent the greater part of his
leisure moments, moments spent, however, in close and concentrated study of scientific phenomena. It also enabled him
to indulge his hobby of photography. This new art made a
strong appeal to his active, enquiring mind ; and he contributed
an article to the *Quarterly Review* about it. It is one of the only
two contributions he ever wrote for it which were not on a
political or ecclesiastical topic ; and he took the opportunity
to give vent to a rare indulgence of his humour. In the main
it is a beginner's guide to the " processes by which the exquisite
works of art which they admire are brought into existence ".
The art appealed to him particularly, perhaps, because " photography is never imaginative, and is never in any danger of
arranging its records by the light of a preconceived theory ".
He compares its value in portraiture with that of painting, and
warns would-be artists in photography against attempts to avoid
a too sharp and too truthful delineation of the human face by
methods, advocated by amateurs of the day, which could, in
his opinion, only present the sitter to the world " with an
elongated mouth, two noses, or one nose the size of two, and
eyes squinting outwards ". The play of light upon the sitter's
face must be most carefully considered. " If you take a dark-
browed man, with eyes deeply sunk, and a prominent cheek-
bone, and photograph him under a vertical light, you will produce upon paper the figure of a scowling and hungry murderer.
The heavy shadows under the eyes lend a savage ferocity to the
countenance. . . ." As usual, Lord Salisbury casts his mind
forward into future possibilities, and sees the immense value
of photography to criminal investigation and the preservation
and proliferation of historical records. He guardedly foretells
the coming of coloured photography from what had already
been achieved by this infant prodigy of science—which had
" forced the sun to write down his record in enduring characters,
so that those who are far away or those who are yet unborn may
read it ".

And he botanized ; rather less agilely and more scientifically than when he had rambled over the same country as a little boy, sometimes as much concerned, in those days, to keep away from the house as to find new species. But now, in so far as his heart was set upon earthly things, his treasure was in his home. His children, five sons and two daughters, were reaching an age when he could take an intelligent interest in them ; and it delighted him to go up to the nursery from time to time and talk with them, not in baby language, but in polished chaff which, according to one of them, they sometimes found quite mystifying. He covered the walls of the nursery floor with pictures from the illustrated papers, showing the events of the day, so as to inculcate their minds with current history. Their religious education he entrusted to their mother. When they left the nursery for the schoolroom he decreed that their hours of work, which had at first been five, should be reduced to four ; and it remained a maxim for them all their lives that in their father's opinion the amount of really concentrated work of which the human mind is capable on one day is strictly limited, and cannot usefully be exceeded. As they grew older, so his intercourse with them became more general and more intimate ; and his principle of the importance of individual personality was impressed upon them in their earliest years by the absolute freedom of opinion which he allowed them. The only condition he stipulated, and it was an absolute condition, was that they should have made an effort to know something about their subject before they put forward their view. He argued with them, guided them, influenced them ; but even on those matters of theology and belief about which he felt most intensely he relied only upon reasoning and persuasion. On one occasion he tossed across to a daughter of fifteen an article by Mr. Frederic Harrison, attacking Christianity, for her " to see what rubbish these people can write ". He had complete confidence in the teaching which their mother had given them —though that lady herself, when asked by a friend what her " system " was, answered that she had no system. She taught her children to say their prayers and come with their father and mother, when they were old enough, to Holy Communion. " It is not I who train them," she said, " but the Holy Ghost." It was a happy family life, quickened by Christian love.

Their father would go out rabbit-shooting with the boys,

though he was very short-sighted and never took pleasure in sport of any kind. He was determined that their boyhood should not be joyless, as his had been. He liked a member of his family to accompany him on his walks in the park, especially his son William, afterwards Bishop of Exeter, or Lady Gwendolen, who later acted for a while as his secretary before she became his biographer. He was fond of an occasional game of billiards. He even played tennis in the private court at Hatfield ; and his son Robert (later Lord Cecil of Chelwood) related to me how once Lord Salisbury slipped and dashed his head against the wall. In spite of a nasty bruise on his forehead and the remonstrances of his son, he insisted on resuming the match after a few moments' rest. The Victorian was a very domestic age ; and Hatfield, for all its largeness and splendid associations, was a homely place.

An invitation which, especially perhaps because it reached him at this time of relative oblivion, gave him profound pleasure, was that of becoming Chancellor of the University of Oxford (November, 1869). He suited the office, and the office suited him. He proposed that its conferment should be made at Hatfield. He welcomed the learned deputation in the Long Gallery (the ceiling of which had recently been covered with gold leaf by his father). Standing at the end of its 180 feet of narrow floor he appropriately responded to their address in Latin. According to his daughter biographer, no distinction that he received in after-life was ever valued higher than this academic Chancellorship.

His father, the second Marquess, had made many alterations and practical internal improvements to the Elizabethan-Jacobean structure. He himself, as soon as he took over, turned his attention to the Chapel. He added to it a marble altar and commissioned an Italian painter, Taldini, to redecorate the walls. And at the suggestion of Lady Salisbury he invited the same artist to add paintings to the ceiling and frescoes to the walls of the great Marble Hall. The external shape and pattern of Hatfield was left by him, as by the eight generations of Cecils before him, almost exactly as it was built by James I's Robert Cecil.

2

There was henceforth, of course, no need for Lord Salisbury

to supplement his income by writing; if he wrote now it was because he was roused by something that happened in the world outside Hatfield and compelled him to give vent to his pent-up views. During this first Ministry of Mr. Gladstone the attention of the Government had been taken up almost entirely by Irish affairs, much to the neglect and detriment, in Lord Salisbury's view, of foreign policy. This had become weaker than ever after Lord Clarendon had died in June, 1870, and was succeeded at the Foreign Office by Lord Granville. Soon afterwards the Franco-Prussian war broke out; and when Napoleon III had been defeated at Sedan (September 1, 1870), Bismarck issued two circulars to the European Powers in which he indicated that the terms to be demanded of France would include the cession of Alsace and Lorraine. The proposed seizure of territory that had belonged to France for 200 years and was strongly French in sentiment seemed to Lord Salisbury to be fraught with danger for Europe. He took up his pen to write the shortest and most urgent of his contributions to the *Quarterly*. It was published in the October issue under the title " The Terms of Peace ". Bismarck's circular notes were dated September 13 and 16. The article must therefore have been written in a few days, but in its perception of the action required and of the ultimate consequences of inaction it is the most inspired of all his writings and a brilliant foretaste of the famous despatch, written eight years later and to be known as the Salisbury Circular, which was to give him fame in Europe.

The *Quarterly* article is a fervent plea for British intervention to prevent the transfer of Alsace and Lorraine. " Will England make no sign? " he asked. " Has it really come to this, that the disposal of the frontiers of France and Germany is a matter to us of purest unconcern? Is not the crisis worth some little risk . . . ? We shall not conciliate the goodwill of our neighbours by refusing to contribute to the police of nations." He suggested that the first overtures to both belligerents should be made privately, and be followed by a formal proposal. Even if it should after all be rejected " rebuffs suffered in such a cause would not be dishonourable; they would at least save us from any moral complicity with acts which we abhor, and from the danger of being estopped by a seeming acquiescence at this time from the chances of action which future contingencies might offer."

"A ceded territory", he wrote, "would be a constant memorial of humiliation." Its recovery would be "a holy cause" for France. It will be for her "a sacred duty to keep disaffection alive". "The French youth will be brought up by countless teachers to long for the lost provinces, . . . to look upon their recovery as the first of national duties, and to believe all means lawful, and all opportunities fitting for performing it." Lord Salisbury realized that France would not feel strong enough to recover the lost provinces by her own unaided efforts. "She will not again attack Prussia single-handed." But the time must come when the ambitious dreams of the Germans "will cross the path of some Power strong enough to resent them : and that day will be to France the day of restitution and revenge".

So exactly did he foresee the writings of a hundred novelists and publicists of the Third Republic, the crêped statue of Strassbourg in the Place de la Concorde, the policy of M. Poincaré, the circumstances in which the war of 1914 broke out !

One or two other points have to be noted in this remarkable article. In view of Lord Salisbury's readiness, when he himself became responsible for British policy, to risk a war for a result that he considered necessary and right, it seems appropriate to record the detestation of war which he shows in his opening paragraphs. "The hope of peace", he writes, "is the one solicitude of all who are not maddened by the bloodthirstiness of conflict. . . . Whatever the duties of neutrality may be, men must be of stone who, in the presence of so much misery, can refrain from reflexions such as these "—namely, that "we, who have nothing to lose or gain by the issue", might be able to do something to bring the combatants to a more reasonable frame of mind. And the next article he wrote (January 7, 1871) began with the same refrain : "The war drags its slow length along, adding each day to its huge work of human misery. . . . An ' heroic resistance ' may be lengthened out indefinitely ; that is to say, a few more departments may be desolated, some hundreds more of homes may be burned, some thousands more of human beings may be slaughtered or crippled ; but the broad issue will be the same. The strength of France is broken ; her territory is severed ; the splendid lustre of military fame that has shone for four glorious centuries is quenched."

One more important point emerges from the article of the

previous October. He fully understood the German mentality. In his later years he was accused of showing weakness towards and too much liking for Germany. His attitude to the Empire which Bismarck created will be considered in due course. But at least he knew the kind of man and the kind of people he was dealing with. Of Bismarck he now writes : " In criticizing the statements of such a man, it would be a waste of words to argue on the assumption that his language necessarily corresponded with his thoughts. . . . Though Count Bismarck does his best to find plausible reasons for his own harsh demands, he is probably not deceived by his own sophistry." He recalls the history of the last seven years, since Bismarck took control in Berlin— " The events between 1863 and 1870 must be looked upon as one transaction—as successive acts of the great drama of Prussian aggrandizement ". And after a first moment of doubt and recoil, Bismarck had been enthusiastically supported by the whole German people, led by " imaginative professors, who find out historical reasons for all the minister's robberies ". And the present policy of Prussia is only in accordance with her traditions. " The seizure of Silesia, without notice or declaration of war, was probably the most piratical act that has been committed by any recognized government in modern times. The Prussians cherish the memory of Frederic II "—and here let it be noted that that monarch is never referred to by his usual nomenclature of Frederick " the Great " by Lord Salisbury : he is always just " Frederic the Second ". The Germans, he continues, in no way repudiate his example ; and they have grandiose dreams for the future of their country. The Deutsches Vaterland, in the words of their poet Arndt, extends as far as the German tongue is spoken. " If these mad pretensions were the caprice of a particular minister or potentate, they would be of small moment . . . but they are the freak of a whole people, whose head has been turned with military fame." Lord Salisbury was clearly illogical in writing of the " splendid lustre " of French military fame, while condemning so utterly the military ambitions of Germany ; but logic, he held, had little place in policy ; and he is here concerned with the immense danger to European peace which he saw in a united and militarized Germany.

The other danger to Europe which his prophetic eye perceived at this time was communism. The tragedy of France had not ended with the capitulation of Paris and the loss of Alsace-Lorraine. The capital became the scene of a bitter and bloody insurrection. Defeat brought extremist political theorists and desperadoes together in a wild attempt to establish the Commune ; and the regular troops became as murderous, in their retaliation, as the Communists themselves. Lord Salisbury as usual examined the conflict in its larger historico-political implications, and applied to home politics the lessons which he drew.* He obtained from Paris and Brussels all the latest books and pamphlets published on the Paris uprising and subjected the theory of communism to a searching analysis. He foretold that in time it would " thrust what we call politics into the background, in favour of a social conflict the most critical and the most embittered that has yet shaken the fabric of civilization." He gave proofs of the identical aims of the Commune and the Internationale ; " You have spent every day, from dawn to nightfall, with the spade or the sickle in your hand, and yet you are not rich " would be the battle-cry of both. " Of course they wish ", he writes, " to exterminate the landlord as well as the capitalist."

And since it was an international creed it would spread to this country. Mr. Frederic Harrison, he pointed out, was already writing favourably about it, or at least putting the best interpretation he could upon it. " The people of Paris believe not in any god or any man," Mr. Harrison had written ; " but they have a religion of their own." One of the first articles of that " religion " was to abolish the right of bequest and inheritance. This leads Lord Salisbury to his basic argument against communism. " Natural affection, and in fact the very existence of the family, would interpose a serious obstacle even to this mitigated robbery. Accordingly, they find themselves forced to declare war against the family and as a necessary consequence against religion altogether."

All this ground has been well trodden since ; but for Lord Salisbury at that time it was new country, and his exploration of it strengthened his bias against any form of drastic change. He begins by saying that " a theory of constant immobility is as

* *Quarterly Review*, October, 1871 : " The Commune and the Internationale."

irrational as a theory of constant progress ". And what, he asks, is meant by " progress " ? " The doctrine that the present age is superior to all that has gone before it has been a favourite one at various times, especially among the younger portion of each generation. . . . A fervent belief that we have progressed, are progressing, and must progress, not only in things material, but in the excellence of our political arrangements and in what is called pure religion, is an article of faith which all who aspire to popular favour must surely believe, or at least profess." Then he makes a point which was cardinal in his philosophy. " If this confident belief in the future progress of our corner of the earth were confined to material things, no criticism could find fault with it." But moral progress is another matter. " Peace and goodwill will not be the result of some clever contrivance which men by much debating and many experiments may hope to hit upon. If they attain it [at] all, it will be by rooting out the selfishness which good fortune nurtures, and the recklessness which springs from misery." He did not believe that legislation could find a remedy for every evil. A vast amount of evil was irremediable. Some political reformers had the same kind of courage that a disbelief in the existence of reefs would give to sailors. It would be a small consolation to mariners when that illusion had brought their ship against the rock.

And so he comes to the main conclusion of his article, which guided his political action to the end of his life. The " party of movement "—in this case the Liberals—" lives upon discontent " : " The party of resistance rests upon the satisfaction which the nation feels, or is presumed to feel, with its present institutions." " And as each successive cause of discontent is removed . . . the party of movement, in order to sustain its existence, must find some new subject of complaint." The one thing that is necessary to the party of change is discontent ; and as the original reformers grow older, they see young reformers growing up who have to discover a new grievance. " There are rewards which can only be obtained by men who excite the public mind, and devise means of persuading one set of persons that they are deeply injured by another. . . . The invention and exasperation of controversies lead those who are successful in such arts to place, and honour, and power." So each generation of reformers outbids the last.

He did not expect English workmen to exhibit " the fanaticism of the Parisian Socialists ", but if, he perceptively observes, they are promised " an elysium of high wages and little work, as the result of pillaging other classes of the community, it would be too much to expect that they should be keen-sighted enough to see through the delusion and refuse the tempting bait."

As usual, he saw the ultimate event—what he wrote in 1871 fits very well the Socialist and Communist programmes of the middle of this present century.

3

Lord Salisbury was bored by his title. He used often to remark to his family that nowadays it represented nothing. In the old days a dukedom or an earldom carried definite duties and responsibilities towards the monarch on the one hand and vassals on the other. Now, rank was a sham. He most frequently dwelt upon this point at the moment when his father's death compelled him to relinquish his seat in the Commons. He had left that House with resentment and regret. His forced departure from it created a rankling sorrow in his mind—so much so that at the family dinner table the subject was taboo ; and he himself never afterwards re-visited the Chamber in which the first fifteen years of his political life had been spent. But his keen sense of duty, and—paradoxical though it may have been —his firm belief in a governing class, compelled him to turn to account his new right to sit and speak in the Second Chamber. He took his seat there on May 7, 1868 ; and he very soon disturbed his fellow-Conservatives by supporting the Life Peerage Bill introduced by their Liberal opponent, Lord Russell. It enabled the creation of a limited number of peers in any one year, who would have the right to vote, but whose title would not be hereditary. Lord Salisbury did not wish to strengthen the House of Lords relatively to the Commons, whose will should be supreme ; but he did want to make it less narrowly representative. He argued that it had become necessary to have in it members drawn from the growing industrial and mercantile interests ; they must also have men who could speak with firsthand knowledge of the health and moral condition of the people. " We belong too much to one class," he exclaimed on April 9, 1869 ; " we want more representatives of diverse views and more antagonism." But his own combative nature did not find the response he hoped for from his colleagues, who voted him down. In the same session he upset them more violently by some typically candid remarks on their attitude to the Endowed Schools Commission Bill. Its purpose was to grant the Commission powers to modify the trust deeds of charitable bequests. One clause enacted that money left for the payment of doles to old people could be used instead for educational purposes ; and some members had advanced the argument, in supporting the clause, that it was bad for the poor to receive money without working for it. Lord Salisbury, furious and sarcastic, mocked the hypocrisy of a House, which, living for the most part on inherited wealth, was denying the solace of an unearned pittance to the poor. Some of the older members left Westminster, after the debate, muttering misgivings about the value to their House of this dangerous young man who had appeared in their midst.

In other speeches in his first two years among the peers he stated explicitly the proper relations which in his opinion should exist between the two Houses : " If we merely echo the House of Commons, the sooner we disappear the better. The object of the existence of a second House of Parliament is to supply the omissions and correct the defects which occur in the proceedings of the first. . . . I am quite sure you will never consent to act except as a free, independent House of the Legislature, and that you will consider any other more timid or subservient course as at once unworthy of your traditions, unworthy of your honour, and most of all, unworthy of the nation you serve. . . . " But : " When the opinion of your countrymen has declared itself, and you see that their convictions—their firm, deliberate, sustained convictions—are in favour of any course, I do not for a moment deny that it is your duty to yield. It may not be a pleasant process. . . . When once we have come to the conclusion from all the circumstances of the case that the House of Commons is at one with the nation, it appears to me that the vocation of this House has passed away, and that it must devolve the responsibility upon the nation, and may fairly accept the conclusion at which the nation has arrived." He supported this reasoning with the unusual but cogent argument that whereas a Cabinet Minister, if asked to do something contrary to his convictions, could resign, and in similar circumstances a member of the House of Commons could give up his seat, no such course was open to their lordships. They and their House were, so to speak, irremovable. They must therefore be prepared, in the circumstances he had described, to get out of the way, or else they would be regarded as mere obstructionists.*

It would have been against Lord Salisbury's nature and sense of decorum to bring up, spontaneously and so soon after his own first appearance there, the question of reforming the House of Lords. But a clash of the two Houses had occurred as soon as Mr. Gladstone became Prime Minister in 1868. The Disestablishment of the Anglican Church in Ireland had already been proposed by the Liberal leader while he was still in opposition. Under the opportunist direction of Disraeli, the Conservatives did not unambiguously oppose the project ; but the House of Lords had no doubts about it, Lord Salisbury least of any of them. When the question had first been raised in the Commons, Mr. Gladstone had remarked that he had " escaped from the spell of the sentiment in favour of an Established Church " ; and Lord Cranborne, as he then was, had immediately rejoined " that sentiment still exercises a hold over me which I regard as sacred ". When Mr. Gladstone's Government was returned to power with a large majority, the Bill was swiftly carried through the Commons and came before the Second House. Lord Salisbury opposed it both on principle and because he claimed that the Church question was only a minor factor in Irish discontent. Something very different, he said, was behind the Fenian movement. " My Lords," he exclaimed, " it is against the land and not against the Church that the Fenian agitation is really directed. . . . The landlord is a much more complete monument of conquest than the clergyman. The clergyman does not hurt the peasant ; . . . but the landlord holds the property which the peasant in his traditions will remember once to have belonged to his sept. If you seek to appease the danger by mere concession . . . it is to the landlord and not to the clergyman that you should really turn your attention."

Many of his hearers were landlords in Ireland as well as

* For the sake of clarity and brevity, I have brought together Lord Salisbury's views on the House of Lords, expressed in several speeches during the sessions of 1868 and '69.

in England or Scotland. Though they intensely disliked his reasoning and were against Mr. Gladstone's Bill, they had to agree with Lord Salisbury's views, already recorded, that, Disestablishment having been fairly put to the electorate in the General Election and then carried by a large majority in the Commons, it was their unavoidable though painful duty to pass it into law. Two years later the accuracy of Lord Salisbury's diagnosis of the Irish trouble was only too plainly confirmed. The Disestablishment of the Anglican clergy in Ireland brought no decrease of disorder. Crimes and outrages became even more numerous ; and the Liberal Government was obliged to bring in a Peace Preservative Bill. This gave Lord Salisbury the opportunity to define his attitude towards Ireland on general lines, to which he adhered when he became Prime Minister. Here in England, he said, " we are content and have long been content to guide ; in Ireland it is essential that we should govern ".

In 1871 Lord Salisbury's profound belief in the value of an education founded on the Christian religion and his loyalty to tradition combined to make him oppose Mr. Gladstone's abolition of religious tests for entry into the universities. He tried at least to moderate its impact by inserting a clause to the effect that nothing contrary to the teaching of the Old and New Testaments should be instructed. Mr Gladstone, as deeply religious as himself, wrote to Lord Coleridge about this time : " My confidence in Salisbury's honour is such that I should not be in the least afraid of discussing the matter with him personally, if any good should seem likely to come of it." * The Bill however was passed through both Houses without important amendment.

Lord Salisbury had in general not yet passed out of the stage of courageous but vain opposition ; and his old taunting spirit burst out again when Mr. Gladstone suddenly decided to abolish the purchase of commissions in the army. The Minister for War, Mr. Cardwell, had claimed that his Bill would promote " seniority tempered by selection ", to which Lord Salisbury answered that it would be much more likely to produce "stagnation tempered by jobbery ". But he did not oppose, he only sought to ameliorate, Mr. Forster's Education Act of 1870 for making the attendance of all children at school compulsory and providing sufficient accommodation for them.

* Lord Coleridge, Vol. II, p. 177.

And he did introduce one or two minor Bills of his own, which, like most of his amendments of other men's Bills, were rejected. Rebuffed and depressed, he threw himself, as we have seen, into new occupations in the country ; and two other jobs, not mentioned yet, deserve a passing remark—the Chairmanship of the Great Eastern Railway, and arbitration in the tangled disputes of the London, Chatham and Dover Railway. In those days Chairmen of Railways were their own General Managers ; and to the value of his work of arbitration on the Kentish line warm tributes were paid. Both tasks brought him new contacts, and were the more valuable because he seldom voluntarily sought new contacts. But all these activities were by-play to him ; and despite appearances his political reputation had been growing during this period of frustration. The defeat of the Conservatives in the elections of 1868, just after their gleeful dishing of the Whigs, had silently raised his personal status among the more thoughtful members of the Party. His loyalty to his convictions, his courage in isolation, his proved ability even in his failures, had won him more adherents than he knew. He was rapidly establishing himself as the Party's most effective debater in either House with the exception of the Commons' versatile and brilliant chief. With Disraeli himself Lord Salisbury still refused to have any personal relations. The position was anomalous and extraordinary. He was the dominating Tory spokesman in the House of Lords ; yet he had no direct intercourse with the Leader of the Opposition in the House of Commons. The Duke of Richmond had accepted the leadership of the Tories when Lord Salisbury refused to consider it ; and if Lord Salisbury wished to convey his views to Disraeli, or, which was much more frequent, Disraeli wanted to convey his views privately to Lord Salisbury, it was the Duke who acted as confidential messenger. Even so, Lord Salisbury absolutely refused to take part in the counsels of what would today be called the Shadow Cabinet. He was in the strange position of being a leading man of his Party and having a much greater regard for the Chief of the enemy Government than he had for his own Chief. But he had certainly observed the maxim that it is the duty of the Opposition to oppose ; and as Disraeli had as steadily opposed everything that Mr. Gladstone did in the other House, the fellowship of parallel action had ineluctably created a bond between them—especially as a champion of Gladstone's calibre compelled the unity of his opponents. And now the champion was beginning to stumble. Excellent as many of his changes had been, he created an atmosphere of restlessness which did not suit the country at the moment. Moreover, he failed to make England count abroad ; and even the submission of the famous case of the *Alabama* to arbitration was counted against him, chiefly, perhaps, on account of the enormous compensation which the referees ordered the British Government to pay. At the end of 1873 the Government was defeated in the House of Commons. At the General Election held in February, 1874, Mr. Gladstone was beaten ; Disraeli became Prime Minister with a handsome Conservative majority behind him.

4

His first care was to secure Lord Salisbury. The business required all the human touch and diplomacy of which Disraeli was master. He chose Lady Derby as his go-between. This Lady Derby was Lord Salisbury's stepmother and about his own age ; she had married the son of the Prime Minister Lord Derby after the death of Lord Salisbury's father. Her stepson called upon her by arrangement. Two days later Disraeli wrote to Lord Salisbury to say that Lady Derby thought it " very desirable " that the two of them " should have some conversation on the state of public affairs ", and invited Lord Salisbury to call on himself. Lord Salisbury had written the day before to his wife (she was abroad with their youngest boy, who was ill), declaring that the prospect of having to serve again with " this man " was " like a nightmare ". It was typical of him that while the business of Cabinet-making was going on, with himself the problem figure, he fled to Hatfield, to settle the fierce questionings of his own mind in solitude. Great was the vexation of his soul. No compromise solution was possible. He must either become a subordinate colleague or remain a critical outsider. For seven years he had been resolved that he would not collaborate with Disraeli ; and he had never concealed his determination from anybody. Now he felt the choice lay between humiliation and isolation—the humiliation of eating his own words, which he had never been known to do, of serving one whom he distrusted and disliked, and of submitting to a leader whom he described in another of his letters to Lady Salisbury as " very arrogant " ; for, he wrote, if he were to take the bit into his mouth, Disraeli would certainly " make him feel it ". Or, in the alternative, he must abandon all hope of office and power for at least several years. " I never knew what perplexity was before," he exclaims to his wife.

A deep innate propensity of his nature decided him. The antennæ of his mind, for all the new interests he had acquired in country pursuits, reached out instinctively in the direction of active politics. And to shrink from a difficult and responsible post—he knew India was in Disraeli's mind for him—might appear ignominious. His few intimate political friends seemed to think so and wrote pressing him to join the new Ministry. After three days of communing with himself and his God at Hatfield he knew his mind. He would serve.

From that moment he cast all questionings behind him and plunged into public work. From that moment also Lord Salisbury became more of a politician.

He had, as we have already noted in an earlier chapter, made up his mind on theological problems and formed a religious basis of action which he never abandoned. But just as science had not been allowed to weaken his faith, so his religion was not now to blunt the point of his political skill. In the days of his ancestor Burghley, Sir Francis Bacon had prayed that " human things may not prejudice such as are Divine " and that our minds " being purged from fancy and yet subject to the Divine will, there may be given unto faith the things that are faith's " ; and in that same spirit Lord Salisbury did not now confuse religion and politics—he rendered unto Cæsar the things that are Cæsar's. The Bench of Bishops had their job to do, and he had his. The State, he held, is a material entity. The craft of government is a practical business. The interests of his country are paramount to a statesman ; they are a trust committed to his care. And he might have agreed with the words of the great Prime Minister of our own days who wrote : " The Sermon on the Mount is the last word in Christian ethics. Everyone respects the Quakers. Still, it is not on these terms that Ministers assume their responsibilities of guiding

States. . . . The safety of the State, the lives and freedom of their own fellow-countrymen, to whom they owe their positions, make it right and imperative in the last resort, or when a final and definite conviction has been reached, that the use of force should not be excluded." * For Lord Salisbury, as for Winston Churchill, God was the God of the Old Testament as well as of the New—in an even greater degree, probably, for in Lord Salisbury's day the Old Testament was much more familiar to Bible readers than it is now, and God was in very truth the God of might, who led his chosen people to victory and smote the Amalekites. The song of Moses was still read : " The Lord is a man of war, the Lord is his name. . . ."

Lord Salisbury accepted Disraeli's offer and on February 21, 1874, he went to Windsor to be sworn in, for the second time, as Secretary of State for India.

His period of study and apprenticeship was over. We shall see now how the principles he had formed for his guidance served him when they were subjected to the test of practical responsibility.

* Winston Churchill, *The Second World War*, Vol. I, p. 251.

PART II
ACHIEVEMENT

s.

G

INDIA OFFICE—A MISSION IN EUROPE

Lord Salisbury had immediate scope to show what administrative gifts he possessed, and his four years on the southern side of the famous Whitehall quadrangle were not merely time spent in a waiting-room until he should move across to its Horseguards front. India was still recovering from the effects of the great Mutiny of 1857 ; the restoration of respect for the law and the revival of prosperity were its prime needs. These were charges which Salisbury delighted to perform. But the old India Office was also a comprehensive training-ground for a future Prime Minister. The Secretary of State and Viceroy between them were responsible for the government of a microcosm of races differing in creed, caste, language and culture. No branch of administration but came within their purview. Lord Salisbury took over these manifold duties at a moment when they were complicated by an outbreak of the worst famine India had suffered for a hundred years. During his brief tenure of the same post in 1866 a lesser outbreak had struck Orissa ; and he had then left the local authorities to find remedial measures. These had been remissly devised. A million persons had perished ; and he had blamed himself afterwards for not having intervened more actively and earlier. Now he was determined not to be found backward ; and the result was that in Bengal, where the new and larger famine raged, he was more zealous than he need have been. For the Lieutenant-Governor of Bengal, Sir George Campbell, was an able and resolute man, and the Viceroy, Lord Northbrook, was even more able and better versed in the Indian way of life ; and the Secretary of State soon became involved in difficulties with both. The Lieutenant-Governor hotly demanded that the export of corn from India should be absolutely prohibited. The Viceroy demurred. The whole grain trade of India would be dislocated, he argued ; there was plenty of rice available, which must be directed to the famine areas. Lord Salisbury decided on the course favoured by the Viceroy. He explained in the House of Lords that there was a sufficiency of grain in India to feed the whole population and leave some over for exportation ; the difficulty was to " bring the supplies to the houses of the starving population ". To this redistribution, and to the import of more rice into Bengal, he bade the Government of India address itself. These services were well performed ; the loss of life from hunger was very small ; and *The Times* was able to write a year later that the Indian administration had won " one of the greatest and noblest campaigns ever fought in India ".

Having supported Northbrook in this transaction Lord Salisbury fell foul of him in others that followed. The Secretary of State, in accordance with a decision of the Cabinet, had publicly pledged himself to remit Indian duties on cotton as soon as the state of Indian finances made that possible. Yet in the summer of 1875 the Governor-General's Council, without informing the Home Government, passed a Tariff Bill confirming these duties. Faced with the dilemma of crossing Lord Northbrook or going back on his own pledge, Lord Salisbury disallowed the Bill. And in another question he found himself at loggerheads with the Viceroy. Lord Northbrook had been appointed by Gladstone ; he was a Whig-Liberal ; and, true to the tenets of his Party, was opposed to a policy of expansion of any kind. Lord Salisbury, on the other hand, was anxious to protect British interests across the northern frontier, and particularly desired to establish closer relations with Afghanistan. As a modest beginning, he proposed that Britain should appoint agents to Kabul and Herat, and possibly Kandahar too. Disraeli fully supported his proposal. The Prime Minister argued that a policy of drift would almost certainly involve us in complications not only with Afghanistan but with Russia ; for the emissaries of the Tsar held permanent posts in Kabul and had the ear of its ruler. Northbrook nevertheless resisted any such appointments—unless, he said, the Ameer agreed, and he believed that he would not. Lord Salisbury regarded the issue as vital to British and Indian interests ; and as always in such cases he was uncompromising to the point of ruthlessness. " I do not propose to send a mission to Afghanistan against the Ameer's wishes," he wrote in a confidential memoir to Disraeli ; " but I propose to tell the Government of India to make the Ameer wish it." The Ameer, he believed, was genuinely frightened of Russia ; and there was the double danger either " that he would play us false, or, remaining true, might blunder into operations which would bring us into collision with Russia ".

There was a further difference of view between Secretary of State and Viceroy over a misdemeanour of the Gaekwar of Baroda ; and it was no surprise to Disraeli or Salisbury that Northbrook soon tendered his resignation. The public, however, was surprised when it heard that Lord Lytton, then in charge of the British Legation in Lisbon, was appointed in his stead. Lytton was a diplomatist by profession and a poet by nature ; and an explanation of his appointment which was suggested at the time was that the first qualification satisfied Lord Salisbury that he was the man required for over-persuading a reluctant Ameer, and the second seemed to Disraeli to supply the touch of imagination for giving splendid effect to the imperial plan which already the Prime Minister had in mind for his Sovereign.

It was typical of Lord Salisbury that, having felt qualms about the number of telegrams he had despatched to Northbrook during his first months at the India Office—so contrary to his normal inclination, and an offence which was seldom to be chargeable against him in the future—he wrote to him privately to apologize, and explained how he believed he had remained too silent nine years before. He also pressed upon an unwilling Disraeli the conferment of an earldom upon the retiring Viceroy. " I don't think he deserves an earldom," wrote Disraeli, " but you deserve anything—and therefore if, on reflection, you wish it, he shall have five balls."

In 1875 the Prince of Wales, afterwards King Edward VII, was sent on a tour of India ; and this first innovation was followed next year by the still greater one of proclaiming Queen Victoria Empress of India. His Sovereign joyfully accepted the darling project of a mind over which the East exerted its mesmeric influence.

Lord Salisbury heartily supported Disraeli in these bold conceptions, as he did also in insisting at all times on a better regard for the feelings of Indians than was in those days customary. He hated such expressions as " the native fellows " ; and when Disraeli wrote to him about " the habit of our officers " of applying the term " niggers " to them, the Secretary of State went to Cooper's Hill, the Indian Engineering College, and uttered a stern warning against race arrogance. He cordially supported

Florence Nightingale in her plans for the welfare of the Indian Army, but his habitual parsimony in public finance frustrated the vast schemes of sanitary improvements and of irrigation which she was advocating.

It was Lord Salisbury's own initiative to create a new Department of Works, its Chief to sit on the Viceroy's Council ; and, with Lytton at Calcutta, his relations with the Government of India became harmonious. The forward policy on the north-western frontier was quietly adopted. It led to untoward complications ; but before they occurred Lord Salisbury had relinquished direct responsibility for Indian affairs into other hands.

2

An indirect result of their common and concordant consideration of Indian problems had been to draw Lord Salisbury and his Chief much nearer together. Their collaboration in office had begun none too well. It so happened that among the items of domestic legislation during the first year of Disraeli's Ministry were two Bills in which the religious feelings of the country were deeply involved. An Endowed Schools Bill was designed to transfer certain powers from the Schools' Commission to the Charity Commissioners ; and it upset the churchmen in the Cabinet. Lord Salisbury was inevitably their spokesman. He found his position " very disagreeable ", and describes a Cabinet meeting on the subject as " very unpleasant ". He failed to secure the inclusion of safeguarding clauses demanded by his friends. But " the matter is too small to resign upon ". Would he have been so acquiescent six months before ? we may ask ; now he confines himself to writing to his friend Carnarvon that " Dizzy has not lost the fatal habit of giving more consideration to the one trimmer who wants humouring than to the ninety and nine staunch men who need no persuasion ".

The old antagonism flared up, less sharply indeed, but more publicly, during this first session of 1874, when the Public Worship Regulations Bill was introduced. It was anti-Ritualist in character and designed to check the anarchy of rubric and ritual which was creeping into Church practice ; and Lords and Commons tended to take sides against and for, respectively, the rigidity of its clauses. Lord Salisbury liked the " rash innovations " no better than the extremists who pressed for their suppression by law ; but he had his usual doubts as to the efficacy of legislation for achieving that purpose. A member of the Upper House spoke in favour of accepting an amendment passed by the Commons, not because he agreed with it but because he was afraid that otherwise the Bill would be lost altogether. This kind of expediency still roused Lord Salisbury to all his leonine wrath against unprincipled tactics. He spoke about the " bluster " of the language used in the Commons and declared that " I for one utterly repudiate the bugbear " of its majority. The amendment was accordingly rejected by the Lords—and, as Lord Salisbury foresaw, was dropped by the Commons. But its members, though politically acquiescent, were infuriated and mortified by Lord Salisbury's scornful allusion to themselves. Disraeli decided to champion the dignity of his House, and told its members that his noble friend was " not a man who measures his phrases ". Then he added the celebrated taunt : " He is a great master of gibes and flouts and jeers." The House of Commons was delighted ; but Disraeli was less pleased with his own quip. He himself had not measured his language ; and he sat down in the Prime Minister's room in the House and wrote an apologetic note to the Minister with whom he was most of all concerned to work in harmony. Describing his phrase as " playful ", he sent the note round to the India Office by hand so that Lord Salisbury received it before he knew what his Chief had been saying about him. Lord Salisbury did not wait to learn from the newspaper next morning the nature of the " playful " abuse ; he answered at once in a most conciliatory tone ; and when he saw the phrase in print he paid much less attention to it than did the political gossips inside and outside Parliament, who scented a first-class row. In fact, this acrid exchange proved to be the last shots of the Disraeli-Salisbury duel. By January, 1875, Disraeli was writing to Lady Bradford, after an hour's discussion of Central Asian matters with Lord Salisbury, " It is impossible for anyone to be more cordial " ; and by springtime in that year letters from the one to the other no longer began " My dear Lord " and " Dear Mr. Disraeli ", but just plain " Dear Salisbury " and " Dear Disraeli ".

Before finally closing the subject of the religious debates of the year 1874 we should put on record the passage of a speech he made in June, in which Lord Salisbury gave almost casual expression to one of the conclusions of much religious and scientific meditation : " There are three schools in the Church ", he said, " which I might designate by other names, but which I prefer to call the Sacramental, the Emotional and the Philosophical. They are schools which, more or less, except when they have been crushed by the strong hand of power, have been found in the Church in every age. They arise not from any difference in the truth itself, but because the truth must necessarily assume different tints as it is refracted through the different *media* of different minds."

Lord Salisbury's new political pliancy and readiness to work closely with Disraeli led him to participate in a series of beneficent reforms giving effect to the Prime Minister's Tory Democracy. Notable among many new laws was the first great Public Health Act of 1875 ; and there was one for preventing any further enclosure of common-land, which Lord Salisbury approved, as he also approved the laws to ameliorate material conditions in factories and in slums. In a special Act of 1878 the whole remaining unenclosed portion of Epping Forest was secured for ever to the London public. The Agricultural Holdings Act helped farmers, and the Artisans' Dwellings Act produced " model " houses for townsmen. This Conservative Ministry also has an excellent record in promoting popular education— notably the Act of 1876 which made it universal and compulsory. In no Cabinet to which he belonged could Lord Salisbury ever be a mere passenger. He may not have been pleased by Disraeli's Acts which gave the Trade Unions their freedom to picket and made the common law of conspiracy inapplicable to industrial strikes ; but he was an influential member of the Government which, frankly and of necessity devoting the latter half of its life mainly to foreign affairs, nevertheless established unassailably the claim of the Conservatives to be a party of the people. It practised Disraeli's maxims that all government exists solely for the good of the governed ; that those who are entrusted with public functions are trustees, not for their own class but for the nation ; and that existing rights should be maintained as long as they do not impede the acquisition of new and just rights by others.

3

Little did the mountaineers of Herzegovina realize, when they rose against the tyranny of the Turk in 1875, that they were setting in motion a whirlpool in Europe which has not ever again subsided into the stagnant pond the Balkans had been under Ottoman domination. For three centuries the Turks had ruled the provinces they had overrun in Europe like soldiers in an armed camp, administering them in military fashion, and subsisting upon the toil of the conquered. No independent country in the world has in recent times made more rapid strides in the art of government than Turkey ; forgotten now are the methods of bribery and corruption by which public offices brought sustenance to the Treasury, and which gained the support of the venal part of the population while brutally suppressing all persons who showed a taste for free political activity. One of the good results of the French Revolution and the Napoleonic Wars had been to spread ideas of freedom to the uttermost parts of Europe ; Greece gained her freedom with the help of Britain and France ; Serbia, helped by Russia, had won almost complete independence. The rest of the Balkan Peninsula, including Rumania, had till now remained under the blight of a new form of Byzantine misrule.

The rising of the Herzogovinians was followed next year (1876) by that of the Bulgarians ; and soon atrocious reports of Turkish methods of repression stirred the public opinion of Europe and diverted the eyes of the British people and of Disraeli's Government from the home to the foreign scene. A despatch from Constantinople to the *Daily News* took London by storm. That newspaper's correspondent had obtained access to a vice-consular report which had never been delivered to the ambassador to the Porte, Sir Henry Elliot. Formidable bands of armed irregulars, known as Bashi-bazouks, had then, it appeared, descended upon the unhappy insurgents, armed mostly with agricultural implements, and had simply destroyed them. Villagers who had given to Turkish officials evidences of wealth were subjected to tortures before being put to death, in the hope that they would reveal caches of treasure ; others were reported to have been slowly roasted, or had their ears or nose or hands or feet cut off. Some hundreds of luckless fugitives had barricaded themselves in a church at Batak. The emblems of

Christianity only roused the fanatical rage of the Mussulman against the Giaour ; the tiles were torn off the roof, petroleum-soaked rags were flung in and lighted, and the refugees who were not burned to death were struck down, when they bolted, by the yataghans of the watchers outside.

The British public had not yet become inured to horrors ; and it was stirred to a fever pitch of indignation by these " Bulgarian atrocities ". Mr. Gladstone was roused from his lair and the righteous anger of his eloquence expressed the feelings of the majority of the British people.

But it was impossible for the Government of Lord Beaconsfield (as he became in August, 1876) to go all the way with Mr. Gladstone. Ever since Russia had unilaterally abrogated the Black Sea clauses of the Treaty of Paris referring to the Straits (1870), she had been steadily consolidating her position in the Near and Middle East—and a threat to Constantinople or Alexandretta was a threat to Britain's route through the Eastern Mediterranean to India. Moreover, the virtual annexation of Turkestan, Khiva and Bokhara had brought Russia a long step nearer to the Indian frontier. The maladministration of the Porte was indeed enough of itself to cause the Balkan uprisings ; but when the princes of Serbia and Montenegro joined the Herzegovinians in fighting the Turks, and when Russian volunteers crossed the Danube in their thousands to join the insurgents, the British Government had strong reason to believe that the various revolts had in fact been deliberately fomented from St. Petersburg. The policy of Russia was, as it has ever been, a compound of idealism, intrigue and force. Undoubtedly her people, her government and the Tsar sympathized with the sufferings of their fellow-religionists, the Orthodox Christians of the Balkans ; but their readiness to help was not so altruistic as to exclude the hope of territorial expansion. And it was an opinion widely held in the British Isles, from Queen Victoria downwards, that the occupation of Constantinople by Russia would be a national disaster.

Gladstone's missionary zeal for turning the Turks " bag and baggage " out of Europe had therefore to be resisted. And further information from the Balkan Countries, trickling through with a gradualness hard to conceive today, showed that, savage as the Turkish reprisals had been, they were not so widespread as had been supposed ; and it also became clear that the subject races themselves were capable of an almost equal cruelty. The Russian Government, it was found, had, for its own purposes, exaggerated the Turkish horrors ; and the British ambassador to the Porte, the Turcophil Sir Henry Elliot, allowed his sentiments to carry him too far in the opposite direction. In an unfortunate phrase he described as " coffee-house babble " accounts of atrocities which afterwards were proved to be correct ; and Beaconsfield, taking his cue from the ambassador's report, had spoken of " bazaar gossip " in one of his speeches. His levity shocked the country ; and one of its worse consequences was to create an increasingly bitter personal feud between the Conservative and the Liberal leaders at a moment when an agreed foreign policy would have been particularly valuable.

Lord Salisbury, though Secretary of State for India, soon became as active a participant in the Cabinet discussions on policy as the Foreign Secretary himself. He understood the pro-Turkish tendencies of Beaconsfield, and the rather lukewarm pro-Russianism of Lord Derby, while committing himself to neither. They could all agree, however, that the Foreign Office should urge an armistice upon the Turks and propose that a six-Power conference should be convened in Constantinople. But the conflicting arguments as to the policy to be pursued at the conference, should it be held, are reflected in the letters which Lord Salisbury wrote every week to the Viceroy. He saw dispassionately the reasons for opposing Russia and for helping Russia ; for keeping Turkey in charge of the Straits, and for forcing the administrative reforms upon her which Russia demanded. The Treaty of Paris of 1856 still bound us, he considered, to respect the integrity of Turkey ; but " The Turk's teeth must be drawn even if he is allowed to live ". As was his wont, Lord Salisbury gave vigorous expression to different and conflicting points of view until such time as he had made up his mind what action could be taken. That was always the aim, the sole aim, of discussion—to decide upon action.

At the Guildhall Banquet of that year, 1876, Beaconsfield declared that " there is no country so interested in the maintenance of peace as England. . . . But although the policy of England is peace, there is no country so well prepared for war as our own. If she enters into conflict in a righteous cause . . . her resources are inexhaustible." The very next day at Moscow the Tsar announced that if Europe failed to come to the rescue of the Christians, Russia would act alone on their behalf. The ostensible cause of quarrel was plain and undeniable ; it placed in flagrant opposition Russia and Turkey ; but behind the championship of the Christians loomed the ominous aspect of the Pan-Slavists ; they stretched their theory of a united Slav-dom to include the acquisition of Constantinople ; and so far from being officially discouraged, they were known to have fervent adherents at Court and in the Army. If war were to break out between Russia and Turkey, Britain might be involved in it.

The only way to prevent this catastrophe was to call the conference which Britain had proposed. Russia was unexpectedly willing. The five other " Great Powers " of those days, therefore, quickly agreed that it should be summoned forthwith by the Russian Government ; and Russia herself, Austria, Germany, France, Italy and Britain chose their representatives to meet the Turks at Constantinople.

Lord Salisbury was the obvious choice for this country. So far, indeed, he had only spoken and written on diplomacy ; but he had spoken and written so effectively, he had shown so much grasp of every successive question as it arose, he had so well combined openness of mind with firmness in decision, that the Prime Minister had no hesitation in giving him the opportunity of proving his talents in diplomatic practice. He was invited to set out for the Turkish capital before the end of that month of November.

Lord Salisbury accepted the mission with his usual inward eagerness and outward scepticism. " I am afraid there will not be much reality in the Conference," he wrote to Lord Derby ; and to his wife he expressed himself with characteristic gloom : " An awful nuisance—not at all in my line—involving seasickness, much French, and failure." However, he persuaded Lady Salisbury to come with him, and to bring their eldest boy, and their eldest daughter too. On hearing of the departure of this family party Beaconsfield wrote to Lady Bradford : " He [Lord Salisbury] had several secretaries and, I think unhappily, several members of his family. I fear these latter will not be as serviceable as his secretaries. The French papers say the Conference is delayed because M. de Salisbury is accompanied by Mme. de Salisbury and several children ! " If there was any delay in his arrival on the Bosphorus, it was not on account of his family, but because Lord Salisbury wisely took this favourable opportunity of meeting the chief statesmen of Europe. Leaving England on November 20 he travelled first to Paris, where he saw the Duc Décazes, then Foreign Minister. By November 23 he was in Berlin, and made the personal acquaintance of Bismarck ; he was also received by the Emperor William I and entertained by the Crown Prince and his English Princess. Thence to Vienna, where he had long talks with the Austro-Hungarian Chancellor, Count Andrassy. On the way to Rome he stopped in Florence, where he penned long letters to Lords Derby and Beaconsfield and an official despatch to the former. On this journey, as well as later in Constantinople, he often sent home several despatches and letters on the same day. In Rome he met the Foreign Minister, Signor Melegari, also the King and the Crown Prince. The last despatch of the journey was posted in Brindisi. Almost all his official conversations had been conducted in French.

These personal contacts had special value for a future Foreign Secretary of the Victorian epoch. In no respect has the work of the Foreign Department changed so much since Lord Salisbury's day as in its mobility. Not only the Foreign Secretary himself, but most of his officials, may now be travelling any day to meet their opposite numbers on any Continent ; they often get to know foreign colleagues intimately by attending a series of conferences, major or minor. These personal acquaintances were far rarer then, and Lord Salisbury was particularly unwilling to go out of his way to meet people—a reluctance for which he was later reproved by Queen Victoria. Beaconsfield had on this occasion, in spite of his jests about the family party, heartily encouraged him to pay his round of European visits. " You must remember," he wrote, " we suffer from a feeble and formal diplomacy and that there has been little real interchange of thought between the English Government and foreign Powers. . . . You should personally know the men who are governing the world, and it is well to know them under circumstances which will allow you to gauge their character, their strength and their infirmities." And his letter contained another acute observation : " This is a momentous period in your life and career. If all goes well you will have achieved a European reputation and position which will immensely assist and strengthen your future course."

How different was this heartening prophecy from the gloomy forecast of failure made by Lord Salisbury himself!—And yet both predictions were fulfilled. The Constantinople Conference was a failure ; but Lord Salisbury returned from it with his name well and favourably known to Europe.

He arrived in the Turkish capital on December 5, took up his quarters in the Hotel Royal, and lost no time in making the acquaintance of his Russian opposite number, General Ignatieff. The General was Russian ambassador to the Porte, where he enjoyed the unusual reputation of being the most talented liar on the Bosphorus. He was distrusted and disliked by the British colony of Pera in general and in particular by the British Ambassador—who was an able, formal diplomatic veteran, and had held his present post since 1867. But by an unfortunate freak of opposite temperaments Lord Salisbury found the company of the Russian ambassador much more congenial than that of Sir Henry Elliot. Ignatieff, with all his tricks, was an animated, witty companion ; moreover, he afforded Lord Salisbury his first personal acquaintance with an eastern European mind— and soon Lord Salisbury perceived what untravelled Englishmen do not always understand, that there is a sharp difference between the western and eastern European mentalities, and that Talleyrand's gibe about language being invented to conceal thought still unmasks a characteristic of eastern diplomacy. The young envoy had his first lessons in distinguishing the thought from the words when he went round to talk things over in Ignatieff's study —without taking Elliot with him. Their conversations were informal, and the Conference itself was to be held in the Russian Embassy ; so his conduct was not irregular. But it naturally displeased the British Embassy ; and the whole British colony, which was in the main strongly Turcophil, received a shock when one day they saw Lord Salisbury and his Russian friend walking arm-in-arm down the tortuous main street of Constantinople.

Sir Henry Elliot had done his best to prime his young colleague in the wiles of Russian diplomacy, but apparently in vain. However, Lord Salisbury accompanied him readily enough to an audience with the Sultan. This " gentleman of exquisite manners ", who was " as mean a villain as could be found in the purlieus of his capital ", had some strange vagaries. At a later time he could not bear to look at anything written in black ink, and documents had to be copied in red before His Imperial Majesty could be induced to give his attention to them. Another obsession, a dread of fire, got hold of him to such an extent that except in his own apartments, he would not allow a lamp or a candle to be lighted in the whole of his vast Palace, its innumerable inmates being forced to grope about in the dark from sunset to sunrise. A more realistic obsession was fear of assassination. This more than eccentric despot, however, received the British envoys with all the courtesy of a grand seigneur, and graciously expressed himself, at their audience, as deeply impressed by the bearing of the new distinguished visitor to his Court. He professed an earnest desire to be guided by the advice of the special envoy of the British Government, which had always been such a good friend to the Ottoman Empire. If Lord Salisbury would let him know the concessions which Her Majesty's Government considered ought to be made to Russia, and the reforms which should be introduced, he (the Sultan) would go as far as was compatible with his independence and the interests of his Empire. The British envoy replied that he must first have some communication with his Cabinet and colleagues, but that in a few days he would be in a position to speak more plainly. The Sultan, recalling the magic name of Lord Stratford de Redcliffe, and renewing his protestations of regard for the latest representatives of British courtesy and civilization, the charming Sir Henry Elliot and himself, extended an invitation to them both to let him know as soon as they had received the necessary communications and then to come and dine with him. The Sultans of Turkey did not often invite strangers to dine with them, or allow them to name their own date ; still more rarely has it happened that the invitation has been spurned. But Lord Salisbury never dined at the Yildiz Kiosque. Messenger after messenger came to the British Embassy to enquire when His Majesty might expect him and the ambassador, and was turned away without an answer, excuse or explanation. Sir Henry Elliot was distressed at this brusque indifference to Abdul Hamid's importunity. He considered that a second visit might enable Lord Salisbury to win from the Sultan the promise of all that he was empowered by the British Government to ask ; and he—probably rightly—attributed his refusals to the influence of General Ignatieff.

Lord Salisbury certainly created a delicate situation by thus slighting the autocrat and throwing himself, as it seemed, into the arms of the representative of Russia. At the first official meeting of the foreign delegates in the Russian Embassy Ignatieff was able to announce that the resolutions he was presenting had been drawn up by Lord Salisbury and himself on the principle of " making a pretence of maintaining the fiction of the independence of the Turkish Government ".* The truth was that the persuasive General had managed to convince Lord Salisbury that he must be Turkey's friend or Russia's : he could not be both. Loyal co-operation was the only possible method if the will of Europe was to be imposed on Abdul Hamid ; and the argument fitted well with Lord Salisbury's categorical and loyal temper.

But he was hardly justified in accepting the Russian's thesis to the full extent of branding the future independence of Turkey as a fiction. His own instructions postulated her independence. His sense of community with the other Powers, his own ardent desire to impose and maintain reforms in the European provinces of Turkey, had carried him across the limit of deviation allowed him by the Cabinet. As the meetings at the Russian Embassy proceeded the British Ambassador, who acted as second delegate, became more and more embarrassed. With his ten years' experience of the country Sir Henry Elliot considered he could gauge the situation better than his Chief. He knew that in the Ottoman administration the functions deriving from various offices by no means corresponded to the titles attached to them ; the duty prescribed in Stamboul looked very different when it was carried out in Macedonia. The contrarieties of Turkish rule could not be mastered in a few days. The very names which constantly recurred—mutessarif, zaptieh, vilayet, vali, muderlik, nahieh and the rest—familiar enough to Elliot himself and to Ignatieff, conveyed wrong impressions to Lord Salisbury without long explanations. Moreover, for the senior delegate, unswerving support of Russia and the closest collaboration with the other Great Powers had priority ; the junior but older delegate advocated only as much collaboration with Russia as was absolutely necessary to avoid a rupture. Elliot held that it would be most impolitic to press upon Turkey any reforms

* " Faire semblant de maintenirl a fiction de l'indépendance du gouvernement Turc "—Elliot, *Diplomatic Recollections*, p. 390.

which she might be counted upon to reject. He believed that it was the very purpose of Russian diplomacy to urge demands which were known to be unacceptable and so to procure a plausible reason for breaking off relations and then making war. This view was supported by British advices from St. Petersburg and indeed by Ignatieff's own career and character ; and Sir Henry Elliot was so convinced of it that, perplexed by the conflict between his convictions and loyalty to his Chief, he composed a long despatch to the Foreign Office in which he set forth his own views, and showed the draft to Lord Salisbury. Lord Salisbury begged him to suppress it : such a demonstration of divided policy, he said, would damage his authority, and the British case must suffer.

Then, a fortnight later, Lord Salisbury went further. He recommended to Lord Derby that Sir Henry Elliot should be recalled. He argued that, while he advocated this action reluctantly, his removal might be made to appear a protest against Turkish recalcitrance. Unluckily for his request, General Ignatieff, with the over-cleverness of an inveterate intriguer, had contrived to convey precisely the same request by a roundabout route to the British Government ; and what Beaconsfield and Derby might have accorded to the trusted envoy they could not grant at the bidding of a foreigner.

Lord Salisbury included in his character the element of suspicion without which no British envoy or Foreign Secretary would be fully equipped for his job. He accepted Napoleon III's maxim that a statesman's heart should be in his head. If he allowed himself to be influenced by Ignatieff's reasoning it was because of its soundness and not because he was fooled by it. Only two days after his disembarkation at Galata he had written to Lord Derby : " All is very smooth between us " (himself and Ignatieff), and added: " I am puzzled by its smoothness—and naturally look for a snare." The Russian envoy might perhaps be " trusting to the obstructiveness of the Turk—a very sure reliance, I fear ". A few days later his suspicions of the General's trickery were confirmed in a singular manner. At one of the meetings in the Russian Embassy the plenipotentiaries had agreed upon the line of a new frontier for Southern Bulgaria, which was duly traced upon the map. At the next day's meeting Lord Salisbury's quick eye discovered that the line had been substantially altered during the night in the direction which Russia had desired. The British envoy, ready as he was to appreciate Ignatieff's wit, did not hesitate to draw attention to this piece of sharp practice, and sat back—this detail his biographer-daughter could have had from nobody but himself—with a feeling of irritated discomfort to hear what plausible explanation General Ignatieff would give. The nimble Slav instantly found the only possible way out. He shrugged his shoulders ; he admitted the " mistake " with disconcerting ease of manner ; and smilingly observed : " Monsieur le Marquis est si fin—on ne peut rien lui cacher." No wonder that by the end of the month the British envoy was writing home with more than his wonted cynicism about those with whom he was called to do business. During the Conference a change of Grand Vizier had been made, and the Sultan now had as his chief adviser the leader of the " Young Turk " movement, Midhat Pasha. " Midhat is fond of saying ", wrote Lord Salisbury, " that Ignatieff has proposed a separate peace to him. Ignatieff is fond of saying that Midhat has proposed a separate peace to him. They are the biggest pair of liars to be found in Europe, but I am inclined (though with much diffidence) to think that Midhat is the falser of the two."

In these circumstances the slender chance of effecting an international agreement rapidly evaporated. The reforms to be pressed upon Turkey were reduced to the barest minimum, and still they were refused. The Porte apparently had never ceased to believe in the fundamental friendship of the London Cabinet, though it was known to be divided ; Lord Salisbury was said by local mischief-makers not truly to represent it ; and the Turks seem also to have believed in the military weakness of Russia. When the final proposals of the Powers were presented to the Porte, the rejection was summary. The Conference broke up. The six plenipotentiaries decided to redeem their failure by a formal concerted demonstration of displeasure. They would all shake the dust of Constantinople off their feet simultaneously ; every one of them would leave next day, Monday, January 22. At the appointed hour a terrific storm was raging in the Bosphorus ; and it made a mock of the intended diplomatic *démarche*. Lord Salisbury alone went aboard. He spent a miserable night while the captain of the Austrian Lloyd vainly strove to put his liner out to sea.

He had at the outset of his mission foretold three things—
sea-sickness, much French, and failure. The second and third
prophecies has already come true, and now the first was fulfilled.

4

He travelled home alone via Italy and rested for a few days
at Naples. He was no sightseer, and the love of natural beauty
came to him only late in life. We may imagine him therefore
roaming, as he liked to roam, through the less frequented ways,
which from Naples lead eastward, and turning his back upon the
beautiful bay and islands of that enchanted coast. And though
his habit was not to indulge in retrospection, but rather to ponder
on what the next step should be, it is fair to assume that on this
occasion, after his first direct contacts with the leaders of Europe,
he must have allowed his mind to dwell on the new characters
he had met ; the different faces of Europe's capital cities, its
varied races, each flowing through history like a broad river
with many twists and windings and numberless eddies, but
each tending to keep to the course prescribed for it by geography
and nature. He had learned much. His eye was keen and
discerning ; his mind still open ; and the main impressions
which he gained can be found in the multitude of those letters
and despatches which he sent home. Certainly he must have
felt very glad to have had that long talk with Bismarck, the
outstanding figure of Europe. A formidable fellow, because,
like all great men, a compound of different and seemingly opposite characteristics. Bluff, frank, even brutally frank. But a
deceiver too. Machiavellian. And wise as well as Machiavellian. Had he not foretold almost exactly the conditions in
which the Conference would fail ? And his *Schadenfreude* was
patent when he detailed the difficulties Russia would encounter
when she invaded Bulgaria—as he was sure she would ; and no
doubt he was right (so Lord Salisbury's thoughts must have
run *) ; but he had done his best to convince Ignatieff that
" occupation " was something the British Government could
never acquiesce in. Bismarck didn't want a war between us

* This imagined soliloquy is entirely based upon the letters and despatches sent home by Lord Salisbury during his voyage to and residence in
Constantinople.

and Russia ; but he did, probably, wish for one between Turkey and Russia ; and the German Embassy seemed to have a good deal to do with the wrecking tactics of those last few days which ruined the remaining chance of agreement. Pity he had had to carry Elliot on his back. Time he went somewhere else. But to go back to Bismarck. It was swashbuckling of him to suggest that we should " take Egypt " as our share of the spoils of Turkey. And how cynical and contemptuous he was about Gortchakoff ! * What a good thing he had scored that passage about his sarcasms out of his despatch from Berlin. Derby would have passed it on to Lady Derby, and she would certainly have imparted it at the first opportunity to the Russian ambassador in London. But he had told Dizzy, in the letter from Florence.

Andrassy was the most talkative man he had met but not the most coherent. He seemed to be playing junior partner to Bismarck, though that was the last thing he'd like to be said about him. In any case he wanted to be on good terms with England and Austrian interests coincided with ours. Certainly neither Andrassy nor Melegari wanted to see Russia entrenched in the Balkans. He had himself told Franz Josef at Vienna that peace would only be seriously threatened if Russia insisted on an occupation of Turkish territory. The only man besides Bismarck who seemed to view that prospect with equanimity was Décazes. Andrassy never joked, like Bismarck, but he aped him in phrases such as " un vieux farceur " about Gortchakoff. Both Bismarck and Andrassy expressed the opinion that even if Russia were to occupy Bulgaria she would not absorb her. White † was good about the Balkan races, and he too seemed to think the Bulgarians are a tough and indigestible people. Fear was brooding over Europe. Even Bismarck had his nightmare. The Germans obviously were living in terror of a coalition against them.

His French had stood the test of all these conversations pretty well. That's about all he could congratulate himself upon. But it was hard work actually negotiating in French in Constantinople. And it didn't bring success to the Conference. He thought he would fail. And he had failed.

* Chancellor of the Russian Empire.
† British Agent and Consul General in Belgrade. Afterwards Sir William White. He had acted as one of Lord Salisbury's advisers in Constantinople.

CHAPTER VII—1877–1878

WAR BETWEEN RUSSIA AND TURKEY—THE FOREIGN
OFFICE

Lord Salisbury was both perplexed and pleased when, on his
return, the Cabinet greeted him almost enthusiastically. The
Prime Minister improvised a little speech of welcome ; the
Queen, to whom his despatches had gone straight from the
Foreign Office, was " satisfied and very civil " ; the Lords gave
him a cheer as he entered the House. They all seemed to feel,
if we may resort to the language of cricket, that the British
representative had been sent in to bat on a very difficult wicket ;
he had not made enough runs to win the match, but he had
defended skilfully and carried his bat. He had not been bowled,
or caught out, or stumped. He had made a draw of it ; and
the least they could do was greet him with applause as he returned
to the pavilion. At the India Office, too, the staff were pleased
to see him back ; they had been fidgeted by the indecisions
and fussiness of Carnarvon, who had been in charge during the
Constantinople visit.

Lord Salisbury was at once immersed in current business,
for there had been a recrudescence of famine in Bengal, and the
forward policy in Afghanistan was casting ominous shadows
across the north-west frontier. But in addition to his departmental duties the Indian Secretary had to find time for long and
repeated discussion of foreign policy ; the experience gained on
his mission had given him greatly enhanced authority in the
Cabinet. From this moment the ageing Beaconsfield leant more
heavily and more trustfully upon the shoulders of the younger
man ; and foreign affairs were the first care of the Government.
Lord Salisbury discouraged the Prime Minister from taking
serious notice of vague hints of alliance put forward by Bismarck,
whom he by now quite mistrusted ; and he was inclined to hope
that Russia was hesitating, on the very brink of war, because
she felt " powerless for a distant blow ". The Tsar's Government had proposed that the Powers should join in a final formal
protest to Turkey for having rejected the reforms. Lord

Salisbury, determined to maintain the collaboration of the Great Powers which had been the only gain of the Constantinople Conference, advised acceptance of this possibly pointless *démarche*. He was embarrassed rather than encouraged by the unexpected arrival of General Ignatieff in western Europe. His boon political companion of Pera wrote to him from Paris to propose himself to Hatfield for a visit to his friend and colleague. Lord Salisbury managed to postpone his arrival for a week, but the General was importunate and Lord and Lady Salisbury could no longer refuse. They specially invited to meet him two members of the Opposition, Lord Hartington and Mr. Forster, so as to dispel the idea of a private political meeting. But this precaution had an unexpected sequel. On the day on which the guests dispersed, the two Liberal statesmen called upon Lord Salisbury at the India Office, to inform him that his Russian guest had pressed upon them a number of diplomatic confidences which he thought would be useful to them for attacking the Government in the House of Commons !

The Joint Protocol of the Powers was signed in London on March 31, 1877. It contained a request to the Turkish Government to reduce its armed forces and reiterated the demand for the adoption of reforms, with guarantees for their enforcement. The stubborn Turks said " No " once more ; and Russia, by no means displeased, declared war on April 24.

Lord Salisbury's intense desire to define and pursue a clear line of policy was never so severely buffeted as during the next few months. According to his daughter-biographer, his own personal wish was for the partition of European Turkey. He was in fact secretly in sympathy with the bag and baggage programme of the leader of the Opposition. But his own leader would have nothing to do with it ; to put it forward formally would be to break with Beaconsfield. That he was determined not to do. The Viceroy, too, was fervent for the defence of Constantinople. And as Indian Secretary he was bound to consider the pro-Turkish views of Moslems. Moreover he knew that partition of Turkish territory must bring Russian influence one way or another down to the Straits and the Aegean Sea. That was a proposition to which Queen Victoria would never in any circumstances agree ; and admittedly Britain's position in the Eastern Mediterranean would thereby be rendered precarious, since she had no foothold nearer to the Straits and to Suez than Malta. The idea soon began to form itself in Lord Salisbury's mind that such a foothold must be acquired. And he also came gradually to the conclusion, which remained with him all his life, that any firmly directed policy was better than no policy at all. Whenever the pros and cons of every line of action were so evenly balanced, the temptation was great to pursue no policy, to adopt a negative attitude, to wait and see. That was now the attitude of the Foreign Secretary, Lord Derby. Lord Salisbury never ceased to chafe under it ; and the gulf steadily widened between Beaconsfield's favourite counsellor and the man officially responsible for his foreign policy.

In these difficult circumstances it took the Cabinet two weeks to decide upon an official Proclamation of Neutrality (May 6, 1877). It was accompanied by a warning to Russia that England was particularly interested in the Suez Canal, in the Persian Gulf, and in the future of Constantinople and the Straits —interests which Gortchakoff promptly promised to respect. The Cabinet also managed to agree upon seeking a close under-standing with Austria-Hungary, Lord Salisbury having found that of all the statesmen he had seen in Europe Andrassy's views were closest to his own. And this moment was chosen to make a change in the embassy in Constantinople. Elliot, who had been withdrawn as an additional mark of British disfavour to the Porte, was now transferred to Vienna ; and Mr. (afterwards Sir Henry Austen) Layard was appointed in his stead. Layard had won fame as the excavator of Nineveh and was an even more devoted Turcophil than Elliot ; but he was considered to have a more " commanding mind " than Elliot, and to be " not *too* scrupulous ". The phrases are Beaconsfield's ; and most people who know the East would agree that at least an astute under-standing of tortuosity is a valuable asset there.

2

Lord Salisbury's mind was all through this critical summer of 1877 harassed by the special anxieties pressing upon his own Department. The Viceroy sent home one report after another of Russian troops advancing southward from Turkestan. It was only a few years before that she had occupied the area lying south of Lake Aral and reduced Khiva and Bokhara to vassalage ;

now she was pushing down from the north-east towards the frontiers of Afghanistan ; and Lytton and his military advisers were urging immediate counter-action by the British army of India. It will be necessary to return to this theatre of Russo-British antagonism later on ; for the moment it is enough to indicate the balanced view of Lord Salisbury on the supposed threat contained in the reported activity of the Tsar's troops beyond the mountains of the north-west frontier. In private letters to Lytton he declared that the occupation of this town or that hundreds of miles beyond the Hindu-Kush was a totally inadequate reason for embarking on war. It would not matter to us " if they were occupied by Hottentots or Esquimaux ". " You listen too much to the soldiers," he told his Viceroy ; and then delivered himself of a typical tirade against experts. " You never should trust experts. If you believe the doctors, nothing is wholesome : if you believe the theologians, nothing is innocent : if you believe the soldiers, nothing is safe. They all require to have their strong wine diluted by a very large admixture of insipid common sense." And in the House of Lords he used a phrase which at once amused and reassured the public. He had pointed out the weakness of the Russians in military organization. Their irregular cavalry, the Cossacks, were unsurpassed, but they had never yet shown the capacity " to supply large armies at great distances ". And then, replying direct to a member of the House who had spoken as if a Russian invasion of India might occur next week, he gave him the memorable advice to " use a larger map ". A great deal of misapprehension arose, he explained, from the popular use of maps on which " you are able to put a thumb on India and a finger on Russia ". And in private letters addressed to the Viceroy at this time his remarkably auguring mind led him to opine that if England were to become involved in a major war the danger was more likely to come from Germany than from Russia.

In the meantime the Russian armies had advanced rapidly both in Europe and in another part of Asia. They were streaming southward between the Black Sea and the Caspian ; and in the major theatre of war, the Balkans, they were pressing down to and across the Danube, a secret agreement having been reached with Rumania. The Russian Counsellor of Embassy in Constantinople, M. Nelidoff, whom Lord Salisbury had met there, had gone to Bucharest under an assumed name, and there negotiated with the Rumanian Government a Convention by which the Russian armies might pass through the provinces of Moldavia and Wallachia unopposed and would be supported by Rumanian troops when they crossed the Danube. The help of the Rumanian army under Prince Carol—later King Carol I of Rumania—proved to be most timely ; for after their first onrush the Russian armies were held up by Osman Digma Pasha's brilliant defence of Plevna ; and it was only on December 9, when the Rumanian corps had stormed the Grivitza redoubt, that the fortress fell and the road to Constantinople lay open. On the Asian front Kars, which had also held out for some months, had fallen on November 11 ; and international tension became tauter in every capital from London and Paris to Calcutta.

The predicament which Beaconsfield and Lord Salisbury had foreseen was upon them. How could Russia be stopped without a war ?

During a lull in operations when the Russian armies were being held, Beaconsfield, apparently without consulting Lord Salisbury, and certainly without consulting Derby, had resorted to a peculiar method of conveying a *quasi-casus belli* warning to the Tsar. Colonel the Hon. Frederick Wellesley, a gay and gallant soldier, who became a favourite riding-companion of the Empress of Austria when she went out jumping the fences in the Vienna Tiergarten, was at this time the active and intelligent Military Attaché to the British Embassy in St. Petersburg. He joined the Imperial Headquarters when the war broke out ; and in the midsummer of that year, 1877, when the Russian advance had been checked, received a hint that mediation between the combatants might be agreeable to the Tsar. He promptly offered to convey this promising proposal to London, and set off to do so by word of mouth. He saw first of all the Prime Minister, then Derby, who was his Chief, and then Queen Victoria, who received him at Osborne in her late Consort's dressing-room, which was " just as he had left it ". Between them, Beaconsfield and Queen Victoria devised an answer to the Tsar which was something more than a personal message and something less than an official despatch, something more than a warning and not quite a declaration of *casus belli*. He was to convey in conversation to the Tsar the definite impression, formed by himself after audiences with his Queen and his Prime Minister, that "in the event of a renewal of hostilities in the spring ", and "if he [the Tsar] should commence another campaign ", he would find Great Britain allied with Turkey against him.

Queen Victoria at first made objections to this irregular method of conveying the message—behind the back of the Foreign Secretary ; but she withdrew them on the consideration that "He tells Lady D—— and she tells all to Schouvaloff."

Thus the Foreign Office and the Cabinet remained in common ignorance of this very important diplomatic action.

Wellesley delivered his message with great tact and skill, giving the Tsar to believe that it was only his personal impression which he was conveying, but an impression formed after long conversations with Queen and Prime Minister. Lord Salisbury seems to have had nothing to do with this manœuvre, though he must no doubt have been informed of it as soon as he himself became Foreign Secretary. Sir Victor Wellesley, who edited and published his father's account of his mission, claims that it succeeded in preventing " a second campaign " by Russia. That is however only half the truth. Its first result was to spur the Russians to greater efforts. The Wellesley message was a delayed-action ultimatum, designed to explode when and if the Tsar renewed the campaign in the spring ; but its arrival at Gorni-Stooden, in Bulgaria, where the Tsar had his military headquarters, produced the immediate effect of stimulating the Russian command to a prompt renewal of active warfare, which was then continuously sustained till March of the following year. On the third of that month the Russians were on the outskirts of Constantinople.

Some time before this the Turkish army had ceased to be a fighting force, and already in December, 1877, at a hint from Beaconsfield himself, the Sultan had appealed to London to mediate. In spite of Lord Salisbury's attitude during the Constantinople Conference, the Porte's belief in England's readiness to come to the help of her ally of the Crimea had never faded ; and it had been justified by the known convictions of both Queen Victoria and her Prime Minister that Constantinople was untouchable. " What the Queen wishes to repeat again and to *insist on* is that the Emperor should be told distinctly though confidentially that we will *not allow* him to go to Constantinople and that that would be a ' casus belli '," was the Queen's way of putting it in a private letter to Beaconsfield. But Derby was still Foreign Secretary ; and Derby was known to be utterly averse from authorizing the use of force either on behalf of the Turks or against them—during Lord Salisbury's mission he had terribly weakened the envoy's authority with the Sultan by informing the Turkish ambassador in London, Musurus Pasha, that the British Government would not consent to, or assist in, coercive measures to put the proposed reforms into effect. Moreover, every pacifist Minister in every country is sure of support ; and at least half of the British public applauded his efforts to keep Britain out of these eastern European complications. Whenever any kind of action against the " liberating armies " of Russia came into the discussion, Gladstone's voice was raised in eloquent rebuke. Beaconsfield raged against Gladstone ; and Queen Victoria, in private, raged against Derby. But Derby was one of the Prime Minister's oldest personal friends ; and Lord Salisbury, as his successor-elect, refrained from urging his removal. Carnarvon was another Cabinet pacifist ; and he was a particular friend of Lord Salisbury. Carnarvon threatened resignation almost as a habit : he had his vast Berkshire home in which to live the life of a county magnate and entertain political friends ; the very mention of the word war was enough to make him turn his thoughts towards Highclere. Lord Salisbury, late one evening—and a February evening too—walked with him round and round St. James's Square trying to persuade him to remain ; these divisions in the Cabinet must not be made manifest to Russia and the whole world, he argued ; but he argued in vain. Carnarvon went ; but Derby remained ; and Beaconsfield inwardly wondered which was the greater misfortune.

Beaconsfield and Derby both tried to draw Lord Salisbury to their side in the dispute. Beaconsfield quoted Wellesley's advice from the theatre of war to fight Russia now ; Lord Salisbury did not think the advice was sound. Derby declared his affection for the Prime Minister but wrote strangely of him : " He believes thoroughly in prestige—as all foreigners do." Lord Salisbury answered him at some length but non-committally. Talk of " the war-party " and " the peace-party " in the Cabinet became the commonplace of society discussion ; the public was restive, but was as equally divided and uncertain as the Government ; the foreign Chancelleries began to think that England was suffering from paralysis.

The Sultan's request for mediation added fuel to the heart-burnings of the Cabinet. The Foreign Office at length replied that it would enquire at St. Petersburg whether overtures for peace would be accepted. St. Petersburg retorted that the Turkish Government must address itself direct to the Russian Commander. A month passed before the Turks received the British recommendation to approach the Grand Duke Nicholas. He replied that no armistice could be granted until he himself knew what the general terms of peace were to be. In the meantime his armies moved on. The British ambassador remonstrated at St. Petersburg. Gortchakoff explained that the terms of peace were too important to be sent over the telegraph lines and must be committed to a special courier—who, in the conditions prevailing in the Balkan mountains, might take some time to reach the army headquarters. The Imperial Chancellor admitted that he had previously informed Sir Andrew Buchanan that the necessary instructions had been dispatched to the Grand Duke ; but he had never said they had arrived. The British Government, roused by his chicanery, decided to despatch the Mediterranean fleet to the Dardanelles. That very afternoon an assurance from the Tsar, previously demanded and previously despatched to London, reached Whitehall to the effect that Constantinople itself would not be occupied by the Russian forces. So the British decision was revoked before the fleet had moved. But the British Government now agreed to address a formal warning to St. Petersburg that they could not regard as valid any settlement between Russia and Turkey unless and until its validity was endorsed by all signatories of the last peace treaty covering the Balkans and Turkey, the Treaty of Paris of 1856.

The Russian armies drew nearer and nearer to Constantinople. A " corps of observation " was sent to Gallipoli. The Turkish plenipotentiaries for the armistice were cut off from the Turkish capital. No information could be obtained about the terms which were being demanded of them. Once more the London Cabinet decided to send the fleet to the Straits. Then news came of the terms posed by Russia ; and at the same time news of their acceptance by the Sultan. Once more counter-orders were despatched to the British admiral, who this time was just entering the Dardanelles. Lord Salisbury was absent from the meeting when the counter-orders were sent, and greatly regretted them. Derby had resigned when the ships had begun to move, and withdrew his resignation when they were brought to anchor—to the satisfaction, apparently, of Beaconsfield, but much to the annoyance of Queen Victoria.

As soon as the British ironclads halted, the Russian armies resumed their advance. No notice was taken of the Sultan's acceptance, which had not yet been communicated to his pleni-potentiaries. For a whole week, indeed, nothing was heard of them. The Sultan's messages had to be delivered into Russian hands ; and it was explained afterwards that the post which received them was forty miles away from the Turkish envoys' camp and the messages had to be carried over snow-clad moun-tains on foot. Russian troops were reported on the coast of the Aegean at Dedeagatch ; others appeared on the fortified out-works for the defence of the capital at Tchataldja. There was panic in Constantinople.

Now parliamentary and public opinion in Britain was roused in favour of action. Even the voice of Gladstone was tem-porarily silenced ; and the voice of the people expressed itself in the jingle :

We don't want to fight ; but, by Jingo, if we do,
We've got the ships, we've got the men, we've got the money too,

which became suddenly much more popular than when it had first been sung on the boards of a music-hall. A country constituent, Sir Henry Drummond Wolff relates, wrote to his member wishing to know where the remains of Lord Palmerston were buried, as he wanted to present his backbone to the Government. For the third time the order to advance was sent to the British fleet, now anchoring close at hand in Besika Bay. For the third time it was stopped. As soon as it had got under steam the Grand Duke Nicholas threatened that he would occupy Constantinople if the ships approached any nearer. The Sultan, now panic-stricken, himself besought the British Govern-ment to stop them. Lord Salisbury could contain himself no longer. " If, after all that has been said," he wrote urgently to the Prime Minister, " the fleet once more returns to Besika Bay, our position will be utterly ridiculous." His view prevailed. For the fourth time the fleet was ordered to proceed. By now the Sultan was nervous that the move would finally provoke the Russians into occupying Constantinople and no longer wanted the British warships for which earlier the Turkish people had so eagerly but in vain scanned the waters of the Dardanelles. But Layard skilfully overcame his fears, and this time the ironclads steamed right on into the harbour of the capital. There they lay, in the Golden Horn itself; and the Russian armies stood just outside Constantinople. Only a few miles separated the rival forces. The Tsar angrily talked of occupying the city. But Alexander II was a man of his word, and did not wish to break it. The British Government ordered the fleet to move a little further off, and to anchor in the Sea of Marmora. So an explosion was avoided. For six months the elephant and the whale, to use Bismarck's expression, lay watching one another, within reciprocal range of observation but unable to strike each other down.

The Russian Government had evasively and imprecisely accepted the view of the British and Austro-Hungarian Governments that the treaty to be signed with Turkey should not modify the clauses of the Treaty of Paris without the consent of all the signatories of 1856. Early in March, 1878, however, the news percolated to London that on March, 3, at San Stefano, a village not twenty miles distant from Constantinople, the Russians had dictated a treaty to their prostrate enemy; and little by little its terms became vaguely known; not until the 23rd of the month were they officially communicated to London. Without waiting until the official transmission had confirmed the extreme severity of the peace conditions, the British Government, on March 8, repeated firmly to Gortchakoff the conditions on which, and only on which, they could attend a peace conference, which the Russian Chancellor had in the meantime provisionally agreed should assemble in Berlin. Every clause of the Treaty of San Stefano, the British Government insisted, must be open to discussion and modification. The Imperial Government returned another evasive reply. On March 13 the British Cabinet repeated its demand. Still no definite acceptance came from St. Petersburg. Austria-Hungary, which had hitherto supported the British view, began to vacillate ; the other Powers were inclined to think that Russia was having her way, and to back the winner. But the British Government were displaying a new firmness ; and on March 21 their demand was concisely repeated, with the request that the Imperial Government should send a precisely affirmative or negative reply. In the meantime preparations were made for war. A special vote of £6,000,000 had already been approved by the Commons. Indian troops were ordered to embark for Malta—a move which could be executed on the instruction of the Secretary of State for India without the publicity of obtaining the authority of Parliament. These, or other forces from India, were to occupy " two important posts in the Levant ", as Beaconsfield wrote to the Queen—which were understood by all the members of the Cabinet to be the island of Cyprus, and Alexandretta on the coast of Syria, bases being thus provided from which to oppose any further southward advance by Russia in nearer Asia.

Gortchakoff's reply, when it arrived, was in the negative. He would not agree that every clause of the Treaty of San Stefano was liable to modification.

The Congress was lost. Now the British Government added to their previous precautions the calling out of the reserve of the home army.

All these precautionary measures were finally approved at the Cabinet over which Beaconsfield presided on March 27. Only one member of it dissented. Derby, at last, definitely resigned. " An unmixed blessing," exclaimed the Queen to her Prime Minister when she received the information ; and she confirmed his supersession by Lord Salisbury as soon as his name was submitted—but for a brief moment she seems to have thought that the post might be given to Lord Lyons.* Political opinion would have been sorely puzzled if the ambassador in Paris, or any other person but the Indian Secretary, had been nominated.

The general expectation was that the change at the Foreign Office meant that something would be done ; what, nobody liked to guess ; but something would be done.

Something was done.

Lord Salisbury composed a despatch.

* Lord Salisbury himself offered the Foreign Secretaryship to Lord Lyons eight years later.

CHAPTER VIII—1878–1880

THE SALISBURY CIRCULAR AND BERLIN CONGRESS

Lord Salisbury did not wait to be formally gazetted to his new post—on April 2—before he wrote the despatch which was surging in his brain. Derby lingered on in the Foreign Office —on April 1 we find him still there, writing a note of thanks to Beaconsfield for having offered him the Garter, which he declined, honourably aware that it was an offer from a friend rather than from the Prime Minister. Lord Salisbury, on his part, had business to complete at the India Office, which occupied the days of March 28 and 29. On the evening of the 29th he and Lady Salisbury were dining out. He kept the engagement ; and then, excusing himself, he left early for his home in Arlington Street, where he locked himself in behind the double-doors of his study, not to emerge thence until three o'clock next morning. Without help from any outside source, driven and guided only by his own knowledge, experience, convictions and impulsive literary talent, he composed the Salisbury Circular which Lord Rosebery later described as one of the " historic State papers of the English language ". It proved itself, in its immediate and ultimate effects, as decisive a document as has ever gone forth in the name of the Foreign Office—and, paradoxically, it was written by a statesman who had never served in the Foreign Office, and was circulated to Europe before he was officially installed in the Foreign Secretary's chair.

The despatch was passed by the Cabinet in the afternoon of the day on which Lord Salisbury had finished writing it ; and two days afterwards, on April 1, it went out to the capitals of the other five Great Powers—to St. Petersburg, Vienna, Berlin, Paris, and Rome.

Lord Salisbury intuitively judged that the plan to hold a Congress in Berlin was not quite lost ; and in his view the alternatives were the Congress or chaos ; a hazard must be taken to save it. Even when he was more mature and more cautious Lord Salisbury did not consider a riskless existence to be a worthy ambition for a great nation. Now, politically young, he openly challenged Russia. The Treaty of San Stefano must be undone. Otherwise, Britain would have to fight. He took the lesser risk to avoid the greater.

The outstanding condition of the Treaty which had been imposed upon prostrate Turkey was the transference from her to Bulgaria of a vast stretch of Balkan territory extending from the Black Sea to the Aegean in the south and to the borders of Albania in the west. This new realm, recalling the Bulgarian Empires of the Tsars before the Turks had entered Europe, was to be ruled by a Prince owing only nominal allegiance to the Porte ; more real, it seemed, would be his allegiance to Russia ; for a Russian Commission was to supervise the Bulgarian Government for two years, and for the same period the country was to be occupied by a Russian army. In addition to this extension of Muscovite influence in Europe, the conquests of the Tsar's armies in nearer Asia were to be retained. Batoum, Kars, Ardahan and Bayazid were to stay in Russian hands ; and Turkey was to pay a war indemnity of 300 million roubles. The Treaty bore the signature of General Ignatieff. Lord Salisbury's old colleague and rival had been at San Stefano and had won this second round of their contest. At the end of the first, at Constantinople, they might be said to have been equal on points. The third and final round was now beginning ; and Lord Salisbury landed the first blow.

With cogent logic, in terse and virile language, his famous Circular set out the reasons why the Treaty of San Stefano should not be allowed to stand. Russia could not be sole arbiter of the peace settlement. Every article must be subject to the approval of the Powers who had signed the Treaty of Paris of 1856 and the Treaty relative to the Black Sea of 1871. " Any Treaty concluded between the Government of Russia and the Porte affecting the Treaties of 1856 and 1871 must be an European Treaty " ; and accordingly " Her Majesty's Government could not accept any partial or fragmentary examination " : and " they could not acquiesce in the withdrawal from the cognisance of the Powers of Articles in the new Treaty which are modifications of existing Treaty engagements and inconsistent with them ".

Passing thence to a detailed examination of its clauses, the Circular proceeds : " By the articles erecting the new Bulgaria, a strong Slav State will be created under the auspices and control of Russia, possessing important harbours upon the shores of the Black Sea and the [Aegean] Archipelago, and conferring upon that Power a preponderating influence over both political and commercial relations in those seas. It will be so constituted as to merge in the dominant Slav majority a considerable mass of population which is Greek in race and sympathy. . . . The provisions by which this new State is to be subjected to a ruler whom Russia will practically choose, its Administration framed by a Russian Commissary, and the first working of its institutions commenced under the control of a Russian army, sufficiently indicate the political system of which it is to form a part."

Further points of the Circular were that " the compulsory alienation of Bessarabia from Rumania, the extension of Bulgaria to the shores of the Black Sea, which are principally inhabited by Mussulmans and Greeks, and the acquisition of the important harbour of Batoum, will make the rule of the Russian Government dominant over all the vicinity of the Black Sea ". And the combined effect of the provisions, Lord Salisbury considered, " is to depress, almost to the point of entire subjection, the political independence of the Government of Constantinople ". He concluded his despatch with a firm but not aggressive statement of the position of his own Government. Her Majesty's Government " would willingly have entered a Congress in which the stipulations in question could have been examined as a whole, in their relations to existing treaties, to the acknowledged rights of Great Britain and of other Powers, and to the beneficent ends which the united action of Europe had always been directed to secure. But neither the interests which Her Majesty's Government are specially bound to guard, nor the well-being of the regions with which the Treaty deals, would be consulted by the assembling of a Congress whose deliberations were to be restricted by such reservations as those which have been laid down by Prince Gortchakoff in his most recent communication."

The Circular despatch was issued to the Press as soon as its contents had been presented to those to whom it was addressed ; and it produced a galvanic and unifying effect both in this country and in Europe, where the western and eastern States, with the obvious exception of Bulgaria, thoroughly disliked the San Stefano proposals. But they had also all been afraid of challenging a Russia flushed with victory. Now the British Government's new sense of direction was as welcome to Turkey, Rumania, Servia and Greece as it was to Austria-Hungary and the Mediterranean Powers. Sir Henry Drummond Wolff, travelling on the Continent soon after the publication of the despatch, wrote of it : " It seemed to have stirred up all Europe and to have restored the credit of England from freezing to fever-point." The longed-for lead was given. " England is bent on preventing Europe from becoming Cossack," exclaimed one of Wolff's eminent foreign acquaintances. Bismarck's immediate reaction was favourable. Prince Gortchakoff prevaricated. He understood what the British Government did not wish ; he would welcome, he said, a less negative and more positive statement of their views.

That was quite encouraging ; the Cabinet readily agreed that before the Congress could usefully meet an understanding must be reached on major differences, and the prospect of detailed agreement must appear reasonably good. Much delicate preparation would be necessary ; and Lord Salisbury began the preliminaries at once. He rightly judged, for all his mistrust of Bismarck, that the German Chancellor desired to preside over a European conference, but that the fervour of his desire varied in proportion to its prospect of success ; and he believed that, if it were held, he would act there, in his own words, as an " honest broker ". Lord Salisbury also saw clearly, as Derby had not, the use he could make of Lord Odo Russell, the ambassador in Berlin, who had established terms of intimacy and independence with the Iron Chancellor. He urged immediacy upon the ambassador, for peace was in danger as long as the Russian army and the British fleet lay in close proximity to each other and within striking distance of Constantinople—with another still mobile Russian army on the fringes of Asia Minor. Bismarck undertook to mediate, and was as good as his word ; but he was struck down by a complication of rheumatism, erysipelas and shingles before he had done more than make the first overtures.

Lord Salisbury had to redouble his own exertions. His first care was to get Russia to consent to redraw the frontiers of Bulgaria along approximately the same lines to which she had agreed at Constantinople the year before. For this purpose he entered into secret negotiations with Count Schouvaloff, the Russian ambassador in London, and by the end of May had not only succeeded in securing agreement on this point but was able to sign, on May 30, a Convention covering most of the differences to be formally discussed at Berlin. No doubt the actual arrival of Indian troops in Malta had something to do with the relatively acquiescent spirit of St. Petersburg. But, as ever, Russia had been more intransigent in Asia than in Europe. She declined to relinquish Kars, Batoum and Ardahan.

Almost as soon as the ink was dry on the two signatures, the contents of the secret treaty were published in the *Globe* newspaper. Lord Salisbury's annoyance was extreme. He was asked by Lord Grey in the House of Lords whether there was any truth in the newspaper report. " The statement to which the noble Earl refers, and other statements which I have seen," the Foreign Secretary replied, " are wholly unauthentic, and not deserving of the confidence of your Lordships' House." The published version was in point of fact remarkably accurate, the only incorrectitude being the alleged withdrawal by Britain of her support of the Turkish claim to maintain troops in the southern half of Bulgaria. The terms of the treaty had been memorized by a temporary clerk in the Foreign Office named Marvin, who had previously been a journalist ; and out of gratitude to his former employers, as he afterwards explained, he communicated to them this sensational information. When, later, he was arrested and prosecuted, it could not be proved that he had stolen a document ; and as at that time no Official Secrets Act had been put on the statute book, his only punishment was to lose his job.

Lord Salisbury was ready at all times publicly to defend secret diplomacy. To discuss differences openly was to hamper the process of give-and-take ; it aggravated divergences and " made retreat on either side a loss of honour ". The time for publicity would come when the Congress met ; his immediate task was to enable the Congress to meet with hope of success. He and Schouvaloff had therefore bound themselves to keep their conversations confidential, and their decisions secret until the Congress disclosed them. So when a near-accurate summary of them was prematurely made public the Foreign Secretary felt himself bound in honour to discredit it. He was not the man normally to tell a lie ; but he believed he should sacrifice his own feelings on the altar of national good faith. Candour in such conditions, his daughter-biographer pleads with justice, would involve active complicity in a public breach of trust. Having made up his mind to pretend that the secret treaty did not exist, he carried the deception to its logical conclusion. When, on June 8, Lord Salisbury notified Lord Odo Russell that he was to be third British representative at the Congress, he instructed him upon the general principles " on which a settlement should be effected ". He also sent to him on the same day a full statement of an arrangement he had made with Turkey. This included the British undertaking to defend Turkish territory in Asia Minor, where Russia had so resolutely refused to give up her conquests. Yet in his despatch of general instruction to his ambassador the Foreign Secretary never once made the slightest reference to his agreement with Schouvaloff, signed ten days before. On the contrary, he wrote as if the fate of the conquered places in Asia Minor were still undecided. Russell was urged to continue to press upon all representatives of the interested foreign Powers in Berlin, including the Russian, " the justice of abstaining from annexations in Asia Minor ". Having provisionally signed away these annexations, Lord Salisbury played out to the end his little game of make-believe.

But the British public, and the European Chanceries, accustomed as they were to secret diplomacy, were nevertheless astounded to learn, some weeks later, that Lord Salisbury had also achieved a secret Convention with Turkey, and that this one had, of course, an anti-Russian bias. Its actual negotiation had been remitted to Mr. Layard in Constantinople. By its clauses Britain was to guarantee to Turkey her territory in Asia —only in Asia—" against further encroachment by Russia ". And holding firmly to his maxim of statesmanship never to undertake more than he could perform, the new Foreign Secretary made the condition that British forces must be allowed to use Cyprus as a base of operations. For this purpose the " occupation and administration of the island shall be assigned to Her Majesty " ; but its sovereignty remained the Sultan's, and any excess of revenue over expenditure was to be paid into the treasury of Abdul Hamid. Moreover, if the Russians should after all withdraw from the Batoum area, " the island will be immediately evacuated ". A further stipulation of the Convention was that, " the British Government not being prepared to sanction misgovernment and oppression of the Christian races in the

Balkans ", the Porte must undertake to introduce the necessary reforms.

In three long personal letters, dated May 2nd, 9th, and 10th, Lord Salisbury had set out his policy to Mr. Layard in all its details. Then, on May 24, with the signature of the Russian Convention coming nearer every day, the Foreign Secretary sent urgent " personal " instructions to the ambassador to press Abdul Hamid to sign the Cyprus Convention at once. His Majesty was to be informed that, if he did not accept it within forty-eight hours, Britain would abandon her opposition to Russia's further advance and could do nothing to prevent the partition of his Empire. Layard's provisional reply was in the following terms : " Therapia. May 25. 7.30 p.m. Secret and most confidential. Your three personal telegrams arrived this morning. I have seen the Sultan, whom I found ill and very much depressed in consequence of recent events. He has given orders to the Prime Minister to act entirely upon my advice, and I have every reason to hope that the proposed arrangement will be signed tomorrow."

The dominant position held by Britain in Constantinople, to which the conclusion of this Convention so astonishingly testifies, makes it all the more remarkable that Lord Salisbury should have been perfectly ready to throw over his pro-Turkish policy. The truth is that all through the Near-Eastern crisis he had hovered between two opposite policies, just as Derby had hovered when he was in control of the Foreign Office. Derby's hesitations had meant inaction ; Lord Salisbury's only meant that until the last moment he could not be sure which of two contrary courses of action he would vigorously pursue ; and in the meantime he kept both doors open until he could clearly see through which he had better go forward. Until the end of May he was ready either to support Turkey, or let her be destroyed. Lady Gwendolen Cecil relates how, at a Foreign Office reception on May 25 in honour of the Queen's birthday, her father appeared " singularly undisturbed ". Yet May 25 was the intermediate day between the presentation of the ultimatum to the Sultan and the receipt of his reply. Had he refused to sign, Lord Salisbury would within thirty-six hours have had to recast his whole attitude towards Russia as explained to Schouvaloff, and acquiesce in the dismemberment of Turkey.

The prospect did not apparently in the smallest degree derange his imperturbability. That evening, his daughter reports, he seemed a little gayer than he was wont to be at social functions.

What had been happening in Constantinople during those critical forty-eight hours deserves to be recounted in detail. Fully briefed by the three earlier letters, Layard knew exactly how to present the British case when he received the urgent telegrams, commanding action, which arrived on May 24, and in the early hours of the 25th—and which all had to be deciphered by himself with the help of his wife alone, owing to Lord Salisbury's imperative order of absolute secrecy. Layard asked for an immediate audience and went to the Yildiz Kiosque, where he found Abdul Hamid, as has already been mentioned, in a highly nervous condition. But the interview is best described as Layard recorded it in his unpublished Memoirs :

I found the Sultan suffering from great depression of spirits and looking very ill. Instead of receiving me, as was his usual habit, in his small private room, he was standing on a raised place in one of the corners or recesses of the large hall on the ground floor, where he could be seen, although not heard, by his attendants. I observed Osman Pasha and a number of Circassians in one of the Chambers opening into the hall. He drew back when I approached him, and his frightened look surprised me. It was evident to me that he was in a highly excited nervous condition.

After he had given me his hand, and keeping as far away from me as he well could, he said that he was suffering from a severe headache in consequence of having passed three sleepless nights, owing to recent events—alluding to the incident at Tcheraghan. I endeavoured to soothe and cheer him by representing to him that although that which had occurred was deeply to be deplored, yet it had, at least, had a good result. It had proved to him that his people and army were loyal and faithful to him and that the attempts to mislead them had signally failed. It would also put an end to the exaggerated rumours and fears of conspiracies and consequent disorders which had recently disturbed the public mind. I informed him that I had been directed by the Queen to express to him her own personal sympathy in his troubles. Her Majesty's message pleased him much.

I heard some time after that he was then labouring under delusions, and that he had actually believed that I was about to assassinate him and to have him carried off by force to an English ship-of-war, and then to place his brother, Murad, on the throne ! He had accordingly given orders that precautions should be taken, and the armed guard of Circassians, which I had observed, should be in readiness in the event of any such attempt being made upon him ! As I spoke in a very low voice so as not to be heard by persons who were in the hall and might have been listening, this added to his alarm and made him draw back from me, with an expression of terror, when I approached him—I had every reason to believe subsequently, that these delusions and hallucinations were encouraged by certain people about him and by the enemies of himself and his country in order to break off the intimate relations which had been established between him and me, and to supplant the influence of England by that of another Power.

The only person who took part in this important interview, besides Mr. Sandison,* was the General Said Pasha [Chief of the Sultan's Household], who apparently then still retained His Majesty's entire confidence. I suggested that he should send for his Prime Minister, who was in the building, but he was not disposed to do so, suggesting that I might afterwards repeat to him what I had to communicate. I then told him that it was absolutely necessary that the most absolute secrecy should be maintained as to the communication which I was about to make to him, and I asked him to give me his royal word that it should not be disclosed. He readily gave it to me, I then proposed that in order not to be overheard he should see me in his private room. He excused himself, saying that it was cooler where we were. What then took place is fully related in a most secret and confidential dispatch which I sent to Lord Salisbury personally—I cannot therefore do better than transcribe it. " As His Majesty was evidently suffering severely, both physically and morally, I did not enter upon an explanation of the proposal of Your Lordship as fully as I should otherwise have done. I merely observed to His Majesty that he had now received so many proofs of the friendship and sympathy felt by the Queen and Her Government for himself and his country that he could not doubt that the suggestion that I was about to submit to him was made in the true interests of himself and of his Empire. To this remark His Majesty warmly assented—remarking that England and the Queen were his only friends and generously adding that he had the utmost confidence in me. I went on to say that His Majesty was no doubt aware that the policy and action of England were necessarily founded upon, or controlled by different and in some respects opposite considerations. She was at the same time a European and an Asiatic Power. As a European Power she was bound by

* Chief Dragoman, or interpreter, at the British Embassy.

Treaties and by her international relations which to a great extent prevented her acting alone in great European questions. In Asia such was not the case. On that Continent her policy was mainly guided by British interests, and she was perfectly free to take such measures as she thought fit to maintain and promote them. I begged His Majesty to keep this distinction in view in considering the proposal that I was about to make to him.

"I then remarked that although Her Majesty's Government entertained the most serious objections to such of the Clauses of the Treaty of San Stefano as were opposed to the Treaties of 1856 and 1871 and were endeavouring to annul or modify them, they were under a certain obligation to act in doing so with their co-signatories to those two Treaties. I had good hopes I said, that through the decided action of Her Majesty's Government important modifications of such parts of the Treaty of San Stefano as affected His Majesty's European dominions would be obtained, that amongst them would be the limitation of the autonomous province of Bulgaria to the north of the Balkans, a matter of the utmost importance to the future of his Empire. I had further reason to believe, I said, that Her Majesty's Government were endeavouring, with some prospect of success, to obtain the withdrawal of the Russian army from the vicinity of Constantinople. If they succeeded in doing so, freedom of action would be restored to his Government, and a constant source of the gravest danger would be removed.

"His Majesty, who seemed very much overcome and rising from his seat, asked me to communicate what I had stated to him to the Prime Minister as he felt so ill that he was quite unable to continue the conversation. I told His Majesty that he had only heard a part of what I had to say to him and that I was instructed to submit a proposal to him for a defensive alliance with England which would secure, there was every reason to hope, his Asiatic dominions from all aggression from Russia in the future. I was unable to add more as His Majesty was evidently so ill that I could not with propriety further detain him. He earnestly begged me to see the Prime Minister at once, and I accordingly joined His Highness in another room.

"Later, whilst I was still in the Palace, His Majesty sent for Mr. Sandison, and requested him to explain to me that owing to his long want of sleep he felt unequal to receiving the important communication that I had begun to make to him, and that when I retired he felt as if he were about to faint. He begged me to believe that he was deeply moved by the friendship shown to him by the Queen and Her Government, which was far beyond anything that he could have expected, and he expressed unbounded satisfaction with the proposal that they had made to him. He hoped that I would excuse the abruptness with which he had been obliged to leave me. Subsequently when I was with the Prime Minister, His Majesty sent Said Pasha to tell His Highness that it was his wish that any advice I might offer, or any proposal I might make, should be accepted."

Lord Salisbury's proposals, including the occupation of Cyprus, were unanimously agreed to by a specially summoned Council of Ministers, and whole-heartedly approved by the Turkish Sovereign. Layard had not even had to use the threat, authorized by Lord Salisbury, that in the event of refusal the help of England would be withdrawn, " and the capture of Constantinople and the partition of his [the Sultan's] Empire will be the immediate result ".

The Cyprus Convention was signed in the Yildiz Kiosque on June 4th ; the secret of its signature was to be kept until the moment for publication should be considered opportune at the Congress to be held in Berlin.

In the meantime Bismarck had been able to resume work after his illness and had come to an arrangement with Andrassy by which Austria-Hungary should take over the administration of the Turkish provinces of Bosnia and Herzegovina as compensation for the increase of Russian influence in the Balkans. Russia was also to keep the whole of the province of Bessarabia, of which the southern part had belonged to Rumania. The surrender of this broad strip brought Russia down to the mouths of the Danube. In exchange for her loss, Rumania would receive the marshy district known as the Dobrudja, which lies between the Black Sea and the south-north course of the lower Danube.

Thus every vital issue was settled beforehand ; and Bismarck could send out his invitations to the Great Powers to meet in Berlin on June 13, there to discuss all the clauses of the Treaty of San Stefano. It was a notable triumph for the British point of view. The Cabinet lost not a moment in despatching its formal acceptance (June 2).

2

While Beaconsfield made a slow and stately progress to Berlin, " right royally " entertained on the way by the King and Queen

LORD SALISBURY AT THE AGE OF 48

By kind permission of the 5th Marquess of Salisbury

Portrait by the German artist Anton von Werder. Painted as a study for the head of Lord Salisbury in the picture of the Berlin Congress, 1878, which was commissioned by the Emperor William I.

of the Belgians, and eagerly sought at successive railway-stations as the Oriental who had achieved a unique record in British annals, Lord Salisbury travelled unobserved, eluding even the members of his own staff and accompanied only by his eldest son. He was joined in Berlin later by Lady Salisbury, who brought with her their sons William and Robert, then quite young boys.

The Congress was opened at 2 p.m. on Thursday, June 13, in the Radziwill palace in Berlin, which had recently been presented to Bismarck for an official residence. Port wine and biscuits were consumed while the various envoys were assembling in full uniform. At the horseshoe table Bismarck rather unexpectedly had Andrassy on his immediate right and Waddington, the French Foreign Minister, on his left. The British delegates sat on the right of the Austrians, and had on their right Prince Gortchakoff. Beaconsfield had cherished the notion of delivering his opening speech in French ; but the ambassador and his own devoted Private Secretary, " Monty " Corry, knowing the imperfections of his pronunciation, persuaded him by a stratagem that the assembled diplomatists were eagerly looking forward to this unique opportunity of hearing " the greatest master of English prose address the Congress in his own tongue ".

The ground having been so well prepared, the Congress was not long drawn out ; and there is no need to recapitulate the detailed discussion of issues which private negotiation had already settled in principle. The first few days were taken up with Royal audiences, sumptuous banquets and gala performances. Beaconsfield delighted in them ; Lord Salisbury was bored. Both spent the first weekend with the Crown Prince and Princess at Potsdam. Beaconsfield wrote home rapturously, Lord Salisbury apologetically. A week later the Foreign Secretary was there again and wrote to Lady Salisbury : " Six hours out of my day have been taken away by that tiresome Princess asking me to lunch at Potsdam." At a later weekend he travelled all the way to Dresden to worship in an Anglican church, there being none at that time in Berlin—" to forget the cares of diplomacy in the consolations of religion ", *The Times* wrote ; but probably it was also in order to escape the fatigue of entertainments, if there was any additional motive over and above his always deep desire to attend Holy Communion on Sunday.

The most important point left open for settlement in Berlin was the right of Turkey to keep troops in the southern part of the newly-created principality of Bulgaria. A mountainous watershed, running east and west, separates the two halves of the Bulgarian race ; and Lord Salisbury was supported by Beaconsfield in insisting that the Sultan should be allowed to hold the passes against the threat of Russian incursions southward. Beaconsfield's championship of the cause of the Sultan provided a dramatic climax on June 21. He let it be known that Britain made the issue a *casus belli*. He ordered a special train to be ready to take the British delegates home. Gortchakoff, not to be outdone, packed his trunks, and let all Berlin know when they were packed. Their diplomatic gestures alarmed Bismarck. He went round to the Kaiserhof Hotel, where Beaconsfield and Salisbury were staying, about four o'clock, and left again less than ten minutes later, having satisfied himself that Beaconsfield was really ready to break up the Congress on the point. He invited him to dine quietly with him that evening—a family party only. We may take up the narrative in Beaconsfield's own words : " Bismarck was very agreeable indeed . . . made no allusion to politics, and, tho' he ate and drank a great deal, talked more. After dinner, we retired to another room, where he smoked and I followed his example. I believe I gave the last blow to my shattered constitution, but I felt it absolutely necessary. I had an hour and a half of the most interesting conversation, entirely political ; he was convinced that the ultimatum was not a sham, and, before I went to bed, I had the satisfaction of knowing that St. Petersburg had surrendered."

Incurably romantic, Beaconsfield packed into this dramatic *tête-à-tête* an issue which had in sober fact been settled by the visit of Bismarck to his hotel that afternoon, following upon Beaconsfield's earlier hint to a mutual confidant, the Italian Count Corti, that the Congress would be ended if Russia did not yield. When Bismarck had been convinced by his ten-minute talk with Beaconsfield himself that the threat was not idle, he had immediately got into telegraphic communication with St. Petersburg, as a result of which he was satisfied that the crisis was overcome.

Encouraged by this success, Beaconsfield took up with renewed zest the fate of the port of Batoum on the east coast of the Black Sea. He and the Foreign Secretary had both given up hope that Russia would hand it back to Turkey ; but they believed they could prevent its being made into a fortress or naval base. Lord Salisbury accordingly suggested to Schouvaloff, who was Gortchakoff's right-hand man in Berlin, that it should belong to Russia but should be " *exclusivement commercial* ". The sequel is best told in Lord Salisbury's own account to Mr. Cross, the Home Secretary, in a letter " for his private eye " : " But Gortchakoff got at Beaconsfield yesterday morning when he was very ill, and persuaded him that the two words (*essentiellement* and *exclusivement*) meant the same thing—and that the latter would be offensive to the Emperor. I have been only able, therefore, to get some words on to the Protocol indicating that it was to be " only commercial ". The Foreign Secretary further made it clear that in consenting to the *status quo* in respect to the Straits, he did so only on the condition that Batoum was not to be constituted into a menace to the Bosphorus.

Lord Salisbury had also hoped to create an independent hinterland for Batoum, where the bulk of the population was Mussulman. Here again he was thwarted by Schouvaloff passing the matter on to Gortchakoff for settlement with Beaconsfield. The boundary line agreed upon between himself and Schouvaloff for the new Khanate had quite a different appearance on the map when it was laid before the full Congress. Whether Beaconsfield ("who is short-sighted and ignorant of detail ") had really agreed to the new line, Lord Salisbury could not say. In any case Schouvaloff " acknowledged that we were done, but professes his inability to help ". Lord Salisbury had had similar difficulty over the precise definition of the frontiers of Bulgaria. He was painfully reminded of Ignatieff's light-hearted trickery with the maps at Constantinople the year before.

Such episodes as these prevented the Congress from being the smooth-running affair which Lord Salisbury's elaborate preparations had been designed to make it. The very completeness of his preliminaries, indeed, became a cause of extreme discomfort and embarrassment to the British delegation. Soon after the Congress had begun its regular meetings, the British Cabinet in London ordered the prosecution of the clerk Marvin —for which it was soundly berated by Beaconsfield from Berlin ; and the *Globe* took the opportunity to publish now the whole text of the Anglo-Russian Agreement, of which the summary had been declared by Lord Salisbury not to be authentic or worthy of credence. This time its authenticity could no longer be impugned ; and the prosecution—and acquittal—of Marvin only made matters worse. " What in the name of Heaven, or rather Hell," wrote Beaconsfield to Stafford Northcote, " could have induced you all to arrest, and prosecute, that poor wretch Marvin ? . . . this sad wretch entrusted with secrets of State with a salary of 8*d.* an hour ! " ; and his heated language gave the measure of his embarrassment. Then, at the beginning of July, the corridors round the Congress hall began to hum with rumours of Britain's other secret bargain ; so Lord Salisbury promptly made up his mind to impart the information of the Cyprus Convention to the French plenipotentiary ; for it was from Mediterranean France that he expected the most hostile reaction. Before he left London he had written a facetious forecast of events at Berlin to his close friend Stafford Northcote ; it included the following playful entry : " June 27. British P.P. [Plenipotentiaries] communicate the [Cyprus] Convention : Waddington tears his hair, and telegraphs wildly to Toulon." In order to prevent M. Waddington from tearing his hair Lord Salisbury had already—and no doubt he repeated it on this occasion—given a hint to Paris that " We should not have the slightest jealousy or fear " if French statesmen sought an extension of their African territory in the direction of Tunis. And he was now pleased to find that Waddington did not telegraph wildly either to Toulon or Paris. Nevertheless, the confidence was made only just in time. He disclosed his second secret arrangement to the French Foreign Minister on July 7 ; on the very next day the *Daily Telegraph* published the substance of the Convention ; and the Government accordingly announced its text to the House of Commons the same afternoon. It was another awkward moment for its author ; but the foreign delegations were on the whole envious rather than indignant. Nevertheless, at a reception at the Austrian Embassy that evening the Russians showed a kind of sullen fury, and their ill-humour created a certain malaise at the party. Beaconsfield, however, walked quietly along, his countenance sphinx-like, a certain jauntiness in his gait. Princess Radziwill, as she records in her Recollections, asked him : " What are you thinking of ? " " I am not thinking," he replied, " I am enjoying myself." He might have been playing a part in one of his own novels.

Agreement over Batoum was only reached on July 12 ; next day the Treaty of Berlin was signed, a month exactly since the Congress began.

3

The two British plenipotentiaries were accorded a tumultuous welcome on their return, first at Dover, then in London. Beaconsfield came ashore with Lady Salisbury on his arm, and as soon as he reached the train an eager crowd demanded a speech. He put his head out of the window of his carriage and said : " Gentlemen, we bring you peace, and, I think I may say, peace with honour." Then it was Lord Salisbury's turn to be called upon to speak ; he, however, remained in his seat and continued to read *The Times*—though, according to an eyewitness, he unbent to the extent of " shaking his head and smiling ". When they reached London, Whitehall was vibrant with enthusiasm. With the pleasant informality of those days they drove from Charing Cross in an open carriage in which also sat Lady Abergavenny and Lady Northcote ; and Lord Salisbury, in high good humour, entered 10 Downing Street with his Chief. Both men appeared at windows in Downing Street ; and this time Beaconsfield coupled Lord Salisbury by name with himself in having brought back " peace, and a peace, I hope, not without honour "—the phrase which has become historic, and was repeated at the same window by one of Beaconsfield's successors just 60 years later, but with less good cause. Lord Salisbury was now also induced to address the crowd : " I thank you heartily, and gather from this great assembly that you will always continue to support a Government which supports the honour of England." The rest of his words were drowned in cheers.

Queen Victoria was if possible even more jubilant than her people. She had felt very grievously the decline of British influence abroad during the 60's and 70's. At the beginning of 1878 she had written to Beaconsfield : " The Queen is really distressed at the low tone which this country is inclined to hold. She thinks every opportunity ought to be taken and every effort made to show them that the Empire and even their low sordid love of gain will suffer permanently and most seriously if this goes on. The country should be frightened as to the results. . . . She feels she cannot remain the Sovereign of a country that is letting itself down to kiss the feet of the great barbarians [Russia], the retarders of all liberty and civilization that exists. . . . We shall never be friends again till we have it out. This the Queen feels sure of." Depressed then to the point of considering abdication, Queen Victoria was so elated three months later by Lord Salisbury's Circular Note that she promptly offered the Garter both to him and Beaconsfield. The Prime Minister protested that the honour would be " rather premature " at that moment. Now, however, he gratefully accepted it for himself on the understanding that Lord Salisbury, who had plied " the labouring oar ", should receive it at the same time.

To have raised the prestige of Britain all over the world was indeed the immedi te and most notable result of the two statesmen's exertions dur ng the short period since Lord Salisbury had been at the Foreign Office. A sign 'of the increased respect felt for Britain was afforded in the following year, when the great Bismarck renewed his approach to London for the conclusion of an alliance, with Austria as a third member. Beaconsfield, with the concurrence of Lord Salisbury (" he and I are the same ", he said to the German Ambassador when Count Muenster asked that the proposal should be kept entirely to himself), mentioned the objection that Anglo-French relations would be prejudicially affected ; and the preliminary offer, made in such a highly confidential manner, was not officially or formally repeated.

The best treaty in the world is not immune from criticism, least of all by an Opposition Party in a democratic country ; and the first shots were soon fired in Westminster, in spite of some organized and much spontaneous acclamation outside. Lord Salisbury was pugnaciously ready to meet the critics ; he now released his pent-up exasperation in withering flames of caustic oratory, directed against those who had attacked and hampered his every effort at bold peace-making during the past three months. Mr. Gladstone's speeches had been, and continued to be, diffuse and passionate denunciations of the Government. His final speech in the House of Commons on July 30 took $2\frac{1}{4}$ hours to deliver. On another occasion, at Southwark, he denounced the Cyprus Convention as " an insane covenant ", and its secret negotiation as " an act of duplicity of which every

Englishman should be ashamed, an act of duplicity which has not been surpassed and has, I believe, been rarely equalled in the history of nations ". It was this diatribe which roused Beaconsfield to his famous description of Gladstone as " a sophistical rhetorician inebriated with the exuberance of his own verbosity ".

Mr. Gladstone was also aghast at the " largeness and vagueness " of the commitments we had undertaken for the defence of Turkish territory in Asia. If we were to make them effective we would have to reform the judicature, the police, the finances, and the civil service of Turkey. Lord Salisbury replied in more sober language than that of his accuser or his Chief. His opponents, he said, were trying to persuade the country that " the duty of England, the interest of England, is to confine herself solely to her own insular forces, to cultivate commerce, to accumulate riches, and not to entangle herself in foreign politics "—a passage which should be remembered every time that Lord Salisbury's so-called policy of isolation is brought up for discussion. What he himself had in mind, he said, was " to extend to others the blessings which we ourselves enjoy ; . . . The one object we have in view is that peace and order shall be maintained, and that races and creeds which for centuries back have lived in feud shall henceforth live in amity and goodwill." Even Gladstone had "thankfully and joyfully" acknowledged that a great work of emancipation had been achieved for the Slavs who lived under Turkish rule in Europe. Yet he opposed the attempt to extend these blessings to the Asiatic domains of Turkey. It is an interesting example of the streaks of reciprocal respect and sympathy which lay deep in these two rigidly Christian statesmen that Lord Salisbury had borrowed Gladstone's Liberalism in regard to Turkish reforms in Europe, and the Liberal had borrowed Lord Salisbury's Conservative caution in not desiring that Britain should undertake in Asia greater responsibilities than she was able to bear. And in regard to Greece, both men greatly regretted that the liberation from the Porte of the provinces of Thessaly and Epirus had not been effected. Turkish misgovernment of their Greek inhabitants had often suggested the solution that these territories should be transferred to Greece. But Lord Salisbury had written to Odo Russell before the Congress began : " If the Greek kingdom were stronger, it might be possible to give Western Thrace to it, but it is too young for such a charge. Another period of transition must be passed through, at the end of which the Greek heritage will no doubt fall to the true heir." The British Government nevertheless prevailed upon the other participating Powers to allow envoys from Greece to appear at the Congress. Their presence availed nothing. Their country had, partly on British advice, played no part in the events that led up to it ; and they had to console themselves with Beaconsfield's epigrammatic advice : " Greece has a future ; and I would say, if I might be permitted, what I would say to an individual who has a future, ' Learn to be patient.' "

" Save me from my friends " must have been Lord Salisbury's heart-cry when he found himself engaged in his bitterest personal controversy in the House of Lords, not with his opponents, but with his former Conservative colleague in the Cabinet, Derby. The ex-Foreign Secretary had more than once stretched rather far the licence allowed to a Cabinet Minister when he makes a personal statement on his resignation. Mortified, maybe, by the success which had attended the policy of his supplanter, he now, on July 18, four months after the event, gave an account of the Cabinet discussion on Cyprus. Of his many " revelations " Lord Salisbury remarked that, no record being kept, they must in the nature of things be liable to error. But the reiteration in a formal debate in the House of Lords, that the Cabinet had decided to seize Cyprus, " if necessary without the Sultan's consent ", roused the Foreign Secretary to cold fury. He likened his predecessor to the celebrated plot-inventor Titus Oates, and with more than his usual directness described Derby's account as " not true ". When the noble Lords, though sympathizing with the Foreign Secretary, murmured their dislike of this unparliamentary expression, he substituted the words " not correct ". Both men left the House, in high dudgeon, unreconciled, and separately ; but the imp of mischief was busy that night and directed the footsteps of one and the other to the then well-known dining club, Grillion's. The sprite arranged, too, that they should be the first arrivals ; and when, a little later, Lord George Hamilton and Gladstone's austere disciple John Morley arrived from the House of Commons, they found two big, very confused figures standing in the remotest corners of the anteroom, each ignoring the other's presence. No one else came to dinner ; so Hamilton, who tells the story in his Reminiscences, and was himself the friend of both embarrassed giants, had to exercise all the agreeable intelligence for which his family was famous, and which is so happily apparent in the Memoirs of himself and of his brother.

The advent of the grouse-shooting season soon took most of the House of Lords north beyond the Tweed, and Lord Salisbury to Puys, where he had built himself a chalet a few years before. A letter to Beaconsfield dated September 2. '78, is headed : " Châlet Cecil, près Dieppe " ; but its contents show that he was still engrossed there in international politics ; and his concluding sentence, " Probably I shall run over if the Note really makes its appearance ", reminded his Chief that he was closer to hand in Dieppe than he would have been in Scotland.

4

The remainder of Lord Salisbury's first period of office as Foreign Secretary was notable mainly for two unhappy events in Afghanistan and Zululand. For the first he had indirect responsibility, for although Lord Cranbrook was now Indian Secretary, it was he who had inaugurated the forward policy on the Indian frontier. Lytton sought to counteract the growing influence of Russia at Kabul by compelling the Ameer to sign a treaty of alliance and receive a British resident in his capital. When the request was refused, a British army invaded Afghanistan. Sir Lewis Cavagnari was duly installed as the representative of Queen Victoria in the capital ; but soon after the troops had been withdrawn the populace rose and rioted, and killed Cavagnari. A second and more serious war began ; and another disaster befell the invaders when General Burrows was totally defeated at Maiwand. The balance was redressed by General Roberts, who here first displayed the military skill which was to make him a Field-Marshal and Commander-in-Chief of Britain's army. A brilliantly executed march from Kabul to Kandahar brought tardy victory to British arms.

Beaconsfield and Lord Salisbury could plead that the arrival of the Tsar's special mission to the Ameer just a month after the Treaty of Berlin had been signed made it clear that Russia, thwarted in Europe and checked in Transcaucasia, was moving her point of pressure to middle Asia. The need of the successive invasions was none the less judged inadmissible by the British public ; they also felt that what had been ill conceived was clumsily executed. And while the war beyond the Indian frontier was still being waged, another began in Zululand ; and here, too, disaster and humiliation followed. At Isandhlwana a whole British battalion and a thousand native auxiliaries were exterminated by the most martial and best trained of Africa's warriors. Natal was only saved from invasion by the heroic exertion of a handful of troops at Rorke's Drift ; and three sanguinary battles had to be fought in the campaign of that year (1879) before the Zulus were subjected. These simultaneous wars on two continents were very unpopular. They offered ready ammunition to the Liberal critics of the Government. Gladstone found wide support when he declared that the Conservatives had " weakened the empire by needless wars, unprofitable extensions and unwise engagements "—with special references to Beaconsfield's annexation of the Transvaal in 1877, and the " filching " of the island of Cyprus from the Porte. To these ministerial misdeeds was added a succession of bad harvests. So when Beaconsfield appealed to the country in March, 1880, it was not inexplicable, in spite of the Government's good record in Europe, that he was soundly defeated.

5

Like so many Victorians, Lord Salisbury had a cold bath every morning ; and even February and a slight chill did not prompt him to relinquish the hardy habit in this year 1880— when he was just fifty years old. The result was that he fell ill of a fever. He insisted nevertheless on continuing to attend to business, at Hatfield and in bed ; and, when he was fit enough to move to London, the Cabinet meeting which decided on dissolution was held, on March 6, in his house in Arlington Street. Only then did he agree to submit to doctor's orders, and departed for Biarritz—the more readily as peers were prescriptively debarred from taking part in Elections. His final act of friendship to Beaconsfield was to put Hatfield at his disposal while he himself was away in the sunshine of Navarre. There the results of the polls reached him day by day for three weeks. The unfavourable returns did not surprise him. He knew better than the Prime Minister how poor were the cards which the Conservatives held. The recent misfortunes in Asia and Africa were bound to lose them tricks, and the Berlin success was not the trump card which Beaconsfield thought it was. In the words of his nephew, Algernon Cecil, he had strongly disapproved of the organized fanfaronade which was kept up after their return ; he instinctively disliked any display of feeling ; and above all, he hated being regarded as " the friend of the Turk ". He also realized how angry the Commons had been at the movement of Indian troops to Malta by departmental order ; and he appreciated at its true value the tremendous impression which Gladstone's exploitation of Conservative mistakes, and even of Conservative achievements, had made and was making all over the country. The success of the famous Midlothian campaign, indeed, had a lasting effect on Lord Salisbury and moved him to carry his own oratory, which had hitherto been confined to the two Houses of Parliament, into the country.

Lord Salisbury's personal reputation was, however, greatly enhanced by his first tenure of the Foreign Secretaryship. Even political opponents admitted the apparently inborn and certainly most unexpected aptitude for diplomatic negotiation of this former *enfant terrible* of Westminster. He had taken over an almost desperate position, when many believed that England would be drawn into war on the side of Turkey, had challenged Russia from it, and had forced her, without war, to reduce her pretensions. He had won a name for strength and resolution, in spite of having wavered between two opposite policies ; he had earned the confidence of the country, in spite of having told a famous lie and resorted to ruthless methods. He had become a European figure. " You would hardly believe ", the British ambassador in Vienna had written to Beaconsfield two days before the Berlin Congress opened, " the change in the position of England in Continental estimation that has been operated within the last two months "—and the ambassador being Sir Henry Elliot, whose advice had been disregarded by Lord Salisbury in 1877, the compliment to the author of the Circular Note was a compliment indeed. And at the time when the election was being fought Lord Salisbury's forecast that Bulgaria would become a Russian province seemed to be proved entirely correct. In the new Bulgaria all the chief administrative posts were filled by Russian officials. Russian officers were training the newly-formed militia. The high-water mark of Russian influence was reached in 1881, when the Prime Minister and the Ministers of War, of Justice and of the Interior were all Russian Generals. Subsequently the Bulgarians, a tough, ambitious race, re-asserted themselves and proclaimed their independence from Russian and Turk alike ; and men may ask whether after all it was not a blunder to deprive them of the historic San Stefano boundaries. Territory torn from the Turk was restored to the Turk ; till well into this century Macedonia remained a cause of friction not only between the Balkan States themselves but also between the Great Powers. The bloody Balkan Wars of 1912–13 were necessary before Turkey was again reduced to about the same dimensions as were allotted to her at San Stefano. And quite recently Bulgaria has become the pawn of a Russia more tyrannical than the Russia of the Tsars. A final judgment will perhaps never be passed, for there is no finality in Europe. Lord Salisbury himself was later in his career to admit that he had misjudged the Bulgar character. And he was haunted by the regret that the reforms he had projected for the Christian subjects of the Porte were never made effective.

The most justifiable criticism of his policy between 1878 and 1880 is that the settlement he obtained was based on consideration of the interests of the Great Powers rather than the interests of the people immediately concerned. He was never proud of it. In private conversation, recorded by his daughter, he expressed the wish that his foreign policy should never be judged by the events of 1878. This diffident estimate did not correspond with the opinion of Lord Rosebery—himself a brilliant though transient Foreign Secretary, who might have gained a higher place in English history if he had not abandoned the Foreign Office for the Premiership. In 1904 Lord Rosebery was invited to unveil a bust of Lord Salisbury at the Oxford Union, and he said : " I think that he reached the greatest moment of his life in 1878. It was not that he returned from the Congress at Berlin in that year with flowers, acclaiming of crowds, illuminations, and " peace with honour ". The great moment of Lord Salisbury's life, to my mind, the moment when he set his stamp on his country and on his own fame, and achieved for himself a European reputation, was when he went to the Foreign Office, succeeding Lord Derby. . . ." And his triumph in that spring of 1878 was his own. With extraordinary self-confidence he had, as we have seen, written his Circular of April 1st without consulting anybody in the Foreign Office ; and when he entered that august building he immediately formed an inner secretariat to carry out a policy of which even the Under-Secretaries were kept in ignorance. His " secret department ", as it was called, was composed of his private secretary and one or two specially selected members of the Office who copied out and deciphered despatches for him. The discomfiture of Russia at San Stefano was probably the most single-handed achievement in the whole long history of British diplomacy.

OPPOSITION

In the character of great men it is often a sign of their greatness that they are able to combine opposite qualities in the same personality—in a personality not split by contradictions, but integrated by an over-ruling self-control, which knows how to apply those opposite qualities opportunely and to the degree required by circumstance. And if this is true of nations, the English may surely claim to be a great people, for they are kindly, but on occasions most ruthless ; peace-loving almost to a fault, but at a crisis fiercely combative ; then mild to administer those whom they have conquered ; humble, and audacious ; easy-going, and severely practical ; having a firm belief in personal liberty, but esteeming authority ; often called unimaginative, but having produced the finest volume of poetry of any modern nation ; loving tradition, but welcoming novelty hardly less ; strongly conservative and strongly progressive. And for giving effect to this last combination of attributes the two-party system has served them politically very well. It has provided appropriate expression to opposite moods. The alternation of periods of progress and stabilization, which occurred almost regularly and more or less rhythmically from the death of Palmerston in 1865 until the " Khaki " election of 1900, gave scope to the people's desire for drastic reforms at home and vigorous expansion overseas, for a liberalization and enlargement of the constitution, and for the maintenance of governmental authority. Lord Salisbury was always favourable to this swing of the pendulum, as he called it, even when it swung against himself. In this year 1880, for instance, when he was exhausted and ill at the end of his first long period of office, he felt that he was in no condition to govern. The physical freshness which alone imparts initiative to policy, instinct to judgment, and confidence to decision, was, in his view, a *sine qua non* of statesmanship. And it had deserted him. But Opposition gave him the chance to nurture himself and coax his briskness back. Quiet country life, long moments of the solitude which kindled his thought, and many hours in the laboratory which he had built in the basement of his house—these made the five years which followed the final preparation for the thirteen years of premiership and eleven of the foreign secretaryship * which were to render almost intolerably arduous the last seventeen years of his active life.

He spent the five years between 1880 and 1885 mainly at home, with a family now growing up and going out into the world. He conscientiously performed the duties of a landlord in Hertfordshire, and of an Opposition leader in London ; and took a regular annual holiday abroad, almost always in the pleasant land of France, which he loved above all other foreign countries. There he could wander without being gazed at ; from its literature, as from its varied scenery, he drew his greatest refreshment of mind. We find him now at Dieppe, now on the Riviera ; at one time at Royat, at another at Biarritz ; and often in Paris, where he bought books old and new. " My gin-shop", he used to say, borrowing a phrase from his Australian experience, " are the book-stalls on the *quais*."

When he was at Hatfield there was early chapel and some-times also a walk, before breakfast. Luncheon was a brief and simple meal ; after it he often walked again in the park, accom-panied probably by one or more members of the family, if he had not to go up to the House of Lords. The interest he took in his boys' careers was startlingly shown when, towards the end of this period, he was found immersed in a military manual. He was strongly antipathetic to the profession of arms ; but when his son Edward decided to join the army, he forced himself to study the regulations to which his boy would henceforth have to conform. He was always a stickler for eight hours of sleep. Though he probably would have agreed with H. G. Wells in nothing else, he felt, like him, the need for " eight hours of dreamless, motionless sleep. . . . If I do not get that allowance [said Wells] my nerves and mind are threadbare." Lord Salis-bury was even happier, according to his biographer, if he could get nine. And he never forewent the weekly refreshment of a quiet Sunday.

So Lady Salisbury had the windows shuttered in their London house and the furniture dust-sheeted. Almost as soon as that had been done, however, the house was opened up again ; for

* Making just thirteen years with the two years 1878–80.

early in the year 1880 John Henry Newman returned from Rome with his Cardinal's hat ; a reception was given in his honour at Norfolk House ; and Lord Salisbury insisted on going up for it. Perhaps Newman's vehement opposition to the Ultramontanism of Manning had something to do with Lord Salisbury's keenness to go ; but in any case his own staunch Anglicanism had never for a moment weakened his deep respect for the nobility, sincerity and intellectual force of the 79-year old Cardinal, to whom he now paid public tribute.

He made another special journey to London when Beaconsfield died at Eastertide of the following year ; and he went on from Arlington Street to Hughenden. After the funeral he wrote to a friend : " I have just returned from the old chief's funeral. It was a very striking sight and to me inexpressibly sad. It seems like the passing away of an epoch. What is it that lies before us ? " When, after the recess, tributes were paid to the departed statesman in both Houses of Parliament, Lord Salisbury's speech, though he was never at his best on formal occasions, profoundly moved the peers. The old antagonism between the two men was only hinted at in order to render more vivid the subsequent tribute to his " patience, his gentleness, his unswerving and unselfish loyalty to his colleagues and fellow-labourers ". The peculiar character of his genius, Lord Salisbury declared, was " the wonderful combination of qualities rarely found together ". His success proved that there was for every Englishman, however humble, an open career leading to the highest positions under the Crown ; and " zeal for the greatness of England was the passion of his life ".

The death of the Party leader raised in an awkward form the question of his successor—peculiarly awkward, because the Duke of Richmond had been leader in the Lords when Disraeli was still in the Commons, and when he went to the Upper House Stafford Northcote was appointed leader in the other place ; and Lord Salisbury was universally regarded as having far stronger claims than either. But this was a candidate who lacked the first qualification of a candidate, which is to desire the vacant post. In a letter to Lady John Manners, who had written to him urging him to accept the leadership, he replied that he was disposed to " leave alone for the present all questions of ' party ' leadership ".

He had by now unequivocally accepted all the implications

of the Reform Bill of 1867. " Our absolute sovereign is the people of this country," he exclaimed a little later in the House of Lords ; and he honestly believed that the primacy which had been conferred upon the House of Commons excluded him for ever from the premiership. A compromise was eventually reached, according to which he himself was to be the Conservative leader in the House of Lords and Northcote in the House of Commons ; and they were to be joint leaders of the Party in the country. Northcote had been for a time Lord Salisbury's colleague in the representation of the two-seated " rotten " borough of Stamford, and they were close and trustful friends. So there was not likely to be any difficulty on personal grounds ; and the arrangement did in fact work very well until the moment came for the Conservatives to form a government—and by then Lord Salisbury had proved himself so decidedly the greater man that no challenge to his election came from anybody—least of all from Northcote.

He had shown himself not only to be much the abler politician, but, which was more surprising, by far the more popular in the constituencies. It was at this period that he took to public speaking in the country. Hitherto he had confined himself almost entirely to Westminster. He had become a most effective debater ; but his expert expositions of large issues, his range over European complications, and his quick eye for the fault in an opponent's argument, had not prepared either supporters or opponents for his success before popular audiences. But he was more adaptable than they thought. He had been deeply impressed by the immense influence upon the electorate of Gladstone's Midlothian campaign. Beaconsfield, who alone could answer him, was dead. He must himself stump the country.

He took the greatest trouble about preparing these speeches. Not one of them was ever machine-made. Each was integrally individual, the offspring of his own thought. He would work out his sequence of argument ; he made no notes ; but spoke the speech over and over again beforehand to himself, impressing one or two key words on his mind. His method thus combined logical continuity of argument with freedom of phrasing. He could think standing just as well as sitting in his study, though he often paused in delivery for several moments till he found exactly the word or phrase he wanted. He was never glib ; he was having a talk with the people. It was his way of keeping in touch with them. He was completely frank with them. He said what he thought ; and he therefore committed many " blazing indiscretions ", for which he felt it quite unnecessary to apologize. The public came to appreciate his speeches immensely. They knew perfectly well that he cared little for their opinion. But he had often shown that he cared just as little for the opinion of his fellow-peers. And they often felt that he was exactly expressing their own feelings. They trusted him. And he never talked down to them. He used rather different language, of course, than that demanded by cut-and-thrust debating. He spoke in a more free and easy style. But he expounded principles and discussed the large issues of the moment, whether relating to home or foreign affairs. And like all men of principle, he was essentially simple and easily understood by the common man.

Always his outlook was subjective rather than objective. It was the problem that mattered, and his convictions on the subject. He did not contradict himself, because the truth as he saw it was his guide and not the people or the audience to whom he happened to be speaking at the moment. His indifference to their adventitious or fortuitous wishes was illustrated by an incident during a speech at Oxford. A reference to " the English " evoked an interruption from a member of the audience who obviously came from north of the Tweed. " British," he cried. Lord Salisbury took no notice ; next time he said " the English " again. " What aboot the Scots ? " bawled the Scotsman, and one or two others backed him up. Lord Salisbury went on with his speech still saying " England " and " the English ". After two or three vain attempts to deflect him the interrupters relapsed into unsatisfied silence. Lord Salisbury's obstinacy on this particular point had perhaps rather more substance than mere indifference to the prejudice of some of his hearers. The Cecils have always had a slightly anti-Scottish prejudice. Like so many great political families of Britain—the Pitts, the Churchills, the Stanleys, the Cavendishes—they are English of the English. Lord Salisbury's oldest known ancestor may have come from Wales ; but one of his own chief characteristics, as Algernon Cecil once said of him, was his " Englishness ".

Lord Salisbury never laboured to produce an epigram ; but

buried in the midst of his speech there was often found a profound political maxim or a terse and characteristic reflection of his own philosophy. In one of the rare addresses he had delivered to his constituents at Stamford, in 1865, when his mind was under the shock of the Liberal Government's mixture of bluster and in-effectiveness during the Schleswig-Holstein crisis, he had said : " In foreign policy what we have to do is simply to perform our own part with honour ; to abstain from a meddling diplomacy ; to uphold England's honour steadily and fearlessly and always to be rather prone to let action go along with words than to let it lag behind them." What sagacious statesmanship is compre-hended in those simple phrases !

Self-government for Ireland, having been proposed by Glad-stone, formed at this time the staple of many of Lord Salisbury's speeches both inside and outside Parliament. The violence of the Fenians supplemented Parnell's torrent of exciting eloquence ; and a series of bad harvests contributed the additional misery of hunger to the unsettled and backward peasantry. The " Land League " organized terrorism with the avowed aim of making an end of the landlords. At Liverpool, in April, 1882, Lord Salisbury declared that liberty had become a farce there and constitutional rights a mere superstition ; " repressive measures " must be adopted. Gladstone's Government wavered between excessive conciliation and excessive coercion. Parnell and his immediate followers were first favoured, then seized and im-prisoned, then released. Afterwards the ex-prisoners were to be called into consultation with Gladstone. The Prime Minister's Irish Secretary, as well as the Viceroy, resigned. Lord Frederick Cavendish accepted the vacant Secretaryship, and went to Dublin, where, with his Under-Secretary, Mr. Burke, he was murdered in Phoenix Park in open day. That was in June of 1882—two months after Lord Salisbury had urged repressive measures. Now Gladstone imposed them in an almost savage Crimes Act.

In a speech at Edinburgh later in the same year Lord Salisbury challenged the claims of the " new Radicals ", led by Mr. Joseph Chamberlain and Sir Charles Dilke, exclusively to represent the " poorer classes ". He condemned the dependence of these self-appointed champions upon " the existence of discontent ". A Party whose mission it is to live upon the discovery of grievances is apt to manufacture them. The Conservative Party was on firmer ground in offering the people economic security, and the unity of the nation instead of its division into mutually hostile classes. The important thing was that capital should flow, that wages should fertilize the channels of commerce, and enterprise be free. On the other hand, " it is right to be forward in defence of the poor ; no system that is not just as between rich and poor can hope to survive ".

If that point of view shows the limitations of its period on social questions, his remarks in another speech in Edinburgh about the growing army of permanent officials have their application today. The constant pressure of their influence, he objected, increased the power of the centre and diminished that of the locality. " You are handed over to the great modern dictator— the inspector—an image made of wood and clothed in red tape." Most of all he detested the " doctrinaire theorist ", who was in his eyes the enemy of a sane social and political system. In the following year his chief out-of-parliament speech was delivered in St. James's Hall in London. It contained a hearty pat on the back for the man with the crossbench mind. He appealed to " the large intermediate body " between extreme Conservatives and extreme Radicals to maintain the equilibrium of the Constitution and to throw their weight into the scales against whichever extreme seemed likely to become predominant.

2

The appearance of the man who was proving on public platforms that he was something more than an average Party politician has been admirably portrayed for posterity by Sir John Millais, whose three-quarter-length picture of Lord Salisbury was painted in this year, 1883, and now hangs in the National Portrait Gallery. We see a large, solemn figure, habited in the long frock-coat of the period—black coat and plain black waistcoat. His hands are crossed behind his back—as they must so often have been, one imagines, at his public appearances, for no man gesticulated less than he. A folded double eye-glass is strung round his neck and rests on his chest. The black hair on his crown is very thin, but carefully trained, except at its fringe, where it curls raggedly upwards. He has a full moustache, a beard bushy but well trimmed ; the whiskers are grizzled. His eyes are turned upwards, and impart a curiously dreamy aspect to his countenance, of which the main characteristics are nevertheless thoughtfulness, power and authority. This is a man to be reckoned with, the picture seems to say ; and the books on the table at his side convey the love of study and scholarship which mark Lord Salisbury as one of the most learned of our Prime Ministers.

3

An occasional bout of melancholy was Lord Salisbury's only form of self-indulgence ; and in the autumn of this year he let himself go in an outpouring of his spirit in the *Quarterly* (October, 1883), which ended with the cry, " How long can the final disintegration of the Empire be postponed ? " Though it was apparently not so named by the writer, the essay almost automatically took the title " Disintegration " from the number of times the word occurred in it ; and it most truly expresses the theme. He saw a dangerous breach being formed in the ranks of the British people by the new class-conscious Radicalism. For him, patriotism and unity were, or should be, indissoluble. He had often protested against the notion that the working classes were a special and separate element of the community ; and now he saw " those who lead the poorer classes industriously impressing upon them that the function of legislation is to transfer to them something from the pockets of their more fortunate fellow-countrymen ; and it is too much to hope that a doctrine, which teaches that a disregard of the Tenth Commandment is the highest duty of citizenship, should not gradually impress itself on the minds to which it is addressed ". He came forward as the champion of the " sacredness of property " ; and expressed a strong preference for the old form of parliamentary government which was controlled by the Crown and the aristocracy. It was their task, he argued, to arbitrate between contending classes in the State. A House of Commons could never be an arbitrator—it was itself a cockpit of contention. Moreover a democracy, " consisting of men who must be ordinarily engrossed by the daily necessities of self-support, only attends to public affairs partially and fitfully ". The " people ", he wrote, " as an acting, deciding, accessible authority, are a myth ".

Radicalism was pursuing the objects of " equality not only of conditions but of extermination of religious dogma ", and

pursuing them " by the method of political disintegration ".   He
charged the Radical with painting spoliation in the colours of
philanthropy and with being the " organizer of decay " ; and
he regarded a conflict between possession and non-possession as
a disease which could have no other than a fatal issue.   It
" eats out the common sentiments and mutual sympathies which
combine classes into a patriotic State. . . .   It slowly kills by
disintegration."

There can be little doubt that Lord Salisbury afterwards regretted the publicity given to this article.   It was written anonymously, as was the practice for the *Quarterly* of that day, and it
was placed, as all his previous contributions had been, the last
of the issue in which it appeared.   Lord Salisbury's style, however, though somewhat reminiscent of Macaulay, had become
strongly individual and well known in political circles.   The
essay was therefore recognized as being the product of his pen
and was freely discussed as such.   The identification greatly
annoyed him ; and he always refused publicly to acknowledge
the authorship.   It had indeed expressed his innermost thoughts ;
but it had been written as an essay, not as a political pamphlet ;
and he was soon to prove that his acceptance of democracy in
action was genuine and uninhibited, and that to criticize him as a
politician, on the strength of his writings as a political philosopher,
was to misjudge him.   Moreover the essay itself contained, near
its beginning, a passage which corresponded to his own political
actions, but which was swamped by its later criticisms of the
democratic system and generally overlooked when the article was
denounced on the platform and in rival reviews.   " The object
of our Party is not," he wrote, " and ought not to be, simply to
keep things as they are.   In the first place, the enterprise is impossible.   In the next place, there is much in our present mode
of thought and action which it is highly undesirable to conserve " ;
and he favoured the disposition which some of his followers
showed to substitute " Constitutional " for " Conservative " as
the name of his Party.   As a political thinker he might work out
organic change to its logical conclusion and condemn it ; but
as a man of action he sought only to make it gradual and to keep
it within constitutional limits.   His mind was steeped in the
events of 1848 in the western countries of Europe ; he was an
authority on the history of the French Revolution of 1789 ; he

had made a searching study of the communism of Marx and Engels ; and he saw danger ahead in the tendencies he observed around him in his own beloved England. And if the disintegration which his inner eye foresaw has not ruined this country, it is due to his influence, as well as to the political good sense of the British voter, that catastrophe has been averted.*

Lord Salisbury showed his vexation at the public discussion of his unsigned views by declaring that he would never again write for the *Quarterly*—a vow which, as it happened, want of leisure during the next twenty years would in all probability in any case have prevented him from breaking. But he drove home his protest by immediately offering an article to the November number of the newly-launched *National Review* ; and the subject of the article was the housing of the poor. His contribution gave proof of the deep knowledge he had of rural conditions, mainly derived from the Hatfield estates, and he brought a greater warmth of feeling along with it than to almost any other public matter. He extended his researches into the living conditions of town dwellers and spoke cordially of the work of the new Industrial Dwellings Societies and of Miss Octavia Hill. He followed up his article by proposing early next year (February, 1884) in the House of Lords, from his place on the Opposition side, the appointment of a Royal Commission. The Government accepted the motion and invited Lord Salisbury to sit on it in the distinguished company of the Prince of Wales, Cardinal Manning, Sir Charles Dilke, Mr. Jesse Collings and the Bishop of Bedford. Some of his friends accused Lord Salisbury of turning Socialist, for he frankly demanded State action. His answer to them was : " My noble friend may press as earnestly as he will upon us the necessity of leaving every Englishman to work out his own destiny, and not attempt to aid him at the expense of the State ; but, on the other side, he must always bear in mind that there are no absolute truths or principles in politics " (House of Lords, February 22, 1884).

" No absolute truths or principles "—as a traditionalist, he was against organic change and wished for the continued existence of an aristocratic ruling class : as a religious philosopher he was convinced that in this world fullness or indigence are

* The last part of " Disintegration " was devoted to Ireland and will be mentioned when the issue of Home Rule comes into the narrative.

unimportant accidents: and as a political thinker he believed
profoundly that the business of the State is mainly to create and
maintain the conditions in which individual enterprise should
have the free-est play ; but as a man of action he knew that
those whom his statesmanship must serve were not an aggregation
of philosophers and abstract thinkers, and that rigid adherence
to a principle or theory is not practical politics.   So in this same
year he was again puzzling and confounding his supporters, to
whom he had so often propounded the primacy of principle, by
agreeing to collaborate with Liberal leaders for a wide extension
of the franchise, on condition that a redistribution of the constituencies should be simultaneously devised.   Gladstone's Franchise
Bill of 1884 proposed to extend the franchise to agricultural
workers ; but the Tories believed it would work out unfairly
unless at the same time the boundaries of the constituencies were
re-drawn.   The Liberals tried to manœuvre the House of Lords
into the position of rejecting the Franchise Bill outright and
started a vigorous agitation against them.   Mr. Bright proclaimed
that " the House of Lords shall cease to exist "—and mobs
paraded the streets of London and other of the larger cities bearing the slogan " Down with Lords " ; to which Lord Salisbury
replied in a series of public speeches, in the City of London, at
Manchester, at Sheffield, and in Scotland.   He had the difficult
task, so often thrust upon Conservatives, of proving on a public
platform that an issue which has been simplified into a slogan
may really be very complicated.   The explanation required
close reasoning ; and these speeches, it must be admitted, make
tedious reading today.   Yet the people listened to them.   He
had demanded an appeal to the electorate at the end of the
Session of 1884 ; Gladstone had refused ; and as the campaign
of abuse and generalities on the one side and clear exposition
on the other continued through the late autumn of that year it
became every week more evident that the nation was listening to
Lord Salisbury.   He never showed the least sign of nervousness
about the actual fate of the Upper House ; and he frequently
went straight to the hearts of his hearers with such simple phrases
as, " The question is not what the House of Lords are, or how
they got there, but whether they did right or wrong."
  During the then unusual labours of an autumn session of
Parliament feelings were running very high, and Queen Victoria,

who had strong views herself but detested controversy, pleaded for compromise. Several political leaders on either side were anxious to forward Her Majesty's design ; and on a November night Sir Stafford Northcote had a secret meeting with Gladstone at the house of a friend. Two Tory peers were closeted with Lord Granville. Lord Salisbury made one of his rare appearances at the Carlton Club to meet his own supporters. Finally, on November 19, he and Northcote went to 10 Downing Street and took a cup of tea with the Prime Minister, who had also invited Lord Hartington, Lord Granville and Sir Charles Dilke. A compromise was reached, and the constitutional crisis passed. Among the Tories who pressed upon Lord Salisbury the single-member rule for constituencies, which solved the riddle, was Lord Randolph Churchill, who thus made his début as Beaconsfield's successor in carrying the standard of Tory democracy. The 1884 Reform Act also abolished constituencies having less than 1,500 inhabitants and so suppressed the last of the " rotten boroughs "—without which Lord Salisbury might never have entered the House of Commons.

It was in Ireland that, according to the view of Lord Salisbury, failure to accompany the extension of the franchise with a Redistribution Bill would have the most calamitous results, for it would transfer power from the hands of a loyal minority into those who were hostile to us ; and England's necessity would be Ireland's opportunity. Gladstone's policy of appeasement had begun in disorder and would end in disaster. The Liberal leader had " swept away an ancient Church ", so he wrote in " Disintegration " ; he had " plunged his hands deeply into the coffers of the landlords, and scattered largesse among the Irish tenantry . . . but their appetites have only been whetted for more loot ; their conviction that it can be gained by outrage has been signally confirmed." And at Westminster, backed by forty devoted followers, Mr. Parnell was " purchasing concessions by offering the votes of his detachment in exchange" ; and he based his hope of escape from the rule of England on the readiness of her Parliament to " concede as a matter of mere weakness what they would never consent to on its merits ". But in this, Lord Salisbury wrote, the Irish leader was assuredly mistaken. " The highest interests of the Empire, as well as the most sacred obligations of honour, forbid us to solve this question by conceding any species of independence to Ireland ... To the minority, to those who have trusted us and on the faith of our protection have done our work, it would be a sentence of exile and of ruin ... We have no moral right to abandon our post and leave all the penalty of our failure to those whom we have persuaded to trust in our power." It would not only be a proof of moral and political bankruptcy ; it would also have calamitous strategic consequences. We should be handing the country over to our enemies, and the coast of Ireland, in unfriendly hands, " would be something more than a pistol held to the mouths of the Clyde and the Mersey and the Severn ". Lord Salisbury's conclusion therefore was uncompromising : " The impossibility of England's acceding to Home Rule is too plain to need enforcing. ... If this country had simply to choose between accepting and resisting separation, the decision would be given promptly and without hesitation." We shall see in a subsequent chapter that Lord Salisbury's remedy for the Irish difficulty was simple—twenty years of resolute government.

3

But it was not only in Ireland that indecision and incompetent statecraft were making difficulties for the Liberals. Gladstone's noble and generous aims, his reforming energy and financial genius, his enthralling oratory and prodigious memory, his ardent humanity, his culture and wide learning, his zest for good causes, may entitle him to be regarded as one of the greatest men who have been Prime Ministers of England ; but those same attributes do not make him her greatest Prime Minister. For he lacked political foresight and executive ability.

He was moreover obsessed by his desire to reduce British commitments in the interest of economy ; and his colonial and foreign policy was little less than disastrous. During his five years of office between 1880 and 1885 Britain was everywhere in trouble and her prestige steadily declined. She lost ground in the Transvaal and on the Indian frontier, in South-West Africa and East Africa, in the Congo and in Zanzibar. His deliberate withdrawals may in one or two cases have been justified ; but sometimes they were far from deliberate. In his Midlothian campaign Gladstone had denounced the Conservative Government annexation of the Transvaal ; so when he became Prime Minister the Boers naturally expected a restoration of their independence. Nothing being done, they rose at the end of the year, surprised and cut up a British detachment and occupied Laing's Nek, the pass leading from the Transvaal to Natal ; and in January of the following year Majuba Hill, commanding the Nek, was stormed by the Boers and the British general killed. Then Gladstone granted the Transvaal its independence. " The galling argument was ", writes Lord Morley in the *Life of Gladstone*, " that the Government had conceded to three defeats what they had refused to ten times as many petitions, memorials and remonstrances." Or as another Liberal historian, Lord Bryce, has written : " The Boers saw in the conduct of the British Government neither generosity nor humanity, but only fear." And the British people, in almost every case, subsequently agreed to spend millions of money and thousands of lives in regaining what had been lost. Moreover, the Liberal policy of retreat gave the impression in foreign countries that Britain was finished ; and it was during this period that French colonial rivalry was revived and German colonial rivalry began.

Gladstone's overseas vacillations and ineptitude came to a climax in the tragedy of General Gordon, whom he had sent to Khartum to rescue the Egyptian garrisons, isolated in different military stations of the Sudan. Gordon, one of the knights-errant who appear from time to time on the pages of British history, had shown an extraordinary power of inspired leadership, first over Chinese and then over Arabs and Africans. He could awe the wildest tribe of equatorial Africa by his presence alone ; and he had a passion to free them from the slave-trade which hung like a curse over their lives. His career as Governor of the Egyptian Sudan had been cut short in 1880 on Gladstone's accession to office. The new Prime Minister reluctantly and tardily pursued a vigorous policy in Egypt itself ; but announced that Britain's presence there was only intended to restore, with France, the administrative and financial stability of the country, and would be temporary ; as for the Sudan, he had not the slightest desire to undertake the " costly and difficult " task of reconquering the province on behalf of the Khedive. It was soon seen, however, that the Khedive could not restore order himself, even in his own country, and still less in the Sudan. The fanatic Arabi in 1881 headed a nationalist rebellion against the Khedive and his foreign supporters. Next summer he was virtually master of Egypt ; and in June, 1882, there was an outbreak in Alexandria, during which 200 Europeans were killed. Fleets were accordingly sent by Britain and France to safeguard the lives of their nationals. It became necessary to expel Arabi from the town ; and the British navy was ordered to bombard it. That was on July 11. The French ships were ordered to take no part in the bombardment, and sailed away ; the date of July 11, 1882, marks the abdication by France of the paramount position she had held in Egypt since the days of Napoleon.

Gladstone, still active and purposeful, instructed the British general, Sir Garnet Wolseley, to advance inland against the rebels. He defeated them at Tel-el-Kebir and entered Cairo a liberator and pacifier.

Repressed in Egypt, the rebellion passed into the Egyptian province of Sudan and spread like wildfire during the next two years. The Egyptian garrisons there, whatever the British Government had said, could not be left to their fate, and General Hicks Pasha was ordered to relieve them. He and his army of raw levies were cut to pieces (October 3, 1883) ; and in his dilemma the Prime Minister now turned to the mystic general who had spent most of the year 1883 in quiet contemplation in Palestine, and who was described by one of Gladstone's supporters * as " insubordinate . . . a most awkward fellow . . . a hero and a saint ". Gordon reached Khartum at the beginning of 1884, but within a month of his arrival the place was completely cut off by the followers of Mohamed Achmed, styling himself the prophet or Mahdi—a Mussulman Adventist—who had taken the lead in the Sudan risings.

Lord Salisbury was not altogether sympathetic with the character of Gordon, and in any case considered that he was an unsuitable agent for the task of withdrawal—" a man whose life has been spent ", he said in the House of Lords, " not in retreating, but in advancing ". But his chief criticism was of the total absence of clear thinking and of settled policy. The Prime Minister and his Foreign Secretary, Lord Granville, had once upon a time accepted the Sudan as an integral part of the Egyptian Empire and therefore a matter of concern to themselves. Later they had declared they had no responsibility for it. They had nevertheless sent an army there to its destruction ;

* Lord Coleridge.

and now again the British Government was giving advice to Egypt about what she should do there. And when Parliament met at the beginning of 1884, Lord Salisbury found that the Government were trying to shift responsibility on to a puppet. "We have seen vacillation and delay . . . and now when the matter seems approaching almost to a point of desperation, we are told that it is not the English Government, but the Egyptian Government which is to blame." Was England a mere disinterested spectator? Evidently not quite that, because she was giving the Khedive " a little assistance in scuttling out " of the largest part of his dominions, under British direction. The English Government of the day might certainly be said to be " experts in scuttling out ". This time, in doing so, they were endangering the life of the most gallant soldier they had been able to find.

A week later, as leader of the Opposition in the Lords, Lord Salisbury carried a motion censuring the Government for " the palpable vacillation and inconsistency of its policy ". The latest of their resolves had been to command the Government of Cairo to abandon all the territory south of Wady Halfa ; and they had sent a British subject to the distant capital of the country to be evacuated. Lord Salisbury followed his speeches in Parliament with one at Manchester during the Easter recess ; and, returning to the charge as soon as Parliament re-assembled, he made the following remarkably accurate forecast of events : " I fear that the history of the past will be repeated in the future ; that again just when it is too late, the critical resolution will be taken ; some terrible news will come that the position of General Gordon is absolutely a forlorn and helpless one ; and then, under the pressure of public wrath and Parliamentary censure, some desperate resolution of sending an expedition will be formed, too late to achieve the object which it is desired to gain, too late to rescue this devoted man whom we have sent forward to his fate, in time only to cast another slur upon the statesmanship of England."

No need to recount the sequence. These words spoken on April 4, 1884, were translated into tragic facts nine months later. In the course of the summer the Government despatched General Wolseley—by now Lord Wolseley of Cairo—to rescue Gordon. His little force plodded manfully forward across desert sands in stifling heat; and in January, 1885, won a victory over the rebels within striking distance of Khartum—the result of which was to impel the ferocious followers of the Mahdi to storm the palace and massacre Gordon and his heroic comrades (January 26, 1885).

They struck not only the death-blow of Gordon but also a mortal wound to the Gladstone Government. The old adage, " a stitch in time saves nine ", lies deep in English consciousness ; it is the very pith and marrow of statesmanship ; and the people understood that by this standard Gladstone had failed, and Lord Salisbury had been right from the beginning. Arabi could have been crushed without difficulty at the start of his revolt ; from that moment onward the Liberal Government had trailed on after events instead of foreseeing and forestalling them. The same indecisions had crippled their retarded actions in Ireland ; they had also by now become involved with Russia in a dispute over the frontier of Afghanistan. The Liberals had bungled. Their resignation was only a matter of time. Whether by calculation or by chance, a vote on the Budget gave the Conservatives and some Liberal Home Rulers a majority (June, 1885). Mr. Gladstone resigned and Queen Victoria sent for Lord Salisbury.

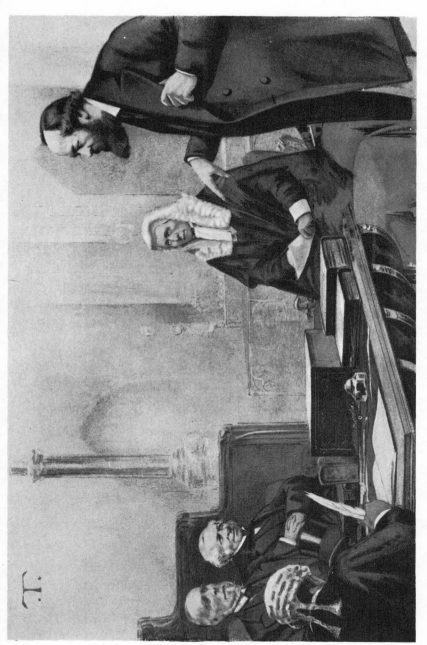

"VANITY FAIR" CARTOON OF LORD SALISBURY IN THE HOUSE OF LORDS, 1882

By courtesy of the Secretary of The Travellers' Club

[*see note, pp. 376–9*]

CHAPTER X—1885 (JUNE)–1886 (JANUARY)

PRIME MINISTER

The summons from Balmoral was delivered to Lord Salisbury in the early evening of June 11, in his laboratory, where he was engaged in experimenting on a piece of wire. Having laid his wire on one side, within a couple of hours he was in the train from Hatfield to King's Cross ; there he caught the night express to Scotland.

He had obeyed the summons promptly but not eagerly. Never an enthusiast, he accepted the prospect of the premiership with a reluctance which even a more sanguine nature than his must have felt in the parliamentary circumstances of the moment. Neither Party could command a majority without the help of the Irish Home Rulers ; and an immediate appeal to the country was impracticable, because the Redistribution Bill, agreed between the Parties, had only just become law; and with its passage the old constituencies ceased to exist, and the new ones had not yet been organized. Nothing could possibly be less congenial to Lord Salisbury than to be dependent on Parnell, especially as Gladstone's last Irish Peace Preservation Act was due to expire shortly—so the new Prime Minister would have the choice between dropping the coercive measures, placating the Irish vote, and risking chaos in Ireland, or renewing the Act and getting on as best he could with Parnell's votes. It was not therefore surprising—and it was quite characteristic of Lord Salisbury —that his first act at Balmoral was to induce Queen Victoria to telegraph to Gladstone to ask him to resume the premiership. This method of escape being blocked by return telegram, the Queen on her part persuaded Lord Salisbury, whose pregnant comments she liked much better than Gladstone's eloquent explanations, to undertake the Government.

The process of choosing his Ministers caused him, in the words of his biographer, " acute suffering "—" I feel sore all over " was his own way of putting it. He was surprised and disgusted, as many new Prime Ministers have been before and since—Peel and Lord Rosebery, for instance—at the depths of

155

artful self-seeking into which the lure of office drags supposedly honourable men. The editor of *The Times*, Mr. Buckle, was agreeably astonished at the cordiality with which Lord Salisbury received him during this week ; and he was soon acquainted with the reason. " You are the first person," the Prime Minister explained, " who has come to see me in the last few days who is not wanting something at my hands—place, or decoration or peerage."

Lord Salisbury was somewhat casual about who took which place in the Cabinet, apart from the key posts. Lord George Hamilton relates in his Reminiscences how he and W. H. Smith had been invited to come and see the Prime Minister-elect at the same time. " Smith," said Lord Salisbury in his incisive way, " I want you to go back to the Admiralty ; and you, Hamilton, to the War Office." Hamilton was disconcerted. He pointed out that he had not very long ago been a junior Ensign in the Guards, under the supreme command of Field-Marshal the Duke of Cambridge, and the Duke, still the Army's chief, would become his subordinate. Many military reforms were necessary ; how could he be expected to overcome the well-known dislike of the Duke to any change whatever ? Ought not the War Office " to be given to an older man ? " Lord Salisbury turned to Smith. " I think there is force in what Hamilton says. Will you undertake the War Office ? " And so it was decided.

And there was no trouble about Sir Michael Hicks Beach becoming Chancellor of the Exchequer ; and very little about Sir Richard Cross resuming the charge of the Home Office which he had held under Beaconsfield. Randolph Churchill, much to Lord Salisbury's relief, seemed quite pleased to go to the India Office ; but, largely on account of Churchill's antipathy to him, the placing of Stafford Northcote provided a vexatious problem. Churchill had sprung into prominence in the 1880 Parliament by the vehemence of his opposition to Gladstone ; but hardly less vehement was his criticism of his own leader in the Commons, Northcote, whom he accused of not reacting violently enough against the Liberal leader—a charge which, it must be admitted, had substance ; for Northcote could never forget that he had early in his career been private secretary to Gladstone, and his natural loyalty and gentleness blunted the shafts which he aimed at his former chief. To Lord Salisbury, also, Northcote preferred always to be obliging and acquiescent ; but he objected sharply when the new Prime Minister offered him a peerage and the office of First Lord of the Treasury. It was not that he objected to a peerage or to a sinecure post ; his objection rested on the fact that Churchill had been saying that Northcote must be kicked upstairs ; and what Northcote would willingly have accepted at the request of Lord Salisbury he was unwilling to take at the instigation of a youthful critic. However, Queen Victoria intervened and he went to the Upper House as Earl of Iddesleigh. Hicks Beach took his place as Conservative leader in the House of Commons.

Before this arrangement was made Lord Salisbury had told Northcote that he would willingly let him take the premiership if the Party agreed. To this proposal the Prime Minister knew the Party would not agree, because others besides Churchill considered the Devonshire squire much too mild a leader ; but the offer had been a perfectly sincere one, for Lord Salisbury would gladly have devoted himself entirely to the Foreign Office. As it was, after fleetingly considering the appointment of Lord Lytton as Foreign Secretary, he decided to hold that post with the premiership in his own hands. It was an unprecedented combination. It involved, even in those days, more work than could comprehensively be undertaken by one man, especially a man who was never content only to look at the surface of things ; and, after this first experiment, Lord Salisbury made several attempts to shift one burden or the other on to somebody else's shoulders.

Neither during this nor his subsequent premierships did Lord Salisbury take up residence in 10 Downing Street. In London he did most of his work in his room at the Foreign Office ; some of it in his own house—and always as much as possible at Hatfield.

When on June 24, 1885, Lord Salisbury kissed hands as Prime Minister he was at the head of a Government of competent men which was nevertheless regarded as a mere stop-gap till the day arrived when a General Election could properly be held. Its leadership was bitter fruit to him. He had not desired it ; but if he were to be Prime Minister, the one condition he would have wished was security. He could not conceive of statesmanship without long-term policies ; and here he was, his tenure uncertain, standing at the head of a team which contained a turbulent potential rebel, and dependent on the votes of Irishmen to whose aims he was immovably hostile. But he had by now convinced himself that politics provided the one congenial opening for the exercise of such talents as he possessed. So, accepting the onerous mission, he tried to secure from Gladstone the assurance that he would be supported in transacting the current business of executive government, such as the voting of necessary credits, and the arrangement of the week-to-week business of Parliament. The Liberal leader refused to give an undertaking in the categorical form demanded ; but this obstacle, too, was shelved by another intervention from Windsor and by the general concurrence of Parties that the Queen's government must be carried on.

From this time onward a kind of chivalrous devotion to Queen Victoria was a mainspring of Lord Salisbury's political action. The trust between them was absolute. The Queen found him to be animated by the same motives as she was herself—an acute sense of responsibility, simple devotion to duty and constant regard for the honour of England, especially in relation to foreign countries, together with a total absence of self-seeking. Lord Salisbury on his side listened with genuine respect to Queen Victoria's views on policy. He was the first of her Prime Ministers who was younger than herself ; and he drew willingly upon her unexampled store of political experience, which had begun to be furnished by Lord Melbourne and been augmented by so many and variously able men of State. He found her advice most of all valuable in foreign affairs. She was, of course, debarred by custom from expressing Party views ; she could only speak as Sovereign. And as Sovereign she was acquainted with, and in some cases related to, kings, princes and princesses of Europe, who in those days greatly influenced the policies of their countries. According to Lady Gwendolen Cecil his friendship for Queen Victoria was, outside of his family, the warmest and closest of Lord Salisbury's life. It was, though less spectacular, certainly more candid and intimate than the much-celebrated relationship between Disraeli and his Fairy Queen.

Even at the Foreign Office his first period of supreme authority had its sour taste for Lord Salisbury ; for his chief occupation during these seven months of office was to demolish part of the structure he had helped to build at Berlin. None had been more determined than he that the new Bulgaria should be divided into two parts, Bulgaria proper on the north side of the Balkan mountains and Eastern Rumelia on the south. He was now called upon to agree to their permanent union.

Most people who know them would agree that the Bulgars are the toughest race in Europe. Slavs of Tartar origin, more sober than most Slavs and with keener political aptitude than any Asiatics, they have an instinctive national sense which silently envisages the future and knows how to abide the moment ; they are brimful of grasping ambition, and unsurpassed in the dourness of their fighting. Though Lord Salisbury had an unmatched feel for western Europe, his brief stay in a Pera hotel in 1877 had not opened his eyes to the portents of power and ambition in this then little known race. They had lain low after 1877 and apparently accepted Russian domination. But all the time the resolve to gain both unity and independence smouldered in the national consciousness. Now the southern province, Eastern Rumelia, which had been left under Turkish rule, suddenly broke into revolt. The northern half of the country, which had been given an independent Prince and placed under the tutelage of Russia, not only sprang to the assistance of its compatriots south of the mountains but showed a complete disregard of Russian commands. On September 18, 1885, the population of the Rumelian capital, Philippopolis, seized and expelled the Turkish Governor and invited the ruler of Bulgaria, Prince Alexander of Battenberg, to come and take over the province. Prince Alexander, half German and half Pole, a soldier and a romantic, responded enthusiastically to their call. He sped forthwith to Philippopolis and proclaimed Bulgaria to be one and indivisible under his own sceptre.

The British representative in Constantinople, Sir William White, telegraphed news of the rising on September 19. The telegram reached Lord Salisbury at Puys, near Dieppe, where he had gone as usual at that season for change of air—" holiday " would not be the right word, for he was never off duty for a day. He immediately opened an exchange of views with the governments of the other Great Powers who were signatories of the Treaty of Berlin. That no time was lost is shown by the fact that on the next day, 20th, he was already in receipt of the reply of the British ambassador in Berlin. Sir Edward Malet had seen Bismarck at once, and reported the Chancellor's response to be that any action taken should be collective on the part of all the signatory Powers. He deprecated any hasty step by any one government; and on the following day he suggested to Malet that the Tsar should be invited to disavow the Bulgarian rebellion. He was in favour of upholding the Treaty of Berlin. With characteristic cynicism he added that a conference should then be held " to drown the question in ink ".

Apart from the last suggestion Lord Salisbury was in general agreement with the Iron Chancellor's views. In a memorandum to Queen Victoria he wrote that England was in honour bound to uphold the Berlin Treaty. Every day that passed, however, showed that nothing but the use of force could undo what had been done by the patriotic fervour of a spiritually united people; and already on September 22 Bismarck declared to Malet that he thought their political union would have to be recognized. Queen Victoria was of that opinion from the first—not only that it would be recognized, but that it should be recognized. Her mind was easily made up. She disliked and dreaded Russia, and she saw at once, more quickly than Bismarck, that this was an anti-Russian move. Moreover, she had a personal and feminine wish to help Prince Alexander. The gallant and handsome young officer had openly cherished aspirations to the hand of the daughter of the Crown Princess of Germany, who was Queen Victoria's own eldest daughter. To the extreme annoyance of Bismarck, Crown Princess Frederick had by no means discouraged these advances; and Queen Victoria supported her daughter. She liked what she heard of the young Battenberg and had no objection to having him for a grandson. So she pressed acceptance of the *fait accompli* on Lord Salisbury. Still striving to maintain the structure of the 1878 treaty, he now urged that a personal union of the two Bulgarias under the same Prince might solve the problem. Bismarck agreed; but added another cynical postscript to the effect that he was personally indifferent to the fate of Prince Alexander.

The other Powers provisionally and half-heartedly agreed with the suggestion, but otherwise stood solid behind Russia in insisting on the *status quo* as established at Berlin. The paradox of the situation was that just as the British Government was beginning to see wisdom in a united Bulgaria, which it had so strenuously opposed seven years before, so now Russia, champion then of a united and enlarged Bulgaria, wanted Bulgaria to be kept disunited—both governments illustrating the unhappy rule of European politics that when the observance of treaty clauses contradicts immediate self-interest it is almost always the observance that gives way. Russia's aim was plainly to dominate the eastern Balkans. Queen Victoria was to that extent justified in writing to her Prime Minister that in upholding Prince Alexander we should be " defending the cause of liberty against Russian aggression and tyranny " ; and Lord Salisbury on his part was by now confirmed in his opinion that the whole Bulgarian people wished the union. He therefore gave instructions to White that the desire of the population of Rumelia was to be the prime consideration.

A Conference of ambassadors met at Constantinople, in which White, upholding this view, found himself in a minority of one. After conducting affairs from Puys for over a week, Lord Salisbury had returned to England ; but his preference for instinctive, unhampered personal direction is shown by the continuance of instructions to the Foreign Office drafted on sheets of private notepaper. On October 27, for instance, his telegram for Sir William White is written out in his own hand on paper with the stamped heading of Hatfield House, and timed 10.45 p.m. He is insisting on " giving satisfaction to the people of East Roumelia " ; and he writes : " Take care that discussion on this point is fully protocolled. It is of vital importance to our policy in Turkey that Russia should stand on record as the opponent of Bulgarian wishes." Austria-Hungary, Germany and Italy, all aspiring to extend their influence in the Balkans at the expense of Turkey, still supported Russia, even though their hoped-for extension of influence would probably have to be gained in rivalry with Russia ; and France, ever burning with sullen anger at her defeat by Prussia, also favoured Russia as being her potential ally in the day which would bring the chance of revenge. Lord Salisbury, having by now completed his *volte-face* on the Berlin arrangement, remained rock-like in his new stance on Bulgarian ground. The British envoy was forbidden to make the slightest concession. After a month of futile discussion, therefore, the Constantinople Conference broke up.

The question had been " drowned ", as Bismarck had fore-seen—but not in ink, nor yet in talk, but in blood. For in the meantime a minor war had been fought between Bulgaria and Servia. King Milan of Servia felt unable to remain a passive spectator of Bulgarian aggrandizement ; he too had ambitions for his country—which were to be gained at the expense of Bulgaria. Since the members of the Conference paid no heed to his claim for " territorial compensation ", he had decided to march, encouraged by the Tsar's withdrawal of all Russian officers from Alexander's army. The Prince, however, was un-dismayed. He turned to fight Milan, and led his enthusiastic levies with such inspiring bravery that he routed the Serbs at Slivnitza, and would probably have entered Belgrade, had not Austria intervened to save a country which she regarded as a present protégé—and perhaps a future victim. Greece, too, had been putting forward claims to territorial compensation ; but her opportunism was checked by Lord Salisbury's known readiness to despatch the British fleet to the Piraeus.

The Powers had not been able to coerce Bulgaria when she was still unsettled and distracted ; it was the less possible for them to restore the *status quo* now that Bulgaria was victorious and settling down. The opposition to the British policy of recognition therefore finally crumbled, and Lord Salisbury's solution was accepted. The Italian and French envoys had hinted to the Porte that sanction might be given to a Turkish " campaign of repression ". The hints were hastily disavowed. Austria explained that Servia had been overrash, and she could now do no more for her. Bismarck had been indifferent through-out. Russia was not prepared for war. Single-handed, Lord Salisbury won a victory of the one over the five.

Prince Alexander's tenure of the throne was formally limited to five years—the one unanimous decision of the Constantinople Conference ; and even that was quickly rendered otiose. The gay venturer into Balkan politics met a Balkan fate. In the summer of next year, 1886, he was kidnapped by partisans of Russia in his own palace at Sofia. The mirage of a " San Stefano Bulgaria " undoubtedly dazzled the imagination of this ambitious young ruler ; but since the vision (which still floats before Bulgarian eyes) was of an independent and not a Russian-ized greater Bulgaria, it no longer appealed to the Tsar. Battenberg was compelled to abdicate ; and his projects of empire and of a royal marriage simultaneously vanished into the limbo of history's forgotten dreams.

Lord Salisbury's shrewd anticipation of events had once more served him well ; and his extraordinary gift of political long-sightedness is demonstrated in the warning he gave to the Sultan when the Turkish Government was preparing to mobilize against Bulgaria. " The next time," Lord Salisbury told him, " Bulgaria will arrange with Servia and Greece beforehand, and organize a combined attack which will be fatal to Turkey." The " next time " was twenty-seven years later, when the three countries he mentioned combined to drive Turkey back from the frontiers of Austria-Hungary almost to within sight of Constantinople. Lord Salisbury never exulted, even when his successes were more congenial to him than that which his *volte-face* had just brought him ; but on such occasions he let his caustic humour run free. " Europe may now rest for a couple of months," he said, " watching the interesting process of a Tsar recovering his temper."

Throughout the Near-Eastern crisis Lord Salisbury had worked closely with Bismarck. In his dealings with the Great Powers his aim was to establish and maintain a " Concert of Europe " ; and he went about it by contacting most closely its strongest representative. He did not make the mistake of trying to help its lesser members by posing as their champion— which would at once create a rivalry of leadership. His one apprehension in regard to Bismarck was that Germany would make a deal with Russia and dominate the Continent—which was the reason why, in 1879, when the news came that Germany had signed a " defensive and offensive " alliance, not with Russia but with Austria-Hungary, he had exclaimed with almost biblical ecstasy, that he had " news of great joy ". He was the more ready to conciliate the Iron Chancellor because the latter had bitterly complained of the tergiversations of British foreign policy under the parliamentary party system. Bismarck later gave full expression to this criticism in his autobiography. " England ", he wrote, " is one of those dexterous Powers with whom it is not only impossible to form any lasting alliance but who cannot be relied upon with any certainty, because in England the basis of all political relations is more changeable than in any other State ; it is the product of elections and the resulting majorities."

The reversals of policy by Gladstone in 1880 had strongly stamped this belief upon his mind ; but the advent of Lord Salisbury encouraged him to hope for better things. He sent a private message to him saying that he had found it impossible to carry on business with Gladstone's Government. They never knew their own mind or case, and at times would not even answer his letters. But he felt he could establish better relations with Lord Salisbury.

Lord Salisbury took advantage of the Chancellor's goodwill to settle with him a sharp triangular dispute which had broken out between Britain, Germany and the Sultan of Zanzibar, who derived large profits from his trade in slaves from the neighbouring coast of East Africa. Then he used the credit he gained with him there to get his support in both Turkey and Russia. " He is rather a Jew," he wrote to Iddesleigh ; but the Jew appears to have helped him to settle yet another dispute which had arisen between Britain and Russia over the Afghan boundary. While Granville was at the Foreign Office, the St. Petersburg Government had jumped a claim to Penjdeh, a strong-point which was generally considered to lie within the border of Afghanistan. Bismarck had at that time publicly alluded to the loquacious futility of the British Government. In spite of the jibe, however—or goaded by it—the Liberal Cabinet reacted with unexpected vigour when the local Russian forces occupied the frontier fort with great slaughter of its Afghan defenders. Britain was bound by treaty to uphold the integrity and independence of Afghanistan ; so military reinforcements intended for Suakin were diverted to strengthen the army of India. For some weeks in the spring of 1885 England and Russia once more stood upon the verge of armed conflict. Now, nourished by the Liberal Government's firmness, and supported with great tact and skill by his friend, Lord Dufferin—who had been appointed Viceroy of India by Gladstone in the previous year—Lord Salisbury soon reduced the issue between the two countries to the dimensions of a regrettable incident. Dufferin gained from the Ameer the unexpected admission that Penjdeh did not, after all, lie within the boundaries of his kingdom ; and the dispute between Russia and Britain was settled by the Protocol signed on September 10, 1885.

Dufferin was an equally successful executor of Lord Salisbury's policy in Burma, where he showed, in the phrase of his biographer,* that his pliancy had the quality of a steel wand. During the period of Liberal feebleness and vacillation abroad the rivals of Britain took heart and tried to improve their position in all parts of the world ; and the French in Indo-China came to an agreement with their neighbour, King Theebaw of Burma, which extended their influence to the very boundaries of India. Dufferin's demand that a British resident should be admitted to reside at Mandalay and advise upon Burmese policy was scornfully rejected by Theebaw ; but by this time Lord Salisbury had taken charge in London. Secure in the knowledge that he would be supported at home, Dufferin declared war on Theebaw ; and a small British force of 10,000 men drove the Burmese before them, with hardly any losses on either side, entered Mandalay, and took the King prisoner. The country was annexed to India.

This was the first addition to the domain of the British Crown made by Lord Salisbury ; and it is worth noting that the alternatives, as they appeared to him, were not whether Upper Burma should be taken over or left independent, but whether it should be taken over by Britain or controlled by France. The postscript to the decision he then took is that after a period of sixty-three years, during which the natural resources of the country were enormously developed, a capacious modern port built for it at Rangoon and a university founded there, its independence has been restored and the government handed over to rulers who, whatever their shortcomings, are less tyrannical and less primitive in their outlook than were King Theebaw and his notable queen Soopaya-Lat.

2

In home affairs, as was inevitable, the period of Lord Salisbury's first administration was one of marking time. He had no majority of his own ; he could only hope to pass through Parliament measures agreed upon by both Parties. He had however the great satisfaction, in this category, of giving practical effect to the recommendations of the Commission on the housing of the working-classes for which he himself had moved during Gladstone's Ministry (in February, 1884).† The pioneering impulse was still strong in him ; he was still ready to defy his

* Mr. Harold Nicolson : *Helen's Tower.*   † See Chapter IX, p. 147.

most Tory-minded supporters. The Bill he introduced penalized landlords who let tenements proved to be insanitary, and the Local Government Board was empowered to pull them down. This measure of social reform, however Socialist in complexion, entirely fitted in with his theory that the main *raison d'être* of government is to enable the people to live their lives in the best possible conditions of health and personal freedom.

As soon as the electoral register was ready, Lord Salisbury dissolved Parliament (December, 1885). But the resulting General Election did not give him a majority. The deadlock was reproduced, in slightly altered proportions ; the Parnellites remained the decisive force. The Liberals and the Irish together, indeed, had a large majority ; but it was only a majority on paper ; for it was becoming apparent that in a vote on Home Rule, which was by now a dominating issue, the Liberal dissidents would outnumber the followers of Parnell. The Prime Minister was nevertheless left dependent upon the help of Parnell for a majority on any lesser issue. More than ever Lord Salisbury regarded the position of his " Caretaker " Government as intolerable and untenable. More than ever did he wish to resign ; in January, 1886, he was writing to his friend Carnarvon : " I am feverishly eager to be out ; internally as well as externally our position as a Government is intolerable."

When Lord Salisbury had formed his Ministry in the previous June, he had not entirely rejected the idea of giving larger control of their own local affairs to the Irish people ; and he had sent to be Viceroy his trusted colleague, Carnarvon, whom he knew to be a man of warm feelings and one who believed in the value of personal contact much more than he did himself. And the new Lord-Lieutenant, almost as soon as he had been installed, began to travel about the country, and met and conversed with every grade of Nationalist and with leaders of the Roman Church. He even arranged, with the personal concurrence of the Prime Minister, to meet privately, in London, the arch-agitator, Parnell himself, who up to this time had not had private intercourse even with Gladstone.* The conversation between him and the Viceroy was to be secret ; the fact that they met at all was not to be known. Neither the Cabinet nor even Queen Victoria was to be informed. But even in those days such an assignment

* See Hammond, *Gladstone and the Irish Nation*, p. 438.

as this could not long be hidden from public knowledge. As Lady Gwendolen Cecil puts it, " somebody talked " ; the story leaked out ; and as it leaked it grew larger and became a stream of bubbling rumour. As there had been no third person present at the meeting, none could deny the rumours, except the participants, who were vowed to silence.

In the following year, Parnell stated at Westminster, in public debate, that a Minister in the late Conservative Government, by whom he can only have meant Carnarvon,* had informed him that the Conservative Party was ready to offer a statutory legislature to Ireland. Carnarvon had, of course, no kind of authority to make any such suggestion, even informally, and he denied the imputation. The British public believed his and Lord Salisbury's disclaimers ; but the Prime Minister's easy-going tolerance of his colleague's vagaries caused him acute moments of embarrassment. He had not mentioned the Carnarvon-Parnell meeting to the other members of his Cabinet ; while Parnell, on his part, had hastened to pass his own account of it to Gladstone—and no doubt in the exaggerated version which he later gave to the House of Commons. It is thus a fair assumption that Gladstone consequently believed that the Tory Party was once more preparing to " dish the Whigs ", and that this suspicion was one of the motives that prompted him to go all out for Home Rule as soon as he again became Prime Minister.

In any case, in December of this year, 1885, just after the indecisive election, the mis-called " Hawarden Kite " was flown, bearing the Home Rule colours. It is known now that it was Mr. Herbert Gladstone, the Party leader's son, whose kite it was. He had not intended it for the public gaze ; and the kite was flown not from Hawarden but from London, in the form of an "authoritative " newspaper article. It carried the first announcement that " Mr. Gladstone has definitely adopted the policy of Home Rule ", but declared that that did not mean " separation ". But it undoubtedly did mean that Ireland was to have her own legislature ; and that was further than Gladstone had yet said he was prepared to go. He had spoken often enough of devolution, but had steadily denied that he meant to repeal the legislative union of the two countries. This announcement, made in the Press in London through his son's misplaced trustfulness,

* The Viceroy was also a Cabinet Minister.

167

was of course attributed to the Liberal leader and did in fact accurately reflect his views and intentions. The father had not known what his son was doing and was temporarily vexed by the disclosure.

Confusion of opinion and exacerbation of feelings now over-spread politics. Both parties were shaken and split. The Gladstonian hints about complete Home Rule frightened Lord Hartington and other prominent Liberals who had just been returned to Parliament as his supporters. Lord Salisbury, holding the view that the " National League ", which by now formed a kind of unofficial government in Ireland, should be suppressed, was hotly opposed in his own Cabinet by both Churchill and Hicks Beach. The two objectors were eventually persuaded to agree to the introduction of a Bill for its suppression ; but no sooner had Hicks Beach announced in the House that he was going to introduce it than the Liberals and Parnellites combined—over an agricultural proposal for the compulsory creation of allotments ("three acres and a cow ")—to vote against the Government and defeat it. Lord Salisbury immediately and readily resigned (January 28, 1886).

3

Paralysed though he had been at home by the lack of a majority, Lord Salisbury had yet managed to make this brief first premiership notable by his successful conduct of foreign policy. He had above all raised British prestige. Such a feat is now sometimes regarded as out of date and even considered, paradoxically, to be discreditable. But the country reinforced by prestige carried decisive influence. Lord Salisbury's Govern-ment had known what it wanted, had pressed its own view persistently, but had sought to fit it as far as possible into a consensus of views ; and it had gained its ends. It had gained them by proving its good faith no less than by proving its correct judgment. Prestige was its reward ; and prestige gained by such methods brought the long-term benefit to Lord Salisbury of being both respected and trusted by the foreign Chanceries. He did not thereafter exploit British authority by trying to have his own way every time—which would have antagonized the others instead of retaining that confidence which is as essential an element of prestige as fear is the essential of power-policy. Power may command ; but prestige influences and gains assent, which is the proper function of diplomacy and produces lasting results. Prestige is no mere *panache* of a Cyrano de Bergerac ; it is the diplomatic essence which brings success without war.

Lord Salisbury himself probably only felt that he had gained some valuable new experience ; and he must have been confirmed in his view that in foreign affairs the *sine qua non* is to have a policy and pursue it consistently. He had also found by practice that he could govern the country from the House of Lords—rather, perhaps, that from the House of Lords alone could he hope to direct both home and foreign affairs. Its unhurried temper allowed him a freer mind for elaborating long-term policy. There he was less subject to the cross-examination, which is the much-cherished right of Members of Parliament, but which can be so harassing and hampering to a Foreign Secretary—and which is far less obstructively exercised in the Upper than in the Lower House. In diplomacy it is even more impossible than in other spheres to give a plain answer, " yes " or " no "—though to ask the plain question is easy enough, especially if it seems likely to score a Party point. Lord Salisbury could not have had the repose in the House of Commons which he felt to be necessary for clear-sighted leadership. Prompt and decisive action is occasionally, though not usually, as essential in diplomacy as it is in war, and Lord Salisbury had by the end of his first period of combined direction of home and foreign affairs gained a strong enough position to act with the minimum of explanation and delay. He was, moreover, by nature and inclination, much better fitted to lead the country from the Lords than he ever would have been from the Commons. That close student of the Victorian era, the late Mr. John Bailey, held the opinion that this " lonely, august, intellectual man " nevertheless had " an inborn capacity for democratic leadership in his time ".

At the moment we have now reached in his career he was receiving cordial tributes of praise from people of high and humble degree. The majority of his countrymen regarded him as a trustable John Bull. Lord Lytton—a partial judge, no doubt—described him as " out and away the greatest Foreign Minister we have had in my time ". Queen Victoria was enthusiastic about " the triumphant success of his conduct of foreign affairs, by which he had in seven months raised Great

Britain to the position which she ought to hold in the world ".
She was proportionately chagrined when he threw up his double
office, and especially at the obvious relief with which he did so.
She coaxed him with the offer of a Dukedom. He respectfully
declined it ; and as soon as he was free returned to his Hatfield
laboratory. There he looked for the piece of wire on which he
had been experimenting on the day when the Queen had called
him to Balmoral. A flicker of annoyance passed over his face
when it could not be found. It had been exactly the right
thickness for his experiment.

GLADSTONIAN INTERLUDE

The conversion of the Liberal leader to Home Rule, and his choice of Lord Rosebery as Foreign Secretary (in the place of Lord Granville), were destined, in their respective spheres of home and foreign affairs, to have so great an influence on Lord Salisbury's career, that we must turn aside for a moment from our main theme, the study of Lord Salisbury's statesmanship, and briefly narrate the course of Mr. Gladstone's third premiership.

The flying of the Hawarden Kite, as we have seen, had brought perplexity and disorder into both the great Parties of the State, and made an arbiter of Charles Stewart Parnell, who had gained immeasurable popularity in his native land by his skill in parliamentary obstruction at Westminster, and by his leadership of the agrarian agitation in Ireland. His Land League had been suppressed once, and he himself had been thrown into prison by Gladstone ; now the League was active again and he was at large. The last General Election had made him the most important cog on the parliamentary wheel.

In these circumstances Queen Victoria had, in December, 1885, when the result of the election was already clear, expressed her wish to Lord Salisbury that he should try to bring about a " Coalition of all moderate and intelligent people ". Gladstone also approached the Conservative leader through his nephew, A. J. Balfour, and suggested that the Irish question should be settled on a non-party basis. To both overtures Lord Salisbury turned a deaf ear. Gladstone had unfortunately, in his talk with Balfour, expressed the belief that unless a settlement were quickly reached, " violence and assassination " would get the upper hand in Ireland. That was precisely the argument most likely to set Lord Salisbury firmly against any compromise. What he might accord to reason he would flatly refuse to the threat of violence. For him a fundamental principle of statesmanship was involved. It was precisely Gladstone's readiness to " concede as a matter of mere weakness what they [Parliament]

would never consent to on its merits " which he had condemned
in " Disintegration ".

Gladstone, then, accepting his dependence on the Irishmen's
vote, had chosen the personnel of his third Ministry (not without many vexations), by the end of the first week in February
(1886). Routine and incidental business occupied the first two
months of the new Parliament. Then, on April 8, the Prime
Minister introduced his first Home Rule Bill In it he proposed
to create a legislative body which would sit in Dublin. It would
deal with all exclusively Irish affairs. Ireland would tax herself
in all branches of revenue except Customs and Excise ; and the
balance from Customs and Excise, after discharge of obligations
still due from Ireland to the British Treasury, would be refunded
to the Irish Exchequer. Certain powers would be reserved to
the Imperial Parliament, in particular those which referred to
the Crown, to the Colonies, and to the Army and Navy. There
would be two Houses in Dublin, the Upper House to have power
only to delay measures passed by the wholly elected Second
Chamber. There would still be an English Viceroy ; he
would hold his office permanently, and he might be a Roman
Catholic. The Royal Irish Constabulary would remain under
Imperial control ; but the Prime Minister hoped they would
soon be disbanded.

The Bill was read a first time without a division ; but it was
immediately evident that many of Gladstone's followers besides
Hartington would oppose him on this issue.

The Prime Minister followed these proposals with the introduction of a Land Bill to buy out the English landlords and
make over their properties to the Irish occupiers.

The debate on the second reading of the Home Rule Bill itself
began on May 10. Lord Salisbury's opposition to it was uncompromising. It was neither factious nor solely political. For
him at that time the safety of the Empire and certain matters of
principle were at stake. His faith was deeply rooted in loyalties,
and his belief was in unity—the unity of Ireland, the unity of
the British Isles, the unity of the Empire. His loyalty was engaged not only to the Crown, but also to the Unionist minority
in Ireland, north and south. The Protestants all over the
country—especially of course the Ulstermen, or Orangemen as
they were then usually called—put all their trust in the Con-

servative Party ; they, and particularly the landowners, would
be ruined, in Lord Salisbury's eyes, if they were abandoned to a
Dublin Government ; he felt " bound in honour " not to let
them down. " The landlords of Ireland may be a small class
comparatively," he had said when discussing the claims of
evicted tenants for compensation from the landlords to whom they
had refused their rent, " but after all they are a class, many of
whom assumed their present responsibilities and incurred the
dangers which they are now running at the hands of a Liberal
Government, because they trusted to the word of Parliament, and
invested their money in Irish land on what they thought was
Parliamentary security." He computed the loyal minority at a
million and a half persons altogether ; so the Liberals were proposing to put 95 or 96 per cent of the representation of the
country " into the hands of those to whom the epithet ' loyal '
could not be applied ".

This consideration seems actually to have been uppermost in
the Conservative leader's mind. But his passion for the principle
of unity caused him to regard the separation of Ireland from
England as a gross, wanton and unnecessary violation of it. His
mind always ran on to the logical conclusion ; and he foresaw
that the limited legislative separation which Gladstone proposed
would inevitably develop into complete severance. The Irish
always regarded one concession as a jumping-off board for the next ;
and it was their nature never to be happy without a grievance.

The strategic reasons against separation he had set out in
his article " Disintegration "—they have been quoted in Chapter
IX. And his historical sense revolted against the parcelling out
of the United Kingdom at a moment when national impulses
elsewhere tended the other way and units were growing ever
larger and more formidable. In his lifetime he had seen Prussia
become the leader of united and militaristic Germany, and Italy,
also, gather a number of minor principalities into one kingdom.
The United States was now firmly welded together, north and
south ; Russia had steadily expanded her frontiers during the
eighteenth and nineteenth centuries and showed no inclination to
discontinue the process. How fatuous to choose this moment
to partition the British Isles ! Especially, he argued, because
one had to bear in mind that Ireland was " not a nation, but
two nations ".

Mr. J. L. Hammond, in his *Gladstone and the Irish Nation*, complains that " the trouble about Lord Salisbury was that he was one day the wise and careful Foreign Minister, the best Foreign Minister who served England in his lifetime, thinking of the needs of the future ; and another the rash and violent Saturday Reviewer enjoying the excitement of the hour ". The criticism is hardly fair either to Lord Salisbury or to the *Saturday Review*. It is true that his language was at times intemperate. But so was Gladstone's. Public polemics were vehement in those days, and never were feelings so exacerbated as over Home Rule ; Randolph Churchill coined the phrase—which was again freely used in 1914—" Ulster will fight and Ulster will be right ". And if Lord Salisbury was too ready to imply that Gladstone was primarily motivated by " greed of office ", and the need to win the Irish vote if he hoped to retain power, he on his part was exasperated by the language used by the Liberal leader. For personal attacks on himself Lord Salisbury cared nothing ; but he felt the hurt of blows struck at his political principles. When a man of Gladstone's authority gave the lawlessness in Ireland as a reason for granting her demands, Lord Salisbury felt as if he had received a personal wound ; he was hit again when Gladstone used a phrase about a battle between the classes and the masses in Ireland. At such moments Gladstone appeared to him to be little better than a political anarchist ; and he hit back with all the vigour of an angry political pugilist. Then, no doubt, his discretion sometimes deserted him. One of his outbursts deeply wounded the feelings, not so much of Gladstone, perhaps, as of the Irish people. In his speech in St. James's Hall, delivered on May 15 of this year 1886, he explained that to have absolute confidence in a nation was a prerequisite to granting them any form of self-government ; and in the course of his general disquisition on the subject he reflected as follows : " You would not confide free representative institutions to the Hottentots, for instance. Nor, going higher up the scale, would you confide them to the Oriental nations whom you are governing in India—although finer specimens of human character you will hardly find than some of those who belong to these nations, but who are simply not suited to the particular kind of confidence of which I am speaking." He went on to mention the Russians and the Greeks as being doubtful repositories for the privilege of self-government—though " what was called self-government was really government by the majority ". He concluded his brief excursion into the philosophy of self-government by observing : " When you come to narrow it down you will find that . . . it works admirably well when it is confided to people of Teutonic race, but that it does not work so well when people of other races are called upon to join in it." Taken as a whole, the speech was an able and vigorous denunciation of Home Rule, and it was interrupted throughout by the enthusiastic applause of his Conservative audience. But the unhappy phrase about Hottentots— which *The Times* described as " not altogether discreet "—was a gift to his enemies and an embarrassment to his friends. He had not likened the Irish to Hottentots ; but the brief passage quoted above—which was about one-fortieth part of the whole speech—obliterated the careful arguments of the thirty-nine other parts. " The pungency of the indiscretion ", Lord Morley writes, " kept it long alive "—so tenaciously alive that even after Lord Salisbury's death John Redmond, paying a graceful tribute in the House of Commons to his memory, could not forbear to recall the unfortunate comparison uttered seventeen years before.

Among many interesting points of the speech was his firm declaration of faith in local government. " Local government is a very good thing," he said ; " personally I have always been anxious to press it forward. . . . It gets rid of the harshness and unbending woodenness which is the character of all Governments which are directed exclusively from the centre." But before the Irish enjoyed local government they must cease " to shoot the agent or vivisect his cows because they do not agree with him ". What the Liberals called " coercion " was simply the maintenance of the law. Apply the principle of good government " honestly, consistently and resolutely for twenty years, and at the end of that time you will find that Ireland will be fit to accept any gifts in the way of local government or repeal of coercion laws that you may wish to give her ". In responding at the close of the meeting to the " three cheers for Lord Salisbury and three cheers for Ulster ", he went so far as to give his sanction to the use of force by Orangemen to defend themselves and to check the " insane career " of the Prime Minister and his friends. The bluntness of his language certainly pleased his hearers on this occasion ; and there is not the slightest doubt that his appalling frankness did in general make a big appeal to popular audiences. People crowded to all his meetings with the feeling that this man was something more than a politician—that he would say what he really thought, and that what he thought would be worth hearing.

One of Gladstone's arguments had been that, under the Union, law was given to Ireland " in a foreign garb ". To Lord Salisbury that was no objection. " In this country " [England], he said in another speech, " you are content to guide ; in Ireland it is essential that you govern." Good government rather than self-government appeared to him to be the prime need of that time. And since the political priorities of one epoch are not necessarily, or even usually, those of the next, it does not follow that, because sixty years later national self-government is a wise and fashionable principle, the same principle would have produced happy results then for nations which were less instructed and less mature than they are now. Timeliness of action was one of the distinguishing marks of Lord Salisbury's statesmanship.

In any case it was this Irish issue which rallied the majority of the British people to him. The Home Rule Bill which had been introduced on May 10 was heatedly debated for four weeks ; and on June 7 the Liberal Prime Minister rose to deliver what many who had often heard him speak described as the finest speech that even he had ever delivered. He countered every argument of his critics, Conservative and Liberal alike ; but in vain. When the division was taken the figures were : For the Bill, 313 ; Against, 343. The Irish Nationalists had of course voted for it, although Parnell himself showed no great enthusiasm for so moderate a type of Home Rule ; but 93 Liberals had decided the issue by voting against it.

Lord Salisbury heard the news at Hatfield, at 3 o'clock in the morning, the youngest one of his sons having kept watch at the Post Office to bring up the telegram announcing the result. It was unlike Lord Salisbury to wait upon news. He was not the kind of leader who keeps his ear to the ground and makes his attitude conform to changing murmurs of public opinion. His statesmanship was made of sterner stuff. A government governs and a leader leads, such was Lord Salisbury's philosophy ; and the result of this vote in the House of Commons, whichever way it went, would not have impelled him to change his attitude to Irish self-government by the fraction of an inch. But he regarded the issue as a vital one for the Empire's future ; and he may have had an inkling that it would also make or mar his own career. Was Parliament going to stand behind him in opposition to Home Rule, or was it going to follow his rival ? The vote showed that it was going to stand behind him, and created for him a majority not only in Parliament but also in the country. About one in three of Gladstone's supporters had refused to follow him into the Home Rule camp. They remained Liberals ; but they preferred to serve Lord Salisbury. The Irish question substituted him for Gladstone as the dominant figure in British politics and within the next decade brought him that fusion of Conservatives and Liberal-Unionists which lasted half a century.

2

So much for home affairs. In foreign affairs the assumption of the Foreign Office by Lord Rosebery inaugurated a new phase of continuity. No longer were the abrupt reversals of policy, which had accompanied previous changes from a Conservative to a Liberal Government and vice versa, to cause dismay to friendly foreign countries.

Lord Rosebery—one of the brilliant might-have-beens of British politics—had had all the advantages of upbringing for the making of a Foreign Secretary. He enjoyed frequent opportunities of visiting European countries ; and he had travelled round the world via the British Empire. His brilliant farewell speech to Australia contained the memorable and prophetic words : " There is no need for any nation, however great, leaving the Empire, because the Empire is a commonwealth of nations "—a phrase which, as his biographer, Lord Crewe, observes, became a commonplace of political terminology, but was then the announcement of a new gospel.* He had a most vivacious imagination, ready address, and the knack of remembering what he had to say to any particular person the moment he met him. He was popular at home as a patron of the turf ; but, unlike Lord Salisbury, he had never had to face financial stringency in his early years, nor had he ever been a member of the House of Commons. His ascent to office was too easy ; he was unaccustomed to opposition ; he was very highly-strung ; and when at the age of 47 he became Prime Minister the rough-

* The speech was delivered at Adelaide on January 18, 1884.

and-tumble of politics broke him down. He suffered from chronic insomnia ; from which he recovered sufficiently to remain the brilliant writer and speaker and to become known as " the orator of empire ".

When he took over the Foreign Office in January, 1886, on the particular prompting of Queen Victoria, he came to it with the deliberate intention of following in the footsteps of Lord Salisbury, whom not only he, but by now also Gladstone, regarded as a master of foreign affairs. At the moment of the hand-over in Whitehall the fleets of the Great Powers were assembled in Suda Bay, where Lord Salisbury had reluctantly sent a British squadron, for the purpose of preventing Greece from seizing Thessaly—which Lord Salisbury considered should belong to Greece, but the seizure of which from Turkey would certainly re-open hostilities in the Balkans. Rosebery found the mood of the Greeks to be even more bellicose, now that the great Philhellene Gladstone had become Prime Minister. The mayor of Athens sent a congratulatory telegram to Gladstone and the Greek Government postponed their reply to Lord Salisbury's last communication, confidently expecting a reversal of British policy. Rosebery, however, brought the international fleet, which was under the command of an English admiral, to the Piraeus. The inhabitants of Athens could hardly believe their eyes ; and their Government still refused the request which Lord Salisbury had made, and which the new Foreign Secretary supported, that they should demobilize the Greek army. Rosebery, like his French opposite number at the Quai d'Orsay, Monsieur de Freycinet, did not " quite see his way to shelling the Parthenon " ; but he did see his way to blockading the Greek ports and sending an ultimatum to the Athens Government. Greece capitulated, and a potential Balkan war, which would almost certainly have brought in Servia as well as Turkey, was averted. The action to maintain peace was, of course, concerted between all the Powers ; and Rosebery had shown delicacy as well as firmness in giving united effect to it.

In July the Emperor of Russia abruptly announced his cancellation of Article 69 of the Treaty of Berlin, whereby Batoum had been constituted " an essentially commercial " port. It will be remembered that its non-military status had been the special achievement of Lord Salisbury at the Congress eight years before.

178

What was Rosebery to do ? He could not go to war with Russia over the status of a Black Sea harbour. In the circumstances, was a protest worth while ? Britain had little or no material interests involved ; her trade with Batoum was small. But Rosebery decided that a vigorous protest was required ; and the words of his despatch to St. Petersburg are worthy of record:

> One direct, supreme and perpetual interest is at stake in this transaction—that of the binding force and sanctity of international engagements. Great Britain is ready at all times and in all seasons to uphold that principle and she cannot palter with it in the present instance.
>
> Her Majesty's Government cannot, therefore, consent to recognize or associate themselves in any shape or form with this proceeding of the Russian Government. They are compelled to place on record their view that it constitutes a violation of the Treaty of Berlin, unsanctioned by the Signatory Powers, that it tends to make future conventions of the kind difficult, if not impossible, and to cast doubt at least on those already concluded.

In matters of Colonial policy, also, which were so closely linked to our relations with foreign States, the Liberal Imperialist saw eye to eye with Lord Salisbury, the benefit of which was reaped by the latter in the question of the New Hebrides when he returned to office. Lord Salisbury could follow Rosebery as smoothly as Rosebery followed him—as was proved again in 1892 and 1895. When Lord Salisbury had returned to the Foreign Office in 1885 and consulted the documents concerning Britain's position in Constantinople, he had exclaimed in disgust : " They [the Liberals] have just thrown it away into the sea, without getting anything whatever in exchange." He never had reason to say so again. Lord Rosebery and he between them lifted foreign policy out of the factiousness of Party ; and Rosebery was justified in the claim which he made later at the Albert Hall, in the speech he delivered there in 1895 just a fortnight after he had finally left active politics behind him—" If there is one thing in my life I should like to live after me, it is that, when I first went to the Foreign Office as Secretary for Foreign Affairs, I argued for and maintained the principle of continuity in foreign administration. My view was this, that whatever our domestic differences may be at home, we should preserve a united front

s. 179 N

abroad, and that foreign statesmen and foreign Courts should feel that they are dealing, not with a Ministry, possibly fleeting and possibly transient, but with a great, powerful and united nation " (July 5, 1895).

3

Mr. Gladstone dissolved Parliament immediately after his defeat on the Home Rule vote which (as already mentioned) had been taken soon after midnight on June 8. At the following General Election, the rejection of self-government for Ireland was overwhelmingly confirmed by the country. The Gladstonian Liberals dropped from 335 to 196 ; the Tory numbers rose from 251 to 316 ; and with them, on the crucial issue at least, were 74 dissentient Liberals, henceforward known as Liberal-Unionists. Parnell retained his old strength numerically, but only numerically ; since he no longer held the balance, his parliamentary importance shrunk to that of the leader of a splinter Party. Lord Salisbury had used the whole of his influence before the Election to see that Liberal-Unionists were not opposed by Conservatives ; he was splendidly rewarded by winning a clear Conservative majority and by gaining as well much goodwill from the Liberal-Unionists. The moment the electoral contest had actually begun, he had hurried off to his beloved France for a real holiday. But Gladstone of course resigned ; and this time it was from Royat that Queen Victoria summoned Lord Salisbury to come and form a government. In her letter to him of July 22 she said she was grieved to cut his holiday so short ; but he knew " what confidence she reposed in him "—the words " what confidence " were underlined. Her faithful minister returned next day ; and on the morrow (the 24th) he set out, not for Osborne, but for the house of the leader of the Liberal-Unionists, Hartington, to invite him, to reason with him, to beg him to take the premiership. In vain. So in the afternoon Lord Salisbury travelled down to Osborne ; and embarked there, at his Sovereign's bidding, as captain of the ship of State a second time. This fresh voyage over uncharted seas—for the sea of politics remains uncharted for every embarking Prime Minister, be his ship never so trim and his crew never so skilled—was destined to be very much more prolonged and more prosperous than his first had been.

TEAM-BUILDING—IRELAND

During his first Ministry a friend had commiserated with Lord Salisbury on having to carry the burdens of both the premiership and the Foreign Office, and according to Lady Gwendolen Cecil he then replied : " I could do very well with two Departments ; in fact I have four—the Prime Ministership, the Foreign Office, the Queen and Randolph Churchill." He had now one way or another to lessen the strain. Obviously he must still frequently make journeys to Windsor, to Osborne and even occasionally to Balmoral, and write as well those regular confidential reports which Her Majesty so much enjoyed receiving and answering. Nor could he leave Randolph Churchill out of the Ministry now to be fashioned ; for his brilliant thrust in debate was an indispensable asset to a Front Bench of competent mediocrities, especially at a time when the Irish contingent in the Commons was making the proceedings of the House anarchic. Ireland might indeed be said to constitute a fifth " Department " for the Prime Minister.

So Lord Salisbury came to the conclusion that in the circumstances he would not repeat the experiment of combining Foreign Office and premiership. Hartington had refused to take the latter ; whom could he find for the former ? He sent Sir Philip Currie, his favourite at the Foreign Office, to try to persuade Lord Lyons, the seasoned ambassador in Paris, to come to Downing Street. That wary old diplomatist, who boasted that he had spent five years in America without making a speech or taking a drink, was not to be inveigled into public duties so different from those on which he had silently built up his reputation.* In despair Lord Salisbury invited Lord Cranbrook, who pleaded the original excuse that he could not speak French. So Lord Iddesleigh was bidden to take over the Foreign Department, Lord Salisbury no doubt reckoning that so cautious a politician and so confiding a friend would at least not go far wrong.

Sir Michael Hicks Beach had senior claim to be leader of the

* Lord Newton, *Lord Lyons*, p. 432 (Nelson Library).

House of Commons, but self-effacedly volunteered to forgo his right in favour of his more sparkling junior, Randolph Churchill, to whom Lord Salisbury also entrusted the Exchequer, while Hicks Beach himself took the thankless Chief Secretaryship of Ireland. W. H. Smith, as in 1885, took the War Office and Lord George Hamilton the Admiralty. The Prime Minister's nephew, A. J. Balfour, was given his first governmental post four months later when he became Secretary for Scotland ; and Mr. Henry Matthews (afterwards Lord Llandaff), a member of the Catholic Church, accepted Lord Salisbury's offer of the Home Secretary-ship—thus becoming the first Roman Catholic ever to serve in a Conservative Cabinet.

The Liberal-Unionists had followed their leader Hartington in declining to take any part in the Government ; so Lord Salisbury was left at the head of a purely Conservative Administration backed by a composite majority in the Commons. Hartington and his immediate associates actually sat on the Front Opposition Bench. The Government has often been referred to as a coali-tion ; but it was an alliance rather than a coalition, substantial in Parliament, but unrepresented in the Cabinet. The live wire between its non-Conservative adherents and the Cabinet was Churchill. He was the Tory leader of the House, and the most Liberal member of the Cabinet. In Downing Street he was indeed a sharp thorn in the flesh of Lord Salisbury ; but in the Commons he was the rapier that could pierce Mr. Gladstone ; for his hatred of Home Rule was as great as his Chief's ; and he was always ready to do battle with the Irish members. In the opening speech upon the Address, when Gladstone delivered one of his less felicitous speeches on Home Rule, implying that the British people, in spite of the figures of the General Election, were really in favour of it, Churchill's reply electrified the House. The oldest member, who recalled the Grand Old Man's duels with Disraeli, could never remember seeing him so discomfited and crushed. During this first short session of 1886 Churchill was, moreover, more even-tempered and courteous than he had been in his earlier parliamentary career. At the Treasury he was assiduous and patient in discussion with its officials ; he had a passion for economy second only to Gladstone's ; and in his preparation of the Budget his first purpose was to effect a sub-stantial reduction in taxation.

But while meekly learning the secrets of national finance at the Treasury, and discovering the meaning of " those damned dots ", as he described decimal points, he was also making speeches in the country which roused enthusiasm but went far beyond the orthodox tenets of Conservatism. More ; he was fond of having long conversations with ambassadors accredited to the Court of St. James ; and Lord Salisbury soon became aware that he was telling them many things which neither he himself nor Foreign Secretary Iddesleigh would have mentioned, and that he often expounded a foreign policy which was certainly not that of the British Government. Churchill indeed made no secret of his dislike of Britain's attitude in the Near East at this time. He openly championed the expulsion of Turkey from Europe, a project with which, as we know, Lord Salisbury was in private sympathy but which he deemed dangerous to British interests, and therefore undesirable. Churchill, at 37, was becoming a political prodigy, and irrepressible. In the Cabinet he opposed the views of the Foreign Secretary, for whom he felt no respect ; and in the country his popularity seemed to grow with every speech. He began to think himself the key man of the Government. And as his power grew, so did his elation, and his earlier irresponsibility returned. By November of that year —1886—Lord Salisbury came to the conclusion that there was no room in the same Cabinet for himself and Churchill.

It was Churchill himself who threw down the challenge. He had publicly pledged himself to economies ; and when the estimates of the several Departments of State were presented to him, he sharply demanded reductions in those of the War Office and the Admiralty. Smith and George Hamilton were two of his friendliest supporters in the Government ; but the Chancellor had taken his stand on the Liberal principle of less money for armaments and more for social requirements. Lord Salisbury came down firmly on the side of his Service Ministers. He judged their demands to be by no means excessive in view of the international situation. Even so, Hamilton was soon able to come to a verbal agreement with the Chancellor ; and Smith was obliging ; but Churchill had expected, and led others to expect, drastic reductions ; and drastic reductions could not be made.

The Christmas recess arrived ; and in mid-December the

Cabinet formally adjourned for some weeks. Lord Salisbury went to Hatfield to spend a quiet Christmas with his family. It was rudely interrupted. On December 21st, in the morning, he received a letter from Churchill, written on the notepaper of Windsor Castle, requesting " to be allowed to give up his office and retire from the Government ".

The Prime Minister spent most of that day making (in his own hand) copies of the Chancellor of the Exchequer's letter and sending them off to his principal colleagues of the Cabinet. Then on the 22nd he replied to Churchill himself. He expressed his " profound regret " ; but, without saying it in so many words, he accepted his resignation.

The reply was a sharp shock to Churchill. Undoubtedly he had " hoped to prevail ", in the phrase of his son and biographer. During his tenure of the India Office in Lord Salisbury's first Administration he had offered his resignation in a moment of pique over a minor issue. His Chief had then been conciliatory and had persuaded him to continue in office. But now he understood at once that the Prime Minister's mood was obdurate. He therefore accepted his dismissal as being definite ; but with characteristic cleverness he forwarded to Hatfield a long letter to explain that he had offered his resignation not only on account of the reason given in his letter from Windsor—the Service estimates—but because the domestic legislation proposed by the Government " fell sadly short of what the Parliament and the country expect and require ", and because " the foreign policy which is being adopted appears to me at once dangerous and methodless ".

Lord Salisbury is generally considered to have been lacking in the " common touch ", and is notorious for having failed about this time to recognize one of his own colleagues at a breakfast-party ; but—as Mr. Winston Churchill has ruefully recorded— he was a master of tactics in the management of men ; and he checkmated Randolph Churchill. He took no notice of his protestations of differences on general policy. He concentrated, in the subsequent controversy, on the actual point of severance, Churchill's own chosen ground of dispute—the estimates ; and on that ground the Prime Minister undoubtedly had both Parliament and the country behind him. He caught Churchill on the wrong foot. A quarrel over a Budget that had not even been presented to Parliament and which, from all they could learn, endangered the defences of the realm at a critical conjuncture of international rivalries, gained little sympathy from the people. Moreover, Churchill had lately shown himself somewhat erratic. He had contradicted himself. He was impatient and mercurial, palpably over-combative and over-strained. Many of his recent statements had been most intemperate. He had given the news of his resignation to *The Times* before it had been accepted by the Queen. He seemed an unsafe custodian for the Treasury ; men preferred the solidity and wariness of their Prime Minister. They showed it in the extraordinary calm with which they received the news of his sudden fall. In the clubs the Churchill affair was the sensation of the year ; the crowds outside, whose plaudits had sounded so sweet in his ears a few weeks back, were now dumb. Political gossips speculated whether the Government would survive ; among its supporters Hicks Beach thought it should resign at once, and Drummond Wolff noted " I think that the Government will inevitably fall." Among opponents so percipient a parliamentarian as Joseph Chamberlain prophesied its immediate collapse. Even Lord Salisbury had his moments of pessimism.

For all his dislike of Churchill's restless temperament he well understood that the young man had genius, and represented something that was not found in his own Toryism. But he had tried the experiment of collaboration, and it had failed ; and from this moment Lord Salisbury's political outlook became more fixedly conservative. The history of the next twenty years would have been differently written had Churchill been an easier man. His inspirations were too vivid and too wayward for his Victorian colleagues ; and after his defeat he counted no more in the country at large. But he had set going political currents which took their course underground, beneath the placid crust of Salisburian Conservatism, to re-emerge in 1905 when a Liberal Ministry, of which his son was a member, gave effect to some of the progressive ideas of his fertile brain.

Lord Salisbury was in no hurry to appoint a successor, for the reason that once more he contemplated getting his friend Hartington to take over the premiership. Hartington stood midway between Radical and Tory ; he himself, Lord Salisbury, was inwardly yearning to take direct control of the Foreign Office,

where Iddesleigh had made the mistake, particularly distasteful
to his Chief, of pursuing in the Near East a meddling and ineffective policy. Hartington was in Rome. The Prime Minister
telegraphed his proposal to him, and begged him in any case to
come home quickly. Hartington was not to be hurried. He
took several days over the journey ; and when he arrived the
project of a Liberal Prime Minister had been rendered impossible by the absolute refusal of the Conservative rank and file
to endorse their leader's self-denying proposition. They knew
him not only as their leader, but as a leader by nature, a leader
born, a leader in spite of himself. Lord Salisbury duly made
his offer when the traveller at length arrived in London ; but
Hartington now firmly, and for the third time, declined the
premiership.

To find successors to Churchill, at the Exchequer and in the
Commons, was a baffling puzzle ; no Conservative member of
the Cabinet seemed to be obviously fitted for either post. Lord
Salisbury had previously, it is true, offered the leadership in the
Commons to Beach (as he had always called him) ; but Beach
was finding the vituperation and obstructive methods of the
Irish M.P.s too much for him ; and his eyesight was giving him
serious trouble. Iddesleigh, too, was manifestly failing in health.
The Prime Minister still wanted to have a Liberal-Unionist in
his Cabinet ; but the Liberal-Unionists remained aloof and
detached. The Government was a ship awash ; no wonder
quidnuncs in plenty prophesied that it would sink ; no wonder
that when messengers were seen passing to and fro between
Downing Street and Churchill's house in Connaught Place the
know-alls asserted positively that the Prime Minister was negotiating the ex-Chancellor's return to office.

Lord Salisbury was doing no such thing. Succinctly he had
expressed his feelings to a private questioner : " Did you ever
know a man who, having a boil on his neck, wanted another ? "
He persisted in his search for a Liberal recruit. Hartington would
not join personally ; but he was inclined to be helpful, and had
earlier suggested Goschen as the likeliest collaborator. George
Joachim Goschen had shown himself to be an expert financier,
both in London and in Egypt ; he had written an authoritative
volume on Foreign Exchanges, and had served with distinction on a special mission to Constantinople. He was the very

man Lord Salisbury wanted. The Prime Minister played him through Hartington. There was breathless suspense for two days. Then he was able in a moment of unwonted elation, to announce to his family : " You know we have landed our fish." Very soon after he had taken up his duties, Goschen dexterously converted a large part of the National Debt. Churchill, in his own mortified phrase, had " forgotten Goschen " ; and Lord Salisbury's shrewd choice was vindicated. No less fortunate was his selection of a successor to Churchill in the Commons. He could not hope to find anybody who would equal Churchill in brilliance ; he would therefore choose one who had the opposite qualities of imperturbability and soundness of judgment. He invited W. H. Smith to take the post. Smith said he would undertake the arduous business if he were relieved of the War Office. To this Lord Salisbury unwillingly consented, and, so that he might not be without Cabinet rank and remuneration, resigned to him his own post of First Lord of the Treasury. He himself was deprived by this constitutional innovation of any formal place in the Cabinet. The premiership not only carried no salary—a matter of indifference to Lord Salisbury ; it had not even any official existence. So Lord Salisbury gave this anomaly as the reason why he must take over the Foreign Office ; he must, he explained, if he was to lead the Cabinet, have a Cabinet post !

His other reasons he kept to himself. The criticism of Iddes-leigh was indeed general, and his impaired health had prompted him to place his office in the Prime Minister's hands as soon as the re-shuffling of places had begun. Lord Salisbury had not at once accepted his resignation ; but he had so definitely made up his mind to assume the post himself that he had mentioned it confidentially to one of his rare journalist friends, Mr. Alfred Austin, then a leader-writer on the *Standard*. Austin imparted the secret to his editor, as journalistic custom prescribes, under the seal of confidence. Unfortunately the news leaked out to a Press agency, which published it. The Editor of the *Standard*, conceiving his obligation of secrecy to be thereby removed, con-firmed the announcement of Lord Salisbury's decision ; and Iddesleigh, at his home in Devonshire, first read the news of his own supersession in the public Press. Lord Salisbury was hardly less mortified than the unhappy Iddesleigh. He despatched a telegram, followed quickly by a letter, to his closest colleague, explaining briefly the sequence of accidents and asking him to come and see him in London and receive a fuller account. Iddesleigh came to town, and on the appointed day drove to Downing Street. First he went into the Foreign Office for the last time and had a long talk with the Parliamentary Under-Secretary, Sir James Fergusson ; then he walked across to No. 10 and went upstairs to the Prime Minister's anteroom. There he collapsed and was placed on a settee. Lord Salisbury hurried out to make amends to his old friend. But his explanation was never spoken ; for Iddesleigh lay unconscious and died in twenty minutes. It was the most tragic shock of his life for Lord Salisbury. For the first time since he and Stafford Northcote had stood together as young candidates on the hustings at Stamford, he had hurt his friend's feelings ; and now, for the first time he saw a man die, and that the man to whom most in the world he wanted to speak. . . . Randolph Churchill showed his warmth of heart by writing to condole with his former Chief ; and Lord Salisbury, in an almost affectionate reply, wrote that " politics was a cursed profession ".

So it was in a moment of sadness that he resumed personal control of foreign policy (January, 1887). But now, he felt, he could manage the two departments whose headquarters stand, in mere dimension of brick and stone, like dignity and impudence on either side of Downing Street. Of the five " departments " that had given him headaches, one had been removed, another, Ireland, was beginning to be less painful, and the three that remained, the premiership, the Foreign Office, and the trans-action of business with Queen Victoria, were three that were interlocked and that he would not really have been happy to see in other hands than his own. Every important despatch was not only seen but commented upon by the Queen ; she clung to the prerogative, re-established by the Prince Consort,* that foreign policy was the business of the Sovereign ; and British ambassadors in those days were not only prescriptively her personal representatives but were also so regarded in practice, and she concerned herself with their appointment. While the Foreign Office had been in the hands of Iddesleigh, moreover, Lord Salisbury realized how much he missed the confidential

* See Roger Fulford, *The Prince Consort.*

conversations with foreign envoys and his consequent inability to influence them by informal hints and suggestions. Nor could he be sure, in spite of the devotion of Iddesleigh, that he himself was seeing everything he wanted from the private reports of British representatives abroad. He knew that nobody outside the Foreign Office could keep his finger continuously on the pulse of the tendencies of foreign Chanceries. The Foreign Secretary alone could estimate correctly the relative values which should be attached to different movements of opinion in foreign countries. His integral attention was needed to range over the entire field and make every factor and every incident contribute to the policy which he had himself conceived, in conformity with the general purpose of Parliament and the nation. And again, Lord Salisbury had come to understand the immense advantages of being Number 1 in every sphere concerned with foreign policy ; and, the corpus of public business being much smaller in the 'eighties and 'nineties than in the present century, Lord Salisbury decided that the double burden was just within his physical capacity. It involved the renunciation of any complete holiday. Foreign affairs never stood still. The Red Boxes pursued him everywhere. Lady Gwendolen Cecil, who often acted as his secretary when he went abroad, seems to imply in an allusive sentence that he never enjoyed two days in succession of complete rest from public business from the year 1886 until 1892 and again from 1895 until about 1899. But he had a great aptitude for hard work without overwork. He regulated his tempo even when he could not regulate his hours. He habitually worked late into the night. But he never lost his sleep. He showed how a great monument of achievement can be raised without overstrain on any single day.

And the double task was eased by the gradual removal of the Irish incubus. On March 5 the reconstruction of Lord Salisbury's Ministry was completed by the appointment of Arthur Balfour to the Irish Secretaryship. His sister's son had shown promise of unusual parliamentary proficiency during the few months he had been at the Scottish Office. But that was child's play compared with demands of the Lodge in Phoenix Park. A shout of laughter went up from the ranks of Ireland at the nomination of this elegant young man, whose languid air, fair, drooping moustaches, pince-nez and spats were the delight of the cartoonist.

They had made things too hot for Hicks Beach ; they would make short work of this weakling. But one or two of the Westminster Irish had noticed that for all his kid gloves he could handle a rapier effectively ; they were all soon to learn that he could also swing a bludgeon.

On March 22 the Government asked for precedence for a Crimes Act over all other legislation ; and on March 28 Balfour introduced, with some drastic additions, a Bill which Hicks Beach had already drafted. From that day until the middle of September Parliament had little time for any other business. Only twice did the House of Commons rise before midnight. Liberals joined with the Parnellites to fight it clause by clause ; and the average hour of rising was a quarter past two. The stiffening section of the Bill against which the Parliamentary Opposition most vehemently reacted was that which enabled the Lord-Lieutenant to " proclaim " an association or a district ; trial by jury disappeared ; the Resident Magistrates were given almost unrestricted powers. The Bill was forced through the Commons by free use of the Closure, a method which had been adopted by Gladstone himself in 1881 for dealing with Irish obstruction. The Land League was then " proclaimed ". Thereafter the Dublin executive had an even more absolute power of preventive arrest than it had been temporarily given by the Forster Act of 1881. Balfour seemed even to friendly critics in England to be going beyond the law in his determination to break the breakers of the law. But it must be remembered that these breakers of the law had been defying it daily with knife and gun, with dynamite and vitriol ; and the boys of the blackthorn brigade were not to be quelled by a week or two spent in jail. Lord Salisbury and Balfour might deplore the clumsiness of the Constabulary at Mitchelstown and they detested the niggardly exploitation of his legal dues by Lord Clanricarde ; but they were determined to re-establish respect for the law. In most parts of the country its servants had been reduced to impotence. The firmness of Balfour in supporting their action, right or wrong, restored their authority and with it made the law of the land more powerful than the threats of the agitators. " What Ireland wants," Lord Salisbury had said in his Hottentot speech, " is government—government that does not flinch, that does not vary." Under the Salisbury-Balfour regime she obtained it.

After coercion came constructive legislation. Admittedly the rent laws bore hardly on the Irish peasants. Balfour brought in one measure after another to amend them. The Land Act was passed in this same year 1887 ; next year came a Land Purchase Act ; the Railways Act, to improve communications and also drainage, followed in 1890. The change that had been wrought by his courage was shown by his being able to travel about western Ireland in a side-car to supervise its application, whereas three years before, even when he was in his native Scotland, he had carried a revolver and been accompanied by detectives. Finally the Land Act of 1891 set up the valuable Congested Districts Board ; and the Crimes Act rested unused in a pigeon-hole of the Dublin Law Courts. With its disappearance Ireland's distemper was cured. She settled down to the twenty years of good government and prosperity for which Lord Salisbury had stipulated. During his third premiership, in 1898, he passed the Local Government for Ireland Act, a first step towards larger self-rule.

The " Irish Question " had brought down in turn Pitt and Peel and Derby and Gladstone. Lord Salisbury emerged from his struggle in a stronger position than he had before enjoyed. The energies of his Government were released for other and greater issues. From 1887 onwards he himself felt such confidence in the ability of his nephew, the " dear Arthur " of many sage and encouraging letters, that he could devote himself to his mani-fold tasks in England, abroad and in the Empire. Moreover, the other stresses of the winter of 1886–7 had left his Government better compacted than they found it. A genius had been lost, but the Ministry had become a more effective team ; a Liberal had been interjected into it, but it had nevertheless become more homogeneous ; above all, Lord Salisbury had been unanimously acclaimed as its indispensable leader.

CHAPTER XIII—1886-1892. THE SECOND MINISTRY
(continued)

SALISBURIAN CONSERVATISM—DOMESTIC LEGISLATION—COLONIAL CONFERENCE

The Salisburian brand of Conservatism had prevailed. No suggestion, now, that the leader of the Party should give way to the Liberalism of Hartington or suffer challenge from the Tory democracy of Churchill. And Lord Salisbury's views were, to all appearances and by all the normal political tests, approved and accepted by the majority of the nation. They felt that he stood for something in which they believed. They only dimly understood his doctrine, but they knew that he had one.

His views had been freely interspersed in the articles he wrote in the *Quarterly Review*, from which numerous extracts have been quoted in these pages. His education and his own reading had steeped his mind in the classical tradition of statesmanship. Disciple of Pitt and Castlereagh, godson of Wellington, brought up on Latin literature, he eschewed the view of the Romantics that " The world's great age begins anew ", and preferred the teaching handed down from Rome that the task of the statesman is to preserve the institutions of civilization from their natural tendency to decay, to maintain form and order, proportion and strength, to mix mercy and authority, and to sustain by constant renovation the political and religious hierarchy.

But the vitality of Salisburian Conservatism, and its acceptance by the electorate, came from its faithful expression of a large part—the Conservative part—of British outlook and belief. It represented not something ephemeral but something persistent in the British character. Lord Salisbury's first and deepest personal conviction was respect for the liberty of the individual, which in his view was inherent in and inseparable from the principles of the Christian religion. He believed in the unalterably individualistic and competitive instinct of man ; and the love of personal liberty made him detest all unnecessary interference with the individual's way of life. And the training of the individual was the first and foremost duty of the parents.

The family was the natural basis of the social structure ordained by God. That the State should in any way weaken the sense of parental responsibility would appear disastrous to Lord Salisbury. And, for the individual, private property was a sacred right. The claim to ownership was basic, distinguishing man from animals, and imparting to him a sense of self-respect and of personal responsibility ; inspiring him also with the noblest incentive for seeking self-advancement and prosperity—that of bequeathing to his children an improved standard of life. The business of the State therefore was to give each individual the largest possible scope of legitimate action ; to enable him to earn benefits, but not to pour them into his lap. Laws designed for such a purpose were never so cunningly devised but they cramped initiative and hampered enterprise. He looked to self-discipline, loyalty and hard work rather than to rules—to moral rather than to legal obligations and controls. Nor had the State any business to be generous with money of which it was, properly speaking, only the trustee. The State must be just, but not munificent. In one of his 1885 Election speeches Lord Salisbury had put his view succinctly : " The Conservative points the working man forward to obtain wealth which is as yet uncreated : the Radical, on the contrary, does not tell him to create new sources of wealth, but says that the wealth which has already been obtained is badly divided . . . and that the real remedy is to look back and fight among yourselves for the wealth that has already been obtained." The business of the State was not to distribute the earnings of private enterprise but to allow the merits of every citizen to win a prize. Moreover, conservation of its accumulated resources should be a primary care of a responsible statesman.

Lord Salisbury therefore frankly gave chief place to the protective and defensive aspect of Conservatism. Therein lay not only its virtue but also, he was convinced, its appeal to the electorate. Government should be efficient but unobtrusive. In a general way he may indeed be said to have disbelieved in legislation. He considered that its nature was primarily restrictive and that it had a more unequivocal capacity for inflicting injury than for imparting benefits. The benefits might be more immediate and more obvious ; but, as the French political economist, Frédéric Bastiat, expressed it, in the formative years of Lord Salisbury's life : " il y a ce qu'on voit et ce qu'on ne voit pas ; et ce qu'on ne voit pas est toujours le plus important " ; the unseen long-term consequences of charitable laws were, in sum, more important than the seen results, and were generally harmful. They diminished the independence and weakened the character of the individual ; and individual strength of character was the greatest asset of a nation. Self-control Lord Salisbury regarded as the noblest and most important of the civic virtues. Legislation, in short, could not improve the individual. Religion could. He frequently dwelt upon the essential inferiority of the political profession to that of the clerical. The evils which the Church fought against were those which mattered most—hatred, malice, idleness, envy, mutual mistrust. These were the harmful things which sapped national strength and productivity, and they were often not assuaged, but actually inflamed, by politicians.

He thought in terms of the nation, of the whole nation, of all classes welded into one unit. Class was then separated from class by common consent ; the divisions were accepted by all with whom he habitually consorted, and he was ready to take advantage, while it lasted, of distinctions which he regarded as the normal fabric of human society. All men are equal before God and before the law, but not otherwise. Equality and similarity are not in accordance with nature, but, rather, contrary to nature. Therefore, Lord Salisbury believed, the graded structure of society is both normal and right—inevitable indeed, for it is found among the most primitive peoples, and is still more necessary in a highly organized community. Nor did he consider that such separation of classes involved hostility or clash of interests. The commonwealth implied for him the co-operation and good health of the whole body politic. But he believed that every class had its special function, and that those who had enjoyed the education of the public school and university had the special responsibility of performing the directive function of the head, or brain ; he believed, in fact, in a ruling class. He believed in the value of tradition, of leisure rightly used, and also of heredity, often incontestably dominant in other avocations —even in games of skill.

2

On the opposite side of the account, Lord Salisbury expected from the ruling class the highest standard of public conduct, a compelling sense of social obligation. Those who had time to spare for the study of history and government must devote to their apprenticeship energy, integrity and self-sacrifice ; their work was harder and more exacting than the daily earning of bread and butter, which moreover made it impossible for the masses to acquire a proper knowledge of political problems. Nobody was so severe as he in his strictures on the nobly-born who failed to respond to what he regarded as the obligations of their station. They must exert themselves or atrophy. He used scathing language about " the smart set " of his day and was contemptuous of the mere " Clubman ". England as a land of Cockaigne was a conception wholly repugnant to him.

From his disbelief in the value of legislation and belief in a class born to rule flowed a strong preference for the importance of administration over the making of new laws. The proper and principal function of the State was to establish and maintain justice—absolute, unbiased, unchallengeable justice between rival interests and all classes of the community. And next to justice came order. Not only at home, but in the Empire, Lord Salisbury gave absolute priority to justice and order. Even foreign countries stood high or low in his estimation according as their regimes were stable and their governments afforded security to the property and rights of their citizens—the yardstick by which he had measured Ireland and found her wanting.

It seems right at this point to observe that his hatred of agitators and loathing of injustice laid a particular onus upon him to discover such injustices as existed and were being silently borne. It is in this respect that he has been properly criticized. There were in the length and breadth of England, and in the factories and coal mines even more than on the land, many thousands of men and women who shared the sentiments of Mrs. Poyser : " And after all, at the end of the year, it's like as if you'd been cooking a feast and had got the smell of it for your pains. As fur as I can see, it's raising victual for other folks, and just getting a mouthful for yourself and your children as you go along." And in another of that wonderful woman's remarkable discourses she says : " I know it's christened folks's duty to submit to their betters as fur as flesh and blood 'ull bear it ; but I'll not make a martyr of myself to skin and bone, and worret

myself as if I was a churn wi' butter a-coming in't, for no landlord in England, not if he was King George himself." Mrs.
Poyser was indeed registering her grumbles against the conditions
that prevailed at the beginning of the century ; but such cases
of hardship continued until its close ; and it is the abiding
blemish in Lord Salisbury's record that he did not take the first
opportunity to investigate them.

His churchmanship no doubt convinced him that though
there were indeed bad landowners and bad industrial magnates
the remedy was to convert them to principles of Christian charity
and justice. He himself, and probably all his personal friends,
treated those dependent on them with the utmost consideration.
But the many others who allowed their agricultural tenants to
live in miserable cottages or their employees to work ten hours
a day for a pittance, while they themselves merely enjoyed life in
London and abroad, on the moors or in their yachts, discredited
a system of free competition in which the vast majority started
with the crippling handicap of acute poverty. No doubt it might
have been fairly operated if all those who directed it had been
animated by the same high motives as Lord Salisbury himself.
But they were not ; and the laws passed since his time have
conclusively proved how much legislation can and must accom-
plish for maintaining and improving the standard of living of
the manual workers—though the process has certainly brought
with it some of the grievous and fundamental evils which Lord
Salisbury foresaw, such as evasion of over-detailed regulations
and consequent disrespect for the law, the increased tendency of
parents to relegate family responsibilities to the State, and the
widely spread expectation of " getting something for nothing "—
the desire to escape taxation and yet receive every benefit which
the State purveys.

In spite of the Prime Minister's " policeman " attitude, however, the legislative record of his 1886–92 Parliament was by no
means blank. For Lord Salisbury there was all the difference
between organic change and organic growth. His views coincided with those of the great thinkers—Bacon, Burke, Cardinal
Newman. He must have agreed with the oft-quoted aphorisms
of Francis Bacon—the contemporary and relative of his own
famous ancestors Lord Burghley and Robert Cecil, the first Lord
Salisbury. " It were good, therefore, that men in their Innova-

tions would follow the example of Time itself, which, indeed innovateth greatly, but quietly, and by degrees scarce to be perceived " ; and " It is good also not to try experiments in States except the necessity be urgent, or the utility evident ; and well to beware that it be the reformation that draweth on the change, and not the desire of change that pretendeth the reformation." His opinion would not have differed from Burke's : " A disposition to preserve, and an ability to improve, taken together, would be my standard of a statesman " ; and he was familiar with the careful definition of true doctrinal development by his own contemporary, J. H. Newman—not yet a Cardinal, nor yet a Roman Catholic, when he wrote his " Essay on the development of Christian doctrine ". Permissible changes, he wrote, were those that did not alter the essential character of a political doctrine. They must preserve the type. They must maintain logical sequence. They must possess the power of assimilation, but assimilate only so as to preserve their chronic vigour, not to corrupt their nature. Just so, in Lord Salisbury's opinion, the British form of government must suffer no violent change. It combined monarchy, oligarchy and democracy, in a well-balanced Constitution. Reforms which did not upset its balance were not only permissible but desirable. The danger was that those who understood its complexities did too little ; the half-ignorant were those most likely to force innovations upon the country. The wisdom of British statecraft was to reform resolutely but soberly, and so to anticipate revolution.

The task of a statesman, then, was to hold the balance justly between all classes of the nation, to make government itself efficient and to give free rein to the diligence and efficiency of private individuals, enabling every section of the nation to apply its whole energy to its own business, and employing as few of the national energies as possible in observing, analysing, enumerating and directing the activities of constructive workers. He knew the value of statistics, but he did not want a nation of observers and statisticians ; and he did not believe in the multiplication of committees. Nor did he consider it in the public interest that the massive energies of the nation's skilled workers should be diverted from their own jobs to that of government, which, like every other difficult trade, required careful training and special aptitudes. The vast majority of the nation had neither time nor talent for government. Only proved wisdom and disinterestedness qualified a man to hold high office, and its business could not all be conducted in the market-place. A Frenchman at that time observed that the strength of the English people was that " they know that they must not know ". The paradox was as palatable to Lord Salisbury as it would be un-palatable to the electorate of today. But equally acceptable to the present generation as to his would be the saying of another Frenchman : " La sagese est le contrepoids nécessaire de la liberté."

3

Guided, then, by principles which were essentially unalterable but adaptable to the needs of a changing world, Lord Salisbury sanctioned the inclusion of momentous domestic measures in the legislative programmes of the years 1886–92. A good example of his attitude was his endorsement of the Bill for making educa-tion a charge upon the State. Lord Salisbury has often been accused of being hostile to the education of the people ; and to have endowed them with free education may indeed seem to be a contradiction of his views on the negative function of the State. The explanation of his apparent inconsistency is simple. He was opposed not to education but to compulsory education. In accordance with his belief in individualism and family responsi-bility he would have preferred that the decision whether and how much their children were to be educated should be taken by their parents. " The duty of sending your children to school ", he wrote to Lord Cranbrook, " is not a natural duty like that of feeding them—it is an artificial duty." But as the State had, under Gladstone's leadership, made education obligatory for all, and as he accepted that decision as " the sustained and deliberate " wish of the country, he considered that the least the State could do was to bear itself the charge which it had imposed upon every family in the land.

Opposition to his Free Education Bill came not only from rigid Tories of the Right, it came even more vehemently from extreme-individualist Liberals. The Liberals wanted in any case to restrict the grants to schools under public control ; and they were supported in this attitude by Wesleyans in the northern towns who provided an excellent but relatively expensive education from which they feared the assisted schools would draw away their pupils. Lord Salisbury faced his critics on his right and on his left, before him and behind him. He had stated his own view during his previous term of office, in 1885 ; and as usual, when he had once made up his mind, he refused to budge from his decision. This measure, like every measure introduced during Lord Salisbury's second term of office, was however delayed not so much by its critics as by the devastating obstruction of all parliamentary business by the Parnellites, and it only became law in 1891.

The one major measure which the Cabinet managed to force through the Commons in its first two years of office was the Local Government Act of 1888. Lord Salisbury thereby not only created the (rural) County Councils, but also the L.C.C.—for his Act turned all towns of over 50,000 inhabitants into County Boroughs. Once more he was opposed by his own diehards, this time mostly by county gentlemen, upon whom he played the full jet of his irony and sarcasm. Nearly all the powers of local magistracy had already, he argued, been transferred from individual squires to public bodies ; but " a sense of their unutterable wrongs will suddenly burst upon them," he wrote ; and " To say you have dethroned the squirearchy when they have in fact no throne left to sit upon is hard upon the squirearchy." The new Act did not provide for the creation of Parish Councils, and three years later, in an election campaign speech, he blurted out a foolish gibe about the rural population being more amused by " a circus or something of that kind " than by having village councils. The phrase was cast in his teeth for many years afterwards, and was, quite erroneously, supposed to prove that he was personally indifferent to his own reform. The only part of his Act about which he had had his doubts was that which entrusted the management of the Poor Law to local bodies—to a majority of men " whose interest it is that the administration should be lax and costly ". He did not want " to leave the cat in charge of the cream jug ".

A measure to which the Prime Minister himself attached much importance, affecting as it did the welfare of the clergy, was the Tithes Bill. Lord Salisbury insisted on transferring the onus of payment from the occupier on to the shoulders of the landlord. Once more the opposition came largely from his own supporters, and once more the delay was caused mainly by the Irish. However, when in 1890 the Parnell-O'Shea divorce case discredited the Irish leader, his parliamentary followers fell into two groups, the pro-Parnells and the anti-Parnells ; their power of obstruction was broken ; and the Tithes Bill went through easily in January, 1891.

Several minor measures of domestic legislation were also passed as the tide of Irish rowdiness receded. Among the " policeman " Acts for the protection of the man in the street was one for the inspection of weighing machines. The safeguard of the Plimsoll Line was reinforced and amplified. And the remarkable expansion of the railway system over the whole island necessitated a long series of new regulations which were skilfully carried through the Commons by Sir Michael Hicks Beach, now President of the Board of Trade. It is interesting to note that nationalization of the railways was proposed by a private member, and opposed by Hicks Beach with the approval of the Prime Minister. They considered that the cost of management would be greatly increased, and they feared that " public corruption might creep into it " at a time when gaining votes might be a consideration in granting or refusing local extensions of track.

Another project which was mooted at that time and has been a subject of controversy ever since was the reform of the House of Lords. In 1888, spurred by a challenge from Lord Rosebery, Lord Salisbury introduced a measure in the Upper House for the creation of fifty life peers, to be drawn from the ranks of the judges, governors, ambassadors, high-placed officers of the Army and Navy and of the Civil Service. He declared that he was willing, if a satisfactory method of elimination could be found, to keep out of the House obviously unsuitable members of the peerage ; but he would in no circumstances abolish the hereditary basis of membership. Therein, he claimed, lay not the weakness, but the strength and value of the Upper House. They must not become a rival to the Commons, but remain a revising and complementary institution. If its members were chosen by election, they would certainly claim equal powers with the other House—and on what grounds could these be refused ? No ; let the Peers stand on the worth of the combination of heredity and talents which the system already supplied ; for to members who were born in an atmosphere of political interests and freedom from financial stringency were added, by the continual creation of new peers, the proved abilities of self-made men.

He was equally insistent that the lack of interest in political life which, in spite of the circumstances of their birth, was shown by many peers, was an advantage and not a disadvantage. He did not want a second assembly of professionals. He disliked careerists ; and a principal justification of the House of Lords was that in the main its members had no axes to grind, and when they voted they did not have to look over their shoulders wondering what effect their vote would have upon constituents. Only those of them who had political aptitude attended the majority of the debates ; the rest formed a background of common sense. " Only a small fraction of us are devoted politicians " was his way of putting it ; and he uttered the warning that if the character of this second, revising Chamber were so changed as to be filled with " determined politicians . . . who attach the same weight and importance to their own opinions as do those who sit in the House of Commons ", then " the doom of our present system of government " would have been pronounced. The main duty of the House of Lords, he said in a later speech, was to provide a check upon hasty legislation. But it was not their function to set themselves against the clear and deliberate judgment of the country.

Admitting, as he did, the important distinction between the momentary and the sustained opinion of the electorate, Lord Salisbury believed that occasions might arise for the Peers when conviction must take precedence over every other consideration. If the House of Lords convincedly believed that a certain policy was right, whatever might be the opposition to it, they must say so and risk the consequences. He once rebuked his old enemy, Lord Derby, for worrying too much about what would be thought of their action " out-of-doors ". " We have a higher responsibility to keep in view," he exclaimed. " I do not believe that the reputation, the character or the influence of any man or body of men is to be preserved by perpetually thinking of what may be thought of their conduct out-of-doors. The motto of the Lords should be ' Be Just, and fear not ' ; and be sure that if you fear you will not long be just."

The Bill of 1888 did not really go further than to confirm and regularize the state of affairs that normally existed ; for the creation of his fifty life members would only have authorized the selection for one generation of eminent men who were likely in any case to be raised to the peerage. Partly for that reason, but mainly because of the congestion of parliamentary business, he dropped the Bill. The dry, impartial words of the *Annual Register* of 1887 were equally applicable to 1888 : " The Opposition has shown itself strong enough and sufficiently united to render all general legislation hopeless."

No doubt Lord Salisbury was also prompted to leave the subject alone by the immense pressure of work that fell upon himself personally when he had once more assumed the double burden of premiership and Foreign Office. In practice the two-Chamber, two-Party system was working well. There was nothing wrong with the British Constitution, he considered. He must devote most of his time and all his energies to efficient administration and sound policy. And for the fulfilment of both tasks his first care was to attend to the national defences. The country had clearly approved of his stand against Churchill in the matter of the Defence estimates. Now, in 1888, he submitted the question of naval strength to thorough re-examination ; and after full consultation with his First Lord and the Admirals, he established the principle of the two-Power standard—which was destined to be maintained until the First World War, and which then immensely contributed to the defeat of Germany ; but it is interesting to note than when the " standard of strength equivalent to that of the combined forces of the next two biggest navies " was adopted, the two unnamed Powers were France and Russia. A five-year programme was drawn up and was almost completed by the time Lord Salisbury left office. To supervise its execution a Naval Committee of the Cabinet was set up in 1890 ; and parliamentary sanction to the programme was obtained by a Naval Defence Act, which was designed to place it outside the scope of Party politics.

4

A happy event with which no Party bitterness was allowed to interfere was the commemoration of Queen Victoria's fiftieth year on the throne (June 21). The celebrations of 1887 were indeed very modest compared with, for instance, the ceremony of King George V's twenty-five years of reign just half a century later. But the Golden Jubilee afforded the opportunity, which Lord Salisbury was quick to take, of one notable innovation. He invited representatives of the Queen's overseas territories to come to London for it ; and in April and May of that year was assembled the first Colonial Conference in British history. It was a very unpretentious affair. The four representatives of Canada, Australasia, South Africa and Newfoundland were received by Lord Salisbury, but the actual discussions were held under the chairmanship of the Secretary of State for the Colonies, Sir Henry Holland (later 1st Viscount Knutsford). For lack of suitable accommodation elsewhere they met in the Foreign Office. Very little was said about their deliberations at the time ; nothing was published as to results. Even *The Times* was silent, except to record the movements of the delegates and the speeches they made at the Mansion House banquet which was given in their honour. And on that occasion the oratory came mainly from native-born Britons—from the Lord Mayor himself, from Sir Henry Holland, from Mr. Stanhope (Holland's predecessor at the Colonial Office), from Lord Rosebery, from the Speaker of the House of Commons, and from Lord Lorne. Sir Alexander Campbell, for Canada, and Mr. Deakin, for Australia, delivered suitable but uninformative replies. Sir Henry Holland gave the only indication of the progress made at the discussions when he said that " he believed this Conference had been successful " and hinted that the defence of the Empire had formed the chief topic of discussion ; but he prided himself that " nothing had come out in the Press ".

On May 4 the four Colonial representatives were received by Queen Victoria at Windsor, when an address was read by Sir Robert Thorburn, the Premier of Newfoundland. He said that during the fifty years of Her Majesty's reign " Your Colonial subjects of European descent have increased from two million to nine million, those of Asiatic race in your Indian Empire from 96 to 254 million, and those of other peoples from two to seven million." The Queen replied briefly and graciously, and the ceremony was over.

At one of the last meetings held in Downing Street a Resolution was passed recommending that an addition should be made to the Royal title to describe Her Majesty as Queen not only of the United Kingdom but also " of the Colonies and Dependencies thereof ". From such a small beginning has one of the world's greatest political institutions grown.

The seeds sown in the secret talks of 1887 were not long in producing a first shoot. In the following year Mr. Stanhope, now at the War Office, introduced and passed a Bill for combined preparation for the sea-defences of the Empire, known as the Imperial Defence Act.

Representatives from India, too, came to London for the Jubilee celebrations. Kuch Behar and his Maharani attended in person, but most of the Princes, and the municipalities of Calcutta and Bombay, sent deputations. The Queen held a special reception for her Indian subjects on June 30.

Lord Salisbury's readiness to innovate was further shown at the end of this same year (November, 1887) when he authorized a special mission to proceed to Pope Leo XIII in order to " express on behalf of Queen Victoria a sense of the courtesy and honour paid to Her Majesty " by a recent " congratulatory mission " from the Vatican. The Duke of Norfolk conducted with a dignity worthy of its setting the first official British visit to the Vatican in the capital of United Italy.

(continued)

PARTITION OF AFRICA

Although Lord Salisbury, as was his wont, had delegated the day-to-day business of the first Colonial Conference to his trusted lieutenants, Stanhope and Holland, just as in domestic legislation he had left the detailed work to Balfour, Hicks Beach and Ritchie, he had still been too tied up with home affairs to pay as much attention as he would have liked to foreign and imperial policy. The Cabinet crisis over Churchill's resignation, the unstable position of a government dependent upon Liberal votes, the preference of those Liberals for keeping clear of imperial commitments, the fact that the Foreign Office was not in his own hands, and above all the distracting tactics of the Irish in London and across the channel, made it impossible for him to master the details of African problems ; and he would not direct a policy until his mind had grasped all the facts and his instinct was free to play upon them. This did not happen till early in the year 1887. By that time public opinion was showing pretty clearly that it preferred the ideas of Disraeli, J. R. Seeley and J. A. Froude to those of the Liberal Little Englanders. Disraeli's first burst of imperialism had indeed proved too impulsive for the British people and they had turned him out after the Afghan and Zulu wars. Then Gladstone's caution and withdrawals were too much for them in the opposite sense, and they dropped him after his tragic failure in the Sudan. Lord Salisbury now came forward as the reluctant imperialist, and the mood exactly suited public taste.

Africa had become the focus of world affairs. Its vast empty spaces attracted the attention and covetousness of several European States ; the questions thus raised were mainly dealt with by the Colonial Department of the Foreign Office ; and it suited Lord Salisbury very well to find himself constitutionally responsible for Africa in his negotiations with the interested foreign Chanceries. Because " l'appétit vient en mangeant ", the British public became more and more imperialist the more territory they swallowed; and Lord Salisbury, at first sharing their sentiments and going along with them, later had to hold in check some headstrong jingoism. He spoke contemptuously of those who " wished to go everywhere and take everything ". Nevertheless it fell to his lot to preside over and direct the most urgent impulse of expansion that had moved the people of England since the days of his Elizabethan ancestor—and it is a coincidence worthy to be noted that during his youth the Hakluyt Society was formed, and took its name from the famous geographer of oversea discoveries who owed so much to the powerful patronage of Sir Robert Cecil.

The scramble for Africa, as it has been called, came to a head suddenly in the 1880's. There had of course been numerous incursions of Europeans, for at least two centuries before that. But only relatively few settlements had become permanent; and there was ample room for all of them. In 1880 four countries —all western European and maritime—possessed defined territories in Africa—Britain, France, Portugal and Spain; to which should be added the Boers of Dutch origin. During the 'eighties there appeared on the scene in growing numbers Germans, Italians and Belgians. Their enterprise was fostered by their respective governments; and soon seven European governments were eagerly competing for the pastures and swamps, the forests and the veldts, the lakes and the mountains of Central Africa, East Africa and West Africa.

The greatest single cause for the political rush to Africa was the cutting of the Suez Canal, which opened up its eastern coast to European shipping, and especially to British shipping. But many other causes converged to the same broad flow of national energies. Germany and Italy had both recently achieved their unification and entertained new notions of imperial expansion. France, too, having been vanquished in the 1870–1 war, wanted to recoup herself on the other side of the Mediterranean and was encouraged by Bismarck to turn her eyes in that direction and away from Alsace and Lorraine. The astute King Leopold of Belgium saw an opportunity of gaining a vast store of wealth from the Congo, which he exploited first on his own account and then for the benefit of his country. These rival colonizers tended to establish trade monopolies; and a new incentive to Britain was the determination to create and maintain the largest possible area of free trading—free trading not only for ourselves, but for all. " We only desire territory," said Lord Salisbury, " because we desire commercial freedom."

And there were other reasons besides the lure of empire and the bait of riches. The great dark continent held more unexplored secrets than any other part of the globe ; and sheer love of adventure drew travellers of every kind to its hidden interior. In Victorian Britain there was such a super abundance of energy seeking an outlet overseas that, as Lord Salisbury put it, " the number of our adventurers is far larger than that of our rivals ". Englishmen, indeed, expressed themselves in those days more easily in action than in words. Nor was it by any means only love of adventure that impelled them. Many went out on expeditions of scientific discovery ; others were moved by an ardent missionary zeal ; many more by the desire to promote business. Among the missionaries, Scotsmen were particularly prominent in the early stages. The best known and the greatest had been David Livingstone, both missionary and explorer— predominantly missionary in his first journey, predominantly explorer in the later ones ; he was the first man to cross the great continent on foot from coast to coast. Other notable explorers of the nineteenth century were Mungo Park, Clapperton, Laing, Kirk, Grant and Cameron—all Scots—Burton and Speke, and H. M. Stanley ; the fervent road-builder James Stevenson, Baker and a hundred more, whose achievements stirred the imagination of the home public ; and their foreign counterparts roused similar feelings of pride and territorial appetite in their own countries.

One motive—and the noblest—for the new interest of Europeans in things African remains to be mentioned—the new humanitarianism which vowed to bring to an end the wholesale trade in slaves. Britain, which had been the greatest offender, had by now become the protagonist for its abolition ; and in this Lord Salisbury was the true representative of his country's temper. He was no evangelist, for all his deep religious faith ; but " his only crusading impulse ", to quote his daughter's phrase, was totally to suppress this accursed traffic. It was he who made the proposal to summon an international anti-slave-trade conference in Brussels in 1889 ; and throughout these years of territorial ambitions the motive of civilizing Africa was ever present in his mind, though hardly ever on his lips. Once in a speech he referred to the irruption of European standards into Africa as " a great force—a great civilizing, Christianizing force " ; and another time he called upon a reluctant Chancellor of the Exchequer to provide the means to do " a great work of civilization without hope of economic reward ". More often he was content to refer to his business of staking out land-claims with a detached, deprecatory, semi-humorous irony ; but all the same, whereas Georgian England had gone to West Africa to make slaves, Victorian England went to East Africa to set slaves free ; and it cannot be doubted that Lord Salisbury took over vast territories in East and Central Africa in a spirit " of service rather than of seizure ".

That the work then begun has indeed been a civilizing enterprise is surely proved by comparison of the status of native-born Africans today with their habits and institutions of the middle of last century. The conditions then prevailing can best be studied in the numerous accounts written by contemporary travellers. Away from the coastal strips the natives lived innocent of clothing or of calendars, without wheeled transport, unencumbered by any kind of currency, though beads might supplement the process of barter. The first explorers found whole tribes sunk in the degradation of cruel rites and institutional injustice, witch-craft, blood-lust, slaughter of enemies, domestic slavery, unheeded suffering, sloth and disease. Semi-starvation alternated with Gargantuan feasts, sometimes of the flesh of conquered neighbours—the lagoon dwellers of Southern Nigeria, for instance, subsisted almost entirely on fish, but indulged, as Mr. Douglas Woodruff writes,* in occasional cannibalism for a change of diet. The rich resources of the soil lay entirely undeveloped, and the boundaries of the various tribes were only vaguely defined ; so when an explorer made a " treaty " with any one of them it was quite uncertain over how wide a region its terms should apply. Moreover, the native potentates were always inclined to sign a better treaty with the next comer if he offered more handsome presents than his forerunner ; and the terms of one bargain often contradicted those of the other. Usually the European government took over territory on the strength of a more or less friendly arrangement with the local rulers, and then had to admit, when

* In *The Story of the British Colonial Empire.*

negotiations began with a rival colonizing State, that its occupation, besides being vague in extent, was without foundation in international law. The British Government, as the first-comer, was often the principal sufferer from this legal disadvantage ; and the need to regulate its position in many places where British dominance had hitherto not been disputed was one of Lord Salisbury's major preoccupations.

At that time the opinion was widely held that empire and democracy were incompatible ; and in assuming official responsibility for fresh territories Lord Salisbury was often perplexed as to how it should be ruled. No man was less of a theorist than he, and no man ever wanted less to impose his views upon others, even upon the Africans of that day. He had no preconceptions about suitable constitutions for them. So, functional above everything, he made it his simple precept to adapt local institutions, purging them of barbarities, mitigating harshness, and substituting laws based on ethical justice. He gave first importance to just and efficient administration. That was to be the main purpose of the British Colonial Service. He instinctively adopted the principle of trusteeship. It came naturally to mind, for his position at home implanted in him the sense of responsibility for others. The white races must not only be masters but, more vitally and lastingly, trustees for the development of a black civilization. He said once in the House of Lords : " They [the native races] will gradually acquire their own proper civilization without any interference on our part." They would, and should, ever remain true to type and to climatic environment.

Lord Salisbury carried his dislike of " interference " so far, that he was occasionally annoyed by the work of missionaries. The native rulers had their own long-established primitive system of laws ; and so opposed was he to any disintegrating influences that he doubted the benefits of conversions. The indigenous systems did supply discipline and enforce authority. Conversions to Christianity inevitably inclined the converts to question the wisdom of their pagan chief and undermined their allegiance to him ; his control over them was weakened ; and it was through him that the British Resident had to govern. The last thing Lord Salisbury desired was to throw Africans off their balance and leave them detribalized, their loyalties confused. And perhaps he did not really believe that a good head-hunter could be converted into a good Christian in the space of a few months or even a few years.

2

After the Napoleonic Wars the British nation had with careless magnanimity restored conquered colonies to their former owners ; and before Lord Salisbury took charge, successive governments, Conservative and Liberal, had as often wished to renounce as to extend their rule over African territories. These were regarded, as Mr. Jorrocks regarded children, as " certain cares and werry uncertain comforts ". And until quite recent times they were the unhealthiest places in the world, full of malaria, flies, vermin, poisonous plants, waterless scrub, where snakes were dangerous and savage animals abounded. We may indeed regret that the Government of the day would not endorse the action of the naval captain who hoisted the Union Jack over Mombasa in 1824 ; but we cannot be altogether surprised when we consider its inaccessibility before the great canal was cut, and the hostility of man and climate. Less reasonable had been some of Gladstone's emphatic renunciations. Besides his declaration about quitting Egypt, which was a thorn in the side of Lord Salisbury throughout the African negotiations with France, and his withdrawal from the Transvaal, he had let the Germans into the area which became known as German South-West Africa. There an adventurous and disreputable trader, by name Lüderitz, founded a factory and hoisted the German imperial flag at Angra Pequena in 1883. Negotiations followed in London. On the British side Pauncefote at the Foreign Office, Derby, the ex-Conservative Colonial Secretary, and Granville, Foreign Secretary, seem to have taken it in turns to deal with the matter, and to have been casual about passing on their information. On the German side the negotiations were taken in hand by Count Herbert Bismarck ; he was specially sent to London by his father—whose abruptness he imitated but whose abilities he did not possess. Derby did not believe that Germany was a colonizing nation. Granville did not know what the Liberal Party wanted—most of them certainly had no desire to possess Damaraland, the northern part of the disputed area. Some German traders had settled there ; and the Berlin Government enquired whether the British Government would undertake to protect them against hostile tribes. The Colonial Secretary, inspired by his Chief's zeal for economy, cabled to the Cape Government, which ardently desired that the whole region should come under British control. Would Cape Colony bear the cost of administering this south-west province ? The Cape Government was in parlous domestic straits and could or would not commit its successor. The extent of the commitment would be as vague as was the extent of the area to be taken over. Negotiations dawdled on between Capetown, London and Berlin, until early in 1884 Prince Bismarck brought them to an abrupt end by proclaiming the annexation of the whole coast, excepting only Walfisch Bay. There the British flag had been hoisted some six years before by Sir Bartle Frere, Governor of the Cape Colony, who wished and who would have been able, had he been allowed, to annex the whole region.

Farther north, too, along the western bulge of Africa, adventurous Germans were pushing into the interior. A commercial traveller, Dr. Nachtigall, asked and obtained facilities from Gladstone's Government to report upon the " state of German commerce " in the Bight of Guinea and up the Niger river. Furnished with British papers and hospitably entertained by British consuls, he made treaties with several native chiefs and planted the German flag in their territories.

Before he resigned Gladstone reacted to these encroachments on British prior claims by granting a royal charter to the Niger Company and by confirming British Agreements with the Nigerian chiefs of the Oil Rivers. In South Central Africa he established British rule in Bechuanaland ; and in East Africa he made treaties with the tribes of the Somali coast and with the Sultan who ruled over Sokotra. The establishment of British control over this island, lying off the Horn of Africa about 600 miles east of Aden, was effected in April, 1886, during Gladstone's six-month Ministry when Rosebery was Foreign Secretary ; and it was mainly due to this Liberal-Imperialist that a granite bastion, which, if fortified by a foreign rival, would have threatened the sea-route from the Straits of Bab el Mandeb to Bombay, was secured for Britain. Three days after the treaty with its Sultan had been signed a German man-o'-war called to enquire to whom the island belonged. The newly delivered Union Jack was immediately hoisted, and the man-o'-war moved on.

In eastern Africa, as in the south-west and west, Germany was showing readiness to step into any shoes left lying about by Britain. Prince Bismarck had at first turned his face against colonial adventures. But public opinion in the new Reich was becoming elated by the performances of its traders and buccaneers, and the old Chancellor, because it suited his policy of challenging England and pleasing France, had suddenly entered the colonial lists ; and in October, 1884, he proposed that all European Powers interested in Africa should meet in Berlin to establish an agreed procedure for making annexations legal. A flag had too often been proved to be not only a portable but also a removable mark of sovereignty.

Two regions where agreement was specially desirable were the lower waters of the Congo and of the Niger rivers—perhaps for the reason that the precise course of neither stream had yet been properly mapped. At the Conference the British Government exerted its influence to secure the principle of freedom of navigation not only on these two but on all the rivers of Africa. The vaguely known area of the Congo, stretching across to Lake Victoria Nyanza, was declared to be an independent and neutral State ; resolutions were passed deprecating the sale to African natives of intoxicating liquors ; and the participating Governments stringently bound themselves to suppress the traffic in slaves wherever their authority extended. As for the establishment of sovereignty, the operative qualification was to be that the occupation should be effectual (February, 1885).

In that same year Britain and Germany appointed an East African boundary commission to report how far inland the " island empire " of the Sultan of Zanzibar might properly be said to extend. The British representative, Lt.-Col. Horatio Herbert Kitchener, was later to win greater fame a little farther north. A Frenchman joined the Commission ; they agreed upon the Sultan's limit of empire and, for their own countries, upon " spheres of influence "—a phrase which was destined to become very fashionable during the next quarter of a century.

3

So when Lord Salisbury was free to turn to the colonial scene he found Germany already well established there ; and Italy was making her first appearance upon it. Italian troops had occupied Assab and the port of Massowah on the Red Sea and were building up her position in the coastal area now known as Eritrea. One of Lord Salisbury's first acts therefore was to grant a royal charter to the British East Africa Company, which had been founded in the previous year by Sir William Mackinnon and Sir John Kirk ; and next year, 1889, he also chartered the British South Africa Company, of which Cecil Rhodes was the moving spirit, and which was working its way up into South Central Africa. These semi-independent Companies traded, built roads, civilized, and organized minor military expeditions ; but Lord Salisbury maintained absolute political control. No political agreement was valid without the endorsement of the Foreign Office.

It is not possible in a one-volume work to follow the vast bulk of Lord Salisbury's official business during this multiparous Ministry of 1886 to 1892. The great massifs of Africa are not more studded with humps than was Lord Salisbury's mountainous labour with high points of policy. He was engaged with all the Great Powers, colonial or non-colonial, including the United States—with whom he had a most vexatious dispute over the seal-fisheries of the Behring Sea. And the danger of a war between the Great Powers breaking out was never very far away. In March, 1887, we find him writing to Mr. Alfred Austin : " I believe that England *will* fight in company with Austria, Turkey and Italy in case Russia should obtain the Balkan States, and it is well the Tsar should know it—though, of course, in a parliamentary State, we can give no specific promises." What might be described as quasi-committal Agreements were in fact contrived in that year by secret exchange of Notes between the Foreign Office on the one hand and the Italian and Austro-Hungarian Governments on the other, their object being the maintenance of the *status quo* in the Mediterranean. But in all such cases Lord Salisbury consistently refused to give positive assurances. He expressed to the Italian ambassador, Count Corti, his desire " to co-operate heartily " in the Mediterreanean. But the character of that co-operation could only be decided " when the occasion for it arises, according to the circumstances of the case ". He explained to Queen Victoria : " We could not, under any circumstances, take part in an aggressive war against France "—to whom the Triple Alliance of Germany,

Austria-Hungary and Italy, concluded in 1882, appeared as a standing threat ; and next year, in a private letter to the British chargé-d'affaires in Rome, he wrote :

The papers are full of suggestions that we have undertaken to protect the coasts of Italy and Austria in case of a war with France. It is needless to say no such covenant exists (February 17, 1888).

In the exchange of Notes with Italy and Austria-Hungary on December 12, 1887, Lord Salisbury had in fact re-affirmed his adherence to the terms of the secret assurances of co-operation which he had given in February of the same year.   But the importance of these secret Agreements has sometimes been exaggerated, so it seems appropriate to give the reasoned opinion upon their purport of Lord Sanderson, expressed by him in 1902, when he was Permanent Under-Secretary at the Foreign Office and when Lord Salisbury had just retired from politics.   Lord Sanderson wrote :

The general result of these communications is, I think, to show that the Agreement between Great Britain and Italy in 1887 did not go farther than a confidential declaration of a community of policy in regard to the maintenance of the *status quo* and the balance of power on the shores of the Mediterranean and adjacent seas, without pledging either country to any particular measures in support of that policy. . . . The same may be said of the Agreement between Great Britain and Austria, which is in fact a complement of that between Great Britain and Italy and closely resembles it.

(Signed) T. H. Sanderson.

In the letter to Mr. Kennedy from which a quotation has already been made (and which is reproduced in facsimile at the end of this book) Lord Salisbury also wrote :

" My impression of what is going on in Abyssinia is not favourable to the Italians.   It looks as if—after a good deal of blustering—they would have to withdraw their troops before anything was done on account of the climate."   In this surmise he was mistaken.   Italy maintained her claims on the Abyssinian Government, and next year (1889) proclaimed a Protectorate over the dominions of the Negus, which nominally remained in force until her army was defeated at Adowa in 1896.   In the same year, 1889, Italy also proclaimed a Protectorate over Somaliland ; and in 1891, Lord Salisbury signed an Agreement with the Rome Government defining (on paper) the boundaries of Italian Somaliland and Eritrea.

The panorama of problems which he had to deal with extended indeed from Europe over all Africa—Mashonaland to Egypt and the Congo to Zanzibar—and from Central Asia to the islands of the New Hebrides and Samoa ; and he himself negotiated or personally directed the negotiations in every case. In Africa he was critically engaged successively and/or simultaneously with Germany, with Portugal, and again at a later stage, and more dangerously, with France a second time. We will follow the course only of those negotiations in which his statesmanship was most typically displayed.

4

The Germans had outpaced us in South-West Africa and out-witted us in West Africa. In East Africa it was a rather different story. Their missionary and medical activities had been efficient and disinterested ; and their traders and explorers, though avowedly desirous of seeing their Vaterland politically pre-dominant, were only engaging in this international game of grab on equal terms with their rivals, though perhaps with rather greater resort to subterfuge. The dominant native power in those parts was Zanzibar. Its Arabian Sultanate had been established in the island for about half a century and had extended its rule into the interior of Africa for the purpose of seizing slaves. Sir Bartle Frere and Sir John Kirk in turn took measures, through the Sultans, to check the traffic ; and when England and Germany settled their respective spheres on the mainland Germany proceeded to purchase outright the northern part of the mainland coast, whereas the British Government continued to recognize the legal rights of the Sultan over a southerly ten-mile coastal strip of British East Africa, where an Arab population lived. The officials of the British Chartered Company managed the administration pretty well, but the Germans were soon in difficulties with the Moslem Arabs who also inhabited part of their coastal strip. The local British were not unnaturally critical of the bungling German administrators and the two white races were soon at loggerheads. The troubles on the German side of the demarcation-line might spread to the northern, where not only English but also Indian interests were at stake. And at the northern end of the British zone the Italians were quarrelling with the Sultan over the lease of the port of Kismayu which was valuable to Italian Somaliland.

The remedy for these disorders seemed quite clear to the governments in Berlin and Rome—bombard Zanzibar; and the German ambassador in London, Count Hatzfeldt, urged that England should at least join them in a blockade of the island for the sake of white solidarity. Lord Salisbury demurred. He wished to maintain the principles of common action with the other Great Powers. But he considered that the demands which both Prince Bismarck and Signor Crispi were making upon the Sultan were outrageous—" in cynical and arrogant injustice it is impossible to surpass Crispi's policy towards Zanzibar ". Moreover, the partly-informed opinion of the British people made them if anything more indignant than the Prime Minister with the two other Powers; and collaboration with them at this moment became intensely unpopular. Lord Salisbury never-theless adhered firmly to his policy. The British navy must remain in touch with the warships of Italy and Germany—not to share in a bombardment but jointly to abstain from bom-bardment. The Germans wanted " to efface " the Sultan; Crispi was longing " to exact what he pleased from him ". The Arab insurrection along the coast continued throughout the winter of 1888–9, and Lord Salisbury's middle course was made all the more difficult because the Sultan was ready to come to terms with Britain at any moment and resented her associating herself with the hostile Powers. Lord Salisbury held to it all the same; and in the spring he had the satisfaction of seeing the whole local German administration overhauled; the revolt died down; Berlin no longer talked of bombardment; and Italy was not prepared to bombard alone.

In the meantime several bold explorers and prospectors of different nationalities were keenly aware of the existence of a vast and unappropriated equatorial region beyond the lands ever claimed even by the Sultan of Zanzibar—the half-discovered country on the confines of German East Africa, British East Africa, the Congo and the Sudan; and into those regions they plunged. One of them, Emin Pasha, an Austrian who had entered the Egyptian Service, lost himself, and others eagerly set out to find him. One was H. M. Stanley; another Karl Peters, a German, who however subsequently frankly admitted that he was out on a " large-scale colonial political enterprise ". Peters was the greatest of German explorers. He had founded the German East African empire; and in the spring of this year 1889 he set out to expand its frontiers. Without the authority of his Government he marched inland with his small force of Zanzibar Arabs through marshes and deserts thought to be impenetrable, reached Uganda, signed a treaty with its king, and persuaded him to declare the country a German Protectorate. This did not prevent the same monarch from agreeing with the pioneers of the British East Africa Company, who arrived just a month afterwards, to place his domain under the protection of the Union Jack; but Peters, oblivious of the double-dealing, continued his self-imposed task of extending the German sphere to the upper waters of the Nile, struck a north-easterly course behind the British East Africa territory, and emerged in 1890 through Abyssinian mountains and bush on to the Red Sea—only to learn that his daring, ambitious and apparently successful enterprise had been checkmated in London.

Lord Salisbury and Bismarck were two heavy-weight boxers who frequently sparred, but neither wished to knock the other out; and they had been having a stiff bout of diplomatic boxing while Peters was on his journey in the jungle. When that intrepid explorer was choosing to make his return trek behind the British settlement in East Africa he was exploiting the German doctrine of the hinterland, which in German eyes had a double and contradictory meaning—one was, in Lord Salisbury's words, that " if you have possessions in an uncivilized country, you have a right to extend those possessions to an unlimited distance inland from the sea "; and the other was, that if you marched round behind another country's settlement, planting flags as you went, you cut off that country from the interior. On the strength of this theory Bismarck was claiming the territory both south and north of Lake Tanganyika, which would have carried Germany across what is now Northern Rhodesia and Uganda, respectively, to abut on the Belgian Congo. The Berlin Government already entertained the notion that the Belgian colony, and even more probably some of the Portuguese colonies, might be obtainable by purchase; and by linking up directly with the Congo the Reich might hope some day to possess a broad band of Africa from east coast to west. On the other hand, in England Cecil Rhodes's grandiose scheme of a uniformly British route from the Cape to Cairo had caught hold of the public imagination. Lord Salisbury was inclined to belittle the idea ; but he also opposed the project of any other country, be it Germany, Portugal or France, to establish the east–west corridor. Interminable arguments passed between London and Berlin about the rights of " previous settlement " and the claims to the hinterland. H. M. Stanley had also been exploring in Central Africa ; he had strong views about what should not be given up, and he expressed them strongly. Large crowds heard him and applauded him. Lord Salisbury seldom took any notice of popular agitation ; but he knew what the country owed to men like Rhodes and Stanley, and he rebutted in a public speech, albeit with wonted sarcasm, the charge that the British Government was surrendering " vast forests and tremendous mountains " which Mr. Stanley had " offered to the British public ".

The main cause of friction, in the Prime Minister's view, was the undefined status of the " empire " of Zanzibar. Its " imbecile Sultan ", as Lord Salisbury called him, was nominally independent, and could therefore be allured with all kinds of propositions by foreign governments, and at the same time he was in practice more or less under British tutelage, and his sins of omission or commission were visited upon us. And in the Arab settlements along the coast, as well as in the island of Zanzibar, pro-German and pro-French parties arose in opposition to the pro-English. The suppression of the lucrative slave-trade was not yet complete and in its later stages was seriously hampered by these pro- and anti-rivalries. It was necessary to establish, legally and finally, British supremacy in Zanzibar. A second place where Lord Salisbury felt that a firm stand was necessary was on the uppermost waters of the Nile. The explorers Speke and Grant had tracked its source from the Victoria Nyanza, and Lord Salisbury ever had in mind the vital importance of controlling its flow for the prosperity of Egypt, which the illustrious administrative ability of Lord Cromer was re-establishing. Finally, there was a long correspondence on the subject of the coastal region of Witu. The Germans had got there first ; but it lay well within the more northerly section of the seaboard, which was agreed to be a British sphere.

By May, 1890, Lord Salisbury had come to the conclusion that in order to obtain satisfaction upon these essentials he must be prepared to give Germany a substantial *quid pro quo*.

Heligoland had been mentioned in an Anglo-German conversation in the previous year by Lord Salisbury's free-lance ally, Joseph Chamberlain, whose imperialism was growing as fast as his radicalism evaporated. He was greatly vexed that his former Liberal colleagues had missed the chance of taking over South-West Africa; and in a conversation with Herbert Bismarck he threw out the suggestion that Germany might hand over Angra Pequena and take Heligoland in exchange. The proposal excited the young Emperor William II to a state of considerable enthusiasm, but it left Lord Salisbury cold. " We are absolutely opposed " to the cession of Heligoland, he wrote privately to Sir Edward Malet, the British ambassador in Berlin. That was in July, 1889. The idea of giving up the island for the gaining of the waste lands of South-West Africa seemed preposterous to Lord Salisbury. Now, however, the stake was bigger. The lands which Rhodes and Jameson were penetrating to the north of the Boer Republics were another matter altogether. And the upper waters of the Nile could be safeguarded, and all the friction about Zanzibar eliminated, by sacrificing the island-counter to Germany. And what real good was Heligoland to England ?

So on May 13, 1890, he offered Heligoland to Count Hatzfeldt and named his price.

The German ambassador thought the price was rather high. But fortunately the Kaiser, who was already dreaming of a large German navy and of becoming the " Admiral of the Atlantic ", passionately desired to possess it, and brushed aside the qualms of his advisers, who since March of this year no longer included the great Bismarck. The cutting of the Kiel canal had been begun ; and the German Press had been given its head over Heligoland. Nothing could suit Lord Salisbury better. After some weeks of negotiation with Hatzfeldt he found that only one point in his African demands could not be gained—that was the prevention of contact of German with Belgian territory north of Lake Tanganyika. Even the suggestion of a British north–

south strip five miles wide connecting Uganda with the northern end of the lake had to be abandoned. On all his other points Lord Salisbury got what he wanted. It still remained to gain the approval of his Cabinet, of Parliament, and of Queen Victoria.

All three were reluctant to agree to the cession of Heligoland. The Admiralty admitted that strategically this " untenable advanced base " was valueless to Britain ; but the curious point was made that the island was a splendid recruiting ground for the Royal Navy. Its inhabitants were described as born seamen, favourable to the British connexion, and splendid material for bluejackets. At the Cabinet of June 3 the majority of its members expressed " much anxiety ". All the same, by June 10 the Prime Minister was able to report to the Queen that its members " unanimously and earnestly " recommended the proposed arrangement to Her Majesty. Queen Victoria still did not like it. It caused her " great uneasiness " that any of her possessions should be " bartered away ". Lord Salisbury's reply was a succinctly worded appeal to royal reason. The island was really a Hanoverian possession, and its retention by the British Crown in 1814 seemed to have been more or less accidental. It had never been fortified, either by Hanover or England. If it were retained by us and still not fortified—and he could not see the House of Commons voting money for the purpose—it would fall into Germany's hands the day she declared war on us. If we ever quarrelled with her, we would merely " incur a humilia-tion " at the outset—and a war with Germany was the only con-tingency in which any possible danger could arise from it. There was no prospect that this case would be made a precedent, " for there is no possible case like it ". Queen Victoria reluctantly gave way ; and the Agreement was signed in Berlin by Sir Edward Malet and General von Caprivi on July 1, 1890.

On the whole the public received the news of the exchange more calmly than the politicians. In both Houses of Parliament there was some keen criticism. The cession of Heligoland alone, however, required parliamentary sanction, and this was obtained without undue difficulty. The Prime Minister gave a full and fair account of the whole transaction, and was only slightly embarrassed when Lord Rosebery asked him whether the wishes of the island's loyal inhabitants had been ascertained ? The Prime Minister replied that they had been ascertained " confidentially ". On being further questioned how public feelings could be confidentially examined he maintained an awkward silence.

In any case he had now secured in international law the rights of his country over Zanzibar, Uganda (without its southern part), and the whole of British East Africa—now known as Kenya —from the boundaries of the Sudan and Abyssinia to beyond the disputed township of Witu in the south. He had made a better bargain than his contemporary critics understood.

The title to Uganda, though lost to Germany, was only vaguely asserted by Britain ; and in the very next year we find the East Africa Company in process of withdrawing from it for lack of capital. Lord Salisbury did not officially oppose the withdrawal ; but he pressed for the construction of a railway to facilitate effectual occupation ; and the growing awareness of public opinion, led by *The Times*, to the importance of Central Africa as a link in the north–south line of communication, together with the protests of missionaries and the Anti-Slavery Society, provoked both the Company and the Government into standing firm instead of walking out. It was left to Lord Rosebery, strongly backed by Cecil Rhodes at the Cape, to carry the proclamation of a British Protectorate over Uganda through a Liberal Cabinet which was at first critical and hostile.

Lord Salisbury's settlement of 1890 did not pass without a challenge from another quarter. King Leopold of Belgium was always lying on the flank of an Anglo-German or an Anglo-French dispute ; and he now attempted to push the Congo frontier eastward to the Nile. In this case Lord Salisbury found an unexpected ally in the French, who had their own project for establishing a west–east band of territory across Africa and were hampered by the Belgian claim. Lord Salisbury lodged a British protest in Brussels ; and under the new imperialism of the French Republic a succession of Paris Governments took the matter up with King Leopold, whose project was abandoned in a Franco-Belgian Agreement drawn up after Lord Salisbury's resignation.

5

But between these years of 1887 and 1892 it was French rivalry, not French help, with which Lord Salisbury became the better acquainted. Successive French Governments, as already mentioned, had the general encouragement of Bismarck to go deeper into Africa, and from her Mediterranean seaboard France pushed her claims southward to meet the settlements which her pioneers had established along the western and southern littoral of the West African bulge. In pursuit of this policy France had made Agreements with the Spaniards, with the Portuguese and with the Germans, who in 1886 had joined her in supporting a Portuguese claim to link East with West Africa—the ambition successively nursed by Portugal, Germany and France, and, thanks to Lord Salisbury, achieved by none.

By the late 'eighties France had not only established a common hinterland for Senegal, Guinea and the Ivory Coast, but had thereby excluded the intervening colonies of their rivals from the interior. Lord Salisbury had few preconceived notions about what he wanted in Africa ; but one of them was to lessen French influence in Egypt and the Nile Valley ; and for that reason he was inclined to be acquiescent about the claims of France on the opposite side of Africa. Incidents had begun to multiply along the west coast in places where colony abutted on colony. Rival flags were hoisted by one team and pulled down by another ; French raiders destroyed villages which were by way of being under British protection ; and Englishmen supported an Arab chief who was obnoxious to the French. So Lord Salisbury decided that the time had come for official intervention. The Paris Government was also of that opinion. The first task of each was to produce maps which presented with some degree of accuracy the rivers and swamps, the forests and the sand-hills of regions unknown to cartographers ; and a peculiar difficulty of the negotiations which followed was that the maps of the two Governments often differed, and were continually being altered, as reports came in from the zealous official surveyors of either party to the dispute.

The best description of Lord Salisbury's policy is that which he himself afterwards gave of it in a long despatch to Lord Dufferin when the latter had just become British ambassador in Paris. " The colonial policy of Great Britain and France in West Africa ", he wrote, " has been widely different." France, he continued, had been pressing inland from the Senegal coast in order to establish herself on the Upper Niger, and had attained this object by a large and constant expenditure and by a succession of military expeditions. " She has overcome by arms the Almamy Ahmadoo . . . and she is now at war with the Almamy Samadu, who lays claims to vast regions in the interior. Great Britain, on the other hand, has adopted the policy of advance by commercial enterprise. She has not attempted to compete with the military operations of her neighbour."

He then recalls to the ambassador the findings of a strong Committee of the House of Commons in 1865, which had come to the conclusion that it would be best to withdraw altogether from West Africa " except probably Sierra Leone " ; and the only British military enterprise which had been sanctioned in those parts was " the punitive expedition to Ashanti in 1873 ". Nevertheless the traders of the River Niger Company had, " without the expenditure of Imperial funds, or the sacrifice of the life of a single British soldier, placed under the protection of the Crown the whole of the Lower, and a great portion of the Central, Niger. . . . The Company had concluded important treaties with several Sultans " ; and it had established an effective administration and maintained security by the agency of a police force and patrolling steamers. Lord Salisbury concludes his despatch by insisting on the benefits of free trade. " British commercial interests are of special importance ; and wherever Great Britain improves and opens up the interior French trade will profit equally." But French agreements had tended to obtain exclusive commercial privileges for France. " No effort should be spared to obtain an understanding that in territories under French influence there shall be no differential treatment " ; and agreement must be sought on tariffs.*

One of the last acts of Lord Salisbury before he left office in July, 1892, was to have this despatch published ; but it left untold his own successful efforts to regularize the positions of the two rivals in West Africa. These took official form in the Agreements of 1889 and 1890. They delimited the frontiers of the British colonies of Gambia, Sierra Leone and the Gold Coast ; and the British Government recognized " the sphere of influence of France to the south of her Mediterranean possession, up to a line from Say on the Niger to Barruwa on Lake Chad ". This allowed to France almost the whole of the Sahara.

* The despatch is dated Foreign Office, March 30, 1892.

France had also obtained a free hand in Madagascar in return for her consent to have nothing more to do with Zanzibar. Bearing in mind the growing anti-clericalism of French politics, however, Lord Salisbury insisted on a clause which secured the freedom of missionary work in both islands. How well his foresight was justified was shown a decade later when General Galliéni, a raging anti-clerical, became Governor of Madagascar, and the French bishop there owed it to this clause that he—and the missionaries, French and British—were not expelled. The final Agreement of August 5, 1890, which embodies the missionary clause and defines the respective spheres of influence of the two countries, is drawn up in two unilateral and identical " Declarations ", one in English and the other in French, the first being signed by Lord Salisbury and the second by M. Waddington. Neither the Anglo-German nor the Anglo-Portuguese Agreement was executed in this unusual form. Possibly it was adopted because in this case the two negotiators were disposing of a vast territory, which was in effective occupation of neither of the States they represented.

Lord Salisbury considered that on the whole he had made a good bargain in having diverted French energies from the north-east to the north-west of the continent. But the vast Sahara territory handed over to France roused the criticism of a public whose imperialism grew more rapidly than its knowledge ; and even *The Times* remarked that Lord Salisbury had displayed " a large liberality ". The Prime Minister answered his critics in two speeches, the first at the Mansion House, and the next, five days later, in the House of Lords. At the Mansion House he allowed full play to his self-deprecatory, caustic humour. He said that he and the French ambassador, M. Waddington, had been engaged in " what perhaps to a satirist may seem the somewhat unprofitable task of drawing lines upon maps where no human foot has ever trod. We have been giving away mountains and rivers and lakes to each other, but we have only been hindered by the small impediment that we never knew exactly where those mountains and rivers and lakes were." They had, all the same, removed possible causes of quarrel ; and he added a comment on the changed conditions of negotiation. " Nowadays," he said, " the electric telegraph has made a terrible change in the politics of the world. In the days of Lord Clive or Warren Hastings if a Dutchman and an Englishman came to blows in the Eastern seas, nobody heard of it for six months, and then everybody felt that it was too antiquated a circumstance to form the subject of a diplomatic correspondence."

He laid the Agreement on the table of the House of Lords on August 11, and again took the line that its importance had been overrated. Having briefly summarized its provisions he seemed to be concluding a rather tired end-of-session speech. "I do not think I have anything else to say," he remarked— and then, unluckily, he had an afterthought. "Anyone who looks at the map," he went on, "and merely measures degrees," would perhaps conclude that France had laid claim to a very considerable stretch of country. "But it is necessary to judge land not merely from extent but also from value. This land is what agriculturists would call very 'light' land, that is to say, it is the desert of Sahara. . . ."

Unfortunately M. Waddington was listening to the speech from the diplomatic gallery. He was deeply chagrined. Not only was he proud of the large acquisition of territory he had procured for France, but his Government had been exploiting his success to revive its flagging prestige. The British Prime Minister's estimate was gravely inconvenient to them. *The Times* in its leading article next morning referred to "the splendid potentialities" of the Sahara and declared that the French had obtained "a really magnificent sphere of influence". But the pained ambassador was not to be appeased by fine phrases about the Sahara's future. He sent round a reproachful note to Lord Salisbury. "No doubt the Sahara is not a garden," he wrote, "and contains, as you say, much light land; but your public reminder of the fact was, perhaps you will allow me to say, hardly necessary. You might well have left us to find it out." Lord Salisbury had nothing to say in reply; and this time he said nothing.

6

For the purpose of his diplomatic work at this time Lord Salisbury had had the walls both of the Foreign Office and his study at Hatfield strung with maps of Africa; but even that large continent by no means contained all the colonial disputes in which he found himself involved. The equatorial rivers and swamps of Africa had their counterparts in equatorial islands and lagoons in the Pacific Ocean. There in 1887 he made the experimental arrangement of a condominium with France to administer the New Hebrides, and the experiment lasted with varying degrees of mutual discomfort till 1906. Two years later German warships appeared off Samoa and seemed likely to rush the island as they had rushed New Guinea some years before. American vessels were on the spot, and only a violent storm which sank the ships of both countries prevented an almost certain battle. (The one British ship there navigated its way out into the open sea.) Here too Lord Salisbury sought a solution by joint rule, but the arrangement worked even worse than in the New Hebrides and was succeeded in 1899 by a partition which placed the rivals in separate groups of islands. One of his so-called graceful concessions was a renunciation of British interest in the small group of the Savage Islands. " I hope you have not annexed the Savage Islands," he wrote to the Colonial Secretary on October 12, 1888 ; " they are clearly in the German ' sphere of influence '."

Though always conciliatory to Germany, as Queen Victoria wished him to be, he steadily rejected the idea of alliance with her which Bismarck once more proposed in 1889. At the beginning of that year the Chancellor instructed Count Hatzfeldt to approach Lord Salisbury, and later he sent his son Herbert to support the ambassador. Bismarck's obvious desire was that the treaty should be directed against France. Lord Salisbury's response was suavely but firmly negative. He must " have time for ripe consideration ". It was " inopportune " at the moment because his parliamentary majority might collapse. According to Count Herbert Bismarck Lord Salisbury also said : " We live no longer, alas, in Pitt's times ; the aristocracy governed then, and we were able to form an active policy which made England after the Congress of Vienna the richest and most respected Power in Europe. Now democracy is on top, and with it the personal and Party system, which reduces every British Government to absolute dependence on the *aura popularis*." However genuinely the above sentiments may have been his own, Lord Salisbury was obviously using the argument which he knew would have most effect with Prince Bismarck, to whom the English Party system was a bugbear. The Bismarcks, father and son, in any case expressed their full understanding of the British Prime Minister's unfortunate impotence and had to be satisfied with his assurance that " the only course possible meanwhile is to go hand in hand ".

Without doubt Lord Salisbury was influenced in his attitude by his profound distrust of the young Emperor William II who had recently ascended the throne. Nothing so antagonized Lord Salisbury as insincerity and pose, and he immediately discerned these glaring defects in the Kaiser. He said to his friend Lord George Hamilton, who as First Lord of the Admiralty met the Kaiser every time he came to England, that he had never met a man " with such a double tongue " ; and that he looked upon him as " the most dangerous enemy we have in Europe ". These remarks, it is true, were made in 1891, two years after the rejection of Bismarck's overtures. But Lord Salisbury's distrust was present from the earliest days of the Prince's manhood. He knew from Queen Victoria exactly what the Queen's own daughter thought about her most unnatural son ; and when the Kaiser committed the vainglorious and egregious folly of dismissing the old Chancellor (in March, 1890), Lord Salisbury watched with dismay his character deteriorating from year to year under the baneful spell of unchecked power.

7

Before recounting the course of the most critical colonial quarrel which Lord Salisbury had with any Power during this six-year period of African rivalries—that with Portugal, which lasted from early in 1889 until June, 1891—a further brief allusion should be made to the Anti-Slave-trade Conference held in Brussels in 1889–90. Owing its convocation to the initiative of Lord Salisbury, it was attended by more States than had ever before met in an assembly of similar importance. In his speech at the Guildhall on November 9 the Prime Minister said : " I do not think any Conference in the history of the world has ever yet met for the purpose of promoting a matter of pure humanity and goodwill." Heartfelt support for outlawing the trade by international law was the one public profession he could make of his latent idealism. And it was idealism supported by action ; for no delegation was more active than the British in adapting the rules of maritime law to the business of suppression.

It marked, he said, a great advance in general European opinion. " Many nations are anxious to join with us, and, whenever we have persuaded all nations to lay aside the various difficulties which prevent them from co-operating, the great object we have in view will be attained." He could add that an immediate result of Zanzibar's coming entirely under British protection was that its Sultan had decreed that all who entered his dominions, or were born within them, should be free—and Zanzibar had been one of the " richest markets of the trade ". In the same speech he told how successful Egypt had been in repulsing, with British help, the inroads of enemies from the slave-hunting south. He also related the improvements, effected in that country, in the application of the law and in the restoration of its finances ; and he said significantly : " We shall pursue our task until the end." The City audience received this affirmation with loud and prolonged cheering (November 9, 1889). In the same year at the Mansion House he had declared that Britain had undertaken not to abandon Egypt " till she was capable of maintaining her own Government in the face of foreign and domestic foes ". Three years later he penned a postscript which had better be recorded here.* " If Egypt goes on improving as rapidly as she is improving now, the time will come when she will insist on being free from Turkey, or England, or anybody else. But I imagine that the result is some distance off ; much too far to enter into our calculations for the conduct of present diplomacy." Even in these almost casual sentences of an unofficial letter Lord Salisbury is revealed as true prophet and statesman.

8

In the settlement of Africa, Portugal had led the world. As long ago as in the fifteenth century Prince Henry the Navigator (whose mother was an Englishwoman) had won fame by the discoveries along the west coast of the continent, and the great Vasco da Gama had doubled the Cape ; and by 1650 Portuguese colonizers by much outnumbered other Europeans. They occupied a length of the littoral south of the Congo river and a longer strip on the east coast from north of the Equator to south of the Tropic of Capricorn. Missionary enterprise followed

* The letter was addressed to Sir Clare Ford, who had lately been appointed ambassador in Turkey—to whom Egypt still nominally belonged.

discovery, trade followed conversions, and afterwards came the grosser traffic in slaves. One way and another the people of Portugal became immersed in Africa long before their rivals, a point which has to be borne in mind when considering the disputes between England and Portugal in the 1880's. By that time Portugal, having lost her South American dominion, had subsided to a relatively lower place among world Powers ; and by a familiar paradox of human nature the influence upon the temper of a nation which is exercised by past grandeur only seems to be increased by present weakness.

When therefore other countries began to stake out claims in Africa it was inevitable that the Portuguese Government should not only look to its own possessions there but should try to extend them. And when it thought about extension, the most obvious project was to unite Angola on the west coast with Portuguese East Africa. The claim could be supported by indicating that the link already existed geographically in the Zambesi river ; and Portuguese settlers had in fact advanced up its banks for a considerable distance. Regarding Britain as her most formidable rival, Portugal in 1886 turned to France and Germany, and persuaded both these countries, as already mentioned, to agree to a partition of Central Africa allotting to Portugal all the intervening territory between her eastern and western colonies. A map was officially published in Lisbon showing in Portuguese colouring a broad belt of country right across the continent, covering the whole basin of the Zambesi river.

Lord Salisbury lodged a vigorous protest. Domestic difficulties, which have in all countries been the decisive handicap to imperial energy, prevented him for a while from doing more. But he knew that Cecil Rhodes at the Cape was working out the large scheme of a federal South Africa under the British flag. Almost the only things which that remarkable son of a Hertfordshire clergyman and the owner of Hatfield had in common were belief in the Empire and love of the classics. More than once Lord Salisbury had to hold Rhodes in check, as when in 1888 the latter desired the Imperial Government to proclaim a Protectorate over the northern territories beyond the Transvaal. But there cannot be many instances of two men so naturally uncongenial to one another jointly contributing on so large a scale to the same ambitious enterprise. At home this dreamer and schemer contributed to the Liberal and Irish Parties' funds ; from the Cape he built his railways and pursued his imperial purposes with the whole vast financial resources which his genius had accumulated in the diamond mines. Lord Salisbury acquiesced in his scheming ; and now, though he could not yet himself proclaim a Protectorate, he refused to agree to the Portuguese trans-continental plan which would have meant that the whole of Matabeleland, of Mashonaland and Nyasaland would be forever lost to Britain. He knew that Rhodes was also facing the hostility of the Boer populations of the Orange Free State and the Transvaal, whose aim was a Dutch South African Republic. Rhodes had nevertheless achieved many successes with his South Africa Company ; and now in 1889, as already recorded, Lord Salisbury vested the company with a Royal Charter. Henceforward it enjoyed official support and had a monopoly of administration, with the obligation to promote a " civilizing as well as a commercial development ", the Home Government reserving the right of supervision over its policy towards the natives and exclusive control of its external relations.

And at this moment official support became indispensable to the Company ; for towards the end of the year 1889 news reached Capetown and London that a Portuguese explorer, Major Serpa Pinto, had marched up from the Mozambique coast and established himself in the Shiré country south of Lake Nyasa. There he had demanded the submission of the tribe known as the Makololo on the Upper Zambesi. When the tribesmen refused, he shot down large numbers of them. The Makololo had previously placed themselves under British protection. There had been many recent scuffles between local Portuguese and British officials and settlers. But this was graver, and had a direct bearing upon the Portuguese claim to expand from east to west and the British claim to spread south and north. It became an international incident, a matter of prestige, and a cause of excitement and anger in Lisbon and London.

Lord Salisbury immediately pointed out that in the region now reached by Serpa Pinto were numerous British settlers, and that neither there nor elsewhere along the projected east–west Zambesi band of territory had Portugal established anything that could be remotely likened to an administration. She had neither officials nor settlers there, whereas British subjects from the Cape and from the home country were arriving every day. The Portuguese Government retorted that would-be settlers from Portugal were also proceeding thither, that the 1886 Agreements with France and with Germany gave her a legal international title to the region, and that in any case her claim rested upon discoveries made 250 years before and upon occupation for a considerable period. Lord Salisbury was infuriated by these " seventeenth-century " revendications. " Lord Salisbury utterly rejects the archæological arguments of the Portuguese," he wrote to Queen Victoria ; they claimed " half Africa on the supposed cession to them in 1630 of the Empire of Monomotapa, of which event Lord Salisbury can find no account whatever in this country. Nor does he consider that the existence of ruined forts proves any claim, but rather the contrary, since it shows the power that built these forts to have abandoned them."

Recriminatory despatches sped by telegraph and by Queen's messenger between London and Lisbon, without either side convincing the other. Nothing had been settled when at the end of the year (on December 26) Lord Salisbury was struck down by influenza, which that year made its first recognized onslaught on the British public and was known as Russian influenza. For two days he was prostrated ; and it was just at that moment that public excitement and reciprocal official obstinacy were making the situation serious. On the third day of his malady, when he was still very ill, he insisted, to the dismay of his physician,* on having all the relevant Red Boxes brought to his bedroom, and according to Lady Gwendolen Cecil he dictated his despatches to secretaries or, failing them, to members of his family, from his bed. Fortunately he had, with his usual forethought, already discussed and decided with his Cabinet what measures should be taken if the Portuguese Government remained obdurate ; so his direction of policy from a sickbed was not so discretionary as it looked—the advantage of being his own Prime Minister was invaluable to him.

On January 6, 1890—the eleventh day of his illness—the political crisis was reached. He prepared the British minister in Lisbon for drastic action. He instructed him to make no irritating demands on the Portuguese Government for apologies or reparations, but to

* Dr. (later Sir) Douglas Powell.

231

insist upon the evacuation of territory occupied by British subjects or native tribes under British protection ; and if this demand was refused he was to leave Lisbon. Two days later Lord Salisbury was at pains to show that this was no ultimatum. " The private telegrams of the 6th [i.e. those relating to shutting up the Legation] were only intended to warn you privately and are not instructions to be acted upon." On the same day Mr. Petre was authorized to spend another £100 on secret service.

Lord Salisbury was beginning to suspect that the truth about what was happening inland from Mozambique was being concealed from Mr. Petre ; the bland assurances which now fell from the lips of the Portuguese Foreign Minister, Senhor Barros Gomez, did not tally with what the British Government heard from its own agent in Mozambique. On January 4 the consul there had reported that Major Serpa Pinto's expedition remained in the Shiré, though its leader had returned to Mozambique— and Pinto had himself boasted to the consul not only that his men remained *in situ* but that " Andrade was organizing an expedition into Mashonaland ". The Foreign Minister had informed Mr. Petre that Serpa Pinto had been ordered to withdraw. But what kind of withdrawal was this ? Lisbon was speaking with one voice, Mozambique with another.

So two days later, on January 10, more explicit instructions went from Hatfield to the British Legation in Lisbon. " The guarantee H.M. Government require is an order to the Governor of Mozambique to withdraw all Portuguese troops that are on the Shiré or in Makololo country or in Mashonaland." Unless such an order was sent and a copy shown to Mr. Petre " H.M. Government must consider the Portuguese assurances as illusory ". And if a satisfactory reply to this demand had not been received at the Legation by 10 p.m. on Saturday, January 11, Mr. Petre was to telegraph to the *Enchantress*, then at Vigo, to come to Lisbon and take him and his staff away, leaving the archives in charge of the acting consul.

This was still technically no ultimatum, and there was no word, official or private, of war. The idea of despatching an ultimatum in form repelled Lord Salisbury. He was keenly aware all the time that Portugal was England's oldest ally, and that she was the weaker nation. He had denounced in scathing language in his *Quarterly Review* articles the tendency of the

British Government of the day to grovel to the strong and bully the helpless ; and here he was himself, while well on the way to settle disputes amicably with Germany and France, using threatening language to Portugal. But he was convinced that the Portuguese Government, itself in great difficulties with its own public, was trading on his reluctance to go to extremes and on her own helplessness. Moreover, there was an element of chicanery in the divergence between the instructions sent from Lisbon and their effect, or lack of effect, in Africa. This suspicion of chicanery was confirmed on January 11 by another message from the British agent in Mozambique, who reported that the official Gazette there stated that " Katunga and other Mokololos had sworn allegiance " and that " the Governor had declared to them that the Portuguese reassumed possession of the entire Shiré Basin and region, and will administrate [sic] them henceforth."

On that same day, January 11, the ultimatum went forth. Even now there was no mention of war ; but a broad hint of it was given by another method. The Channel fleet was ordered to sail for the coast of Portugal under sealed orders ; and at 8 a.m. on that very morning the whole of the British squadron in East African waters left Zanzibar and headed south. Both of these naval moves became quickly known in Lisbon, as they were meant to be. But the only actual threat in the language to be used by Mr. Petre was still that he and his Legation would quit—that is to say, that diplomatic relations would be broken off. The British demands remained unaltered—Portuguese forces, officials " and expeditions of any kind whatever " must be recalled from the territory claimed by Britain, and H.B.M.'s Government " desired and insisted " that urgent instructions be forwith despatched to the Governor of Mozambique to withdraw all Portuguese forces " on Shiré and the territories of the Makololo and Mashonaland ".

The Portuguese Government yielded. The necessary telegram was sent in the terms prescribed ; and a copy was handed to Petre. Street rioting broke out in Lisbon and other towns. The windows of the British Legation were broken. The coat of arms was wrenched from its stand at the British Consulate and carried derisively round the streets of the Capital. The mob also broke the windows of Senhor Barros Gomez. The

Foreign Minister courteously apologized to the British envoy next day ; and he considered his own broken windows as having justified his stubborn support of Pinto until he was " in presence of an imminent rupture with Great Britain ".

The issue was decided, but frontiers had not yet been exactly agreed ; and their definition and demarcation proved to be a protracted and vexatious business. Lord Salisbury declined the Portuguese suggestion of arbitration, because the dispute between the two countries was not a question of fact and because there was no system of law or admitted code on which a ruling could be based. The only accepted criterion was that which had been agreed upon at Brussels—effectual occupation. As to whose occupation was the most effectual there might indeed have been much argument, especially in the Shiré. But for the rest of the disputed territory there was little doubt that British settlers were the most numerous and the better organized, while the Portuguese claim, Lord Salisbury repeated, " rested almost entirely upon transactions which are said to have passed two or three centuries ago ". " Great Britain ", he added, " rests her claim almost entirely upon the title that has been established by the self-sacrifice and successful exertions of British missionaries and traders within living memory." The invocation of missionaries in this connexion is a little surprising, and their inclusion in the argument possibly owed something to the undoubted state of extreme fatigue to which the Prime Minister–Foreign Secretary had by now been reduced. Having never ceased attending to his duties, though he had had to summon the Cabinet to meet in his London house, he had not yet been able to shake off the after-effects of the influenza which struck him down in December. Now at last, in April, he escaped to the Riviera. Even there, however, he continued to supervise the negotiations with Portugal. By August a Convention was agreed by the two Governments.

The Cortes rejected the Convention out of hand, and once more the outlook was black. But the British pioneers and traders in the disputed regions went ahead, and before the end of the year a distracted Portuguese Government was calling upon Lord Salisbury to hold back his own people and re-establish the boundaries of the abortive August Convention, some of which had been overstepped. Lord Salisbury minded this request less

234

than the argument which was advanced at the same time from Lisbon that unless Portugal were better treated Dom Carlos might lose his throne. That plea annoyed him as much as it worried Queen Victoria—one of her royal relations even persuaded her that the gallant young Queen-Regent of Spain would also be driven out if the monarchy disappeared from Lisbon. Lord Salisbury nevertheless briskly responded that " we do not think it worth while to submit to unreasonable terms for the sake -of preventing the Lisbon populace from overthrowing the Portuguese Monarchy ".

This mild form of blackmail failed to shake Lord Salisbury; and one Foreign Minister succeeded another in Lisbon. Meanwhile the agents of the Royal South African Company were pushing outwards in all directions and consolidating as they went. Lord Salisbury insisted to Rhodes upon his restoring one considerable area—that of Macequece. Macequece (or Massi-Kessi) lay on the route to Beira, and Colonel Heyman was successfully leading a small expedition thither when he was halted by orders from the High Commissioner in Capetown. Lord Salisbury would allow no designs on territory that had long been effectively occupied and administered by any other nation. But delay was worsening the situation for Portugal ; and in May, 1891, her Government announced its readiness to sign. This time the Cortes ratified the agreement, and the Treaty was signed by Petre (now Sir George Petre) and Conde de Valbom in Lisbon on June 11, 1891.

Britain acquired the whole of those splendid, spacious lands which extended from the Boer Republics northward as far as Lake Tanganyika and from Portuguese East Africa across to Angola in the west. The new territories were named Rhodesia, and their southern capital was called Salisbury. Thus was appropriately celebrated the distant and not always harmonious collaboration of the two men who in their different ways had brought this ample addition to the Empire ; their names are now forever linked, in closer partnership than during their lifetime, in one of the most English of the African States.

9

Lord Salisbury's period of office was drawing to its close. It included many happenings which there has been no room to record ; but, in spite of the important Local Government and Free Education Acts, his 1886–92 Ministry will be remembered mainly for its Chief's colonial achievements. Lord Salisbury would have been the last man to think of his as a one-man Ministry ; and perhaps it was in fact just that perfectly balanced combination which has a master mind directing the whole policy of the Government with the loyal support of competent, disinterested, and large-hearted men of State. They did their own jobs quietly and unobtrusively ; and in the dominant issue of the day, the colonization of Africa, they believed in the civilizing work which awaited the white races in Africa and in the special vocation of Englishmen for that work. Their faith has perhaps been better expressed by a modern French writer * than they could have expressed it themselves : " L'Angleterre prouve par l'exemple ce qu'est la civilization. Au lieu d'en chercher sans cesse une théorie, elle se contente de la pratiquer." Lord Salisbury's untheoretic methods have stood the test of time. Even in the case of Heligoland, about whose cession his critics have been the most vehement at that time and since, his decision stands ; although twice in the last thirty years Germany has lain prostrate in defeat we have not attempted to recover the island. Another attribute of his statesmanship which lent permanence to his settlements was this readiness to take into his calculations the just claims of others—as he had at Macequece. No mere grabbing, no ruthless exploitations can be charged against him.

Seldom, if ever, in peacetime has a Ministry so enhanced the position of Britain in Europe and the world as did Lord Salisbury's second Administration. It has claims to be regarded as the greatest warless Ministry in British history, at least in so far as international affairs are concerned. But, true to its favourite principle of the swing of the pendulum, the British electorate turned it out of office in the General Election of 1892. The voting gave the Conservatives a slight majority of seats over the Liberal Party. But the Irish again held the balance as in 1885, and Lord Salisbury was outvoted at the first trial of strength on August 11. He resigned immediately and retired to spend a quiet autumn at Hatfield, without resentment, and consoled by the conviction that a period of rest was overdue and would not be prolonged.

* M. André Thérive in the *Figaro*, July 19, 1938.

BALCONY AND RECESS IN LORD SALISBURY'S STUDY

By kind permission of the 5th Marquess of Salisbury

OUT OF OFFICE—HOME HABITS—LEADING THE OPPOSITION

In the brilliant address which Lord Rosebery delivered, when he unveiled the bust of Lord Salisbury in the Oxford Union, he questioned whether Lord Salisbury appreciated " the magnificent palace which he had inherited at Hatfield " ; and in another sentence in the same speech he gave the answer : " The luxuries purchased by wealth, the swell of honours and titles . . . were dross to him." Lord Salisbury was born to these things. He accepted them. He did not scorn them ; but he was supremely indifferent to them. Asceticism, indeed, he once described as " a most deadly error " ; but few men in the position of Lord Salisbury have so sincerely taken to heart the words of St. John : " Love not the world neither the things that are in the world." For him it was literally true that a man's life consisteth not in the abundance of the things he possesseth. Hatfield was just a good place to live in ; and he made it serve him well. It was far enough from London to be rural and restful ; it was near enough for him to keep his finger on the pulse of public affairs. He subordinated its amenities to his requirements ; and one of his needs, since he did so much official work at home, was to have a safe place for his confidential papers. In his study, therefore, on the ground floor of the east wing, he built an alcove into the wall some six feet above floor-level. It was approached by a miniature gallery ; and the gallery itself could only be reached by a small ladder, which was removed every night. Within this recessed alcove were a number of labelled pigeon-holes ; there, behind a solid locked door, his most secret documents lay secluded from inquisitive eyes. And into his broad leather-topped writing-table he had two slits cut, on the right side and on the left, each like the mouth of a pillar box, opening into the two top side-drawers. Into the one, of which only he possessed the key, all his incoming letters were dropped ; into the other, of which the footman also had a key, he dropped his outgoing mail. So his correspondence never littered his table ;

and early or late he could attend to it or lock it up, and none of it would be disturbed—even by the most efficient housemaid ; nor was anything likely to spill over to the floor, for in his time the surface of the desk was bounded by a low rail. In the corner of the room nearest to the writing-desk he had a small spiral staircase constructed, which led down into the laboratory where he sought diversion from affairs of State ; even in the room itself there was a large window-cupboard where he kept retorts and other of his scientific accessories. These, and the bookshelves, gave the measure of his private interests. The books in this room were mainly about science and theology and botany—a work on the " Grasses of Scotland " still bears witness to the thoroughness of his earlier studies in this department of knowledge.

His classical and historical tomes he kept in the large library in the west wing of the house. But he had pocket editions of many of the classics, which he liked to take away with him on his holidays. He especially enjoyed reading the Greek dramatists. He did not care for poetry, though he read Pope and Dryden, and greatly relished Goethe's *Faust*—which, like the Greek works, he read in the original language. Of novelists Scott and Jane Austen were his favourites. He would now and again pick up a " shilling shocker ", and could be seen in the corner of one of his clubs reading the best French novels of his day. At home he had a large collection of books on the French Revolution. The theatre afforded him only an occasional diversion. He preferred to see a Shakespeare play, but in his younger days the comic operas of Offenbach held a great attraction for him.

Lord Salisbury was about 6 feet 4 inches in height and large in proportion. He therefore chose, from a dozen available ones, his sitting-room and bedroom on the ground floor ; and his bulk also prompted him to make a novel bath for himself, into and out of which he could walk easily on three or four steps, as in a swimming-pool, without clambering. He had a lift built to carry him up to the first floor, where the drawing-room, as some who were present have told me, shook as with a minor seismic disturbance when he entered it. All his gadgets, it will be noticed, served a practical purpose, and enabled him to devote every ounce of his vital energy to his work.

It was still his one happiness in life to sit at the head of the big dining-room table with his family round him. His sons, even after they were married and had children, were encouraged still to regard Hatfield as home. Lady Salisbury expected all her grandchildren to gather yearly round her Christmas tree. And at dinner, over the port, for which Lord Salisbury had a fine palate, he would still be an enlivening, humorous, caustic conversationalist and renew, for maturer minds, his role of guide and kindly critic which he had played in the eager adolescent discussions of ten years before. But more frequently now he and Lady Salisbury presided in the state dining-room, filled with the celebrities of the day. Political leaders of both Parties, kings, courtiers and clerics were bidden at the weekends. Mr. Gladstone came, and Lord Crewe and other eminent Liberals ; all his own colleagues in turn ; young Winston Churchill ; the Prince and Princess of Wales ; Royalties and semi-Royalties from all over Europe—of whom there were many; the Shah of Persia ; the great Li-Hung-Chang of China ; and county neighbours too. Lord George Hamilton tells the story of a dinner-party at which a smart young politician and a rather rustic squire were present, and a sharp discussion arose between them, in the course of which the younger man accused the older of being a Philistine. He used the expression more than once, and at last the exasperated country gentleman, for whom Lord Salisbury had regard, testily exclaimed, " I don't know what you mean by a Philistine." " Don't you ? " interposed Lord Salisbury. " A Philistine is a gentleman who is annoyed by the jawbone of an ass." The bumptious young man dried up.

Lord Salisbury still took exercise regularly, often before breakfast, in a constant but vain endeavour to diminish his girth ; and on his walks preferred to be accompanied by a member of the family or a congenial guest. Archbishop Lang, then Dean of Divinity at Magdalen College, Oxford, spent a weekend at Hatfield when Archbishop Benson and Dr. Talbot were also guests ; and one day he, Lang, and Dr. Talbot went out walking with their host. The talk was about religious education ; and the future Archbishop of Canterbury noted in his diary that night : " The Conservative leader took a characteristically pessimistic view," and added : " There is, with all his goodness, too much of the pride of intellect about him." * Perhaps the young

* J. G. Lockhart, *Cosmo Gordon Lang*, p. 113.

clergyman foresaw the course that religious education was to take less clearly than the old statesman ; but certainly Lord Salisbury was pessimistic about the future of religion. " We have been warned," he said to Lady Gwendolen Cecil, apparently about this time, " that Christianity could know no neutrality, and history has verified the warning. It is incapable of co-existing permanently with a civilization which it does not inspire ; and any such as came into contact with it withered. How much more must this be so with one that had been formed under its auspices and had subsequently rejected it. Such a society must inevitably perish." His voice and manner, his daughter writes, grew heavily oppressed as he spoke, and his eyes seemed to be filled with a vision of gloom.

Solitude was as much a necessity to him as it had been for his hero the younger Pitt. His cloistral habit of mind was so great that even in his double-doored study he did not feel sufficiently insulated, and he liked to go down to a secluded part of the grounds beside the river Lea, known as the Vineyard, which was cut off from the rest of the park by a stone wall and locked gate. Here he was *incomunicado*. His " impulses of deeper birth " sprang to mind in such moments. For he still had an intensely strong inner life, though by now he had externalized himself. In public he had become a public man. But this compelling desire for secrecy, for solitude, for communing with himself still subsisted. When he was seeing the world through " that inward eye which is the bliss of solitude " then, he felt, he was really *living* ; so far from being slowed-down, life was quickened.

And quite apart from his longing to ponder undisturbed he had in extreme form the Victorian's craving to be regarded as a private gentleman. He avoided rather than sought personal contacts. He headed off the determined attempts of hero-hunters like Ouida to meet him ; he had no desire whatever to make new acquaintances ; he met so many persons in the ordinary course ; and he preferred that each one should count. Even friends who greeted him with excessive heartiness produced a nervous recoil. When crowds invaded the park on Bank Holidays —for even in those days the house and grounds were thrown open to the public—Lord Salisbury and the family would take refuge in Miller's wood and picnic there.

To the outside world he had become by this time something

of an institution ; but to those who gained access to him he was very human—gravely courteous, sometimes surprisingly unreserved, always friendly and helpful. His grand-niece, Mrs. Blanche Dugdale, relates * how once, when she was a little girl, she caught him unawares alone in the summer drawing-room, " his great head sunk in thought, his thick grey beard spread over his vast chest ". With the temerity of extreme youthfulness she asked him : " Uncle Robert, what is the Plimsoll line ? " He slowly raised his head, gazed at her with his serene eyes, and explained all about the topic which was filling the newspapers.

Only to strangers was he painfully ungenial. At dinner, on the rare occasions when he dined out now, he might speak no word to the lady at his side if he did not know her or was not interested in her. He combined with his genuine lowliness of spirit a certain patrician arrogance. And he expected to be obeyed, even in the smallest matter. A story is still told of him at Hatfield which illustrates this. His tastes were more frugal than Lady Salisbury's, who was inclined to magnificence in her entertaining. He kept an extraordinarily close eye on the household accounts ; and one day he came to the conclusion that too many pineapples were being grown and consumed at Hatfield. So he issued an order that no more were to be grown. Some time afterwards he saw a multitude of them in one of the conservatories. He went in, pulled them up and threw the lot away.

His need of exercise drove him to tricycling when, in his declining years, long walks became too fatiguing. Then he had most of the paths in the nearer part of the park asphalted. For this recreation he used to wear a kind of sombrero hat and a special short sleeveless cloak with a hole in the middle, which, together with his greying beard, rather gave him the appearance of a cowled and hirsute monk. If he intended to ride up and down some of the more sloping paths he would order his under-coachman to come with him. The young " tiger " helped to push him up the hills, and then, coming down again, he would as often as not be told to " jump up behind " and stand on the axle. The " tiger " rested his hands on the Prime Minister's broad shoulders, and the two of them would sail downhill together with the front wheel rocking and zigzagging over the irregularities of the asphalt.

* *Family Homespun*, p. 108.

Perhaps Hatfield made, and unmade, him. Its ease, its soothing serenity, the clock-like regularity of service from a score of footmen and another score of maidservants, with steward and housekeeper taking even the ordering of them off the hands of Lord and Lady Salisbury. . . . He was waited upon all his life. Never was this leisure abused. . . . No shadow of wastefulness or sloth or dissipation marred the high standard of honour, of *noblesse oblige*, of daily work, of duty to one's neighbour and the never-failing sense of responsibility. The comforts were easements of tasks that had to be done, not mere superfluities. But by long habit they became necessaries. The well-being and contentment of Hatfield rendered possible that continuing inflow of ideas and outflow of action which made him the great man he was ; but the solid comforts of Victorianism ended by enveloping him. He seemed now to see no further than his own estates except when he raised his eyes to look overseas at foreign countries, at Ireland, or the Empire . . . there was a hiatus in between . . . hardship dwelt there, discontent, sordid slums . . . he did not seem to notice them . . . but in those slums was being bred a new Socialist movement which would rise up and smite his Party after he was gone.

Lord Salisbury used some of the unaccustomed leisure of these three years to speak in public on the scientific subjects which had so long occupied his spare moments at home. Did space allow, a whole chapter could be devoted to his chemistry and to his correlation of science, religion and politics. About this time he gave the reasons why he preferred chemistry to other branches of science. Astronomy, he said, was largely composed " of the science of things as they probably are " ; and geology " of the science of things as they probably were ". But chemistry is " the science of things as they actually are at the present time ". Chemistry was indeed very much more than a hobby to him. His researches in it had both expressed and further developed the natural attributes and processes of his mind. He liked to mix different elements so as to form certain definite compounds ; such and such mixtures produced such and such results, which he could vary by varying the constituents. And as he sat and watched his test-tubes he must often have mused upon the human and national motives and interests which, mixed in differing proportions, were likely to produce foreseeable results. He observed the transforming processes all the way from known facts and tendencies to ultimate consequences. He carried the method of the laboratory into politics. He studied human nature and national characters, he perceived motives, and he anticipated —and was able to influence—the political issue. Though so often accused of being " inhuman " and devoid of psychological insight, he was uncommonly skilful, as we have seen, at managing men. He watched them dispassionately, as he watched his test-tubes. He took full account of the relevant motives of individuals and of special characteristics of nations ; he usually calculated rightly what would be the reaction of men in specified conditions ; and he was almost infallible in his estimates of mass tendencies.

His laboratory work was taken seriously by eminent scientists of the day ; and in 1894 he was chosen to be President of the British Association, which that year met at Oxford. In his inaugural address he took the opportunity to acquaint his learned audience with his reflexions and conclusions on Darwinism. Here is its salient passage : " It is evident from the increase of heat as we descend into the earth that the earth is cooling, and we know by experiment, within certain wide limits, the rate at which its substances, the matters of which it is constituted, are found to cool. It follows that we can approximately calculate how hot it was so many million years ago. But if at any time it was hotter at the surface by 50° F. than it is now, life would then have been impossible upon the planet, and therefore we can without much difficulty fix a date before which organic life on earth cannot have existed. Basing himself on these considerations, Lord Kelvin limited the period of organic life upon the earth to a hundred million years, and Professor Tait, in a still more penurious spirit, cut that hundred down to ten. But on the other side of the account stand the claims of the geologists and biologists. They have revelled in the prodigality of the ciphers which they put at the end of the earth's hypothetical life. Long cribbed and cabined within the narrow bounds of the popular chronology, they have exulted wantonly in their new freedom. They have lavished their millions of years with the open hand of a prodigal heir indemnifying himself by present extravagance for the enforced self-denial of his youth. But it cannot be gain-said that their theories require at least all this elbow-room. If we think of that vast distance over which Darwin conducts us from the jelly-fish lying on the primeval beach to man as we know him now ; if we reflect that the prodigious change requisite to transform one into the other is made up of a chain of generations, each advancing by a minute variation from the form of its predecessor, and if we further reflect that these successive changes are so minute that in the course of our historical period—say 3,000 years—this progressive variation has not advanced by a single step perceptible to our eyes, in respect to man or the animals and plants with which man is familiar, we shall admit that for a chain of change so vast, of which the smallest link is longer than our recorded history, the biologists are making no extravagant claim when they demand at least many hundred million years for the accomplishment of the stupendous process. Of course, if the mathematicians are right, the biologists cannot have what they demand. If, for the purposes of their theory, organic life must have existed on the globe more than a hundred millions years ago, it must, under the temperature then prevailing, have existed in a state of vapour. The jelly-fish would have been dissipated in steam long before he had had a chance of displaying the advantageous variation which was to make him the ancestor of the human race." His conclusion, expressed with typical irony, shows that in the problem of the descent of man he stood, like Disraeli, on the side of the angels. Lord Kelvin and Professor Huxley were among the scientists who approved his argument ; others dissented *in toto*. At the present moment, I understand, his relation of the age of man to the cooling of the earth's crust is considered to be incorrect.

In the year before he delivered this address, he had been invited to open the overhead electric railway in Liverpool. He dilated upon the effect of scientific inventions upon the course of history. " I know no more interesting study in history," he said, " than those periods when great forces of this kind first appeared . . . when the compass came into existence and enabled Columbus to find the New World ; when gunpowder came into existence and enabled the centralized State to sweep away the vast and powerful complications of feudal times ; when the printing press came into existence and revolutionized the literary and religious condition of Christendom ; when the steam engine came into existence and produced that vast change in the relations of our populations to each other which have borne fruit in the political changes of which this generation has been conscious."

He also, of course, delivered political speeches all over the country, including Ulster. From the character and learning of Lord Salisbury it might be inferred that the speeches would be classical in diction and worthy of preservation in political anthologies. Yet they seldom appear in collections which contain the addresses of far less distinguished men. And the paradox is easily explained. Although every speech produced a passage or at least a sentence of original thought and far-reaching interest, yet, if it was spoken in the House of Lords, it was always very closely restricted to the matter in hand ; and if it was spoken in the country, he adopted a homely, disjointed style and was inclined to be repetitive. He despised rhetoric ; he wanted to have a talk with the people and take them into his confidence. A graphic account has been left by Mr. A. A. Baumann * of a speech which he heard Lord Salisbury deliver in a South London music-hall, at a slightly later date than that which we have now reached, when he had again become Prime Minister and the misdeeds of Turkey in Europe were once more engaging the attention of the diplomatic Chanceries. " The Prime Minister ", writes Mr. Baumann, " wiped his brow with the back of his hand. The familiar gesture at once put the huge audience of shy artisans at their ease. He dealt with the Balkan question. ' I have in my pocket ', said Lord Salisbury, ' a letter from the Sultan of Turkey, which I will read to you ' ; and fumbling in the breast pocket of his frock-coat he pulled out a bundle of letters, from which he selected one, and said, ' The Sultan of Turkey asks me to tell the people of England . . .' and then began to read a few words about Turkish reform. The artisans, clerks and dock labourers gasped with excitement." In the more ingenuous England of that day this patrician simplicity brought him immense, unsought popularity.

When he had left office in the late summer of 1892 Lord Salisbury had quickly escaped to his beloved châlet near Dieppe, where, it may be suspected, he relaxed more easily than at Hatfield. " I mainly employ myself in sleeping," he genially

* In *The Last Victorians*, p. 82.

exclaimed in a letter to his late Private Secretary, the Hon. S. K. McDonnell. And the rest of the letter is very characteristic. He told McDonnell that the " debt of thanks " was all on his own side, not on McDonnell's. " It did not matter to you how I discharged my duties, but it mattered very much to me how you discharged yours. That our term of office was singularly free from quarrels among friends, or party divisions, was in a large measure your work. I am very sorry our official connection is severed, though I have got very sick of office itself. Without your help it would have been unbearable long ago." Perhaps it was because he was in such a hurry to get away to Dieppe that he declined to see Lord Rosebery, who took over the Foreign Office from him. The new Foreign Secretary was naturally vexed, for, as he wrote to the Queen's Private Secretary, Sir Henry Ponsonby, he had " worked hard to make the foreign policy of this country continuous ", and he no doubt considered that a personal meeting might facilitate continuity also in the imperial field in which Lord Salisbury had laboured so successfully.

And valiantly did the forgiving Rosebery carry forward that work, in spite of the snub. In Uganda, as mentioned in the last chapter, he successfully completed the work begun by Lord Salisbury. In Egypt, too, he upheld British authority in a stubborn contest with the Khedive ; during the clash between Britain and Siam he spoke such vigorous language that Lord Salisbury, when he returned to office, found himself toning it down. Lord Rosebery's imperialism also outstripped that of his Conservative *alter ego*. He never concealed his belief that the more territory that came under British rule the better—a view that was shared by Cecil Rhodes and many others, but not, as a matter of practical politics, by Lord Salisbury.

2

The House of Lords had little but formal business to transact during the early part of the session of 1893, and its sittings usually only lasted an hour or two. But if a debate was expected, however relatively unimportant the subject, Lord Salisbury went up to London for it. One who remembers him has described him entering the Chamber, sitting down heavily in his place as the Leader of the Opposition, turning briskly about to say a word or two to colleagues at his side or behind him, then listening closely to the arguments of a Ministerial spokesman. As he became absorbed in listening his foot, or both feet, would drum a tattoo on the floor, his knees twitching vigorously up and down—sure signs, members came to realize, that he himself intended to speak. And familiar also was the way he then heaved himself up with a sideways turn, leaning massively upon one arm. He never made or used notes, however long the debate, however numerous the arguments he rose to counter. His voice was clear and mellowed, resonant without effort. According to Sir Henry Lucy, one of the first and greatest of parliamentary sketch-writers, he looked towards the Gallery as he spoke, except when he was being playfully sarcastic about a previous speaker, in which case he looked straight across the Table at the victim of his banter. Wherever he faced, his sonorous tones carried to the Press Gallery—in spite of the fact that, as Lucy narrates, he "conversed" even his longest speech, whereas Gladstone declaimed even his shortest.

When Lord Salisbury was Prime Minister and Lord Halsbury was his Lord Chancellor, he would sometimes leave the Front Bench and casually sit beside him on the Woolsack, for he valued Halsbury's counsel above most men's. He would also frequently visit the Party Headquarters in St. Stephen's, when he drove away from the Lords, and discuss news and views from the constituencies. But it never occurred to him to go round to the near-by Lobby of the House of Commons, or even to gaze down from its galleries upon the scenes of his earliest parliamentary exploits.

Though the last Parliament had been prorogued in August, 1892, the new one did not meet until January 31 the following year. The question of self-government for Ireland absorbed most of the session in the House of Commons. Mr. Gladstone introduced his second Home Rule Bill on February 13 ; and his first inimitable speech of $2\frac{1}{2}$ hours was followed by a succession of personal interventions in debate which, he being then in his 84th year, dismayed his followers, fearful for his health. Lord Randolph Churchill, after two years' absence from the House, replied with well-phrased argument but in a manner which distressed his hearers and foretold his early collapse. No fewer than 82 sittings were devoted to the Bill, which was eventually passed by 347 votes to 304—figures which showed that apart from the Irish votes there was a majority of 48 against it.

The House of Lords remained serenely indifferent to the controversial excitement "out of doors", as Lord Salisbury would have said, and the second reading of the Home Rule Bill was not taken there until September. The Leader of the Opposition delivered a devastating indictment of it on September 8. He rose about 10 p.m., and began with good-humoured taunts about the evasions and contradictions of Ministerial speakers, many of whom were indeed extremely half-hearted in their support of the Bill. Lord Ribblesdale, for example, had been almost apologetic, and Lord Salisbury took him to task. He was a " defender " who had " made a confession ". " He belongs to what may be called the noble army of confessors in this debate," Lord Salisbury continued, in an analogy which shows so well the texture of his own mind. " Confession is a very interesting element in literature. From St. Augustine to Rousseau, from Rousseau to Lord Ribblesdale (loud laughter), it is a most interesting record of the working of individual minds." He then took up one after another in ordered sequence such arguments as had been advanced by convinced advocates of the measure and countered them on religious, commercial, strategic and imperial grounds. He was especially strong, as he had always been, on the subject of the Protestant minorities scattered all over the island and not only in Ulster. You could not have a common policy for Ireland, he argued, which would please, at the most, more than three-fifths of her inhabitants. " Unity has never existed in Ireland. There has been a deep division for seven centuries." He had a lot to say about the frustration of William Pitt's policy by George III, and declared that the only possible corrective was " fusion in a large community in which such divisions would have no influence ". Even if Mr. Gladstone's Bill were passed, the Irish question would not be settled. The only possible policy was, as Mr. Gladstone had himself once declared, " Patient continuance in well-doing," or as President Lincoln had said in another connexion, " Keep on pegging away." He pointed out the fallacy of the supposed analogy with the British oversea territories advanced by some speakers, and the extreme danger of Ireland unwillingly falling into the hands of an enemy Power. In a peroration of more fervent phrases than he usually permitted himself he proclaimed : " As long as England is true to herself now or on any future occasion, if you allow this atrocious, this mean, this treacherous revolution to pass, you will be untrue to the duty which has descended to you from a splendid ancestry, you will be untrue to your highest traditions, you will be untrue to the trust that has been bequeathed to you from the past, you will be untrue to the Empire of England."

His arguments and his oratory undoubtedly expressed the feelings not only of the House of Lords but of the country. 419 peers voted against Home Rule, only 41 for it. The project was swept out of Parliament, not to return for a decade and a half. Gladstone's personal triumphs in the Commons had availed him nothing.

He did not however at once resign. Only in March of the next year, 1894, did he make way for Lord Rosebery, who was one of the more dubious friends of Home Rule and had no desire to appeal to the country on that issue. His brief and troubled premiership was more notable for Bills introduced than for Bills passed, and a casual vote on a secondary matter brought his unhappy period in No. 10 Downing Street to an end. The Liberal Party, having been disrupted by the Home Rule issue, was routed at the General Election of 1895, which gave Lord Salisbury 340 Conservatives and 71 Liberal-Unionists, with only 177 Liberals against him and 82 Irish members—who moreover were now split into Parnellites and anti-Parnellites. For the first time in his career Lord Salisbury had an unshakable majority behind him ; and the drag on his time, his attention and his energies that was Home Rule had been finally removed.

Perhaps the person who in all the country rejoiced most at the return of Lord Salisbury was Queen Victoria. Her dislike of Mr. Gladstone had spread to all Liberals who favoured Home Rule and his other Radical projects. She nourished the most extravagant distrust of him and his immediate followers. At the mere prospect of a change-over from Lord Salisbury to Mr. Gladstone in 1892 she had written to Sir Henry Ponsonby (July 26) : " The Queen cannot make up her mind to send at once for that dreadful old man (not because she has any personal dislike to him) as she utterly loathes his very dangerous politics, the language he has held, the way in which he has used every artifice to get in and whom she can neither respect nor trust." She considered his colleagues to be " greedy place-seekers who are republicans at heart " ; and she debated with herself whether to urge upon their leader " the gr^t fatigue of the position at his age ".*

However, that was all over now. Mr Gladstone had failed, as she believed he would ; and she would have her dear Lord Salisbury back again. She had at one time, it is true, thought *him* to be rather queer. He had his " peculiarities ". But he had grown out of them ; and he was now her well trusted adviser. She sometimes thought he was the best Prime Minister she had ever had . . . or perhaps Peel. . . . In any case, decidedly Lord Salisbury was a greater man than Disraeli. . . . And he was now Prime Minister again. . . . Perhaps she would never have another. . . .

* Arthur Ponsonby, *Henry Ponsonby, His Life from his Letters*, pp. 216–17.

SECRETARY OF STATE'S ROOM AT THE FOREIGN OFFICE

THE THIRD MINISTRY—FOREIGN COMPLICATIONS

Whether or not Lord Salisbury was Queen Victoria's greatest Prime Minister is a question which will be variously answered by different historians ; what is less controversial is that no Prime Minister in any reign, with the possible exceptions of Palmerston and Walpole, has in time of peace enjoyed such undisputed authority as he did during the years that immediately followed his victory at the polls in 1895.

The Separatists, as his opponents were usually classified at the time, had been routed. The Liberal Party was broken into two sections, one of which allied itself with the Conservatives and supplied valuable talent to the Cabinet. The Gladstonian remnant was impotent, their great chief having finally left the political stage he had so long adorned. Lord Salisbury's majority of 152 over all opponents was the largest any Party had commanded since the Liberals swept the country after the Reform Bill of 1832. The Leader of the Opposition, Rosebery, had dimmed by his premiership the lustre of the reputation he had gained at the Foreign Office. Lord Salisbury was without a rival. Nor was it only at home that he stood head and shoulders above his contemporaries. The once formidable Bismarck was discontentedly growling and dictating caustic reminiscences at Friedrichsruh ; gone too were the one or two other foreign statesmen who had made their mark on history at the Congress of Berlin. He was *consensu omnium* the premier statesman of Europe. As each international issue arose, " What does Salisbury say ? " was now the question to which European Chanceries wanted the answer. It was a good mark for the foreign envoy in London if he could report home an *ipsissimum verbum* of the great man. Lady Gwendolen Cecil has a ludicrous story in this connexion. She and her father were on one of their walks together, when he stepped aside into a stationer's shop, and bought a sharp-pointed wooden paper-knife which he saw in the window. In reply to a surprised question from her, he explained in all seriousness that it would be just the thing to keep himself awake with during interviews with foreign ambassadors. Some of these, it appeared, had developed a habit of asking to see him for no other reason than that their courier was departing a day or two later to their home capital. They wanted to report what Lord Salisbury had to say on current topics. Nothing bored him so much as these supererogatory interviews. He was apt to fall asleep ; so he developed a technique of fidgeting with this paper-knife and occasionally digging its point into his thigh to keep himself awake !

At home his authority had a peculiarly personal quality. It was entirely unsought ; it was, so to speak, unsubstantial. It rested upon his character and achievement rather than upon his office. The premiership, as already mentioned, gave him no official status or legal powers ; he was no longer now even First Lord of the Treasury, having yielded the post to Balfour ; his authority might, without derogation, be compared with that of another typically British institution, the M.C.C. The Marylebone Club has no legal right to legislate for cricket. Yet it not only legislates, but its rulings are implicitly obeyed throughout the cricket world. Its authority is final. Just so was Lord Salisbury's word final. Winston Churchill has recorded * that at this time " there was a tremendous air about this wise old Statesman ". He was the benevolent despot of his own Party, the unchallenged leader of the country. Never within the English Constitution had so humble a man come so near to being a dictator.

At his present age of 65 his blend of physical energy, experience and instructive judgment was at its maturest. His opinions were based on long experience, his intuitions were checked and his instincts guided and controlled. He could take his decisions rapidly and surely. The element of intuition was not then, as it is today, swamped in facts and figures. In the half-century that has passed since his day knowledge has become so very much more widespread and more technical ; statistics and exact information are broadcast daily ; the masses are far more thoroughly coached in political matters. They are consequently more critical and less ready than in Lord Salisbury's time to accept guidance unquestioningly ; the statesman's time is taken up in endless controversies and explanations. In these circum-

* *My Early Life*, p. 179.

stances instinct withers ; and leaders do not seem to feel they can rely on something within themselves. They ponder long over pros and cons. But in Lord Salisbury the old English preference of the man of action to think without verbal expression and to act without explanation was always strong ; and now we find him ever confident enough to take an instant decision, even though that decision might be a negative one. Physiologists tell us that a man's familiar work comes to be directed by reflex action without conscious reference to his brain ; and by this time Lord Salisbury's diplomatic decisions, like the touches of a master-musician on the keyboard, were made by instinct based on the experience of a lifetime.

He never had the same instinct in home affairs. There his technique was more orthodox. He listened to what others had to say. He knew that home politics was a popular art—unlike the art of diplomacy, which was essentially aristocratic before the days of total diplomacy ; and he had not got the popular touch, or any gift for showmanship. His political principles made him distrustful of legislation as the cure for social ills. But he had sufficient political elasticity to realize that democracy demanded it. And he saw that in this year 1895 the public demand for it was growing, and was giving birth to a Socialist Party. The Liberals, as *The Times* had said in one of its leading articles, had " artfully bound up " Home Rule with a revolutionary policy ; and Lord Salisbury rightly judged that it was Home Rule—separatism—that had been defeated, and not the desire for reform. " Constant revolution ", he said in his first speech in Parliament after the General Election, " is not the political food upon which the English people desire to be fed ; but changes there must be." His peroration to this speech (August 15, 1895) is little known, and should be remembered when accusations are heard against Lord Salisbury that he was indifferent to the needs of the " working man ". He said : " We may be successful or we may fail in our efforts to ameliorate the condition of the people by the social legislation we shall propose. We can only do our best and trust to a candid judgement. . . . But it is the improvement of the daily life of struggling millions and the diminution of the sorrows that so many are condemned to bear, which is the task—the blessed task—that Parliaments are called into existence to perform . . . and which

I trust henceforth all Governments will feel to be the highest, the exclusive duty, that any statesman, or advisers of the Queen, or leaders of parliamentary parties can be called upon or privileged to perform."

Like so many very sincere men, Lord Salisbury was apt to be imprecise in his language, relying upon, and expecting to be judged by, the general intention of his words, about which, in this eloquent, almost passionate peroration, there could not be the slightest doubt. But the word " exclusive " must appear to a later reader surprising, if not insincere. It might seem to suggest that foreign affairs were excluded from the purview of the Queen's advisers. Of course nothing of the kind was in Lord Salisbury's mind. The trend of the debate on that August day shows that the contention was between those who wanted revolutionary changes (as the Conservatives considered them), and those who wanted reforms within the established framework of the Constitution. Lord Salisbury wanted to exclude any tampering with the " unity of these kingdoms " (as *The Times* worded it), in any changes that were to be introduced.

It was August, it was even after August the Twelfth, and Lord Salisbury, though he was uninterested in grouse-shooting, had no intention of prolonging the session a day longer than necessary or of calling Parliament together again before the usual time of reassembly, which was February. He therefore waited till the following year before enumerating the reform measures he had in mind—and most of which he was in fact able to get into the Statute Book before the end of his Ministry. But in the meantime he was overwhelmed with a veritable thunderstorm of foreign affairs. Flash after flash broke out in all parts of the sky. Britain came within reach of war against four of the six other greatest nations within the next three years. We are apt today to think of the latter part of Queen Victoria's reign as a tranquil period of English history. It was on the contrary a time of storms and stresses, at least internationally. As Lord Rosebery discovered, " There is never a calm on the political ocean " ; and it was mainly due to the masterly helmsmanship of Lord Salisbury, who once more combined the Foreign Office with the premiership, that this country rode the storms without becoming involved in war against any major Power.

He had actually offered the Foreign Office to the Duke of Devonshire, who fortunately, as was his habit, declined active office ; and he had suggested the Home Office to the other principal Liberal-Unionist who had agreed to serve under him. Chamberlain had different ideas ; and his refusal of the Home Office was the most decisive of several reasons which made the 1895–1900 Government remembered almost exclusively for its imperial and foreign achievements. Lord Salisbury had been quick to see the genius of Joe Chamberlain and the possibility, even when he was the most Radical of mayors at Birmingham, of awakening in him an interest in the position of Britain in the world. Before Chamberlain had even left the Liberal Party, Lord Salisbury invited him to lead the British mission to U.S.A. in the Fisheries dispute between the country and Canada in 1887 ; and when the representative of Britain returned with a first-hand knowledge of the great Dominion and a charming young American bride-to-be, Lord Salisbury had invited him to dinner, and later numbered Mrs. Chamberlain among the few ladies with whom he was always ready to discuss politics. After Chamberlain's break with Gladstone, Lord Salisbury received from him a list of projected reforms which included the establishment of Labour Exchanges, cheap trains for workmen, and the municipal ownership of public houses, and adumbrated Old Age Pensions. After the Conservative victory of 1895, therefore, when Lord Salisbury knew he could count upon the support of the Liberal-Unionists, he invited the Duke of Devonshire and Joe Chamberlain to meet himself and A. J. Balfour at his house in Arlington Street for a private and preliminary allocation of Cabinet seats. Devonshire, as already mentioned, declined the Foreign Office. Chamberlain was given complete freedom of choice. He opted for the Colonial Office, then a minor post. The Prime Minister and his nephew were surprised. Lord Salisbury asked him if he would not take the Home Office. Balfour suggested the Chancellorship of the Exchequer. No ; Chamberlain wanted the Colonial Office—" in the hope ", as he noted in his diary, " of furthering closer union between them and the United Kingdom ".* J. L. Garvin calls this little conference of four men on June 24, 1895, " epoch-making ", and few will dispute the description. Had Chamberlain taken the

* J. L. Garvin, *Life of Joseph Chamberlain*, Vol. III, pp. 4 and 5.

Home Office, the Unionist Ministry of those five years might have produced many of the reforms which did not come till more than ten years later, and the Liberal landslide of 1906 might have been prevented. On the other hand, colonial development would certainly not have received the tremendous impetus which Chamberlain's administration gave to it. The British people would not so soon have been taught to " think imperially ". The Boer War might never have happened. There would certainly have been no Khaki Election in 1900.

Chamberlain had meant what he said in one of his election speeches : " We are pledged on the one hand to maintain the greatness and integrity of the Empire, and equally pledged to a policy of constructive social reform " ; and Lord Salisbury was equally sincere when he spoke so eloquently about the improvement of the daily life of struggling millions. But the truth is that the mood of the country was at the moment prevailingly imperialist. The pride, and perhaps the greed, of the people had been roused by the vast expansion of British dominion in eastern, central and western Africa and in other parts of the world ; they were more than ready to be taught to think in terms of empire ; and Lord Salisbury could justly assume, as Sir Charles Oman writes in his History of England, that the electorate had given him a mandate " to take in hand a strong imperial and colonial policy ".

So Joseph Chamberlain became Colonial Secretary and almost immediately annexed Bechuanaland—that is to say he incorporated the southern half of that territory, the part known as " British Bechuanaland ", into the colony of South Africa ; and soon afterwards he transferred the administration of Nigeria to the Colonial Office. Later he created the Kingdom of Buganda, and negotiated the transfer of the Tonga islands from German to British protection.

Lord Salisbury turned his own attention to the two inherited dilemmas of deciding what action his Government could take in China, and Armenia ; where in the one case, British missionaries and their families had been brutally massacred, and, in the other, the Christian Armenians were being persecuted by the Turks. He decided at once that in the first case he could do nothing except protest in firm but not threatening language ; and in Armenia he would continue the policy adopted by the

Rosebery Government of insisting upon proper punishment by the Porte of guilty officials—a right of interference which this country possessed under an Article of the Treaty of Berlin.

2

These were serious but politically minor affairs. On August 7 —just a week after Lord Salisbury had been confirmed in office by the General Election, and eight days before he made his speech promising social reforms—a sudden violent storm broke out under a blue Atlantic sky. The Prime Minister was unpleasantly surprised on that day to receive a long note (which covers twelve pages of Bluebook print) from Mr. Olney, President Grover Cleveland's Secretary of State. The United States Government suddenly claimed a direct interest in the boundary dispute between Venezuela and the British Colony of Guiana, which had been dragging on for many years, and which had long since caused a rupture of diplomatic relations between the South American Republic and the British Empire. Mr. Olney's note asserted that the Washington Government was interested in the dispute because the determination of a frontier in South America came within the orbit of the Monroe Doctrine. It differentiated " Great Britain as a South American State " from Great Britain in Europe. The Secretary of State asked whether the British Government would submit the question in its entirety to arbitration, and added that a negative answer would tend to embarrass greatly the future relations between the United States and Great Britain.

Lord Salisbury had the knack of an inactivity that was recognizable as masterly, not helpless ; and he now decided upon a policy of passive resistance. He held his hand, poised but motionless, until the moment demanded action. For two months he did not even send a reply to Mr. Olney. He knew how inflammable was American public opinion, especially at a time when a Presidential Election was approaching. He turned his attention, amid his many other cares, to a deep study of the boundary problem ; and he recalled to mind, too, the strange episode which had disturbed Anglo-American relations during his previous period of office. The British minister in Washington, Sir Lionel Sackville-West, had then (1888) been sent away by the United States Government in singular circumstances. The envoy had received a letter purporting to be written by a former British subject, naturalized in the United States, asking how he should use his vote in the forthcoming Presidential Election. This same Grover Cleveland was at that time seeking re-election after his first tenure of the office ; and the unknown correspondent expressed doubts whether he should support a politician who had shown such marked hostility towards Canada. The British minister had unguardedly replied, stating in general terms that he did not consider that President Cleveland's re-election would harm Anglo-American relations. The letter was a political trick. The impostor who wrote it published the unwary envoy's reply in the Press. The advice, insipid though it had been, was clearly a breach of international convention : a foreign diplomatist had intervened in American domestic affairs. Sackville-West had then received two American journalists and tried to explain the matter away. His explanations provided material for more partisan propaganda ; and his original letter had been distributed as a fly-leaf in the presidential campaign. The U.S. Government abruptly requested him to leave Washington.

Lord Salisbury had protested against this signal departure from diplomatic amenities, but his protest had been ignored. Now, he would, for the moment, ignore the American demand. The furious flame of Mr. Olney's note, which was being fanned by the American Press, would, he was confident, burn itself out.

The Venezuelans had made their case worse by jumping a small part of the disputed territory and capturing a British Guiana outpost ; and a British schooner had been fired upon by a Venezuelan gunboat. Now, after two months' examination of all the circumstances, Lord Salisbury demanded the withdrawal of the twenty Venezuelan soldiers who remained on what he had decided was legally British soil ; and a month later (on November 26, 1895) he forwarded not one, but two long notes to Mr. Olney. The first dealt with the Monroe doctrine, the second with the proposal of arbitration. It was not difficult for him to show that unless the Monroe doctrine had been much extended since the day of its originator, British action had in no wise infringed it. It was the Washington Government which was going beyond President Monroe's definition. " With the existing colonies or dependencies of any European Power we have not interfered and shall not interfere," President Monroe had declared in that momentous message of December, 1823. His successor's present claim to intervene on Venezuela's behalf could therefore be regarded as interference with an existing British colony, against which Monroe had expressly bound the American Government.

And another of Mr. Olney's points was easy to controvert. The Secretary of State had gone so far as to make the following declaration : " That distance and 3,000 miles of intervening ocean make any permanent political union between a European and an American State unnatural and inexpedient will hardly be denied." " Her Majesty's Government are prepared emphatically to deny it ", wrote Lord Salisbury, " on behalf of both British and American people who are subject to her Crown." He did not fail to point out that the necessary meaning of Mr. Olney's words was that the existing union between Great Britain on the one hand and Canada, Jamaica, Trinidad, many other islands, and Honduras was " inexpedient and unnatural "—a view which Her Majesty's Government were unable to share.

In his second note, sent on the same day, Lord Salisbury took up the arbitration proposal. He declined to accept the American suggestion that the whole dispute should be submitted to arbitration, but he most readily agreed to it for the tracts of auriferous territory near the existing boundary which had until recently been almost entirely unpopulated. But Her Majesty's Government could not consent in any circumstances to " the transfer of large numbers of British subjects, who have for many years enjoyed the rule of a British colony, to a nation of different race and language, whose political system is subject to frequent disturbance, and whose institutions as yet too often afford very inadequate protection to life and property ".

The two despatches arrived by sea in Washington early in December, when Mr. Olney happened to be away on a duck-shooting expedition with the President. There was a lull while the two men considered Lord Salisbury's arguments ; but the address of Grover Cleveland, now nearing the close of his second presidency, to Congress on December 17 was a most alarming thunderclap. The boundary dispute had reached such a stage, he told his legislators, " as to make it incumbent upon the United

States to take measures to determine with sufficient certainty for its justification what was the true divisional line between the Republic of Venezuela and British Guiana ". He proposed that Congress should make an adequate appropriation for the expenses of a Commission which should investigate on the spot and determine the proper boundary line. Then he added : " When such a report is made and accepted it will, in my opinion, be the duty of the United States to resist by every means in its power, as a wilful aggression upon its rights and interests, the appropriation by Great Britain of any lands . . . which after investigation we have determined of right to belong to Venezuela. In making these recommendations I am fully alive to the responsibility incurred, and keenly realize all the consequences that may follow. I am, nevertheless, firm in my conviction that, while it is a grievous thing to contemplate the two great English-speaking peoples of the world as being otherwise than friendly competitors in the onward march of civilization, and strenuous and worthy rivals in all the arts of peace, there is no calamity which a great nation can invite which equals that which follows supine submission to wrong and injustice and a consequent loss of national self-respect and honour."

This defiant misapplication of a sound principle was all the more threatening to peace because the Venezuelan Government had by now appealed to the United States for help. The President's words, moreover, were received with tremendous applause in Congress ; and next day Senators streamed into the White House to offer their congratulations to Grover Cleveland. Within three days the money for the Boundary Commission was voted ; and in the words of an American historian, " All the world was apprised how ready the Congress was to support the President to the very utmost in his new and vigorous assertion of the Monroe doctrine." * H. M. Stanley wrote in the next number of the *Nineteenth Century* in London that " Americans hate England " and President Cleveland's message was a " public warning to prepare for war ".

The British nation, trustful in Lord Salisbury's sagacity, remained phlegmatic. The Prime Minister never in his life retreated from a conflict once he had entered into it. He

* The historian was Professor Woodrow Wilson, afterwards President of the United States (*History of the American People*, p. 247).

upheld the principle of arbitration, properly applied ; and he continued his delaying tactics. Rosebery put forward through Sanderson at the Foreign Office the suggestion that a third Power should be invited " to offer its good offices between the U.S. and us ". Sir William Harcourt, the Opposition leader in the Commons, urged unlimited concession upon Chamberlain, with whom he remained personally on cordial terms. Chamberlain reported his view to the Prime Minister in Cabinet, to which Lord Salisbury replied that " if we were to yield unconditionally to American threats another Prime Minister would have to be found " (January 11, 1896).

The deadlock was complete, but Lord Salisbury remained unperturbed. He declined an offer of help from an unexpected quarter. The Prince of Wales had received a cable from Mr. Pulitzer, powerful owner and director of the *New York World*, who had once met the Prince and knew him to be a well-wisher. The newspaper now asked him for a statement of his views. The Prince of Wales, afterwards to be known as King Edward the Peacemaker, drafted a friendly reply and submitted it to the Prime Minister—Foreign Secretary. Lord Salisbury begged him not to send it.

But a suggestion of help which came from Chamberlain was entirely congenial to him. Through his recent (third) marriage Chamberlain had many American contacts ; he knew well the ambassador in London, Mr. Bayard ; he had met Mr. Olney. He therefore suggested that he should make an informal and confidential approach to Bayard. Lord Salisbury agreed at once, but stipulated for a doubled indirectness of approach, through a mutual friend of Chamberlain's and Bayard's. This roundabout method of negotiation continued for some months. At the end of it Chamberlain was able to report a definite improvement of feeling and a clear desire to reach a settlement, and proposed that the time had come for himself and Mrs. Chamberlain to pay a " private " visit to the States. Once more Lord Salisbury readily agreed.

Before that time opinion in America itself had begun to veer. The war-scare had had a deplorable effect on business and brought many sharply back to sobriety. The Administration was assailed almost as vigorously as earlier it had been hulloa-ed on. Pulitzer described President Cleveland's policy as " jingo bugaboo ".

The friends of Britain showed their heads all over the country. So the Chamberlains set off hopefully. At the first interview with Olney the American Minister was quite obdurate ; but after this tactical repulsion he became steadily more friendly, and it was soon agreed that, in the area of the disputed frontier, territory " continuously occupied " by British subjects for a " long period " should be excluded from arbitration. Then Chamberlain handed over the negotiations to the British ambassador, Sir Julian Pauncefote, who, agreeing to fifty years as the qualifying domiciliary period, carried them to a successful conclusion. What might even then have caused embarrassment was the fact that an American Arbitration Commission had actually proceeded to Venezuela and was still investigating. But Lord Salisbury was by no means nonplussed. He chose not to officially recognize their existence, so he made no protest against their proceedings ; on the contrary, he allowed numerous British documents to be placed at their disposal, as a friendly gesture, by the Colonial Office. He regarded their investigations as those of private individuals who were interested in the upper waters of the Orinoco. In the meantime, with the full concurrence of Mr. Olney, he concluded a Treaty of Arbitration with Venezuela ; and the British and American Governments signed an Agreement on February 2, 1897, according to which the Guiana–Venezuela boundary was to be determined by a joint Anglo-American Commission with a neutral chairman. The chairman chosen was Professor de Martens, of the Russian Foreign Ministry. They did their work so thoroughly—their researches extending back to the days of Raleigh's last expedition to Guiana—that their report was not presented until October, 1899 ; and their chosen frontier coincided, apart from some small local variations, with that originally proposed by Lord Salisbury.

The episode has been worth recording in some detail because it affords an example of the elasticity and the remarkable " address in avoidance and subtlety in persistence " which J. L. Garvin regards as characteristic of Lord Salisbury's diplomacy ; and it was also, we may hope, notable in history as being the last occasion on which the two branches of the Anglo-Saxon race came to the brink of war.

Their two Governments were in fact, upon reflection, so disconcerted by their narrow escape from a fratricidal war that they drafted an Agreement making arbitration applicable to all serious matters of dispute between them. The Treaty was signed on January 11, 1897, thus paving the way for the Agreement on the boundary dispute which was signed three weeks later. It was rejected by the Senate and so did not come into force ; but its spirit survived to assuage future quarrels. Lord Salisbury's view on arbitration was expressed in the following words : " All the great triumphs in the past have been in substitution of judicial doctrine for the cold, cruel arbitrament of war. We have got rid of private war between small magnate and large magnate in this country ; we have got rid of the duel between man and man ; and we are slowly, as far as we can, substituting arbitration for struggles in international disputes." War was still the final and legitimate weapon of diplomacy ; Lord Salisbury used that weapon himself in the decline of his days ; but what he regarded as " great triumphs " were the successive stages in the elimination of war as a means of resolving disputes.

3

During the earlier phase of the quarrel with the United States Lord Salisbury had had to turn his attention to an equally disturbing incident in another continent—a sharp clash between Boer and Briton occasioned by the buccaneering exploit of the friend and right-hand man of Cecil Rhodes, Dr. Jameson, who served the Chartered Company as Administrator of Rhodesia. On a fine African summer morning, December 29, 1895, Dr. Jim, as he was popularly called by the white population of south and south-central Africa, invaded the Transvaal at the head of a troop of horse, intent upon obtaining redress for the Uitlanders living in the Boer Republic. The recent development of deep-level gold-mining in the Rand had brought a vast influx of out-landers, or foreigners, mainly British, to Johannesburg ; it had also provided a new and apparently inexhaustible supply of revenue to the primitive, patriarchal government of President Kruger. He, fearful that the Boer leadership would be over-whelmed in his own capital city, refused to grant them any political rights whatsoever, though he took full toll of their in-dustry. It was not surprising therefore that an unusual band of conspirators, mostly clubmen and millionaires, was secretly formed ; they were supplied with arms from the Cape, and pledged themselves to rise at a given signal in order to obtain the ordinary privileges of citizenship by force. Nor was it surprising that the Government in Capetown, headed as it was by Cecil Rhodes himself, should view their conspiratorial intentions with sympathy, and should order Jameson to be at hand, in the neighbourhood of Mafeking, to offer them help in case of need. The adventurous Dr. Jim was not the most patient of men ; and when December 27, the date provisionally settled for the rising in Johannesburg, passed, and nothing happened, he decided to force the hand of the plotters by marching on the capital. The news was instantly telegraphed all over the world by Kruger. Rhodes exclaimed that Jameson had upset his apple-cart ; the British Government issued urgent and repeated orders to the invader to return at once to his base. Dr. Jim, anticipating some such reaction in London, took care to cut the telegraph wires as he went along. One of Chamberlain's messengers actually reached him, but was brushed aside. The doctor and his 500 horsemen got to within a day's march of Johannesburg ; but the city conspirators were cowed and divided, and Dr. Jim's own men were completely exhausted by sleeplessness and lack of food ; moreover the Boers were quite ready for them. Kruger knew all about Jameson's force and had several thousand of the best mounted sharp-shooters in the world waiting for them. On the fifth day of their adventure, at Doornkop, the marauding force was surrounded and all who were not killed surrendered.

The raid was not only a military fiasco ; it was a political disaster which had unhappy repercussions far beyond the veldt of Africa. In Capetown Cecil Rhodes was driven from office ; a young barrister, Jan Christian Smuts, was turned away from his British connexions for ten momentous years ; the smouldering rivalry between Boer and Briton blazed into hatred ; " the entire course of South African politics ", as Winston Churchill has written, " was turned away from peaceful channels ". The British settlers henceforward looked to London for protection, the Dutch race in Cape Colony and in the two Boer Republics, the Transvaal and Orange Free State, looked to President Kruger as their champion. Worst of all, Kruger looked to Berlin.

For the Kaiser had intervened, and by his intervention had turned a local dispute into an Anglo-German one, in which the sympathies of other European countries, especially of Holland, were shown to be on the side of Germany. Germany's challenge to Britain, which was to last almost exactly half-a-century, was given a good start.

On January 3, 1896, the Kaiser sent a telegram to President Kruger, congratulating him and his people on having maintained the independence of his country against the " armed bands " which had broken into it " as disturbers of the peace ". The message, much watered down by his advisers, might appear innocuous ; but what had the Kaiser got to do with it at all ? That was the question which Britons indignantly asked themselves. He had always posed as the friend of this country. Only six months before—in August—he had visited Cowes for the yacht-racing, and had been treated as an English sportsman. The political problems of the moment, however, had not been forgotten ; and Lord Salisbury, rather reluctantly, had travelled down to the Isle of Wight to pay his respects to the Emperor, as well as to his own Sovereign. He had a long conversation with the German Emperor on August 5, which ended in complete disagreement on the point of how to deal with the Armenian-massacring Turkish Government. Lord Salisbury next day reported to Queen Victoria, and during the course of his visit received an invitation to see the Kaiser again that afternoon. He had arranged to return to London ; and he returned to London. He made (according to Sir Valentine Chirol) no explanation or apology ; and the Kaiser, who had waited for him, was naturally very angry indeed.

Lord Salisbury, *more suo*, recorded nothing of a conversation that had been abortive ; and when the Kaiser's version of it was later brought to his notice his observation was that it showed the expediency of having a third person present when talking to the Emperor. The British public of course were in total ignorance of what had passed between their Prime Minister and the supposedly friendly Emperor ; and were therefore a great deal more surprised and hurt than Lord Salisbury was when now, in January, 1896, the Kaiser launched his telegraphic incitement to President Kruger.

Personal pique against Lord Salisbury probably had more to do with the telegram than has generally been supposed. He was by all accounts almost in a state of hysteria at the time. His Chancellor, Prince Hohenlohe, records that he was " talking

wildly " of declaring war on England. He tried—but in vain—
to inveigle the Tsar and the French Government into supporting
him ; and he did in fact instruct his ambassador in London to
enquire whether the British Government approved the raid ; if
the answer was an affirmative, he was to break off diplomatic
relations. Hatzfeldt, dismayed, took these instructions in written
form to the Foreign Office. Most fortunately Lord Salisbury
was absent ; and the ambassador was able to retrieve the Note
unopened. The Kaiser also ordered German marines, who happened to be in East African waters, to land at Delagoa Bay. The
move was particularly disturbing because it seemed to prove that
there was a local understanding between Germany and Portugal,
which only later information showed to be untrue.

The British people were the more incensed because the sympathies of the majority, in the jingo mood then prevailing, were
heartily with Jameson. Winston Churchill unblushingly writes
in *My Early Life* : " I need scarcely say that at 21 I was all for
Dr. Jameson and his men." Even the sobriety of *The Times*
was shaken to the extent of publishing a poem entitled " Jameson's Ride " by the new Poet Laureate, Alfred Austin, the second
verse of which exemplifies with lamentable accuracy the public
feeling with which Lord Salisbury had to deal :

> Let lawyers and statesmen addle
> Their pates over points of law ;
> If sound be our sword, and saddle,
> And gun-gear, who cares one straw ?
> When men of our own blood pray us
> To ride to their kinsfolks' aid,
> Not Heaven itself shall stay us
> From the rescue they call a raid.

(The words were supposed to express Jameson's thoughts.)

The *Economist* wrote that we were bound to resist a " piece of
gratuitous insolence ", even if resistance cost us a great war ; and
the *Saturday Review* declared that we had no wish to provoke war
" even with Germany ". It explained " even " by adding that
Germany was our trade rival and " we stand to win much and
lose nothing by a war with her. But between the dislike of war
and the degradation of tamely submitting to undeserved insult,
only one choice is possible. Lord Salisbury must remember that

we hold command of the seas. . . . Lord Salisbury should now tell Germany and her allies to mind their own business."

Lord Salisbury was not likely to forget that the two-Power naval standard, his own creation, was the bulwark of peace with Europe ; and amid all this talk of war he knew that there was in fact much less danger of it from German blustering than from the crisis created by the American President's commitment of his country in the Venezuelan affair, which reached its climax just at this time. The need was only to keep his head even though others were losing theirs.

Moreover the South African imbroglio was primarily Chamberlain's affair. He trusted Chamberlain ; and he at once adopted the Colonial Secretary's proposal that a flying squadron be formed, and not secretly, but " by ostentatious order " ; and that it should lie ready to move in any direction, towards African or European shores. This decision settled the international crisis. The German Emperor came to his senses and a catastrophe was averted. But he smarted under the impotence which naval inferiority had imposed. From this moment he was determined that the disparity must be removed. He had already called Tirpitz to his side. The Transvaal quarrel was used by Emperor and Admiral to convert the Reichstag and the German people to the construction of a formidable fleet. The long-term consequences of the " flagrant piece of filibustering ", as Chamberlain had called it as early as December 31 in a note to the Prime Minister, were thus equally disastrous in Africa and in Europe.

At home one of its most notable effects was to raise the prestige and influence of Chamberlain. His treatment of the raiders was admitted to have been correct and vigorous even by his Liberal opponents. And in his speech when Parliament re-opened in February he announced that he was determined still to obtain justice for the Uitlanders and that he had invited President Kruger to come to London and discuss the difficulty with him. Immediately afterwards he re-opened negotiations with the old Boer peasant-President by despatch. Lord Rosebery, who had lost Chamberlain, was sore and scornful. " In the vigorous practice of the new diplomacy," he said, " the Colonial Secretary went to a public dinner and said that the administration of President Kruger, the gentleman he had invited to England and whom he was anxious to conciliate, was eminently corrupt. That is a very new diplomacy indeed." These strictures did not impress the British public. Joe Chamberlain was the man of the moment. Lord Salisbury may have shared some of Rosebery's misgivings ; but if he did, he kept his doubts to himself, and was as loyal in supporting him as Chamberlain had been loyal in consulting his official chief.

It was about this time that the phrase " splendid isolation " entered into common usage. There was a suggestion of it in Chamberlain's speech at a Queensland banquet held in London on January 21, 1896. He was referring to the " unexpected hostility " shown towards England by foreign countries in the days that followed the Raid : " We were confronted with suspicion, even with hate " ; and he went on : " Three weeks ago, in the words of Mr. Foster, the leader of the House of Commons of the Dominion of Canada, the great mother-Empire stood ' splendidly isolated '." To this portion of Chamberlain's speech The Times gave the cross-heading in capital letters " SPLENDID ISOLATION ". That was perhaps the first prominent use of the phrase that was to become so famous. In any case, Lord Salisbury himself neither invented it nor was in the habit of using it.

But even if he did not much like it, the caption expressed well enough the consequences of his policy of steadily refusing to commit his country to any entangling alliance at a time when Britain's influence and power were growing.

4

During this same troubled winter of 1895–6 the Austro-Hungarian ambassador approached Lord Salisbury, as he had done during his previous administration, with a view to obtaining a British assurance of help against any attempt by Russia to change the *status quo* in the Near East and Mediterranean area. The request is only worth recording because it produced one of the clearest statements of Lord Salisbury's attitude towards all requests for pledges of future action in unspecified circumstances. " I told Count Deym ", Lord Salisbury wrote to the British ambassador in Vienna (February 4, 1896), " that in this country it was impossible to take any engagement involving an obligation to go to war, as the power of H.[er] M.[ajesty's] G.[overnment] to do so depended on the political sentiment prevailing at the moment when the necessity arose : and that sentiment it was impossible to foresee. . . . I could not therefore consent to enter into an engagement on behalf of H.M.G^t. which I had no certainty of their being able to fulfil. . . . No Brit. Govt. could venture to pledge themselves beforehand, without running the risk of being forced to be unfaithful to their word." The Austrian ambassador nevertheless pressed Lord Salisbury on the same point later in the month (February 26, 1896) ; and the British Foreign Secretary repeated his refusal with even greater emphasis : " No Government in this country would ever pledge itself to go to war in some future contingency, of which the exact circumstances could not possibly be foreseen." But beyond a refusal to enter into any such pledge, Lord Salisbury added, " I said nothing which could throw doubt upon the continuity of English policy in the East of the Mediterranean."

5

A British Foreign Secretary must be prepared for the labour of Sisyphus. He rolls the huge, almost unmanageable stone, the danger of war, to the summit of the hill, and just as it seems about to disappear over the crest it rolls back to the bottom, and the wearisome uphill toil has to be undertaken all over again. The danger of war with Germany had been removed as it had with the United States. Next year it reappeared in the Far East, in Russian guise.

The xenophobia of the Chinese, as mentioned earlier in this chapter, had recently been expressing itself in the murder of European missionaries ; and seemed at first to be directed less against Russians than against foreigners who came from further west. Russia in any case was better placed to confront any hostility shown to her nationals ; being moreover semi-Asiatic herself, she knew how to take advantage of the perennial divisions of Chinese factions ; and while serving her own ends, how to pose as the friend of China against foreign intruders. Russian engineers had just completed the great project of a trans-Siberian railway connecting St. Petersburg with Vladivostock ; and it now appeared that the Tsar's Government was determined to link it with a port which, unlike Vladivostock, was ice-free all the year round. The chosen terminus was Port Arthur, at the southern tip of the Liaotung peninsula ; and with the help of the leading Chinese general-statesman, Li Hung Chang, and other mandarins, whose scrips, by commmon report, bulged with Russian roubles, the Imperial Government obtained 25-year leases both of Port Arthur and the neighbouring commercial harbour of Talienwan, now known as Dairen.

Lord Salisbury well understood the desire of Russia to possess somewhere a warm-water port ; she had been thwarted in her quest in the Black Sea and in the Persian Gulf ; and there might be advantages in her seeking it at the further end of Asia. So long as he could, Lord Salisbury looked the other way—and he had plenty to look at elsewhere. But unfortunately Russia forced him to take notice of what she was doing in the Far East by tactlessly and unnecessarily dismissing British advisers and engineers from the service of the North China Railway and the Korean Customs. Other European countries, moreover, were becoming directly involved in the affairs of China. Two German missionaries had been murdered ; whereupon the Berlin Government had ordered an armed force of marines to be landed at Kiaochow and to raise the German flag there ; and the Emperor sent his brother, Prince Henry, eastward in a battleship, to " strike with his mailed fist ", should it be necessary ; and shortly afterwards it became known that the Chinese Government had granted a 99-year lease of the port to Germany.

That was in January, 1898 ; and the Chinese themselves proposed then that Britain should have a similar lease of Wei-hai-wei, which was temporarily occupied by Japan. Lord Salisbury at first rejected the proposal, which ran contrary to his policy of maintaining the integrity of the Chinese Empire ; but seeing that that empire appeared to be disintegrating from faction fighting and external pressures, and that public opinion at home was becoming restive, he agreed on second thoughts to occupy it, " in order to restore the local balance of power ". The British public, he explained, clearly demanded " some territorial or cartographic consolation in China. It will not be useful, and it will be expensive." So, reluctantly, and " as a matter of pure sentiment ", he sent Commander Napier and a hundred blue-jackets to raise the Union Jack in Wei-hai-wei on May 24, 1898 ; and the port was soon provided with a much-welcomed sanatorium, and a cricket pitch. In a more realistic mood he also acquired a 99-year lease of 200 square miles of territory on the

Chinese mainland opposite Hong-Kong—a far-sighted contribution to the defence of the island-colony.

The treachery of Li Hung Chang in signing away Port Arthur and Dairen had roused the Court Party of the boy-Emperor in Peking to fury. The chief mandarin was dismissed from the Imperial service ; another official concerned was sent to the interior and throttled, and even the unfortunate envoy in St. Petersburg, whose only crime was not to have opposed what appeared to be the policy of his country, was recalled and suffered a public execution in Peking. And now the Russians, by another act of unnecessary provocation, stirred the British public into a fresh burst of anger. The Admiral commanding the British fleet in the Pacific had ordered some of his warships to anchor in Port Arthur, which was one of the harbours to which treaty rights with China gave them access. The St. Petersburg Government at once objected. Lord Salisbury, determined to avoid a quarrel if he could, kept their objections to himself. Even Foreign Office officials were not informed. On January 20, 1898, we find a memorandum addressed to him by his Private Secretary, Eric Barrington, saying that he had heard that Russia had complained of the presence of British warships at Port Arthur and suggesting that he should enquire of our Embassy in St. Petersburg whether that were true ? On the same sheet of paper Lord Salisbury wrote, in his usual red ink, yes, it was true ; a week ago M. de Staal, the Russian ambassador in London, had lodged a complaint with him. " I replied ", Lord Salisbury's minute continues, " that I saw no ground of complaint in the presence of British ships in a bay where they had a treaty right to enter. But as a matter of fact they had been sent by Admiral Buller without any orders from us ; and I believed that in the ordinary course they would soon move out to some other anchorage." Still the British public knew little of the matter. But the Russian leaders were intent upon provocation. Two days later they caused the semi-official Telegraph Bureau to announce that official information had been received from London " that the British ships of war at Port Arthur had received orders to leave immediately ".

Lord Salisbury even now only protested that this announcement was " inaccurate and injudicious, and might have inconvenient results ". A long correspondence ensued between the two governments as to the use to be made of the two ports, Port

Arthur and Talienwan, by Russia, whose representatives quibbled and contradicted each other. Commercial shipping would still be allowed to call at both ports. Then, Port Arthur was a fortified place and trading vessels must call at Talienwan. Then, Talienwan was a " Treaty Port " but not a " Free Port ". The Chinese Government, desperately short of ready money, was at this moment asking Britain for a loan. The British Government made a condition that if it were granted Talienwan must be included among the harbours open to commerce of all nations and coming within the administration of the Customs, at the head of which was an Englishman ; and this point was eventually conceded in a rescript by the Tsar. Lord Salisbury also obtained the consent of both the Russian and the Chinese Governments to the assurance that the Yangtse valley and Shanghai, where British merchants were established in large numbers, should never be alienated from China and should be regarded, in fact, as a British sphere of influence.

These minor compensations for the rebuffs which Algernon Cecil has called " the only considerable diplomatic reverses " in Lord Salisbury's career by no means satisfied the British people, who were not accustomed to appeasement in any form. Lancashire operatives thought of the China trade as a kind of monopoly of their own mills ; and the Government received a notable setback in August of that year 1898 when their candidate was defeated at Southport.

Lord Salisbury's moderation throughout these negotiations with Russia was however carefully calculated, and can easily be understood. He had clearly made up his mind from the first that he was not prepared to fight Russia on a Far Eastern issue ; and he had several good reasons.

In the first place, he was deeply concerned to maintain, despite all impediments, the Concert of Europe. " If any one European Power ", he had said in his Guildhall speech in 1897, " had tried, in the teeth of all the others, to settle by itself the problem which the Concert undertook, the only result could have been a bloody and desolating European war " ; and in the same speech : " The Concert, or, as I prefer to call it, the inchoate federation of Europe, is a body which only acts when it is unanimous . . . the Concert has great power, but it is slow." In the same year he proclaimed yet more clearly his hope for some kind of European Federation. " The federated action of Europe, if we can maintain it," he declared, " is our sole hope of escaping from the constant terror and calamity of war, the constant pressure of the burdens of an armed peace, which weigh down the spirits and darken the prospect of every nation in this part of the world. The Federation of Europe is the only hope we have." He was not addicted to poetry, but he quoted with approval from Tennyson's lines in " Locksley Hall " :

Till the war-drum throbbed no longer, and the battle-flags were furled
In the Parliament of man, the Federation of the world.

He was thinking in particular, at that moment, of the Greco-Turkish war which broke out in 1897 and the cognate problem of Crete. Greek impetuosity had provoked hostilities against Turkey in Thessaly, where the Greek army was ignominiously defeated. To obtain the transfer of the island of Crete from Turkish to Greek rule had been one of the motives of the war ; and despite her defeat Greece defiantly maintained her demand, which was justified racially and geographically. Hellenic insurgents were aided and abetted by a small expeditionary force from the mainland and the Moslems were cooped up in the towns. The Great Powers had their responsibilities under the Treaty of Berlin and earlier commitments, but they held different views as to how those responsibilities should be performed. Turkey had to be stopped on the mainland ; to take Crete away from her at that moment would have made it impossible to get her to listen to reason in Thessaly. On the other hand, the Turks had disgraced themselves a short time before when the massacre of Armenians had been carried into the capital city itself and thousands had perished under the eyes of the Constantinople police. Every proposal which seemed to favour Turkey was opposed by Russia and by public opinion in England, stirred deeply, for the last time, by the oratory of the aged Gladstone— " What do they expect me to *do* about it ? " Lord Salisbury groaned to his intimates : " I have no belief in a policy of scold " ; and in public he declared : " No fleet in the world can get over the mountains of Taurus to protect the Armenians." To his ambassador in Turkey he wrote : " It is the common object of the European Powers that the Turkish Empire should be sustained, because no arrangement to replace it can be suggested which would not carry with it a serious risk of European conflict.... It is an object of primary importance that the Concert of Europe should be maintained."

German policy finally precluded joint measures against Turkey. In this her hour of disgrace the Emperor William demeaned himself by posing as the friend of the Moslem world ; and he made the Far Eastern and Middle Eastern complications worse confounded by staging a theatrical appeal to Islam in a State visit to " the pariah Sultan ".* Lord Salisbury, who felt as much anguish as his critics on account of the massacre, most ardently wished that Britain had never come to be regarded— latterly through his own policy—as the friend of Turkey. He lamented, in the House of Lords (on January 19, 1897), the mistake that the British Government of 1853 had made when " we put all our money on the wrong horse ". He even reverted, in a modified form, to the famous proposal then made by the Tsar Nicholas to the British ambassador, Sir Hamilton Seymour, on the eve of the Crimean War, that Russia and Britain should combine to put an end to Turkish rule in Europe. Lord Salisbury now instructed his present ambassador in St. Petersburg, Sir Nicholas O'Conor, to throw out the suggestion that " Russia and England should give way to each other in places where the interests of the other were greater ". For instance, England would give way to Russia in the Ottoman Empire round the Black Sea and down the valley of the Euphrates as far as Bagdad ; Russia to England on the Euphrates below Bagdad and in Arabia and Turkish Africa ; thus there might ensue "a cordial and close understanding between Russia and England ".† Lord Salisbury also at once accepted the invitation of the Tsar to take part in an international conference to " secure the continuance of general peace and put some limit on the constant increase of armaments".

Sir Nicholas O'Conor, however, gravely mistrusted Russian intentions and had thought it well to transmit to the Foreign Office extracts from a newspaper called *Viedomosti*, according to which Russia had " a mission in Asia . . . and the power to destroy British rule in India " ; and " Russia is not only the mightiest of the Powers, but a new spiritual continent, a new psychological

* The late Prof. Seton-Watson's phrase.
† See Sir Nicholas O'Conor's despatch of February 12, 1898.

and colossal world within the sphere of whose irresistible influence all Asia must eventually gravitate . . . the West seems to be losing sight of our immemorial right to be masters of the East ".

The scramble for power was indeed intense in that vigorous epoch when almost every country purposed expansion ; and it was small wonder that Lord Salisbury considered in all the circumstances that the best he could do was to prevent the European Concert from breaking out into complete disharmony, and in general to maintain the *status quo*. Crete had better remain titularly Turkish ; the integrity of China must be juridically observed ; Russia, firmly partnered in Dual Alliance with France in Europe by the military Convention of 1894, must be appeased. He placed on record the " grave objections " of the British Government to the occupation of Port Arthur ; the British Government " retained their liberty of action ". But the liberty to act was not translated into decision to act. And he also made concessions to Germany in Samoa and to France in Tunis and West Africa. And he could do nothing for the Armenians. He was still guided by the principle he had stated at the Guildhall banquet two years before : " Our first duty is towards the people of this country, to maintain their interests and their rights ; our second duty is to all humanity " (November 9, 1896).

The overriding reason why he was so conciliatory to all, and so particularly accommodating in the Liaotung peninsula, has still to be mentioned. It was the probability, nay, in his mind the certainty, that before the end of 1898 Great Britain would be involved in a serious conflict with France, the ally of Russia— in Africa, and perhaps in Europe too. Lord Salisbury's natural inclination was to define a difference, to combat an opposing view or interest. But he knew when concession and compromise were necessary. He measured his undertakings by the strength of his resources and always related his policy to the armed strength of the nation. He abhorred bluff. His attitude in the Far Eastern crisis of March–April, 1898, is best revealed by an episode related by Lady Gwendolen Cecil in one of her un-published memoranda. The news that the Chinese garrisons had been removed from Port Arthur and Talienwan, that the Russian flag was flying in both places, that Russian warships, contrary to promise, remained in the naval harbour and that

2,000 Tsarist troops had been landed there, had shocked public opinion ; and the shock was reinforced by the jubilation of the St. Petersburg Press—the *Novoe Vremya* of April 5 described the Russo-Chinese Agreement as " the undoubted diplomatic disaster of Lord Salisbury's government ". Most members of that government held much the same view themselves ; and a deputation of the Cabinet came to see him at his house in Arlington Street, where he was confined by a severe bout of influenza. Their indignation was as great as that which agitated the public ; and they came to urge strong action upon their chief. The rest of the story is best told in his daughter's own words :

His temperature was high and the doctor absolutely forbade an interview. His colleagues therefore wrote a short draft of the message which they suggested sending to Russia, and I was asked to take it up to him for approval or rejection. He read it over, observed that its transmission would probably mean war, and then, after a short pause, said with the peculiar inflection in his voice and glint in his eyes which warned his intimates against taking his words in any pedantically matter-of-fact sense : " Of course the Russians have behaved abominably and if it would be any satisfaction to my colleagues I should have no objection to fighting them. But I don't think we carry guns enough to fight them and the French together."

" I expressed somehow ", Lady Gwendolen continues, " my incomprehension of what the French had to do with the matter. He turned to me with a look of surprise which he always seemed genuinely to feel when other minds failed to travel as fast or as far as his own. ' What the French had to do with it ? Did I forget that Kitchener was actually on the march to Khartum ? In six month's time ', he went on, ' we shall be on the verge of war with France ; I can't afford to quarrel with Russia now.' " Lady Gwendolen took her father's message down to the waiting Cabinet Ministers ; a despatch went to St. Petersburg ; but its wording was very different from that of the original draft.

Somewhere in the recesses of Lord Salisbury's dispassionate mind was lurking, perhaps, the belief that Russia had the same kind of claim to restore order in the Empire of China, if it collapsed—and only if it collapsed—as he was making for Britain in the Sudan. Another clear glimpse of the Prime Minister's mind, and the fears he entertained at the time of a large-scale European war, is provided in a passage of the speech he delivered in the

Albert Hall after he had recovered from his illness. "Nations may roughly be divided ", he said, " between the living and the dying. . . . For one reason or another—from the necessities of politics or under the pretence of philanthropy—the living nations will gradually encroach on the territory of the dying, and the seeds and causes of conflict among civilized nations will speedily appear. These things may introduce causes of fatal difference between the great nations whose mighty armies stand opposite threatening each other. These are the dangers, I think, which threaten us in the period which is coming on. It is a period which will tax our resolution, our tenacity and imperial instincts to the utmost. Undoubtedly we shall not allow England to be at a disadvantage in any re-arrangement that may take place. On the other hand, we shall not be jealous if desolation and sterility are removed by the aggrandisement of a rival in regions to which our arms cannot extend " (May 4, 1898). It seems a legitimate conjecture that the last sentence referred to Russia in China.

Neither colleagues nor the public were satisfied with Lord Salisbury's attitude of acquiescence and his reputation suffered a temporary decline. He could make no explanation in public, for he was particularly anxious to avoid giving the impression that the Nile expedition, the last stage of which had just been begun by General Kitchener, was in any way directed against France. Its purpose was the redemption of the Sudan from the brutal tyranny of the Mahdi. It was a mission of liberation. In weighing the respective need or merit of having to fight in one place or the other—assuming he could not fight in both—Lord Salisbury's realism and idealism concurred to make him choose the Sudan. In either place the defence of British interests was no doubt his main consideration ; but he saw in the Sudan a chance of serving humanity, of doing the work of Christian civilization, as well as of consolidating the British position in the Nile Valley to which he had always attributed high importance.

The redemption of the Sudan was a policy conceived and executed as wholly upon Lord Salisbury's personal responsibility as constitutional practice allows. This, and the story of Fashoda, marking the culmination of his diplomatic achievement, deserve a separate chapter.

FASHODA

If in the events described in the last chapter Lord Salisbury felt he was able, for the first time in his life, to delegate details of foreign policy to a colleague, he made himself solely responsible for the settlement of the dispute with France in southern Sudan, which may be said to have begun in March, 1895, and which, as he foresaw and foretold, reached its climax in September–November, 1898. Great Britain, as we have seen, had become the leading foreign Power in Egypt in 1882, when France had declined to take part in suppressing the Arabi rebellion. But she still retained rights and interests and the aura of the Napoleonic tradition. She had not only the power, but in many minor matters the right, to interfere ; and she interfered often and obstructively. Moreover, she claimed that her sphere of influence extended over the Nile Valley ; and in 1894 she had secured from the Congo Free State a title to territory reaching to the left bank of that river in the Upper Sudan. Then, in the spring of the following year, when Lord Rosebery's Government was still in office, the rumour reached London that she was preparing to transform the claim into an accomplished fact. French military missions were very active in West Africa, in the Sahara, and on the borders of Abyssinia. Was there a plan to strike right across Africa to the Nile ? It sounded improbable. The Government was closely questioned in the House of Commons ; and Sir Edward Grey, then Foreign Under-Secretary, made an unexpectedly firm and spacious statement in reply. He said that in consequence of our claims and of the claims of Egypt in the Nile Valley, the British sphere of influence covered the whole Nile waterway ; and then, referring to the various rumours brought up by members of the House, he said he did not consider that they deserved credence, but he added these words : " The advance of a French Expedition under secret instructions right from the other side of Africa into a territory over which our claims have been known for so long would be not merely an inconsistent and unexpected act, but it must be

Sculptor Herbert Hampton   *Country Life photograph*

STATUE OF LORD SALISBURY AT THE FOOT OF THE GREAT STAIRCASE IN
THE FOREIGN OFFICE

278]

perfectly well known to the French Government that it would be an unfriendly act, and would be so viewed by England " (March 28, 1895).

In those days of habitual understatement Grey's words constituted a stiff warning, which France would disregard only at the peril of war.

M. Hanotaux, the French Foreign Minister, nevertheless ignored it. His agents continued their activities in Abyssinia and Upper Ubanghi ; and a year later he and M. Delcassé, the Minister for the Colonies, sent Captain Marchand to French Congo, there to organize and equip a mission to undertake the trans-continental journey which had been the theme of Grey's solemn remonstrance. Marchand disembarked at Loango on July 23, 1896, and shortly after plunged into the jungles of Central Africa with a handful of officers and an escort of armed Senegalese, bent upon reaching the valley of the Nile.

By this time Lord Salisbury was again installed at the Foreign Office, and he seems to have received early information of Marchand's departure, in spite of all the precautions of secrecy, and to have had no doubts about his objective—" de donner à notre colonie du Congo une issue sur le Nil ", as afterwards appeared in plain language in the French Yellow Book ; and the project was calculated to obtain for France the power to exercise partial control of the water of the lower Nile.

He decided, with the full consent of the Khedive of Egypt, that the moment had come to redeem the Sudan from the chaos and misrule into which it had fallen after the death of Gordon and the withdrawal of the Egyptian garrison. The writ of Cairo ran no further than Wady Halfa, near the cataract of that name, which completely severed all means of communication with the lost province ; beyond the cataract were barbarism and bankruptcy, rapine, bloody feuds, insurrections and slave-raids which formed a constant threat to the southern frontiers of Egypt. The great work of Cromer and his advisers was jeopardized ; it was the common decision of the Egyptian and British Governments that law and order must be extended southward along the upper courses of the Nile. As Lord Salisbury said later, during the debate on the address in February, 1898 : " Kartum formed a part of Egypt when Mr. Gladstone's Government was in office, and the whole of the Nile Valley as far [down] as Wady Halfa was then taken away, and a barbarous, cruel and desolating despotism was installed in once fertile provinces, which I hope before many months will be restored to Egypt." A complementary motive for deciding upon the forward policy in the Sudan at this moment was a desire to be of service to the Italians in their Red Sea colony of Eritrea. The disaster of Adowa had encouraged the Mahdist dervishes to fling themselves against all foreigners ; and an Anglo-Egyptian advance was calculated considerably to ease pressure on the Italian flank.

Britain was to supply the commander, and eventually the major portion of the troops ; but in the earlier advances General Sir Herbert Kitchener, who had been Sirdar, or C.-in-C. of the Egyptian Army, since 1892, had only Egyptians and Sudanese under his command. In March, 1896, he was instructed to advance as far as Dongola, between the third and fourth cataracts, and to consolidate his position there.

Kitchener was one of the few British generals in whom Lord Salisbury had confidence. He had been a visitor to Hatfield, and Lord Edward Cecil, the Prime Minister's soldier son, wrote afterwards : " My father was much impressed with him. That I clearly remember, for my father was not often impressed." When the Nile expedition was begun, Kitchener appropriately appointed Lord Edward Cecil, who was in the Egyptian service, to be his A.D.C., and told him to write weekly reports home to his father. The General's peculiar genius for organization made him well suited to conduct a campaign in which supplies and commissariat, hygiene and railway building were for two years more important requirements than strategical talent.

Just a year after the British and Egyptian Governments had ordered Kitchener to begin his advance to Dongola Lord Salisbury did an unusual thing. He had had one of his almost regular springtime bouts of influenza, and went to the Riviera to recover. That was by no means unusual, but this time he decided to combine work with holiday, and arranged to meet the French Foreign Minister in Paris on March 26, 1897. He was received by M. Hanotaux at the Quai d'Orsay in the morning, and the French Minister returned the visit at the British Embassy that same afternoon. Neither the French nor the British Press contained anything substantial about their conversations, nor does the Record Office provide any account of them ; but they were of considerable importance, for in the course of them Lord Salisbury proposed that Britain and France should conclude a Treaty of Arbitration.

At the Quai d'Orsay in the morning Lord Salisbury, with the art of the skilled negotiator, mentioned the project almost as if it were an afterthought towards the end of the conversation ; and was disappointed when M. Hanotaux replied with the equally familiar device of agreeing in principle while raising points of practical difficulty, with the implication that they were insuperable. In the afternoon talk at the Embassy Lord Salisbury therefore confined himself to mentioning with extreme regret the breakdown of his Arbitration Treaty with the United States owing to the action of the Senate. He had however also arranged to see in the evening his friend the French ambassador to the Court of St. James's who was in Paris ; and he urged Baron de Courcel to press his arbitration proposal on M. Hanotaux. In de Courcel's own words : " Lord Salisbury me dit : ' Il est une question que je vous prierai de signaler tout spécialement à l'attention de M. Hanotaux, c'est celle de l'organization d'une procédure d'arbitrage pour le règlement de toutes nos petites difficultés mutuelles.' " M. de Courcel, like his chief, gave a non-committal and discouraging reply ; but he, of course, carried the matter to M. Hanotaux ; and it is noticeable that in the circular despatch which the French Foreign Minister sent to the French ambassadors in the principal European capitals a fortnight later, recounting his interviews with Lord Salisbury, he gave a leading place to the Prime Minister's proposal—which was that Britain and France should set up a permanent Arbitral Tribunal consisting of two neutral members.

The conversations of the two Foreign Ministers on March 26 covered indeed many other points, notably the vexatious problem of Crete ; but it hardly seems probable that Lord Salisbury would have departed so far from his common habit as to break his journey in Paris, when he was in weak health, unless he had some important proposal to put forward. We know now that he expected to be on the verge of war with France over Kitchener's southward advance in the Sudan (see Chapter XV, p. 276), and although he spoke to M. Hanotaux of settling " the many little matters which divide us more in appearance than fundamentally " he probably reckoned that an Arbitration Treaty of any kind would help to prevent that war. Moreover on the Cretan question Lord Salisbury showed himself extremely accommodating to the French view ; and he suggested that, as their two governments found themselves in close agreement, they should submit joint proposals to the other Great Powers. M. Hanotaux promptly replied that he could not consent to form a kind of " Concert à Deux " within the " Concert à Six ".

France and Russia, we must remember, had recently signed their secret Treaty of Alliance, the exact terms of which were unknown. Was the Machiavellian thought in the back of Lord Salisbury's mind that he might loosen the attachment between Paris and St. Petersburg? In the conversation with Lady Gwendolen Cecil just referred to he had also said : " I don't think we carry guns enough to fight them [the Russians] and the French together." If any notion of separating them existed, it was quashed by M. Hanotaux's reply. And the second talk had not gone so well as the first. " La seconde conversation ", the French Minister dictated afterwards to his secretary, " m' a paru un peu plus embarrassée." Moreover Lord Salisbury was manifestly unwell. " He was very red," M. Hanotaux notes, " and his breath came with difficulty." When Lord Salisbury went on to see M. de Courcel, the latter also recorded that Lord Salisbury " complained of a certain fatigue ". That he should nevertheless have insisted on holding these conversations seems to be additional proof of the importance he attached to them.

2

Considerable space has been given to this Paris visit of March, 1897, for the double reason that the purport of the three conversations has never been made public before and that it ought to be borne in mind when we consider the story of Fashoda, to which we now return.

Kitchener slowly and thoroughly completed his appointed task of establishing the authority of the Egyptian Government along the Nile up to Dongola. Then in March, 1898, Lord Salisbury decided upon a further military advance to Khartum for the pacification of the whole Sudan. His military advisers recommended a change of command for this active operation ; but the Prime Minister, now firmly supported by Lord Cromer in Cairo, having found a soldier to his taste, refused to consider anybody else's claim. So Kitchener, technically an Egyptian general, but now in command of a force which included British battalions as well as Egyptian and Sudanese, moved forward to dislodge the Khalifa's dervishes from the Atbara river. Highlanders and Sudanese rushed their thorn-hedged zareba together. More transports had then to be collected, more railway-line built. A slow advance upstream and across the sand at the most torrid season of the year enabled the troops, on Spetember 1, to catch their first glimpse of Omdurman and of Khartum, a capital at that time more remote from Western gaze than Lhasa is today. Next day, September 2, religious zeal lent fury to a dervish onslaught ; in the words of the historian Holland Rose : " In that vast amphitheatre the discipline and calm confidence of the West stood quietly facing the fanatic fury of the East. Two worlds were there embattled." But the fanatic fury, or at least the spectacular dash, was not all to be on one side in that picturesque though bloody battle ; for its final episode was the famous charge of the 21st Lancers (in which Mr. Winston Churchill, then a young reporter, having exchanged his pen for a sword, took part). The faithful sons of Mahomet fought gamely, even when the Khalifa mounted his dromedary and disappeared ; but their final rout was complete. The victorious general, defying the snipers, rode at the head of his men into Omdurman. Two days later detachments from every regiment of his victorious army were ferried across to Khartum, and the Egyptian and British flags were hoisted on the ruins of the palace in which Gordon had been slain thirteen years before. Kitchener, without a doubt, always felt himself to be the avenger of Gordon ; and the only occasion in his life when he publicly showed emotion was at the military memorial service which he held in honour of his great predecessor. A day or two later he ordered the destruction of the Mahdi's tomb. The bones of the dead prophet were thrown into the Nile. This grim act of retribution was sharply criticized at home. But Kitchener had done most of his soldiering in Cyprus and Palestine before he came to Cairo. He knew the East of his day and its respect for emblematic justice. He judged it politically advisable to make the gorgeous mausoleum a heap of rubble ; and he was warned by his Mohammedan advisers, so he wrote to Lord Salsibury, that it would be better to " remove " the body, which would otherwise be made a rallying point for his surviving followers.

Having occupied Khartum, the moment had come for Kitchener to open a letter entrusted to him by Lord Salisbury. The Prime Minister had written three identical letters, in his own hand, which he had committed to the Sirdar, to his second-in-command, General Sir Archibald Hunter, and to the next senior officer, General Rundle. They were sealed ; and each recipient was given strict instructions to sew the letter into the lining of his tunic and not to open it until Khartum was reached. The letters, when opened, informed the three military chiefs that Major Marchand, about whom no official information had been made public, had undoubtedly started about two years before on a west-to-east journey across Africa, in pursuance of the French policy of creating a territorial strip across the continent which must prevent continuous British or Anglo-Egyptian occupation from north to south. Lord Salisbury's instructions were that he, Kitchener, was to go in search of Marchand up the Nile, that the second-in-command was to mount the Blue (more easterly branch of the) Nile, and that the third officer, General Rundle, was to remain in Khartum and maintain contact with Cromer in Cairo.

Lord Salisbury's reasons for imparting his orders in this unusual manner were presumably threefold. In the first place he would not wish at the start of the Sudan expedition to give the impression that it was in any way directed against France. Had anything leaked out about such instructions before Kitchener reached Khartum, the French Government might have felt justified in making it a *casus belli*. In the second place, Kitchener being legally and technically in the Egyptian service, Lord Salisbury might not have felt he could properly send him direct orders to Khartum ; nor indeed could he have been confident that he would be able to keep in daily touch with him, wireless being then unknown and telegraphic facilities not so perfect as today. And finally, the British Prime Minister may have considered that it was the simplest method of signifying that he himself proposed to assume direction the moment the military operations against the Khalifa were concluded. The issue would then become a political one between the British and French Governments. It was for himself, Prime Minister and Foreign Secretary, to take personal charge. Behind his retiring nature Lord Salisbury had an imperious character ; from that moment he assumed entire direction, and Kitchener became his very effective ambassador.

When, therefore, three days after the battle of Omdurman, a dervish boat floated down the Nile into Omdurman and reported that it had been fired upon by a band of white men higher upstream, it was an easy guess for Kitchener that Marchand had arrived. The British commander lost no time in carrying out his instructions. Hunter was dispatched up the Blue Nile as far as Roseires ; Rundle remained in Khartum ; and on September 10 Kitchener himself set off up the White Nile, taking with him five gunboats, a detachment of the Cameron Highlanders, two Sudanese battalions and an Egyptian battery. Five days later he captured a small dervish camp, whose chief informed him that three weeks before he had had a fight with " a small body of Europeans " who had entrenched themselves at Fashoda. The flag they flew was unknown to the Emir ; all he was concerned with was to expel them, for which purpose he had dispatched a request for reinforcements to the Khalifa. More confident than ever that he was about to meet the intrepid French leader, the Sirdar pushed on to within twelve miles of Fashoda, where he was met by the chiefs of the Shilluk tribe, who expressed to the victor of Omdurman their delight at the defeat of the Khalifa, and confirmed the occupation of the fort at Fashoda by a small body of whites, whom they supposed to be Englishmen. Kitchener thereupon addressed a letter to " The chief of the European expedition at Fashoda " ; and next day he steamed towards the old fort and scattered huts of which the station was composed. He received *en route*, from Marchand, a reply to his letter of the previous day ; and an hour or two later Marchand himself appeared in a boat coming down the river. He was flying the French flag ; and, accompanied by another French officer, he at once came on board Lord Kitchener's gunboat.

By this time Lord Kitchener was by one means or another in full possession of the points of Lord Salisbury's policy. He received from Cromer a copy of a Foreign Office despatch dated August 2—one month to the day before the decisive battle had been fought at Omdurman. Lord Salisbury began by repeating the instructions for reconnoitring the two branches of the Upper

Nile, which have already been recorded, and proceeded : " In dealing with any French or Abyssinian authorities who may be encountered, nothing should be said or done which would in any way imply a recognition on behalf of Her Majesty's Government of a title to possession on behalf of France or Abyssinia to any portion of the Nile Valley."

The first passages between the two leaders on the gunboat on the Nile were nevertheless couched in terms of the warmest mutual congratulations. Marchand repeated the flattering words of the letter which his Senegalese sergeant had a couple of hours before delivered from his rowboat. There is no reason to doubt the major's sincerity when he congratulated the British general on the destruction of the Khalifa ; for the Khalifa would almost certainly have destroyed Marchand if he had had another month in which to reach him. And the Frenchman went on to speak of Kitchener as incarnating " the contest of civilization against the savage fanaticism of the Mahdi ". Kitchener equally sincerely congratulated his French opponent on his brilliant two-year penetration of the African jungle, with only a handful of men, to reach his present position ; but he informed him civilly that the presence of the French at Fashoda and in the valley of the Nile was regarded by the British Government as a direct violation of the rights of Egypt and Great Britain, and he must protest in the most emphatic manner against the hoisting of the French flag in the Khedive's dominions. The rest of the conversation was later thus described by Marchand himself (text somewhat abbreviated) :

" I have come to resume possession of the Khedive's dominions," Kitchener began.

" Mon Général, I, Marchand, am here by order of the French Government. I thank you for your offer of conveyance to Europe, but I must wait here for instructions."

" Major, I will place my boats at your disposal to return to Europe by the Nile."

" Mon Général, I thank you, but I am waiting for orders from my Government."

" I must hoist the Egyptian flag here," Kitchener next said.

" Why, I myself will help you to hoist it—over the village."

" Over your fort."

" No, that I shall resist."

" Do you know, Major, that this affair may set France and England at war ? "

I bowed, without replying.

Kitchener then, according to Major Marchand's account, gazed slowly round the landscape and in particular at his own well-armed escort of gunboats and 2,000 men. " We are the stronger," he observed ; and then intimated very firmly that he intended to hoist the Egyptian flag over an outlying portion of the fort. After a moment's silence, Marchand signified acquiescence, but added that he would not haul down the French flag from its present position. Kitchener made no objection ; and the two men agreed to leave the settlement of the dispute to their governments.

Their personal relations never ceased to be cordial. After the interview they exchanged presents ; and an interesting point in Marchand's letter of thanks for " le splendide souvenir du Sirdar " was that he addressed him as " M. le Général-en-Chef Lord Kartoum ". This was not the fanciful compliment of a propitiatory rival. Within three days of the victory of Omdurman Queen Victoria had offered her successful general a peerage ; and Kitchener had written to a friend : " The Queen offered me a peerage in such a nice manner. I think ' Khartoum of Aspall ' will be the title I choose. ' Kitchener ' is too horrible a name to put a ' Lord ' in front of." Probably during the intimacy of the whiskies-and-sodas in which they wished each other well in Kitchener's cabin, when their official interview had ended, the new peer had mentioned to his French friend how he felt about the title which was to be conferred upon him.

Kitchener returned to Khartum. Major Marchand remained in his fort at Fashoda, with a French flag overhead which had become a much more powerful protection for him since a battalion of Sudanese and four guns, the whole force under a British officer, had taken station in a neighbouring bastion, five hundred yards away, over which floated the flag of the Khedive.

3

The scene of our story now shifts from Central Africa to London and Paris.

The first telegram from Lord Salisbury which we need notice came, however, not from Whitehall, but from a village in the Vosges Mountains, called Schlucht, which the Prime Minister had chosen this year for his annual autumn holiday on August 11. No crisis deterred Lord Salisbury from taking a period of relative rest in early spring and late summer. Freedom from responsibility it was not. But responsibility never tired him so much as the irksome day-by-day personal contacts, and details for decision on minor matters, from which he escaped. The month's sojourn at Schlucht did not now prevent immediate attention to business. His despatch from the mountain resort was dated September 9— exactly one week after the Omdurman victory. Lord Salisbury had learned from the British ambassador in Paris, Sir Edmund Monson, that the new French Foreign Minister, M. Delcassé (he had succeeded M. Hanotaux in June), had now for the first time alluded to a possible clash between the French Mission and the Anglo-Egyptian flotilla. " If M. Delcassé should revert to this subject," Lord Salisbury telegraphed immediately to Paris, " I request you to point out to him that, by the military events of last week, all the territories which were subject to the Khalifa passed by right of conquest to the British and Egyptian Governments. Her Majesty's Government do not consider that this right is open to discussion." (It is curious to note in the original draft of this despatch, which is written in ink, that its most important phrase " by right of conquest " is added, in pencil, in the margin. The writing is not that of Lord Salisbury, but of course the words could only have been written in by his authority.)

There never were ambiguities in Lord Salisbury's mind or policy ; or if he did allow an ambiguity to exist, it was because he considered that over-precise definition was in that particular case inadvisable. But he decided at the beginning of every diplomatic negotiation where he was ready to make concessions and where he would not. The valley of the Nile was henceforth to be Anglo-Egyptian. About that he had made up his mind ; and if the French Government understood that Britain was ready to fight, there was less chance that it would take up as uncompromising an attitude as he had himself. In no circumstances would he fail Egypt and the Sudanese.

Nevertheless, the French Government was by no means

inclined to yield. And it had a good case. Successive chiefs of the Quai d'Orsay—and they followed each other swiftly—had either directly or by implication warned British Governments that France was not disinterested in the Upper Nile. They moreover reminded the Foreign Office that Mr. Gladstone had declared that Britain would evacuate Egypt and on May 11, 1885, had explicitly stated that in the meantime Egypt limited her sway to a line drawn through Wady Halfa. The authority of the Khedive over the Sudan therefore ceased ; and since the Khedive was still nominally a vassal of the Turkish Sultan, it reverted to the Ottoman Empire, of which it had indeed never ceased to form a part—although there was in fact not a Turkish official in the length and breadth of it. Britain on her part had not unnaturally in the circumstances come to regard this region as a no-man's-land, and in 1890 had signed a Colonial Agreement with Germany by which she annexed the part of it which adjoined Victoria Nyanza. It was not difficult therefore for France to point out that the new British view contradicted the old ; what had been treated as no-man's-land was regarded as a possession of the Khedive, temporarily alienated, and now returning to its lawful owner. The logical French mind also asked why, if it were conceded that the Khedive, under the Sultan, was the legal possessor, the Quai d'Orsay should have to negotiate about it not with Cairo or Constantinople but with Lord Salisbury.

These points of logic and legality did not unduly disturb the British Foreign Secretary, who was able to indicate serious anomalies also in the French arguments. France herself, as we have noted, had in 1894 secured from the Congo Free State a title to the left bank of the Nile ; yet in the following year her Foreign Minister, M. Hanotaux, was to declare : " The region in question is under the supreme sovereignty of the Sultan. And it has a legitimate master—he is the Khedive," a statement which was received with loud applause in the Chamber of Deputies (April 5, 1895) ; and next year, when the decision was taken to begin the advance on Dongola, Hanotaux did his best to provoke the Sultan into enquiring why he, as suzerain of Egypt, had not been consulted.

It was, however, undeniable that British policy had the full approval and active support of the Khedive ; and Lord Salisbury therefore brushed aside arguments of legality which led the disputants into a maze of sophistries as perplexing as the African jungle from which Major Marchand had just emerged. He affirmed plainly in the House of Lords that he regarded " the right of conquest " as " the most useful, most simple and soundest " of the titles on which to base the regime he intended to establish in the Sudan, the other title being the fact that the Sudan had " formed part of the possessions of Egypt ".

It was in vain for M. de Courcel, the French ambassador in London, to repeat his cross-examination of Lord Salisbury on October 10 : " Pour en revenir aux arguments tirés des droits de l'Egypte et du caractère de général égyptien revêtu par Sir Kitchener, j'ai demandé à Lord Salisbury comment il se faisait qu'ils nous fussent opposés, non par un ministre égyptian, ou un représentant de la souveraineté du Sultan, mais par le premier ministre d'Angleterre discutant avec l'ambassadeur de France ? "

Lord Salisbury left the conundrum unanswered. It was indeed unanswerable. But he stated his view fully and cogently to M. de Courcel :

" I pointed out to him that the Egyptian title to the banks of the Nile had certainly been rendered dormant by the military successes of the Mahdi ; but that the amount of right, whatever it was, which by those events had been alienated from Egypt, had been entirely transferred to the conqueror. How much title remained to Egypt, and how much was transferred to the Mahdi and the Khalifa, was, of course, a question which could practically be only settled, as it was settled, on the field of battle. But their controversy did not authorize a third party to claim the disputed land as derelict. There is no ground in international law for asserting that the dispute of title between them, which had been inclined one day by military superiority in one direction, and a few years later had been inclined in the other, could give any authority or title to another Power to come in and seize the disputed region as vacant or relinquished territory."

On that basis he could be logical, as well as practical, in informing the French Government (on October 12, 1898) that " no title of occupation could be created by a secret expedition across unknown and unexplored wastes, at a distance from the French border, by Monsieur Marchand and a scanty escort ".

Similarly, when the French ambassador in London tried to merge the solution of the Fashoda episode in a general Central African settlement between the two countries, Lord Salisbury, who had himself suggested a general settlement to M. Bourgeois, when he was Foreign Minister (for one month) in 1896, now replied that the situation had been quite changed by the victory of Omdurman.

M. de Courcel was still not convinced, especially as about the same time Lord Rosebery made a speech, in which he exclaimed that a flag, after all, was only " a portable affair ". The argument was meant to support the British case ; but it irritated the French ambassador and acutely reminded him of the number of islands and provinces—not to mention a whole continent—which Britain had acquired by implanting a flag on them.

The unequivocal attitude of the Prime Minister–Foreign Secretary was hotly supported in the Press and in the street. British jingoism was then at its zenith ; and responsible political leaders of both the Parties of State were almost as enthusiastic as the crowds. In a great speech at Epsom Lord Rosebery said : " Great Britain has been conciliatory, and her conciliatory disposition has been widely misunderstood. If the nations of the world are under the impression that the ancient spirit of Great Britain is dead, or her population less determined than ever it was to maintain the rights and the honour of its flag, they make a mistake which can only end in a disastrous conflagration." And again, in the same speech : " Great Britain has been treated rather too much as what the French call a negligible quantity in recent periods." Newspapers of the Radical persuasion were only a little less eager in their support of government policy. Lord Salisbury took the then unusual course of publishing the official documents while negotiations were still proceeding, and the public responded to the trust thus reposed in them by showing complete confidence in his leadership. On the French side, also, excitement grew, and the Cabinet of Paris found the exuberance of the boulevards positively embarrassing. Sandwich-men patrolled the Rue de Rivoli with placards proclaiming " Guerre à l'Angleterre ".

M. Delcassé at first showed himself as stubborn as his Anglophobe predecessor. But he realized that German *Schadenfreude* was the chief beneficiary from a Franco-British quarrel. He therefore very soon decided to work for a peaceful solution and an ultimate all-in understanding with Britain. On September 27 the British ambassador " urgently pressed him " to say whether he refused at once to recall M. Marchand. " After considering his reply for some few minutes," Sir Edmund Monson reported, " His Excellency said that he himself was ready to discuss the question in the most conciliatory spirit, but I must not ask him for the impossible."

One of the difficulties of the French Government was that it could not communicate directly and quickly with Fashoda; and therefore in the same interview with Sir Edmund Monson M. Delcassé asked whether Lord Salisbury would consent to allow a telegram from the Quai d'Orsay to be forwarded by British-Egyptian agency up the Nile. Lord Salisbury agreed at once ; and in the despatch giving his consent used the phrase which was to save the peace : "Her Majesty's Government", he telegraphed, " cannot decline to assist in forwarding a message from the French Agent in Egypt to a ' French Explorer ' who is on the Upper Nile in a difficult position." Lord Kitchener, in a message dated three days earlier, had spoken of " the explorer Marchand " ; and Lord Salisbury remembered that M. Delcassé himself, in an earlier conversation with the British ambassador, had denied that there was any " Marchand Mission ". This admission was the more significant because it came from the man who in 1896 had helped to equip the expedition which had been described as intended to give the colony of French Congo an outlet to the Nile. And at that time the French Government was also organizing an east-to-west expedition under an Orléans Prince, which was to emerge from Abyssinia and join hands with Marchand—which it fortunately failed to do. Nothing therefore could have been much more official than the two-pronged attempt to create a French barrier across Central Africa— diplomatic contradictions had certainly not all been on one side.

The denial of a French " Mission " by Delcassé was a clear indication of concession ; and Lord Salisbury, who had called up a reserve squadron of the British navy but was naturally just as desirous as M. Delcassé for a pacific solution of the quarrel, exploited this conciliatory move to the utmost. Thenceforward Marchand was always plain " Monsieur " Marchand, he was an emissary of civilization and a pioneer, his was " the secret expedition of a handful of men ", Monsieur Marchand had got himself into " an impossible position ", " in so false and unreasonable a position ", and so on.

The hard fact of Marchand's helplessness strongly supported Lord Salisbury's contention. Even French chauvinists admitted that as he could not be reinforced he must be got away ; and he could not get away without British connivance and help. The French ambassador in London for a while argued that the gallant major could return by the same route as he had come. Lord Salisbury promptly replied that " we offered no sort of impediment to his doing so ". " Yes, but ", the ambassador continued, " he cannot do so without food " ; and he would require as well fresh supplies of ammunition. Lord Salisbury answered that, with certain safeguards pledged on the word of the French Government, these could be provided. The discussions, courteous but acute, went on throughout September and October. As late as on October 30 Delcassé angrily ordered Marchand to return to Fashoda, which he had just quitted. But Lord Salisbury had his ultimatum ready ; and at last, on November 3,* the definitive order went from Paris to Marchand to " carry out the withdrawal from Fashoda ". The explorer proceeded to Cairo to make the necessary arrangements. On November 14 he returned to Fashoda and evacuated his followers via Abyssinia. He could claim with pride that he had traversed Africa from west to east by a path that no European had ever trodden before.

Lord Salisbury was as conciliatory in the moment of triumph as he had been uncompromising while the conflict lasted. He knew that, in the words of our ambassador in Paris, France felt " staggered and humiliated ". He sought to salve her hurt pride. Nothing could have been more tactful than the way he announced her surrender. It so happened that a banquet had been arranged at the Guildhall on November 4 to greet Lord Kitchener, who had returned to England at the end of October. The Prime Minister was to be there and to make the principal speech. And it was on that day that he himself received the official information that the French Government had recalled Marchand. He therefore introduced the announcement of the

* M. Delcassé's actual decision was taken on November 2.

withdrawal into his speech, but with studied casualness. " I received from the French Ambassador this afternoon," he said, " the information that the French Government had come to the conclusion that the occupation of Fashoda was of no sort of value to the French Republic, and they thought that . . . to persist in an occupation which only cost them money and did them harm, merely because some people . . . thought it might be disagreeable to an unwelcome neighbour, would not show the wisdom with which, I think, the French Republic has been uniformly guided, and they have done what I believe many other governments would have done in the same position—they have resolved that the occupation must cease." Five days later the Prime Minister had to deliver another speech at the Guildhall, this time on the occasion of the Lord Mayor's banquet. The interval between the two speeches had brought a continuous flow of tributes to the Foreign Secretary ; and not tributes only, for the success at Fashoda had radiated repercussions favourable to Britain in other parts of the world. Lord Salisbury referred to the expectations thus aroused. Many people, he remarked, seemed to be anticipating great results abroad from the recent successes in foreign policy. " Some people would say," he continued, " that we intend to seize Syria or to occupy Crete ; and a third view is that we intend to declare a protectorate of Egypt." These last words provoked a burst of loud and sustained applause, which took Lord Salisbury aback. " It is quite clear," he exclaimed, " if some of my audience were at the head of affairs what would be done. But I am sorry to say," he added in his driest tone, " that for the present I cannot rise to the height of their aspirations."

This was the climax of his policy of the last two years, for which he had sacrificed so much. It had ended in a complete triumph. But " triumph " was a word not found in his dictionary of diplomacy.

In point of fact the expectations of the optimists were not altogether falsified, inasmuch as *post hoc et propter hoc* diplomatic advantages did flow to British policy in Crete and in China. Lord Salisbury's accumulated prestige was paying dividends in all parts of the world ; and his wise moderation in the hour of victory prepared the way for a long and prosperous collaboration with Egypt and for that *entente cordiale* between this country and France which M. Delcassé now set himself to achieve. Lord Salisbury's final contribution to the conciliation of France was the obliteration of the very name of Fashoda from the map of Africa. It was renamed Kodok, by which the place is known to this day.

The French had given way, as they gave way many a time in the long struggle for colonial ascendancy, not because they lacked good men on the spot, but because their distant champions, Dupleix, Montcalm, Marchand, were not so effectively supported as their British rivals by administrations often divided by personal rivalries and always fearful of continental complications. In 1898 France was still being distracted by the Dreyfus case, Emile Zola having recently hurled his famous " J'accuse " at the head of the French War Office ; and Paris bitterly comprehended that if a divided France became involved with Britain in Africa, she would soon have Germany on her back in Europe. Above all, the French navy was not deemed to be a match for the British.

By a Convention signed by France and Britain on March 21, 1899, the north–south dividing line between the French and British spheres of influence was agreed to be the watershed between the basins of the Congo and the Nile rivers. In the Sudan an Anglo-Egyptian condominium was established ; and Lord Kitchener, still nominally a servant of the Khedive, became first Governor-General of the province. On January 3, 1899, he had already laid the foundation stone of Gordon College.

The historic drama of 1898, the clash between two great countries, was henceforward officially referred to as an " incident " —one of those " incidents ", however, that change the course of history. A colonial rivalry of two centuries, and a feud much older, disappeared, let us hope for ever, when the French champion quietly quitted his post in equatorial Africa.

CHAPTER XVIII—1895–1899.   THE THIRD MINISTRY
(continued)

SOCIAL LEGISLATION AND DIAMOND JUBILEE

The Queen's speech for the opening of the first session of the new Parliament on February 11, 1896, held but a meagre fare of social measures compared to what might have been expected from Lord Salisbury's impassioned words of the previous autumn, which were quoted in the first section of Chapter XVI.   But the engrossing events recorded in that and the following chapter sufficiently explain why the speech from the Throne gave more space to Siam, Venezuela, Armenia, Dr. Jameson, Ashanti and Chitral than to home affairs.   The Prime Minister was the last man to make the royal speech a political shop-window or to promise more than he believed he could perform.   Public opinion was absorbed throughout this month of February by the enquiry being held upon the Transvaal raiders and the extent of Cecil Rhodes's connivance with them, by the outcome of the dispute with President Cleveland and Mr. Olney, and by the sufferings of the Armenians.   Nevertheless, the Government undertook to introduce an Education Bill, a Workmen's Compensation Bill, an Agricultural Rating Bill, an Irish Land Bill, a Coal Mines Bill, a Truck Bill, and a Military Manœuvres Bill ;   and all except the two first became law before the end of the session. The proposed provision of large funds from the public purse for voluntary elementary schools, giving religious instruction in the Anglican tradition, roused the wrath of the Liberal Nonconformists.   Frustrated by the skilful Opposition leadership of Mr. H. H. Asquith in the House of Commons, Mr. Balfour had to withdraw the Bill with 1,238 amendments still to be considered.   It was pruned and modified by Balfour in the following year and successfully steered through both Houses.   It demanded the highest financial supply ever yet voted for education in this country.

The Workmen's Compensation Bill was both introduced and passed in 1897.   The new conception of making the employer liable for accidents befalling the employed, being one of the many projects of Chamberlain's fertile mind, was made his special charge in the House of Commons, while Lord Salisbury took up its defence in the other place. It was of course attacked by right-wing Conservatives as a Socialist and therefore a dangerous innovation ; but the Prime Minister, with, perhaps, rather more casuistry than conviction, argued that it was the reverse of Socialism because it " threw back the responsibility from society to the individual ". His deepest nature was revealed when he added the argument : " When we pass from property to life the claims of liberty must not be allowed to endanger the lives of the citizens in any well-governed State." Lord Salisbury was taunted for this staunch support of the ex-Radical from Birmingham. But his loyalty to his colleague was absolute. Delegating, as usual, all legislation which was not his primary concern to the responsible Minister—in this case to two Ministers, the Home Secretary, White-Ridley, who was in nominal charge, and to Joseph Chamberlain—he confidently entrusted the passage of the Bill through the Commons to its originator. He characteristically believed in giving full play to the spontaneity which goes with creativeness ; he knew that the father would look after his offspring better than the Minister who was nominally in charge. He was justified in his trust ; and, as Prime Minister, became responsible before the end of the session for a measure which, thirty years before, he would certainly have regarded as ill-advised and revolutionary.

The Agricultural Rating Bill pleased the landed interests without provoking any violent antagonism ; but the Irish Land Bill, which the First Lord of the Treasury's younger brother, Gerald Balfour, introduced in a three-hour speech, provoked the sharp controversy and invective which any law-making for dwellers on the land was certain to arouse in Ireland. In this case it was the landowners who felt that they were being deprived of their rights ; but nevertheless native Irish critics kept the House sitting till the early morning hours with their challenging amendments, and the Bill only became law on the last day of the session of 1896. The Prime Minister certainly owed escape from complete exhaustion to his membership of the Upper House ; and in that calm atmosphere the Secretary of State for War, Lord Lansdowne, easily gained acceptance for a Military Manœuvres Bill for " acquiring space for operations over an extensive district ". It was in the course of a morning ride with Sir Michael Hicks Beach that the idea occurred to the two country squires that Salisbury Plain would be just the place for the large-scale exercises which the War Office was anxious to carry out ; and neither Lords nor Commons raised objections to the project. Lord Salisbury found time to interest himself personally in a Bill which amongst other safeguards for workers forbade house-maids to sit on window-sills when cleaning the outside panes— one of them having fallen from an upper floor and been killed ; and he earned an ephemeral sobriquet of " The Housemaids' Markiss " in the club-rooms of Pall Mall.

He certainly had no reason to be dissatisfied with the achievement of his Government during the year 1896 either at home or abroad ; it was the more discouraging that an unusual rush of seven by-elections in January and February of the next year gave a steep decline to the Conservative–Unionist vote in six out of the seven. 1897 was indeed politically a black year for Lord Salisbury. His foreign policy of conciliation brought him the loss of Conservative votes which he minded more than the temporary decline of his own reputation, though neither the one nor the other deflected him from his settled course. Nor did he forfeit for an instant the confidence and support of his Sovereign (from whom he had accepted in the previous year the time-honoured post of Lord Warden of the Cinque Ports).

A series of minor measures, such as the Infant Life Protection Act, a Merchant Shipping Act, and the Liability of Shipowners Act occupied most of this 1897 session. The House of Commons also gave a second reading to a Private Member's Woman's Suffrage Bill. The Prime Minister's views on it were not expressed in public, but in private conversation he favoured this drastic social-political change which was only to be effected a quarter of a century later.* He spoke favourably, if humorously, of the wearing of bloomers by female exponents of the new craze of bicycling.

2

But this was minor matter in a year which was made memorable by the celebration of Queen Victoria's Diamond Jubilee. On June 20 she had been Queen for 60 years. She spent that day

* See Lord Cecil of Chelwood's *All the Way*.

at Windsor, surrounded by her numerous royal relatives who had travelled from all parts of Europe ; next day she came to her capital, at that moment more dominantly and manifestly the capital of the Empire than at any time before or since ; and on June 22 London saw a pageant of imperial Britain such as had never yet been seen. Every larger colony sent a contingent of troops ; Londoners' eyes were dazzled by the brilliant accoutrement of a troop of Indian cavalry, and gazed with astonished interest at the " dark auxiliaries from our Asiatic and African dependencies ". Even today the capital can be stirred by a pageant on the grand scale over a six-mile route. In 1897 it was a new, an inspiring, an exciting experience ; and when the celebrations had ended with a naval review in the Solent in which 173 warships took part, without a single vessel having been withdrawn from foreign service, John Bull gasped with pride and gave vent here and there to expressions of vaunting jingoism.

Lord Salisbury's was a passive part. " Every day ", wrote J. L. Garvin of Joseph Chamberlain during the Jubilee weeks, " was giddy with endless functions and ceremonies." When officialism required it, the Prime Minister appeared at a dinner or reception, and when absolutely necessary he made a speech, and made it with grace and authority. But he chose rather to preside at a distance, to take responsibility for the decisions of others, and to give particular but discriminating support to his energetic Colonial Secretary. It had been Chamberlain's initiative to invite the troops from overseas, and all of the eleven Colonial premiers—of Canada, Newfoundland, New South Wales, Victoria, South Australia, Queensland, Western Australia, Tasmania, New Zealand, The Cape and Natal—and they were all appointed to the Privy Council.

From their presence sprang the Second Colonial Conference, not deliberately planned by either the Prime Minister or Chamberlain. Nor did it reach any conclusions upon the three major matters discussed—inter-political relations, commercial relations and defence. But the twelve participants found themselves in complete agreement that mutual support was in every case desirable, and that as opportunities presented themselves every measure of closer collaboration should be eagerly furthered. A very agreeable and unexpected offer was that of " an ironclad of the first class ", placed " at the disposal of the Empire " by

Sir Gordon Sprigg, of South Africa ; and Sir Wilfrid Laurier, the Liberal Premier of Canada, impressed audiences in different parts of the country by his thoughtful addresses on imperial topics.

Chamberlain's mind and speeches had been full of projects for federation and a Zollverein. But Lord Salisbury's simple phrases adequately summed up the sentiments evoked and the intangible results obtained by the imperial assemblage : " We are undertaking the great experiment ", he said, at a banquet in the Imperial Institute, " of trying to sustain such an empire entirely upon the basis of mutual goodwill, sympathy and affection. . . . It is the triumph of a moral idea in the construction of a great political organization which is the object and the effort in which we have all joined." And his Guildhall speech later in the year contained a rebuke to the manifestations of jingoism which had in the meantime appeared : " We do not wish to take territory simply because it may look well to paint it red upon the map. . . . We wish to extend the commerce, the trade, the industry and the civilization of mankind." As in home affairs, so in colonial developments he disbelieved in getting results by legislative action ; but, in furtherance of the imperial ideal of freer trade which had been advocated by the colonial premiers and most vigorously of all by Chamberlain, he denounced forthwith, before the end of July, the existing commercial treaties with Germany and Belgium which precluded the colonies from giving a preference to British goods. The denunciation cannot have been easy for him, considering the importance which he was giving at this moment to good relations with Germany. But he put the Empire first ; and he was still able to reply to foreign protests that Britain alone of the imperial Powers did not insist on the exclusion of foreign goods from her colonial markets.

3

The ensuing session of 1898 saw the Criminal Evidence Act, the Inebriates Act and the Local Government for Ireland Act put upon the Statute Book—as well as minor measures covering Vagrancy, Vaccination, Prison Administration and other matters which hardly came to Lord Salisbury's notice. But he attached great importance to the Irish Bill which, in the words of the Queen's speech, was designed " for the organization of a system of local government in Ireland substantially similar to that which, within the last few years, has been established in Great Britain ". It gave the whole of Ireland the largest measure of self-rule she had enjoyed since the Union, and proved to all the world the consistency and good faith of Lord Salisbury's policy of everything for Ireland except a separate Legislature.

In 1899 eleven Acts of Parliament were passed, varying from a Seats for Shop Assistants Act to the establishment of the Gordon Memorial College in Khartum, which crowned the conquest of the Sudan, and from a Sale of Food and Drugs Act to the assumption by the British Government of a Protectorate over Nigeria. This last was, of course, the business of Joseph Chamberlain, who however showed that his zeal for social reform was in no wise abated by simultaneously promoting the Small Houses Acquisition Act, enabling occupiers to become owners. It is significant of the outlook of that decade that Lord Salisbury's entrusting of the Bill to the Colonial Secretary was much criticized by contemporary commentators. A " fantastic arrangement ", said one ; and another charged Chamberlain with being too busy with what did not concern him to pay proper attention to the prevention of tropical diseases—a most unjust accusation, as the pages of J. L. Garvin and Julian Amery prove to the last syllable. Old Age Pensions was another non-Colonial cause which Chamberlain had much at heart. It had indeed many advocates on both sides of the House, and Mr. Balfour announced that the Government would bring forward a measure of its own on the subject. Lord Salisbury's Government was formally committed to the project of Old Age Pensions. That must be placed on record in any account of his administrations. But he himself remained aloof, and probably regarded the schemes devised by private individuals and by Mr. Henry Chaplin's Committee as impracticable on the ground of expense. Even Chamberlain exclaimed to his constituents in Birmingham that " Rome was not built in a day and we are not going to have Old Age Pensions in a week ". The cost of a quite modest scheme was estimated at £34,000,000 per annum ; and if its critics can now themselves be criticized for considering the figure " prohibitive ", let it be remembered that the total Budget figures of expenditure and revenue in that year 1899 were respectively £110,927,000 and £111,157,000. It was left to a young

Welsh Radical, David Lloyd George, who was then engaged in daily tilting at Lord Salisbury and his colleagues in the House of Lords, to prove, twelve years later, that the country could take a much heavier load of taxation than it was carrying at the end of last century. In the meantime even Chamberlain's gargantuan mind had to confine itself to the ever more pressing negotiations with the President of the Transvaal Republic.

4

But before we proceed to the Boer War and the declining days of Lord Salisbury's career, mention should be made of two uncongenial tasks, the performance of which threw light on the non-political facets of his character. He was always irked by the business of personal appointments. Possessing no instinctive judgment of character and cordially disliking patronage in all its forms, even the preferment of Bishops vexed him. " I declare they die to spite me," he exclaimed when two or three episcopal vacancies occurred within a few weeks. And upon him of all men devolved the charge of naming a Poet Laureate in succession to Tennyson. He had died in 1892, and Gladstone had engaged in prolonged discussions and search without being able, not unnaturally, to discover anybody worthy to fill the large place of his admired friend. Lord Salisbury's nature was allergic to poets—he had had no acquaintance with Tennyson, though the views on political evolution of that great figure of the Victorian Age so closely resembled his own and though Tennyson had at least on one occasion voted with Lord Salisbury against the Liberal leader on a division in the House of Lords. The new Prime Minister was not in any case going to waste time over an appointment which seemed to him of minimum importance ; and on assuming office in 1895 he almost at once offered the post to Alfred Austin, who eagerly accepted it (January 1, 1896). Lord Salisbury knew that he was a prolific writer of verse as well as a good journalist and was religiously minded (he was a not very ardent Roman Catholic). He had founded and edited the monthly *National Review* in 1883 ; his Conservatism was irreproachable. The new Laureate was soon—too soon— celebrating public events in rhyme with the same assiduity with which he had previously written his leading articles—but it was

Rudyard Kipling whom the Diamond Jubilee inspired to create the " Recessional ".

William Ewart Gladstone died on May 19, 1898 ; and upon Lord Salisbury devolved the duty of paying a last solemn tribute in the House of Lords. What an opportunity to salute in imposing phrases the adversary whose personality he so much admired and whose politics he so heartily detested ! He might have dwelt feelingly on the contradictions of a character at once speculative and practical, have referred to the vicissitudes of a career which had impinged at a hundred points upon his own. He might, too, have referred to their common devotion to theology and the classics, perhaps also to the literary tastes, contrasting so sharply with his own, which made Gladstone an authority on Homer and Dante, a reviewer of Tennyson's poetry and a translator of Horace and of Leopardi. But to have made the death of a fellow-statesman an opportunity for an oration would have been alien to Lord Salisbury's nature. Instead, he said simply and sincerely what he felt. Moving the Address to the Queen that a monument be erected to him in Westminster Abbey, he asked how it was that Mr. Gladstone was held in such universal esteem ? And he answered his rhetorical question in the following noble passage :

" Of course, he had qualities that distinguished him from all other men ; and you may say that it was his transcendent intellect, his astonishing power of attaching men to him, and the great influence he was able to exert upon the thought and convictions of his contemporaries. But these things, which explain the attachment, the adoration of those whose ideas he represented, would not explain why it is that sentiments almost as fervent are felt and expressed by those whose ideas were not carried out by his policy. My Lords, I do not think the reason is to be found in anything so far removed from the common feelings of mankind as the abstruse and controversial questions of the policy of the day. They had nothing to do with it. Whether he was right, or whether he was wrong, in all the measures, or in most of the measures which he proposed—those are matters of which the discussion has passed by, and would certainly be singularly inappropriate here ; they are really remitted to the judgment of future generations, who will securely judge from experience what we can only decide by forecast.

" It was on account of considerations more common to the masses of human beings, to the general working of the human mind, than any controversial questions of policy that men recognized in him a man guided—whether under mistaken impressions or not, it matters not—but guided in all the steps he took, in all the efforts that he made, by a high moral ideal. What he sought were the attainments of great ideals ; and, whether they were based on sound convictions or not, they could have issued from nothing but the greatest and the purest moral aspirations ; and he is honoured by his countrymen, because through so many years, across so many vicissitudes and conflicts, they had recognized this one characteristic of his action, which has never ceased to be felt. He will leave behind him the memory of a great Christian statesman." Then, after a further reference to Mr. Gladstone's salutary influence on the political and social thought of his generation, Lord Salisbury ended his tribute with the words : " He will be long remembered not so much for the causes in which he was engaged or the political projects which he favoured, but as a great example, to which history hardly furnishes a parallel, of a great Christian man."

Of the many memorial speeches delivered, Mr. Gladstone's biographer picks out Lord Salisbury's as going " nearest to the core "—a remarkable commendation from an avowed agnostic who was a political follower and disciple of the dead statesman.

PART III
DECLINE

LORD SALISBURY IN OLD AGE
From a photograph in the possession of the author's father

CHAPTER XIX—1899–1900. THE THIRD MINISTRY
(continued)

BOER WAR—KHAKI ELECTION

Lord Salisbury was 69 years old in 1899, and it would have been better for his reputation if he had then retired and *finis coronat opus* had been written across his last consummate diplomatic success. The exertions of the preceding four years had made too large a draft upon his energies. His powers of body and mind were declining ; and—which enhanced the evil—his moral authority outlasted his physical vigour. In the eyes of his contemporaries he was still the Olympian arbiter whose decisions it was presumptuous to challenge ; and by posterity, which most easily remembers a statesman as he last appeared on the stage, he is too often thought of as a corpulent, lethargic, rather absent-minded old gentleman who did not recognize members of his own Cabinet or household, and who seldom stirred from Hatfield. And the caricature, like every good caricature, is but disproportioned truth. One incident of many may be related. About this time he was walking in a street near his London house accompanied by his soldier son, when an elderly, well-dressed man raised his hat to them. " Who is your guardsman friend ? " asked Lord Salisbury, to the amusement (though not to the surprise) of his son, for the polite passer-by was his father's butler. Stories of the kind abounded among his acquaintance. But the old Prime Minister thought it was his duty to carry on, and his supporters emphatically thought so too. After all, he reflected, it was normal that nature should have its way, his eyes grow dimmer and his mind slower—while also his girth grew larger and his chest more sunken. He made no effort to stay the course of nature. It probably never occurred to him to take, like Bismarck, stimulants by day and sedatives at night. And he became more careless than ever about his clothes.

And in the summer of this year his burden was made heavier to bear. In July Lady Salisbury had a stroke, from which she never fully recovered, and she died on November 20—the wife who had been the mainspring of his career, his faithful companion, his unfailing counsellor. Now the mainspring was broken. . . . And his other faithful counsellor, Queen Victoria, she too was sinking at last into senility. She could no longer count on the dependability of her remarkable memory ; her eyesight, like his, was cripplingly weak ; she could not read ordinary script. Neither one nor the other gave up working to the limit of the energies that remained to them ; but the Queen had to cut down her letter writing ; and Lord Salisbury gave way to moments of drowsiness. His daughter recounts that he would drop off to sleep, pen in hand, when composing a despatch ; and then, refreshed, resume after ten or fifteen minutes.

It was thus not altogether surprising that he should push his delegation of work one step further this summer by entrusting the conduct of the Anglo-Boer negotiations fully to Chamberlain. He, as Colonial Secretary, had already, as we have seen, been the British spokesman in the preliminary exchanges with the South African Republic ; but the negotiations had by now grown to something much beyond a local dispute ; and this was the first time that Lord Salisbury allowed the actual negotiations of a major foreign-colonial transaction to be wholly conducted by a colleague. " Considerable freedom had been accorded to Mr. Chamberlain by the Cabinet," writes Mrs. Dugdale, who obtained most of her information on these matters direct from her uncle, A. J. Balfour. " Nor was Lord Salisbury ever quick to interfere with the judgment of those to whom he had entrusted responsibility."

So far from interfering was the Prime Minister that he hardly opened his lips to speak publicly on the growing crisis. On April 29 he chose the Royal Academy banquet as the somewhat incongruous occasion on which to announce that he had reached an agreement with Russia on the respective rights of the two countries in China ; but the negotiations with President Kruger were the business of Mr. Chamberlain in London and Sir Alfred Milner in Capetown ; and Lord Salisbury only insisted that the public should be kept as closely informed as possible by the issue of Blue Books—just as he had issued one at a critical moment of the negotiations with France over Fashoda.

The first of these was published on June 14 and showed that Milner's conference with Kruger at Bloemfontein had been worse than useless. The Boer President had rejected outright the proposal that British and other foreign subjects should be granted full civic rights after five years' residence in the Transvaal. And the President's manner made the rejection more exasperating than it need have been. He brusquely claimed that the Convention of 1882 had lapsed and that Britain was no longer the " paramount Power " in the Transvaal. And all the time the British Government knew that Kruger was establishing connexions with the discontented Dutch element in Cape Colony, that he was concluding an offensive and defensive alliance with his neighbours of the Orange Free State, and that he was accumulating a vast store of arms, which he purchased with the money extracted from the unenfranchised but tax-paying Uitlanders. Behind all that was the recollection of the Jameson Raid, which hung like a hangman's rope round the British negotiator's neck ; and the memory of the older Boers brooded on the long trek northward half a century before, with all its hardships, which they had undergone for the very purpose of living their own lives in their own way. These new immigrants, they insisted, must live 14 years in the country before they could expect to be naturalized.

Untoward incidents and fruitless official exchanges continued ; and on August 26 another Blue Book only showed that relations between Pretoria and London were more strained than before, to which point was given by a speech delivered by Chamberlain at Highbury on that same day. Kruger, he said, " dribbles out reforms like water from a squeezed sponge ", and " the sands are running out in the glass ". The " dribbles " of concessions made by Kruger were communicated to the British public on September 1 ; and three weeks later the Colonial Secretary telegraphed to Milner that " it was still open to the South African Republic to secure a peaceful settlement without any sacrifice of independence ". But the formal notice from Kruger to the Colonial Office that he disowned any kind of British suzerainty over the Transvaal was met by a Cabinet decision to reinforce the meagre British forces in the Cape and Natal. Whereupon Kruger handed to the British agent in Pretoria a note demanding that all British forces on the borders of the Republic should be withdrawn within 48 hours and all reinforcements which had arrived in South Africa since June 1 should be sent back to the coast and removed from Africa. The ultimatum was of course rejected, and two days later, on October 11, he ordered his armed burghers to cross the frontiers, called upon the Dutch of Cape Colony to rise, and obtained a simultaneous declaration of war by the Orange Free State—whose forces immediately invaded Cape Colony and " annexed " a part of it.

Lord Salisbury has been criticized for his inactivity and silence during the summer of this year, and perhaps justly ; but the reasons of his passivity will already have been clear to the reader. He was reluctant to assert his right of interference when once he had deputed another to act for him ; and his reluctance was exaggerated by the forcible character of Joseph Chamberlain on the one hand and his own fatigue on the other—the fatigue which was rendered so much more unnerving by his profound depression at the prospect of war and the long drawn-out ill-health of his wife. It was not until war had broken out that he resolved to make a speech. The Lord Mayor's banquet was due to be held on November 9 ; he could not seek to avoid his duty to respond for the Government, even though by that time Lady Salisbury was almost literally dying before his eyes.

He had indeed more than the conventional reason for speaking to the world from the Guildhall. On October 27 he had received a long, confidential and disturbing despatch from the British ambassador to France, Sir Edmund Monson. Well informed by personal friends among foreign members of the diplomatic corps in Paris, Sir Edmund reported that the Russian Foreign Minister, Count Mouravieff, was busy trying to form a European coalition against Britain.

Mouravieff had come to Paris on what was described as a private visit, and had gone on to Spain. In both places he urged in secret conversations that the leading Continental countries should " take common action against the ever-increasing aggressions and expansion of England ". He played upon the soreness over Fashoda that still subsisted in France, and proposed that Spain should be rewarded by securing Gibraltar and a larger slice of Morocco. He implied that he knew Germany was ready to come in—a plausible supposition, since the Kaiser had been posing as the friend of Kruger and the German Press was even more virulently anti-British than that of France, and indeed of most of the other European nations. Portugal and Austria-Hungary were the least unfriendly ; and it was the diplomats of this last country who rendered us the valuable service of divulging the plan to Britain. Both in Paris and in St. Petersburg the British and Austro-Hungarian embassies were on terms of close friendship ; Monson learned all about the plot from a personal friend, and Sir Charles Hardinge (afterwards Lord Hardinge of Penshurst) from Prince Kinsky, the Austrian chargé d'affaires in the Russian capital.

Lord Salisbury referred to these intrigues in the curiously loose language which he sometimes found useful. " I have seen it suggested," he said at the Guildhall, " but it seems to me a wild suggestion, that other foreign Powers will interfere after this conflict and will, in some form or other, dictate to those who are concerned in it what its upshot should be. . . . The interference of nobody else [sic] will have any effect upon us. . . . I am convinced that no such idea is in the minds of any Government in the world."

These apparently casual phrases were no doubt carefully calculated to show the foreign Governments concerned that Mouravieff's plan was known to him, without alarming the British public by hinting darkly at a dangerous plot. And by the time he spoke, his statement that no such idea was in the minds of any foreign Government was supported by the facts that M. Delcassé, despite French public opinion, was resolutely working for a rapprochement, that Kaiser Wilhelm contented himself with urging Britain to make the best of a bad job and come to a settlement with the Boers, and that in Russia the Tsar was steadily pro-British—though his attitude did not prevent the Russian Government from causing us petty annoyances on the Afghan frontier and sending a colonel of sinister reputation to be military attaché at the Boer headquarters.

Lord Salisbury adhered to his policy of peace almost at any price with these potential antagonists. The campaign in South Africa was going badly. Our unpreparedness, for which Lord Salisbury must share the responsibility with his Secretary of State for War, was capped by bad generalship. Buller was defeated at Colenso, Methuen at Magersfontein, and Gatacre by the Dutch irregulars in Cape Colony at Stormberg. The country was shaken at this series of reverses, especially as there were many responsible politicians, chiefly in the ranks of the Liberals, who considered the war to be unjustified and wrongful.

Neither the Queen nor Lord Salisbury nor the Government, however, were for one moment deflected from their purpose. How clearly this had formed itself in the Prime Minister's mind, and how closely it approximated to the ultimate settlement in South Africa, was demonstrated in another passage in his Guildhall speech. " Whenever we are victorious," he said, " we shall consult the vast interests which are committed to our care. We shall consult the vast duties which it lies upon us to perform, and taking counsel with the uniform traditions of our colonial government and of the moderation and equal justice to all races of men which it has been our uniform practice to observe, I have no doubt that we shall so arrange that the issue of this conflict will confer good government upon the area where it rages, and will give a security that is sorely needed, for the future, from the recurrence of any such dangers, or the necessity for any such exertions, and the restoration of peace and civilization to that portion of the world."

The tired, repetitive wording of the speech only served to echo the more faithfully the thoughts which were uppermost in his mind—confidence in a victorious outcome of the war, priority for good government, belief in equal justice for all races, and a longing for the restoration of peace and the extension of civilization.

But if the war was to be won the first and immediate need was to create a higher command capable of winning it. Lansdowne, supported by Balfour, pressed the claims of Lord Roberts to take over the supreme command from Buller. Lord Salisbury demurred, on the unexpected ground that Roberts was too old— not so paradoxical as it sounds, for he spoke as one knowing the infirmities of age. But he allowed himself to be persuaded by his nephew on the condition that Kitchener should also go out as Chief of Staff.* Lord Salisbury forgot to inform the Queen of this important decision, which however ruffled their relations for a few days only. The tide of war was turned as soon as the new High Command arrived in Africa. Kimberley, Ladysmith and Mafeking were relieved, and by June, 1900, Roberts had entered Johannesburg and Pretoria, the Boer regular armies were defeated and dispersed, and Britain now had in Africa the biggest

* Lansdowne, at the War Office, from the first intended that, if Roberts went out, Kitchener should go with him.

army she had ever sent overseas. But Kruger and the Boers refused to give up the struggle. Kruger soon fled from Africa and set himself with only too much success to further inflame Continental feelings against Britain ; and Boer guerilla bands continued to engage and harass the British forces for two years. It was a dreary business of blockhouse warfare, with occasional dashing raids by brilliant leaders like Smuts and Denys Reitz. The Boers were farmers one day and belligerents the next ; so in order to safeguard their families Kitchener devised a system of concentration camps for women and children. Unfortunately the earlier ones were hastily prepared and ill supplied with water. In consequence, hundreds of the inmates died of enteric fever and diphtheria ; and this tragic consequence of what was intended for a work of mercy supplied congenial material for Kruger's propaganda in Europe. Monson wrote from Paris of " the infamous language and shameless mendacity of the French Press " ; Hardinge described the hostility of the Russian Press and society towards Britain as " phenomenal ". The German newspapers were even more scurrilous. But the volatile German Emperor, who had stormed against us at the time of the Jameson Raid, and was to try to form a coalition against us five years later—after the creation of the Entente Cordiale—at this time, after a moment of hesitation, went out of his way to display friendship for Britain. When Kruger, having been received at the Elysée and had an enthusiastic send-off from the Paris crowds, was on his way to pay his respects to the man he fondly regarded as his chief European patron, he received at Cologne a message informing him that the Kaiser would be unable to grant him an audience ; so he omitted Berlin from his itinerary. And before this, in the autumn of 1899, Kaiser Wilhelm had chosen to pay a visit to the Queen, his grandmother, during which, although it was described as a " personal " visit, he made every gesture of friendliness to officials and the public. He went to Windsor, and to Sandringham as the guest of the Prince of Wales ; but he brought his new Chancellor, von Bülow, with him, and he desired to meet the Prime Minister and other members of the Cabinet. Lord Salisbury excused himself on account of the death of Lady Salisbury, which had occurred on the day of the Emperor's arrival. The Kaiser's principal political conversation was therefore with Chamberlain, who was disturbed to find how envied

313

and isolated Britain had become and advocated a " defensive " alliance with Germany—which would be a " natural alliance " for the English, he said in an unexpected outburst of enthusiasm for the project in his famous speech at Leicester on November 30. The proposal was much criticized in England, and turned down brusquely by Bülow, who was by then back in Berlin. Lord Salisbury remained aloof ; from the first he had let it be understood that he was hostile to an alliance. His scepticism and quietly obstructive obstinacy undoubtedly reflected and represented the view of the country.

It also became clear that the German Government was not firmly behind the Emperor ; and the effect of his contacts with the leaders of the nation was marred by his patronizing advice to them on how to win the war, alternating with a strong recommendation to bring it to an end by agreement. An extraordinary example of his fatuity and lack of understanding of the British temper is afforded by the letter which he wrote a short time afterwards to the Prince of Wales. " It would certainly be better ", he wrote to his uncle, " to bring matters to a settlement. Even the best football club, if it is beaten notwithstanding the most gallant defence, accepts finally its defeat with equanimity. Last year in the great cricket match of England v. Australia, the former took the victory of the latter quietly, with chivalrous acknowledgment of her opponent." * His was precisely the kind of intervention which filled Lord Salisbury with disgust, distrust and contempt.

But if the Kaiser's visit had only doubtful success in royal and official circles it certainly made a favourable impression on the British people, who were surprised and vexed by the almost universal abuse they were receiving from foreign countries ; and the Kaiser also made headway in the European chanceries for his project of mediation between Boer and Britain.

The intervention to this effect actually came from a most unexpected quarter—from Washington, prompted by an approach to the United States consul in Pretoria by the defeated Presidents of the Transvaal and Orange Free State. The sequence of events was as follows. On March 5, 1900, the two Presidents telegraphed from Bloemfontein direct to the British Government offering peace on condition that the " incontestable independence

* Lord Hardinge of Penshurst, *Old Diplomacy*, p. 74.

314

of both Republics as sovereign international States " should be recognized and respected. Lord Salisbury received the telegram on March 6 and answered it five days later. He recalled the circumstances in which the war had broken out—the secret preparations of the two Republics followed by the unprovoked irruptions into Cape Colony and Natal—and said that in view of the use to which the Republics had put " the position which they previously enjoyed ", Her Majesty's Government could only answer that they were not prepared to assent to the independence either of the South African Republic or of the Orange Free State.

The two Republican leaders thereupon canvassed the foreign representatives in their capitals, beginning with the American consul ; and two days after the British Government's reply had been received the U.S. chargé d'affaires in London was instructed by Washington to inform Lord Salisbury that he was in a position to communicate a request from the Governments of the two South African Republics to the President of the United States to intervene with a view to the cessation of hostilities ; that the same request had been made by the two Republics to the other foreign representatives in the two capitals ; that the President of the United States expressed his earnest hope that a way to bring about peace might be found ; and that " he would be glad to aid in a friendly manner to bring about so happy a result ".

Lord Salisbury answered promptly, courteously and firmly that " Her Majesty's Government does not propose to accept the intervention of any Power in the South African war ". Not finding it convenient to be in the House of Lords to make the announcement himself, he commissioned Mr. Balfour to make it in the House of Commons, where it was received with prolonged applause, only the Irish Nationalists and some of the Liberals conspicuously withholding their approval.

" Joe's War," Lord Salisbury used to murmur sorrowfully in the privacy of his family . . . he had settled so many colonial conflicts without war ; but he never for an instant refused to accept responsibility for it in public. He had backed the Colonial Secretary throughout the negotiations, though showing himself, in Mr. Garvin's apt words, " disinclined to be hastened ". " I can summon the Cabinet when you please," he had typically written to Chamberlain on September 18, 1899, " but I should not show any symptom of haste yet." Once the war had begun

315

he never wavered in his determination to see it through. In this attitude he had the robust support of the Queen—veteran sovereign and veteran statesman were equally *tenaces propositi usque ad finem.* It was in the worst days of the war that Mr. Balfour went to Windsor on Lord Salisbury's behalf and opened his remarks with a consolatory, reassuring phrase, which provoked the great old lady to make her famous reply : " Please understand that there is no one depressed in *this* house—We are not interested in the possibilities of defeat—they do not exist." And in April, 1900— in her 83rd year—she abandoned her annual holiday in the South of France and went to discontented Dublin instead—the city whose representatives at Westminster denounced the war at every opportunity, but whose citizens gave her a boisterous welcome and sent thousands of soldiers to the front. In all the circumstances it was not surprising that the words Tennyson applied to the aged King Arthur, " Authority forgets a dying king ", were never considered by the British people to be relevant to Queen Victoria, or to her chief Minister.

One of the few cheering features for Lord Salisbury of a war which he hated was the rally of overseas Britons to the mother-country in her days of darkness and difficulty. Australia, Canada, New Zealand and the loyalists of South Africa sent thousands of mounted riflemen who were the best equipped of any arms to beard the Boer on his native veldt.

2

The Boer War was far from being Lord Salisbury's only vexation. Over and above the intricate disputes about contraband and the rights of search at sea which it generated, and to which he gave his personal attention, the question of the Portuguese colonies had been brought up by Germany ; the same country was seeking a concession from Turkey to construct a railway to Bagdad ; and soon China was to be in ferment and become the scene of armed intervention by the Great Powers.

Throughout the prolonged and secret discussions on a possible re-distribution of the African territories of Portugal Lord Salisbury played a negative role, and they need not be recounted here in detail. When he had exclaimed that there were living nations and dying nations, and that the Latin nations were decadent, he was only saying aloud what most people then believed. The world had seen one empire after another crumble and disappear ; in recent history Spain had lost almost all her oversea territories ; Portugal's government had become a scramble of needy political careerists to secure the fruits of office ; and many people would have agreed with the remark of the King of Greece to Sir Edmund Monson in Paris at the time of the Dreyfus trial that " everything seems to be rotten " and France was " decaying " (*en decadence*). It did not therefore seem in the 'nineties unreasonable to suppose that bankrupt Portugal might feel inclined to let the rest of her colonies go, as she had relinquished her hold on Brazil ; and it seemed mere common sense that the potential heirs should reach an agreement among themselves so as to avoid outbidding each other at the auction or, even worse, coming to blows. Portugal's credit abroad was almost gone and her undeveloped colonies were a burden on her exhausted exchequer. She owed money to Germany and Britain and other foreign countries. In 1898 she had wanted more help from this country. We were then already at odds with the Transvaal ; and it naturally occurred to Chamberlain that if we were to lend any more money we must have some guarantee ; and if a guarantee were required what more appropriate security could be offered than the southern part of Portuguese East Africa containing Delagoa Bay, through which foreign arms and ammunition were passing to President Kruger ? Rumours of these proposals reached Berlin, where of course they were interpreted as a British design to seize Lourenço Marques, the port of Delagoa Bay, and where they provoked insistence on Germany's right to share in the spoils. Lord Salisbury refused to bargain with Germany, and insisted throughout that any arrangement between Britain and Portugal must be a straightforward financial transaction. During his absence from England, however, in the spring of 1898, Balfour, his deputy at the Foreign Office, and the ever-eager Chamberlain, took up the negotiations, and pushed them to a conclusion during another of their chief's absences in August. The Agreement with Prince Hatzfeldt, signed on August 30, 1898, was itself inoffensive. In order to " obviate international complications " and " preserve the integrity and independence " of Portugal it was agreed between Britain and Germany that neither country should make a further loan to Portugal without informing the other, which would have the right to take up a share of it ; and parts of the

Portuguese colonies of Mozambique, Angola and Timor were detailed as regions the revenues of which were to be assigned to the two contracting States as security for their money. Attached to the Treaty, however, was a secret Convention, according to which, if Portugal could not maintain the integrity of her colonial possessions, Britain and Germany agreed to oppose the intervention of any third Power. And to this highly secret Convention there was attached a still more secret Note, which laid down that if either party obtained the permanent cession of Portuguese colonial territory the cession should not become valid unless and until the other party had secured analogous gains in its sphere. In defence of the Balfour-Chamberlain policy it can be said that it undoubtedly improved Anglo-German relations and contributed greatly to the friendly attitude of the Kaiser during the Boer War.

Nevertheless, when Lord Salisbury returned from France soon afterwards and was informed of the terms of the Anglo-German bargain, he was very angry. For the only time in his life he used harsh words to his nephew. He knew that Portugal, in spite of all her difficulties, declined to entertain the idea of parting with her colonies, which were her " only guarantee of national importance ". These secret Agreements went far beyond the purely financial arrangement which he had authorized. Portugal was Britain's only ally ; the fact that the Treaty of Alliance was over 500 years old no doubt gave it a special significance to Lord Salisbury. Next year, in the midst of many other preoccupations, he sought a way to remedy the mischief that had been done by his lieutenants. He summoned to consultation the Anglophil Minister of Portugal, the Marquis de Soveral, who had spent almost all his diplomatic career in this country and whose ability, geniality and faultless manners had gained for him the friendship of the Prince of Wales and a special place in London society. His acute intelligence had apprehended something of the Anglo-German bargain which had been made at the potential expense of Portugal ; now he and Lord Salisbury came to terms at the potential expense of Germany—and again without the potential sufferer being informed. This second Agreement, it is true, merely re-asserted the old Anglo-Portuguese treaties in modern guise. It re-engaged Britain " to defend and protect all conquests and colonies belonging to the Crown of Portugal against all his enemies, future as well as present ", and it included a

Portuguese promise not to let arms pass through Lourenço Marques to the Transvaal. The so-called " Windsor Treaty " was signed on October 14, 1899, three days after the outbreak of the Boer War. It was therefore of the greatest immediate value to this country ; and the reaffirmation of an ancient alliance could have afforded umbrage to none had it not been contradictory to, though not legally incompatible with, the secret German Agreement of the previous year. According to Lord Grey in *Twenty-Five Years*, Soveral had told Lord Salisbury that he knew all about the secret Anglo-German bargain, and the British Prime Minister can hardly be blamed for restoring confidential relations between allies who were both colonial Powers immediately concerned in the future of the Boer Republics. All the same the two Treaties created for British foreign policy an embarrassing heritage of duality.

3

Two other harassing questions which need not detain us long were those of Samoa and the Bagdad Railway. The former prompted Kaiser Wilhelm's understandable gibe that " the British Government appears to have two heads " ; for once more Joseph Chamberlain's pro-German policy appeared to be passively obstructed by Lord Salisbury ; but the Kaiser seems to have been thinking less of this duality of control in British policy than of the readiness of England to make any concessions asked for by France or Russia but to haggle over every inch of territory coveted by Germany—a sentiment he expressed in picturesque language to a British military attaché. The galaxy of islands known as Samoa in any case only remotely interested Britain, and the outbreak of the Boer War induced Lord Salisbury to agree to Germany taking one half of them and the United States the other.

Lord Salisbury was less obstructive to German expansion as expressed in the desire to build a railway from opposite Constantinople across Asia Minor to Bagdad. There were several reasons for his acquiescence. In the first place it was a financial and economic project, without, at first, territorial implications. In the second place, he had always been in favour of the development, the civilizing, as he would have said, of nearer Asia by the collaboration of a Western Power with Turkey. There had been a time when he hoped that that Power would be Britain. He and Disraeli had built up a position of predominance in Constantinople which, he considered, the succeeding Liberal Government had " thrown into the sea ". Since then the Suez Canal route to India had been greatly developed and the overland way was of little strategic importance to Britain. He had therefore quite recently, as we have seen, been ready to let Russia take charge of that region of Asia, in pursuance of his fixed policy of the " big brother " in every backward part of the world and in his intense desire to see Russia pacified. Now, however, Germany was coming forward as the friend of Turkey ; and he saw in her occupation the prospect of a lessening of her pressure in Europe, and still more, a counter to Russia. He had not agreed to Russia having " a sphere of influence " down to Bagdad because of love of Russia, any more than he now agreed to Germany building a railway there for love of Germany ; but he was not above confirming a rivalry between two nations which were both rivals of England—and it was their rivalry in the Near and Middle East which was destined to prevent them from uniting against the British Empire in two World Wars. He may have been remiss in not encouraging British financiers to take part in the undertaking, as they were invited to do by Berlin ; but just as he had insisted to Russia that her sphere of interest was to end at Bagdad, and that the region from there to the Persian Gulf was to be British controlled, so now he concluded a secret Agreement with the Sheikh of Kuwait, at the head of the Gulf, whereby the Sheikh pledged himself not to alienate any part of his domain. Similarly Lord Salisbury successfully opposed a French plan to establish a coaling-station at Muscat, situated at the mouth of the Gulf. Where in his opinion British interests were directly involved, he was still iron-firm. But his was no dog-in-the-manger policy. Let others develop Turkey and help her to set her house in order. The spread of good government and civilization in every part of the world was one of his guiding motives ; and he believed, as most men believed at that time, that it was a plain duty of the powerful nations to help and control those which had not reached the same stage of political and material well-being. There were flourishing nations and decaying nations. The vast Turkish Empire was falling to pieces. Its outlying parts were one after another passing into foreign hands. It was important to prevent chaos and make the succession as orderly as possible.

4

And the same reasoning seemed to apply to China, to which he next had to turn his attention. In the spring of 1900 Chinese dislike of and contempt for western European influence, always smouldering below the surface, was fanned into flame by a militant society, calling itself the " Fist of Righteous Harmony ", and commonly known as the Boxers, who murdered missionaries, their wives and children, and many thousands of native Christians ; * finally, the German minister was killed by Chinese soldiers in the streets of Peking and the Boxers, now reinforced by Imperial troops, surrounded and besieged the foreign Legations.

Where exclusive British interests did not exist Lord Salisbury not only preferred but was keenly in favour of common action by the Great Powers ; and in this case the policy was clearly indicated by the common need to prevent their diplomatic representatives from becoming captives of the Chinese. Aside from this one joint purpose, however, their rivalries persisted ; and at one moment Lord Salisbury was writing to Queen Victoria : " Russia, not China, seems to me the greatest danger at the moment." The military party in St. Petersburg, headed by the War Minister Kouropatkin, had the ear of the Tsar, and wished to obtain absolute control of Manchuria ; even the more cautious Witte, backed by the Foreign Minister Lamsdorff, aimed at its " peaceful penetration ". Russian armies were soon in control of most of that province, and were at the same time reluctant to take part in the relief expedition to Peking for fear of antagonizing China.

Lord Salisbury did not in principle react against this expansion of Russian influence ; but a natural consequence of it was that he found himself collaborating most closely with the country which was the most single-minded in the business in hand. The German Emperor threw all his natural exuberance into avenging the death of his minister. He obtained the consent of the other Powers to the appointment of a German field-marshal, Count Waldersee, to be commander of the international force which was to march on Peking and relieve the Legations. He gave

* It is estimated that 30,000 Christians were put to death.

him an enthusiastic send-off from Berlin, garnished by an outburst which dismayed the representatives of the other participant Powers. "Just as the Huns a thousand years ago," he exclaimed, " under the leadership of Attila, gained a reputation by virtue of which they still live in historical tradition, so may the name of Germany become known in such a manner in China that no Chinese will ever again dare to look askance at a German." ; and he urged his troops to take no prisoners. Fortunately, perhaps, Waldersee arrived in China only after the allied contingents had reached Peking and saved the diplomatists. Only a small German unit of 200 men was available to march with them ; and a Russian general had not only taken part on his own initiative but had managed to lead his men first to the gates of the capital. The whole position was full of anomalies and absurdities, which did not make Lord Salisbury's task any easier. The view being generally held on the Continent as well as in England that China was on the brink of dissolution, expert writers in the British Press were severely criticizing Lord Salisbury for not securing a preemptive right in the forthcoming partition. Lord Salisbury may have shared the common error of mistaking the collapse of a regime for the collapse of a nation ; but in China, as in Turkey, what he wished for was the restoration of good government without partition. No doubt the protective and tutorial nation would acquire certain advantages for itself ; but to break up an ancient State was never one of his purposes. He attempted to negotiate Agreements on these lines, separately, with Germany and with Russia. They fulfilled the hopes neither of the partitionists nor of the abstentionists. They did provide a demarcation of spheres of interest. But they were largely stultified by the fact that the two foreign Governments simultaneously reached an Agreement behind his back, by which Germany, having agreed with Britain that the river-ports and the littoral of China were to remain " free and open to trade for the nationals of all countries ", assured the Russians that they might do what they liked in Manchuria without fear of German opposition. Lord Salisbury had to admit to his Permanent Under-Secretary at the Foreign Office that his carefully negotiated pacts had proved " unnecessary "—" useless " would perhaps have been the truer word— " but [he claimed] innocuous ". He was further chagrined by the conduct of the allied troops when they reached Peking and looted the Summer Palace ; and he sorrowfully transmitted the final settlement of the complications left by the suppression of the Boxer Rising to his successor, Lord Lansdowne, who took over the Foreign Office on November 12, 1900.

An episode may be recorded which at this time illuminated the intricacy of Lord Salisbury's character. During the height of the crisis in China he was invited to address a meeting of the Society for the Propagation of the Gospel (June 19). The Prime Minister accepted the invitation. His acceptance was proof of his intense sympathy with the objects of the Society ; but some of his remarks startled and disconcerted his hearers—and were, for that reason, the most cited. He urged discretion upon missionaries, and quoted an Eastern saying : " First the missionary, then the Consul, then the General." It was a terrible hindrance to missionary work, he insisted, that " the notion should get about " that political expansion and missionary work went hand in hand. He went on : " Just look at this Chinese matter. You observe that all the people who are slaughtered are Christians. Do you imagine they are slaughtered simply because the Chinese dislike their religion ? There is no nation in the world so indifferent on the subject of religion as the Chinese. It is because they and other nations have got the idea that missionary work is a mere instrument of the secular Government in order to achieve the objects it has in view. That is a most dangerous and terrible snare."

This zealous Christian knew that statesmanship and crusading were too different things and said so to his audience of zealots—at heart regretting that the two could so rarely be combined.

5

Earlier in this year Australia had been proclaimed a Commonwealth—an event in which Lord Salisbury had no immediate or active participation, but to which the policies and sympathies of a lifetime had contributed in no small degree. Joseph Chamberlain negotiated the agreement of the not too pliant separate Australian State Premiers, and drew up " the first and only Constitution that has ever been framed for a whole Continent ", to quote Mr. Garvin. Lord Salisbury thus presided as Prime

Minister over the transformation of the raw colony he had known half a century ago into a nation, the greatness of whose future he foresaw with an almost mystic confidence.

6

In the meantime criticism of the Boer War was reinforced at home by the growth of Socialism. It was in February of this year 1900 that the " Labour Representation Committee " was formed, the kernel of the Labour Party of today. Its secretary was a young Scot named Ramsay Macdonald ; and the only member of it who had been in the House of Commons was also a Scot—Keir Hardie, who had made his first appearance there in a cloth cap which defied the top-hats of 1892 but who had been defeated (as already mentioned) in the General Election of 1895. The group was therefore entirely unrepresented in Parliament at this moment ; but Lord Salisbury was well aware of the progress it was making in the country and especially in northern England. To some of its aims he had no objection. At its inception the movement was religious in outlook, and among its first objectives were the better education of manual workers, alleviation of the Poor Laws and Land legislation, and the encouragement of municipal enterprise—in housing, lighting, drainage and other amenities—through local government councils endowed with more powers and made more representative. With these practical purposes Lord Salisbury had the greatest sympathy, and it was only preoccupation elsewhere which prevented his giving more time and care to their furtherance. He had expressed not once but often his belief in the " sound political instinct " which was " the natural inheritance " of the British people ; he had justified the formation of Trade Unions and never challenged their right to strike. And his natural courtesy would never have allowed him to use an expression like John Stuart Mill's " the stupidest hodman " ; on the contrary, any and every measure calculated to increase the self-respect of the individual, whether a manual worker or anybody else, was sure of his support. His objections to the formation of a separate Party were made on relatively minor points—he had a horror, for instance, of anything in the nature of " splinter " Parties. Basing his view on the decay of parliamentary rule in France, where every ambitious politician gave a new label to his half-dozen followers, and where British Governments had found themselves dealing with twenty changes at the Quai d'Orsay between his own first spell at the Foreign Office and his last and present tenure of the post, he had come to regard grouping in a legislature as a political disease. The practical results at which the new Party was aiming could, he believed, perfectly well be achieved by the existing Parties. It was rather the theories, and the ultimate consequences of those theories, derived from Karl Marx and advocating class war, to which he was irrevocably opposed ; and he regarded the teaching of such men as Sidney Webb, Bernard Shaw, Blatchford and, in some respects, Hyndman, as being disintegrating and therefore harmful to the political and social structure of the country. For H. M. Hyndman, the top-hatted, bearded clubman, whose great regret was that he had just missed playing for Cambridge against Oxford at cricket, he had no dislike ; but as the friend of Marx and Mazzini and bitter enemy of capitalism and imperialism, as the man who had told Disraeli that what he wanted was not " peace with honour ", but " peace with comfort ", Hyndman roused his fierce an-tagonism. Even now, in his old age, Lord Salisbury was roused to anger, perhaps rather to anguish, by hearing " comfort " put before " honour " as a national ideal—and he felt it especially keenly because he could say nothing about it . . . he who had had every comfort and amenity at his disposal since the day when he had come to live at Hatfield.

It was on these higher and more general grounds that he combated Socialism. He foresaw that it would become mainly materialistic. He knew that already some of its more rabid champions were advocates not only of class hatred but of un-compromising secularism ; that they put the State before God, and while preaching emancipation would bind men and women to a most exacting relationship with the State. The family, in which, according to Lord Salisbury's view, strength of character is normally developed, especially when the parents are truly Christian, would be superseded by a bureaucracy, every en-croachment of which he sternly resisted. He was therefore hostile to Socialism in principle and in practice. He believed in the political efficacy of an informed aristocracy, continually renewed ; and he believed in the capitalist system, in the gradual accumulation of ethical and cultural as well as material wealth. He admitted that the aristocratic and capitalist systems of his day were far from perfect. But the imperfections came from the human shortcomings of the leaders in politics and business. They were not inherent in the systems. Human weaknesses must mar the application of any system, including Socialism. He did not experience or perhaps even realize the truth contained in Hyndman's protest that religion itself was sometimes " twisted to their own account " by the rich and powerful.

7

For the present, however, the Socialists were not formidable opponents. More serious opposition came from the prominent Liberals who regarded the South African War as unjustified ; and the most fiery challenge was that of the extreme Radical wing of the Party, with David Lloyd George as its spokesman. Lloyd George had shown his political antipathies at the early age of 17 by publishing in a Welsh newspaper an abusive attack on landowners in general and Lord Salisbury in particular ; and now he harangued audiences all over the country and— although usually meeting with a hostile reception—became the most outspoken and effective of " pro-Boers ", and an almost daily critic of the Prime Minister inside and outside Parliament. He acted on the same principle as the young Disraeli had : Pick out the biggest man you can find : attack *him*, and everybody will take notice of you. So Lord Salisbury suffered—in silence— the fate of most great statesmen in the decline of their days— the vilification of the Man of the Past by the Man of the Future. But these ceaseless attacks on his leadership made him more inclined to listen to the pressing demand for a new election of his 'most keen and active lieutenant. Chamberlain was himself being attacked even more vehemently than his chief. He drew Lord Salisbury's attention to the " stop-the-war " meetings being held in many parts of the country ; and he argued that proof must be given to the nation and to foreigners that they, the Government, had the people of Britain behind them.

Lord Salisbury's Ministry had two more years to run ; and he himself would have preferred to have carried on until the end of the war before he decided upon dissolution. Nobody then expected the war to last so much longer. Lord Roberts had entered the enemies' capitals, the annexation of the Transvaal had been proclaimed, Kruger had fled. The choice of this moment for a General Election would be regarded as a tactical device to cash in on victory. No doubt it would succeed, for the country was not likely to swap horses in mid-stream, especially when the rival alternative was a divided team. But he always wanted to ascertain the considered opinion of the British people and not its momentary and emotional view. Yet this was precisely what he was now being asked to do.

What Lord Coleridge had written many years ago, at the moment when Randolph Churchill had been taken into the Cabinet,* " Lord Salisbury is always dominated by someone ", had been falsified by the event in 1887 ; but in 1900 the criticism would have been justified. Lord Salisbury allowed himself to be overborne ; Chamberlain had his way ; and Chamberlain became the central figure of the Khaki Election of September–October, 1900. Savagely attacked, he hit out right and left. Now and again he vexed moderate Unionists by his fierce sallies, as when he wrote to a favoured candidate that " Every seat lost by the Government is a seat gained by the Boers ". However, his forecast to the Prime Minister that they would get at least as many seats as in the existing House of Commons was more than fulfilled. The Conservatives and Unionists won 402 between them, giving them a majority over all their opponents of 134— less than in 1895, but six more than at the moment of dissolution. The figures exceeded Lord Salisbury's expectation. Just before the Election he had written privately to Lord Lansdowne : " During the Queen's reign every Minister who, after a year's tenure of office or more, has dissolved Parliament, has been turned out by the Parliament he has summoned. There has been no exception to the rule." Lord Salisbury became the first and the only exception—the first Prime Minister to check the electoral pendulum which had swung so regularly all his political life. It was a notable triumph, to which Chamberlain's combativeness on the platform and Lord Salisbury's stabilizing influence in the background probably made approximately equal contribution.

Whether the victory ultimately benefited the Party that won it is altogether doubtful.

* See Note, Chapter XII, p. 382.

DEATH OF QUEEN VICTORIA—GERMANY—JAPANESE
ALLIANCE—RESIGNATION AND DEATH

How unwilling Lord Salisbury was to continue in office has
been set down by an eye-witness who was much with him at the
time, his son, Lord Robert Cecil, afterwards Lord Cecil of
Chelwood. In an anonymous article contributed to the *Monthly
Review* in October, 1903, Lord Robert wrote : " But probably
the greatest trial of his patriotism and courage was reserved for
the end of his career. Only those in his most intimate circle
know how distasteful office had become to him in his later years.
He hated war, and his hatred of it grew as he grew older. He
was borne down with domestic grief and physical weakness ;
and yet he felt himself unable to lay down his burden lest the
enemies of his country should take courage from the ministerial
and electoral difficulties that might, and indeed did, follow his
resignation. He remained at his post. . . ." Certainly his
motives were of the highest. Love of office was never one of
Lord Salisbury's failings. His faults are only to be found, as
so often with the greatest, in an excess of his virtues ; and his
sense of duty and of responsibility became perhaps exaggerated
in his old age and blurred his perspectives. His natural weaknesses were growing disastrously—the dimness of sight, the
absent-mindedness. The approach of senility was shown at this
time in an incident which I would not record had I not heard it
on unimpeachable authority. Lord Roberts had returned
victorious from South Africa and was among the hundreds of
guests invited to a garden-party at Hatfield. Lord Salisbury
preferred to spend the afternoon in his study ; but he thought
he would do well to have a talk with Roberts ; so he went on to
the lawn to find him. He brought the little white-haired veteran
back to his study, and had a long conversation with him—and
it was only after the guests had departed that he was informed by
his family, to his great astonishment, that it was Sir Harry
Johnston, the African explorer and administrator, with whom

he had been conversing ! Incredible indeed does it appear that a man liable to lapses such as this could be considered suitable to be Prime Minister—though less strange when one reflects that subsequently, and in days of much greater publicity, Ramsay Macdonald and Ernest Bevin have held the highest offices in an equal condition of physical enfeeblement. When gossip-writers were fewer and less well informed, such episodes did not easily reach the ears of the public.

The death of Queen Victoria in January, 1901, accentuated his *taedium vitae*. It would be a truthful generalization to say that women played no part in Lord Salisbury's life ; and yet, paradoxically, two women, his wife and the Queen, exercised far more influence over him than all his male acquaintances put together. Lord Cecil of Chelwood has recounted that his father once asked him if he found it helpful to discuss a point with others before coming to a decision ; and when Robert Cecil, as he then was, answered " yes ", Lord Salisbury was greatly and genuinely surprised. He preferred to reach his conclusions by study of the facts and secluded thought. His wife and Queen Victoria alone commonly helped him to make up his mind ; and the Queen's own desire to talk over every political issue with her most trusted Prime Minister was so great that even when he had been out of office she had, quite unconstitutionally, taken him into political consultation. This mutual respect and confidence was doubtless, in November, 1900, another reason which prompted Lord Salisbury to continue in office.

His reconstituted Ministry contained so many of his own relatives that it was nicknamed the " Hotel Cecil ". The most important new appointment was that of Lord Lansdowne to take his own place at the Foreign Office. Queen Victoria and Lord Salisbury both picked him out as having ideal qualities for a post which the Prime Minister knew he could no longer undertake. But the blame for our unpreparedness for the Boer War had been laid on Lansdowne and his transfer to the Foreign Office provoked violent criticism, by which, of course, Lord Salisbury remained entirely unmoved. He remembered the case of Castlereagh, who had failed conspicuously at the War Office and had as conspicuously succeeded when he became Foreign Secretary. He knew well how different are the qualities required for the two offices ; and Lansdowne had the broad and cultured outlook, the mingled caution and boldness, the tact, the close attention to form, the power to adjust psychological antagonisms, which the conduct of foreign policy demands. Diplomacy is a French art, and Lansdowne had French blood in his veins—the blood indeed of the great Talleyrand himself. So eminent a member of the British Foreign Service as the late Lord Carnock, who served under both of them, is known to have considered Lansdowne a better Foreign Secretary than Lord Salisbury. But that was surely to compare Lord Salisbury in decline with Lord Lansdowne in his prime, and a man who had had to face, and had overcome, a score of international crises with a successor who, largely owing to the older man's skill, had an unusually calm though by no means uneventful passage at the Foreign Office.

Never was transition from one Foreign Secretary to another more smoothly carried through than when Lansdowne took over on November 12, 1900. Even before that date we find incoming despatches initialled (in red ink) by him, showing that Lord Salisbury was leaving the business to him ; and a day or two later we see " L " and " S " appearing side by side at the foot of the same docket—an affecting and surely unique proof of continuity at the Foreign Office ! Lansdowne was very soon to show, however, that this close personal collaboration was not to prevent him from giving a sharp turn to British policy.

But he began by taking up the project for an Anglo-German Alliance, which the Kaiser and, in London, Baron Eckardstein were eagerly putting forward again. Lord Salisbury did not like it ; but the further visits of the Kaiser to England during the last illness of Queen Victoria and for her funeral, following his journey to Cowes during the early days of the Boer War, provoked a warmer response than ever from the sentimental British public, and Hatzfeldt, the German ambassador, claimed that the majority of the British Cabinet were also in favour of it. Lansdowne soon complained that Eckardstein's suggestions were for " an international arrangement of a somewhat indefinite but very far-reaching character " ; so, in the absence of any written proposal from Berlin, the Foreign Office drew up two Draft Conventions based on the verbal proposals of the German spokesmen in London and Berlin. These Draft Conventions looked like business and provoked direct intervention by the Prime

Minister. He had perhaps shown too large a spirit of accommodation in the past—in minor matters. But an alliance—never !
Within two days of receiving the Draft Conventions Lord Salisbury composed an incisive Memorandum denouncing the project
of alliance. J. A. Spender, in his book *Fifty Years of Europe*,
calls it " a classic on the subject of splendid isolation " ; and
Algernon Cecil has commented that, coming so late in his career,
it looks like " his last will and testament " ; so it shall be given
in extenso :

Memorandum by the Marquess of Salisbury.

May 29, 1901.

This is a proposal for including England within the bounds
of the Triple Alliance. I understand its practical effect to be :

(1) If England were attacked by two Powers—say France and
Russia—Germany, Austria, and Italy would come to her
assistance.

(2) Conversely, if either Austria, Germany or Italy were attacked
by France and Russia, or, if Italy were attacked by France
and Russia, or, if Italy were attacked by France and Spain,
England must come to the rescue.

Even assuming that the Powers concerned were all despotic
and could promise anything they pleased, with a full confidence
that they would be able to perform the promise, I think it is
open to much question whether the bargain would be for our
advantage. The liability of having to defend the German and
Austrian frontiers against Russia is heavier than that of *having
to defend the British Isles against France*. Even, therefore, in its
most naked aspect the bargain would be a bad one for this
country. Count Hatzfeldt speaks of our " *isolation* " as constitut-
ing serious danger for us. *Have we ever felt that danger practically ?*
If we had succumbed in the revolutionary war, our fall would
not have been due to our isolation. We had many allies, but
they would not have saved us if the French Emperor had been
able to command the Channel. Except during his reign we have
never even been in danger ; and, therefore, it is impossible for
us to judge whether the " isolation " under which we are supposed to suffer, does or does not contain in it any elements of
peril. It would hardly be wise to incur novel and most onerous

obligations, in order to guard against *a danger in whose existence we have no historical reason for believing.*

But though the proposed arrangement, even from this point of view, does not seem to me admissible, these are not by any means the weightiest objections that can be urged against it. The fatal circumstance is that *neither we nor the Germans are competent to make the suggested promises.* The British Government cannot undertake to declare war, for any purpose, unless it is a purpose of which the electors of this country would approve. If the Government promised to declare war for an object which did not commend itself to public opinion, the promise would be repudiated, and the Government would be turned out. I do not see how, in common honesty, we could invite other nations to rely upon our aids in a struggle, which must be formidable and probably supreme, when we have no means whatever of knowing what may be the humour of our people in circumstances which cannot be foreseen. We might, to some extent, divest ourselves of the full responsibility of such a step, *by laying our Agreement with the Triple Alliance before Parliament,* as soon as it is concluded. But there are very grave objections to such a course, and I do not understand it to be recommended by the German Ambassador.

The impropriety of attempting to determine by a *secret contract* the future conduct of a Representative Assembly upon an issue of peace or war would apply to German policy as much as to English, only that the German Parliament would probably pay more deference to the opinion of their Executive than would be done by the English Parliament. But a *promise of defensive alliance with England would excite bitter murmurs in every rank of German society*—if we may trust the indications of German sentiment, which we have had an opportunity of witnessing during the last two years.

It would not be safe to stake any important national interest upon the fidelity with which, in case of national exigency, either country could be trusted to fulfil the obligations of the Alliance, if the Agreement had been concluded without the assent of its Parliament.

Several times during the last sixteen years Count Hatzfeldt had tried to elicit from me, in conversation, some opinion as to the probable conduct of England, if Germany or Italy were involved in war with France. I have always replied that no

English Minister could venture on such a forecast. The course of the English Government in such a crisis must depend on the view taken by public opinion in this country, and public opinion would be largely, if not exclusively, governed by the nature of the *casus belli*.

[*End of Memorandum*]

Lord Lansdowne nevertheless pursued the negotiations with pertinacity, though with great circumspection. The course of them can be studied in many works, especially those of G. P. Gooch, J. A. Spender, Sir Valentine Chirol and Julian Amery, and of course in the official British documents. We are concerned here to draw the portrait of Lord Salisbury ; and his part was to oppose the alliance with the whole of his considerable *vis inertiae*. Lansdowne, unlike Lord Salisbury, took counsel with all his principal subordinates, of whom Mr. (later Lord) Bertie submitted a long Memorandum strongly deprecating an alliance with Germany but advocating one with Japan (November 9, 1901). Lansdowne took the opportunity of his following Memorandum (November 11) to contest, not Bertie's arguments but those Lord Salisbury had used on May 29. He said that it was not correct to interpret the proposed treaty as laying much heavier obligations on Britain than it would lay on Germany. In regard to " isolation " he wrote : " I fully admit the force of the Prime Minister's observation that this country has until now fared well in spite of its international isolation. I think, however, that we may push too far the argument that, because we have in the past survived in spite of our isolation, we need have no misgivings as to the effect of that isolation in the future." He also recognized that the treaty, if concluded, should make the alliance an open, not a secret one. He nevertheless saw " great difficulties in the way of a full-blown alliance with Germany ".

A month later he drew up the only kind of Agreement he thought suitable. It amounted, in his own words, " to little more than a declaration of common policy ". Even though the treaty was now to be made only with the sanction of Parliament, Lord Salisbury minuted : " I should like to speak to you more fully about this. . . . At present it seems to me full of risks and to carry with it no compensating advantages."

In the meantime the Kaiser had not helped his project by

333

describing His Majesty's Ministers as " a set of unmitigated noodles ". The German Government welcomed the Foreign Editor of *The Times*, Sir Valentine Chirol, to Berlin, where he talked the whole matter over semi-officially with the so-called oracle of the Wilhelmstrasse, Baron Holstein. In vain ; and a little later two public speeches, the one by Mr. Chamberlain at Edinburgh and the other by Count Bülow in the Reichstag, caused the negotiations, official and semi-official, to go up in smoke, or rather in a mist of recriminations about the respective behaviour of British troops in the Boer War and German troops in the Franco-German War of 1870–71.

Lord Salisbury's view on this particular issue had triumphed, but not his general arguments. He indeed gave the appearance of contradicting them himself ; for, having maintained in his May Memorandum that there were grave objections to laying the proposed Agreement with Germany before Parliament, and that no English Minister could bind his country beforehand, because in a crisis public opinion would decide whether the *casus belli* had arisen or not, he proceeded cordially to support Lansdowne's moves for an open alliance with Japan.

Few people now contest Landsowne's view that isolation was not proved to be a suitable policy for the future because England had fared well " in spite of isolation " in the past. Lord Salisbury's arguments had been based, in his own phrase, on " historical " reasoning. Lansdowne, like Chamberlain, was more impressed than he by the bond of envy and enmity which was uniting the European Powers against Britain. It caused him such " misgivings " for the future that he turned towards France as soon as Lord Salisbury had retired. The fact that he waited until that moment, and made no decisive move until the old statesman had died, seems to show that he expected the same *vis inertiae* to be opposed to his projected close understanding with France.

From such study as I have been able to make of Lord Salisbury's complex mind, so full of unuttered calculations, I am persuaded that he would always have been hostile to any preferential compact with any *European* Great Power or group of Powers. He was hereditarily imbued with the " Big Brother " outlook—the responsibility of the stronger State for the weaker ;

and the one system to which he was fervently attached, and which he supported with all his strength, was the Concert of Europe ; whatever the temporary interruptions to its harmony, he ever sought to set it going again at the earliest possible moment. So long as the Great Powers of Europe could march together, there would be no war. It was bad enough that already a Triple Alliance had been formed, between Germany, Austria-Hungary and Italy, and was countered by the Dual Alliance of France and Russia.

He did contrive to get them all five to co-operate when their vital interests were not thereby too obviously affected ; he could speak independently to both sides ; he could hold the balance. He had always agreed with the view of Palmerston (proclaimed when he himself was a youth of 19), that so long as England sympathized with right and justice she would never find herself altogether alone. If she now tied herself to one party or the other, she could no longer hope safely to play this honourable role. The split between the greater European States would become permanent—or as permanent as anything ever has been in Europe's history ; and the " bloody and desolating " war which he had foreboded in 1897 would become a certainty. He had supported the British commitment to Portugal ; he was ready to pledge this country to Japan. But among the leading States of Europe it was vital that Britain should maintain a position of independence. " Isolation " had never prevented co-operation with one or two or three or all of them for a specific purpose. " We are part of the community of Europe," Lord Salisbury had said at Carnarvon in 1888 (April 10), " and we must do our duty as such." Furthermore, the policy of detachment made it possible, if necessary—but only if necessary—to transfer the weight of Britain from the Concert to the maintenance of the Balance whenever the Concert was disrupted. The so-called Isolation thus subserved the supreme and permanent need for Britain to prevent the supremacy of any single Power in Europe.

And Lord Salisbury's view of a treaty was that it served no purpose unless it conformed to the realities of international politics—in itself a treaty of alliance with Germany would change nothing. He understood better than Chamberlain the bitter envy and underlying hostility of Germans to England's great

335

position in the world. He would have dissented profoundly from the view expressed by Mr. Amery in discussing Chamberlain's policy * that " Chamberlain's last bid for a German alliance marks one of the great turning-points in history. Had it prospered, the fate of mankind from that time to this might have been altered immeasurably, and for the better." An alliance, in Lord Salisbury's view, was valueless unless it were dependent upon mutual trust and absence of conflicting interests. Both these essentials were wanting in the case of Britain and Germany. His long political experience, his study of history, his shrewd evaluation of human infirmity prevented him from estimating very highly the worth of international compacts— least of all would he place much faith in the country which had made a hero of Frederick II and was now making an idol of William II. To his few intimates and colleagues who asked him why he was so unwilling to respond to the German Emperor's advances the old statesman would reply in a low, dejected voice, " He's false."

There can indeed be little doubt that Lord Salisbury rendered another lasting service to the country in preventing the British Government from becoming tied to Germany by a bond which, as subsequent events have shown, she would have been ready to snap whenever it suited her. Lansdowne, in his turn also, came to doubt the good faith of the Wilhelmstrasse as much as Lord Salisbury had always doubted the trustworthiness of the Kaiser.

2

As he had done in the case of the Anglo-German negotiations, so also Lord Salisbury left the Japanese negotiations in the capable hands of Lansdowne, with the difference that this time the Prime Minister, to whom every despatch, outgoing and incoming, was submitted, was a most benevolent monitor. He inherited Japanese goodwill from the Liberal Government's policy in 1895 of refusing to join Russia, France and Germany in putting pressure on Japan to evacuate Port Arthur ; and in his alternating moods of opposition to and propitiation of Russia he may have thought of Japan in the same protective terms as those in which, many years before, he had denounced the out-

* Julian Amery, *The Life of Joseph Chamberlain*, Vol. IV, p. 158.

rage of Kagosima. And now the Admiralty were warning him that the two-Power naval stand was becoming increasingly difficult to maintain in the several seas of the world. His naval advisers argued that the Japanese navy would be a most valuable ally in maintaining peace and the *status quo* in the Far East ; and Lord Salisbury and the Foreign Secretary accepted their argument. Actually the first suggestion came from the Japanese themselves—when the minister in London, Baron Hayashi, saw Lansdowne at the Foreign Office on April 17, 1901 ; and the first formal proposals were made in the following October.

In the meantime the indiscretion of the British minister to Japan, Sir Claude MacDonald, who was on leave in England during the summer, put a weapon into the hands of the Japanese Government which they used cleverly to hasten the negotiations. Lord Salisbury knew that there was a strong party in Tokyo which favoured an agreement with Russia, and he confided his fears to Sir Claude MacDonald, who was a personal friend and came to discuss the Japanese proposal with him. Lord Salisbury also told him that King Edward approved in principle the idea of an alliance with Japan ; but he added that such an alliance, being a departure from British tradition, might take some time to negotiate. MacDonald, being on friendly personal terms with Hayashi, repeated to him the gist of his conversation with the Prime Minister. It was a *lapsus linguae* to let the Japanese know that Lord Salisbury feared that Russia might anticipate Britain in coming to an agreement ; and every time the negotiations flagged a hint was given from Tokyo that perhaps better terms might be reached in St. Petersburg. Marquis Ito, the head of the pro-Russian party in Japan, was indeed allowed to go on a visit to the Russian capital ; and according to Langer * he very nearly achieved his purpose there. Lansdowne thereupon challenged the Tokyo Government as to their intentions. They came down firmly for a British alliance, and Ito was instructed to leave St. Petersburg. When he got as far as Berlin, the Russian Government telegraphed to him begging him to return ; but then it was too late. Instead, he went on to London. The Anglo-Japanese Treaty was signed there on January 30, 1902, by Lansdowne and Hayashi. It ordained the maintenance of the *status quo* and the integrity of China, but

* *Diplomacy of Imperialism*, Vol. II, Chapter 23.

Japan was recognized to have "special interests" in Korea, and Britain in China (in the Yangtse Valley). The Treaty was to remain in force for five years.

Though British diplomacy was moving into dimensions unfamiliar to Lord Salisbury, his instinctive wisdom had not deserted him. Logic had never seemed to him a suitable guide in foreign affairs ; and history has vindicated his inconsistency in opposing an alliance with a powerful European nation and readily contracting one with a country which was only beginning to show its mettle. The Japanese, elated at becoming the accepted allies and associates of a great European Power, and at seeing their special interest in Korea publicly recognized, were happy to exercise a particularly close co-operation with the British navy, and rendered invaluable service to Britain in her hour of peril twelve years later. Lord Hardinge of Penshurst, then ambassador in St. Petersburg, records that a Russian Grand Duke congratulated him on what he called the "*coup de maître*" by the British Government—the last master-stroke of her veteran Prime Minister, and the first success of the new Foreign Secretary.

3

All this time a war of attrition was being fought in South Africa against the armed burghers and farmers, who proved more formidable as guerillas than they had been as organized columns. Disappointment at the prolongation of hostilities, grief at the regular and still unfamiliar lists of casualties, uneasiness about the methods of block-houses and concentration camps, filled the public at home with concern and afforded grist to the mill for critics of the Government. Lord Salisbury came in for his share of censure. In an earlier speech (November 9, 1899) he had exclaimed : "We seek no goldfields. We seek no territory " ; and already, even before the war was finished, we had annexed over 150,000 square miles containing the richest gold-mines in the world. His exclamation had been a sincere expression of his own feelings at the time, but its very sincerity made a tardy explanation appear the more insincere. Others rallied to the side of the Prime Minister and expostulated that he himself had never really believed in the justice and necessity of the Boer War. These vicarious excuses vexed him more than the hostile criticisms. In the spring of 1902, at a Primrose League meeting held in the Albert Hall, he delivered his last public speech (May 7) ; and he made a point of accepting full Cabinet responsibility for the war which was, by then, at last drawing to its close. John Morley had recently made a speech which was clearly aimed at Joseph Chamberlain's diplomacy. He had said that if in 1899 members of the Conservative Cabinet had foreseen the results of the policy on which they were then launching their country, not one of them but would have checked it. Lord Salisbury indignantly and emphatically repudiated any such notion. " There is a kind of maudlin sentiment," he declared, " which induces people to pass over the conduct of our assailants," and to admit them to be in the right. " The Boers chose without any right, without any ground for complaint of any violation of international law, to invade our territory and to seize the lands that belonged to our Sovereign ; they chose to convert the rights of our fellow-subjects into that of persons forced to submit to their domination ; they chose to dispute our rights without a vestige of a ground for doing so." After protesting (amid laughter) that " we are not tired out " by the long war or the negotiations for peace which were then being obstinately disputed, he said there was nothing that we wished more earnestly than that the Boers would join us in setting up a political structure enabling them to enjoy " all the order and all the strength which is conferred upon our brother nations by our colonial system ".

The Prime Minister freely unburdened his mind in this valedictory speech, which, as usual, seems to have been delivered without the aid of notes. He began it with a friendly allusion to Randolph Churchill as one of the founders of the Primrose League, which was then an " apostolic " organization whose numbers had bounded up since it was created in 1883. At the back of the hall, for this occasion, was emblazoned in large letters Disraeli's favourite motto, " Imperium et Libertas " ; and Lord Salisbury attributed to " the energy of the Primrose League in preaching its principles " that we were " at present supreme in Egypt " and that in Ireland " we at all events have no longer to fear the support given by any statesman to the insane and suicidal projects of Imperial disruption "—which (here comes the saving compliment to Gladstone) had seventeen years earlier been sustained " by the highest statesman of our time ".

The speech in all its weakness and strength deserves to be examined in detail—this last utterance of a politician, a sage and a seer. Having flattered the Primrose League, he came to the Boer War and the part that Empire troops were playing in it. "All wars are horrible. It is frightful to reflect upon the human misery which they involve and the sorrow and privation which they bring with them to multitudes of our fellow-subjects." But at least now "the power, the prestige, the influence, aye, the magic effect of our great Empire is more potent, more efficient, more admirable than it was" in 1883.

He called the greater colonies—the Dominions of today—"our brother nations"—a forward-looking phrase, well ahead of the thought of 1902, and differently conceived from the projects which that other great imperialist, the Colonial Secretary, was advocating. Having associated himself, in the earlier part of his speech, with Chamberlain in responsibility for the war, he now dissociated himself from his plans for "federating the colonies" and creating an Imperial Council. He earnestly expounded to his hearers his view that "the development of the Empire calls for no legislation". Much better to leave it to natural growth. "They [the 'daughter countries'] will go on in their own power, in their own irresistible power, and I have no doubt they will leave combinations behind them which will cast into the shade all the glories that the British Empire has hitherto displayed."

But we could not safely interfere by legislative action with their natural development. We should not in this case antici-pate events or "foreclose the results, the precious results, which, if we are only patient and careful, the future has in store for the Empire. . . ." "Because their own wretched lives are confined to some sixty or seventy years" statesmen must not imagine that "it is open to them to force an anticipation of the results which the natural play of forces and of affections and the alterations of the judgments and the mutual feelings of various peoples in the world will bring before us. There is nothing more dangerous than to force a decision before a decision is ready. . . . If we will be patient and careful, there is a tremendous destiny before us." Just as in an earlier utterance he had shown himself full of foreboding that a war would break out between European Powers, so now he expressed a premonition that big changes were about to occur, which, however, he made no attempt to define. " We are at the commencement of a movement of causes, of opinions and of feelings which will end in changes largely modifying the present distribution of power and the present distribution, I may say, of allegiance."

Vague as the prophecy is, nobody can deny that now, fifty years after it was spoken, it has come true. In this rough-hewn oration, built up, apparently, as he went along, the rugged stones of his statesmanship stand out clearly enough—his horror of war, his readiness to take risks, and to assume every responsibility, his mistrust of legislation, his belief in spontaneity, in unfettered freedom for growth, in the inevitability of change, in the irresistible growth of the British peoples springing from the wombs of the daughter nations. In one of the phrases of his peroration he declared that this Empire depended not upon territorial contiguity, but upon its naval defences and upon " the feelings and affections of some of the most vehement races upon the face of the earth ".

Having, as the saying is, " let himself go " at the Albert Hall, he was singularly reticent on his next important public appearance, which was in the House of Lords three weeks later, when peace was at last concluded with the South African Republics. It was his duty to make known its conditions to the country, and it might have been supposed that he would have made some comment or even have expressed some feelings of satisfaction on this momentous occasion. Far from it. He murmured an apology to the Peers for the length of the document which he was about to read to them ; and having read through the terms of surrender, he sat down. It was left to Rosebery, the leader of the Opposition, to express in a few felicitous phrases the relief and joy of the nation. On that memorable day (June 2, 1902) the sitting of their lordships' House lasted just three-quarters of an hour.

As usual, he underplayed his hand. The 167,465 square miles which had just been added to the British Empire brought the total of territories acquired during Lord Salisbury's premierships—and acquired, except in those cases of these two new colonies and the Sudan, with hardly any fighting—to some six million square miles, containing populations of about a

341

hundred million—a record which surely no other Prime Minister in British history except the elder Pitt could approach. Mr. Churchill, indeed, has written : " Lord Salisbury played a greater part in gathering together the growing strength of the British Empire, for a time of trial which few could foresee and none could measure, than any other historic figure that can be cited." *

4

But the thought that was uppermost in Lord Salisbury's mind was that now the moment had come when he could with propriety lay down the burden of office. At last he could throw off the harness that had been galling him for these last three years. Only one consideration prevented him from resigning immediately. The coronation of King Edward was due to be held on June 26—courtesy compelled him to defer retirement for a few weeks. But on the 23rd he had to inform anxious questioners in the House of Lords that the King was seriously ill. Next day it was officially announced that the coronation ceremony had been postponed on account of His Majesty's acute appendicitis. The King's recovery was remarkably swift, and the retarded ceremony took place on August 9. But before that day came Lord Salisbury had begged to be released. His health was daily deteriorating. The motive was genuine and indeed self-evident. But it was also true that Lord Salisbury never enjoyed and never could have attained to the same relations of mutual regard for and sympathy with the new Sovereign as he had had with Queen Victoria. Their official relations were always correct. The Prime Minister willingly supported King Edward's wish to assume the additional title of " King of the British Dominions beyond the Seas " when he ascended the Throne ; and the King, on his part, conferred on his retiring Prime Minister the Grand Cross of the Victorian Order. But King and Minister found themselves at variance on several minor matters. As soon as he came to the Throne King Edward agreed with the proposal that a full enquiry should be held into the needs of Army Reform, which the blunders of the Boer War had made so apparent ; but he was most desirous that it should be conducted in private. Lord Salisbury insisted on a public

* *My Early Life,* p. 179.

enquiry by a Royal Commission, to which he considered the Government to be already committed ; and he had his way. The King wished to bestow peerages on several of his personal friends ; and some of them seemed to Lord Salisbury to be unsuited for the honour. According to Mr. Edward Legge * it was the Prime Minister's blank refusal to be in any way associated with the conferment of a barony upon one of them which prompted the actual moment of his resignation. In any case, it was on July 11, 1902—within a month of the new date for the coronation—that the Prime Minister went to Buckingham Palace and there finally tendered his resignation, on the ground of ill-health. On the same plea, Lord Salisbury begged to be excused from attending the postponed coronation, to which the King also assented ; and at the end of the month, Prime Minister no more, he left for a holiday on the Continent, " on doctor's orders ".

Before he quitted office it may be presumed that Lord Salisbury was enabled to exercise the prescriptive privilege of an out-going Prime Minister and advise his Sovereign on his successor. In that matter they were certainly agreed on the choice of Arthur Balfour. During these last two years he had enjoyed the Prime Minister's full confidence and had deputized for him in the func-tions of the premiership, as he had, a little earlier, in those of the Foreign Office. Chamberlain, the only other candidate of equal calibre, had been the more influential, but he had never been Lord Salisbury's confidant in the degree that Balfour was. Foreign Office despatches were invariably marked to be seen by Balfour, but by Chamberlain only if he were personally concerned. Balfour moreover was on the most intimate terms of friendship with Lansdowne ; and King Edward also preferred him, though occasionally finding the nimble discursiveness of his talk hard to follow. Nor could the King entirely dismiss from his mind memories of the day when the republican-tinted Radicalism of Chamberlain had made his visit to Birmingham an entry into the lion's den. He preferred Balfour's urbanity ; and Balfour was the natural political heir of his uncle. Thus an opportunity was missed of infusing the veins of the Party leadership with new blood.

* In *King George and the Royal Family*, Vol. I, pp. 50–1.

5

The end of his work was the end of his life. He lingered on for a while as Queen Elizabeth's oak lingers on in Hatfield Park, as dead as alive. He hoped at first to pick up strength by following the doctor's advice and his own inclination and going abroad. Taking two members of his family with him, he went to Homburg, then becoming renowned as a cure-station ; but he was not very happy among fashionable invalids and very soon moved on to Lucerne. There he recovered something of his strength, but a little later he journeyed south, to the Riviera, where a sojourn in his own villa seemed to set him up again. The slight improvement did not last, and when he returned to Hatfield he was incapable of exertion. Worst of all for him was the deterioration of his eyesight. There is a great renunciation behind most great lives, and his had been the enjoyment of his library. Always his library had been his place of solace and refreshment. How little time he had found to feast his mind on literature since those eager hours of his younger years when he had read and written there from noon till night ! Now he had the leisure, but it had come too late.

Naturally, he followed the fortunes of his nephew, who frequently consulted him. He soon saw him implicated in contention with Chamberlain over Tariff Reform. Lord Salisbury set his face against taxes on food ; and Balfour accepted his view ; while Chamberlain considered a moderate duty on foreign corn and meat to be necessary. Balfour sought to combine a preferential tariff against foreign manufactured goods with the refusal to tax food. The subsequent course of the controversy is well known, and does not concern us here. Lord Salisbury agreed that the Foreign Office should be put in a position to retaliate against tariffs hostile to British interest—he had spoken in that sense as far back as 1892. The theory of " free trade " tied him no more than any other theory, though in practice he had preferred to leave the colonies open to the trade of all foreign countries. But he regarded food taxes as " politically impossible ". Lady Gwendolen Cecil records in one of her private memoranda that during the last few weeks of his life he was still denouncing " a tax on corn or meat ". " For his Party to become associated with any such proposals," she writes,

" he spoke of to the end as a calamity—unquestionable and disastrous."

Equally disastrous to the Party was the " duality of leadership " which the controversy engendered. Chamberlain had his followers, Balfour had his, many were undecided, some—including Winston Churchill—left the Party altogether. One of the few of his former colleagues who came to see their former chief at Hatfield in the last years of his life was Lord George Hamilton, who writes of him : " He was then a doomed man, but for a short time he spoke to me with his old brilliancy and decision." During their short talk Lord Salisbury inveighed against the " dual leadership " which was ruining the Party. Sir Michael Hicks Beach, who also went to see him that year, in July, was shocked to find how weak he was ; his heart was " very bad " ; but even then he " was evidently angry with Balfour for allowing Joe to master him so much "—which was rather hard on Arthur Balfour, whó had to try to carry out the policy recommended by his uncle without his uncle's prestige. He had been, when he was Lord Salisbury's right-hand man, a good balancer, an urbane and most skilful intermediary ; but he lacked that touch of ruthlessness which leadership requires—and which Lord Salisbury possessed.

Those few who saw him now knew that the end could not be far away. In that compendium of English history which is *Burke's Peerage* the first Earl of Salisbury (in the Cecil line) is described as having died " worn out with business ". The same phrase could be applied to his descendant. As the summer of 1903 wore on he was plainly a dying man. He gave up his tricycling at last ; but he still insisted on going every day before breakfast, in a wheeled chair, to a ten-minute service in the Chapel. In mid-August he took to his bed. Thereafter he was, for intervals that ever grew longer, in a comatose or semi-comatose condition. We cannot tell the thoughts that, in his moments of consciousness, passed through the mind of the dying statesman, who had seen so much, done so much, knew so much. . . . But his character being what it was, it would surely be wide of the mark to suppose that the events of his long career passed before his closing eyes, as Lytton Strachey brilliantly imagined for Queen Victoria. Far more likely is it that all the conscious thought that remained to him was turned even then to the future. Death meant to him the beginning of Life. Its shadow, which had lain over him these last months, would be changed into light. He would " see things not seen as yet ". As long as his soul had been held in flesh and bone it could not hope to see God. Now the human habiliment would be cast off, and, like Tennyson, he might hope to see his Pilot face to face. The finite could not comprehend the infinite—that had always been his conviction. As long as the intellect was human, how could it partake of the Divine ? But his faith had been greater than his understanding. Soon he would understand all that had so long been ununderstandable. . . .

He died at sunset on August 22. It was the sunset not only of a day, but of an Age.

The offer of a grave in Westminster Abbey was declined. He was buried where he wished to be, by the side of his wife, in Hatfield churchyard. There in the family burial ground they laid him, among many other Cecils, and a few former servants of the house, old nurses, and faithful housekeepers, who, they too, had had Hatfield for home through long, contented years.

Country Life photograph

FAMILY GRAVEYARD IN HATFIELD CHURCHYARD

The raised tomb in the foreground contains the remains of Lord and Lady Salisbury. In the background can be seen the graves of retainers of the Cecil family. One was Caroline Hodges, "nurse of Lord and Lady Salisbury's children", who "lived in their house for 43 years, a loved and trusted friend". She died in 1906. Another contains the remains of two sisters, Isabella and Ellen Allan, who were respectively nurse and housekeeper at Hatfield for 36 and 29 years. The other graves are all of members of the Cecil family.

No one statesman can represent all the English people all the time, for England is greater than her greatest individual. Few indeed are those who have truly represented the whole country for the briefest time ; fewer still those who have truly impersonated Britain in peace. In wartime a Chatham, a Lloyd George, a Churchill, when the nation's existence was at stake—but in peacetime the fullness of her life, the contradictions of the nation's character, the variableness of her moods require at one time a Peel, at another a Gladstone, at other moments an Aberdeen or a Neville Chamberlain. And for four years, between 1895 and 1899, Lord Salisbury, more than any of these in peacetime, stood for England. To the outside world he was England. He was the England defined as lately as in 1938 by Paul Valéry : " L'Angleterre est l'Empire du fait, le pays du monde où le choix des hommes et des choses revient toujours à l'expérience. C'est là ce qui l'a fait puissante, lente, étrange, parfois inconcevable pour nous. Sa force, son mystère, son charme font songer aux attributs de la nature." Lord Salisbury typified the English character thus defined—and if that character is ever a perplexity to foreigners, so was Lord Salisbury's even to his own countrymen and contemporaries. This is what Mr. Garvin wrote of him : " Salisbury's portrait is one of the hardest to draw. When we study the negative resources of his statesmanship, its address in avoidance and its subtlety in persistence, his own lineaments seem to become fugitive and unseizable." *

His closest political associate, Arthur Balfour, when after his death he was praying the Crown to erect a monument to Lord Salisbury in Westminster Abbey, said there " was a peculiarity which I think he possessed more than any man I have ever known—a certain self-contained simplicity which made it not easy for other men quite to understand him ".† And Lord Curzon, when St. John Brodrick had taken his place as Parliamentary Under-Secretary to Lord Salisbury àt the Foreign Office, wrote to his successor as one who had suffered from too close

* *Life of Joseph Chamberlain*, Vol. III, p. 160.
† In the House of Commons, May 17, 1904.

proximity to impenetrable greatness : "I know what an uphill job it is . . . with that strange, powerful, inscrutable, brilliant, obstructive deadweight at the top." *

On the same occasion as Balfour spoke, the leader of the Opposition, Sir Henry Campbell-Bannerman, supporting the prayer to place the recumbent statue of Lord Salisbury where it can now be seen near the West Door of the Abbey, said in the course of his speech that "to most of the members of the House the late Prime Minister was personally unknown "—and it was the same predominantly Conservative House which had been elected under Lord Salisbury's leadership.

Lord Salisbury even after long study remains unclassifiable. Like others of the greatest he fits into no category. All we can do is to pick out the main features of his character and of his statesmanship—which are inseparable.

He was a traditionalist and Conservative. That emerges self-evident from these pages and needs no further emphasis. It will have been observed, however, that he was never opposed to change, a word which he much preferred to "reform"—change being part of the law of growth, a rule of nature applicable to political life. He was always ready to make timely adjustments while conserving the general structure—for a too rigid institution inevitably survives its purpose. It will also have been noticed that this partisan Conservatism was more trenchant during his early years in the Commons than in his later years. As he grew older he became more and more a national figure ; and he was one of those statesmen, fortunately not rare in English history, who knew how to transform himself, as needed, from partisan to patriot, from a factious politician to the nation's spokesman —and, if circumstances required it, to revert to Party politics next day. But even as a Party politician he habitually thought of the nation as a whole, not of one part of it, or one class of it. He was entirely free from conscious class preference, and reserved some of his sharpest barbs of criticism for men in his own position who did not fulfil the duties implicit in privilege. On the other side his contempt was keenest for politicians who gained notoriety by stirring up envy and class hatred. Class hatred was the only thing he hated in politics. He could be wonderfully sarcastic

* Ronaldshay, *Life of Lord Curzon*, Vol. I, p. 282.

about the extremists of the Left who made the discovery of grievances the staple of their career.

In his later years he was much happier in a national role than as a Party man. Anything in the nature of courting favours or canvassing he abhorred ; and he was apt to be ill at ease and clumsy on the rare occasions when he attempted it. But he always took public opinion into account. He saw clearly enough where the sovereignty of the country lay. He did not like the Party machine, but he never lost touch with it. Only in foreign affairs did he consider public opinion to be a dangerous guide. When I asked Lord Cecil of Chelwood, the son who was most closely connected with him politically, whether he paid much attention to public opinion, the answer was : " Yes, but not very much in regard to foreign policy. He thought it dangerous to pay too much attention to it in foreign affairs because he thought public opinion was not well enough informed. In home affairs he paid very much attention to opinion, especially that of his own Party."

Besides being a traditionalist and a Conservative he was an aristocrat who believed in aristocracy. He esteemed a hierarchical system, whether clerical or lay : his Christianity convinced him that the institutional authority of the Church was as necessary for the political as for the moral health of the community.

The national life was then more deeply imbued with religion than today, and religion teaches reverence ; reverence produces respect for authority ; and authority is necessary for effective leadership. It was still not considered outrageously snobbish to talk about the " Upper ten thousand ", and among the ten thousand were certainly found many to whom authority and leadership came naturally ; and a good proportion of them— though by no means all—had the quality, superlative in statesmanship, of disinterestedness. No man who is not disinterested can have an unwarped judgment ; and it was Lord Salisbury's own crystal disinterestedness that won and held for him the trust of the English people. They knew well enough that democracy in its extreme form signified to him the irruption of ignorance into the highly technical business of government. But they admitted their ignorance ; and he accepted, though he disliked,

349

democracy. In his early years he agreed with the thunderings of Carlyle : " Democracy to complete itself ; to go the full length of its course, towards the Bottomless or into it, no power now extant to prevent it or even considerably retard it . . . Count of Heads to be the Divine Court of Appeal." * Lord Salisbury, for better or for worse, did retard the process. Nothing would have induced him to accept the view neatly paraphrased by Mr. Peter Legh :

> We are a democratic race,
> And like our rulers commonplace ;

but in his later years he would, I think, have generally agreed with the dictum of the Norwegian Ibsen, who was almost his exact contemporary, and who wrote : " Mere democracy cannot solve the social question. An element of aristocracy must be introduced into our life. Of course I do not mean the aristocracy of birth or of the purse, or even the aristocracy of intellect. I mean the aristocracy of character, of will, of mind." And if he had been alive today, he would probably have agreed with Lord Beveridge when he said : " We have somehow to carry on an aristocratic tradition in Britain without the aristocrats." †

His own character and mind, no less than his social position, made him an effortless leader, one who did not shout commands, but who showed the way and was followed. Moreover, he had a profound belief in the sound political instinct which was the " natural inheritance " of the British people.

His ideal for his country would surely be that England should be a nation of noblemen and a nobleman among the nations.

This Conservative nobleman had the startling simplicity of the true aristocrat. For all the intricacies and convolutions of his subtle intellect he set common sense above intelligence and could be as simply direct as the simplest countryman. He was indeed a countryman, springing from the long line of country-dwellers—individualists, self-reliant, according to others respect for their particular personality, learning from familiarity with the ways of nature the wisdom of long-term policy and the folly

* *Macmillan's Magazine*, August, 1867.
† In a broadcast on December 30, 1951.

of the townsman's short-term slickness. There was something anonymous about his character and his policy, which seemed to be drawn out of the past as a folk-song is drawn from the heart of a nation. He was fond of using the countryman's homely phrases. One which was often on his lips in times of difficulty was : " There is always a pass through the mountains " ; and if we seek the maxims of his statesmanship we can find them among the common sayings of the English people : " A stitch in time saves nine ", and " Prevention is better than cure " ; " Waste not want not ", and " Cut your coat according to your cloth " ; " Look before you leap ", and " Strike while the iron is hot ".

It being one of the marks of his greatness that he combined opposite attributes in his personality, his fundamental simplicity was spiced with a superficial cynicism. He wielded sarcasm and cynicism as handy political weapons, which could be used to silence an obtrusive opponent, or to protect himself against the charge of priggishness, or to shield the deep sentiment which he often felt but never allowed to appear ; or else just to express his contempt for experts—as when, coming away from a talk with his Chiefs of Staff, he exclaimed : " If these gentlemen had their way they would soon be asking me to defend the moon against a possible attack from Mars." His caustic shafts went out against the academic as well as the military mind. " One of the difficulties about great thinkers," he once observed, " is that they so often think wrong "—his own thinking being, like truth itself, complex, cautious, comprehensive, and its expression almost always guarded and qualified, except when he took refuge in the brilliant half-truth of an epigram.

The weakness of Moret, the impulsive young politician in Winston Churchill's novel *Savrola*, was that " he had no counter-poise of healthy cynicism ". Lord Salisbury did not suffer from this defect of statesmanship. He was sometimes as discouraging to young men as Talleyrand was with his *Surtout pas de zèle*. At the Foreign Office, Lord Cecil relates, he would startle an official who appeared to him to be anxious or merely over-zealous, with the remark, " Nothing matters." To some of the more bureaucratically minded experts there was always some-thing of the amateur about him ; and he on his part gibed at what he called " Foreign Office jargon ". He certainly never suffered from that insidious malady known to the French as " *la déformation professionelle* ". The late Lord Perth told me of an incident which caused him bewildered astonishment soon after he had entered the Foreign Service. There had for some years been a desultory exchange between the British and German Governments on their rival claims to the possession of Mount M'Fumbiro in East Africa. After a profound study of all the relative documents, the Department concerned composed and sent up to Lord Salisbury a final, carefully considered statement of the British claim. The draft dispatch came back to the Department with four decisive words written in the Foreign Secretary's own hand and in the usual red ink : " M'Fumbiro is a myth."

The word " honour " is now not much used in political parlance ; but it was ever in Lord Salisbury's mind and often on his lips and at the tip of his pen. He was always animated by the directive which he set himself at the outset of his career at Stamford. It has already been quoted ; but let it be set down again : it is the key which unlocks his political mind : " In our foreign policy what we have to do is simply to perform our own part with honour ; to abstain from a meddling diplomacy ; to uphold England's honour steadily and fearlessly, and always to be rather prone to let action go along with words than to lag behind them." The words were spoken in 1865 ; and they were the text of his policy for 35 years—the policy that made Britain's word as good as a pledge, and that built up the prestige that wins a war before it is begun.

But in regard to the last sentence of his self-given directive, we today, when we consider the much closer nexus of nations in this age of U.N.O. can only exclaim : *Felix opportunitate vitae.* Lord Salisbury in his day assuredly knew the delays which obligatory co-operation with other nations caused ; but in many parts of the world the decision he took in Whitehall could be, and was, instantly translated into action. Swift decision, prompt execution, was one of the weapons in his extensive armoury ; equally well could he employ the opposite method of infinite patience and dogged refusal to budge—he knew how to call into his service that " immovable calmness, the patience that no folly,

no provocation, no blunders can shake ", which he had praised
in Castlereagh, or that " subtlety in persistence " which Garvin
had reluctantly admired in his dealings with Chamberlain. And
he was wonderfully well equipped with political foresight. Instances of his uncannily correct forecasts abound in these pages,
especially in his writings recorded in the earlier chapters. His
own intense inner life seemed to endow him with insight into the
unspoken suffering of friends or relations and the unavowed intentions of foreign nations. Lord Vansittart has written that
" the essence of statesmanship is anticipation " ; and Lord Salisbury, having foreseen what was most likely to happen, had the
faith to base his policy on his own forecast and so to act as to
forestall the evil and support the better tendencies, to influence,
to direct, and never to " lag behind ". His master-mind made
incidents subserve the policy he had deliberately chosen instead
of allowing them, as lesser men will, to dictate his course. More
often than to most men it was given to him, as to Wordsworth's
" Happy Warrior ", " to see what he foresaw ", and in a shape
conformed to British interests.

None of these attributes—authority, knowledge, devotion to
duty and to the dictates of honour, commonsense, foresight—
would have availed him had he not possessed the crowning virtue
of courage. Moral courage is the cardinal, the essential quality
of statesmanship. Disraeli said to Lady Gwendolen : " Courage
is the rarest of all qualities to be found in public men " ; and he
added, " Your father is the only man of real courage that it has
ever been my lot to work with." Lord Salisbury could indeed
never have stepped into the political arena at all had he not been
by nature fearless. His eldest brother an invalid, his next
brother having died in infancy, he himself born with a nervous
system which made him, during those early years, a sleepwalker
and a martyr to " nerve-storms " (as he himself called them),
subject for most of his life to severe mental depression, he overcame these disabilities by courage, faith and will-power ; and
those same attributes endowed him with the large serenity which
enlightened his old age.

It was his courage which made him ready at all times to be
" in the right with two or three ", even to defy general opinion
single-handed ; which gave him confidence in his own line of
policy once he had determined it, ability to wait unperturbed,

disregard of consequences to himself, willingness to take up every challenge, undismayed reaction to disaster, undeviating persistence in the face of unfavourable omens, and absolute refusal to take an expedient course which he believed to be wrong.

In private life his courage and faith made him quite unconcerned about the hour when death should come to him. In mid-career he was ready for it. According to Lady Gwendolen Cecil he could not understand the dread of it—" One might as well be afraid of going to sleep," he used to say. The death of others was none the less an ever-recurring profound grief. During the Boer War he actually caused embarrassment to his military advisers by pressing them to have it waged with fewer casualties.

The last manifestation of his Christian valour was during those months after retirement when death, he knew, was near and when it would be welcome. He tried by all means to conceal his physical feebleness lest it should cast a shadow on the lives of those who loved him. He still wanted, amidst the comforts which surrounded him at Hatfield, to help others. He had always been ready, except when working, to sacrifice his own convenience and to render small services to members of the family which they were more than ready to perform for themselves. Deeply embedded in his nature was the sentiment : " Know that the love of thyself doth hurt thee more than anything in the world "—one must read Thomas à Kempis to understand Lord Salisbury.

He matched courage in politics with the opposite quality of prudence. He was as wary as Elizabethan Burghley. He understood too the value and the need of suspicion in international affairs. In his diplomacy he could be very subtle and suggestive. Like Talleyrand, he studied motives ; and often considered it opportune that the course of action he thought desirable should be proposed by somebody else ; and he was content to let that somebody get the credit, if success came. Self-effacement he deemed to be another cardinal virtue of diplomacy ; and it was in his very nature to be self-effacing. His selflessness made him not merely indifferent to his own reputation but even resentful of praise. He sternly discouraged any sign of glorification of success. He loathed the word " score " in its sense of having " scored off " a diplomatic opponent. " I have heard him denounce ' scores ' with vehemence," Lord Cecil of Chelwood has written to me. Lord Salisbury's reasons were both personal and politic. He intensely disliked a fuss being made about anything he did, and he hated hurting the feelings of his opposite number ; but when he was questioned on the point he typically gave a practical explanation. Mr. Iwan Muller, then Editor of the *Daily Telegraph*, once complained to him that it was a pity, and a mistake, to conceal his successes. His reply was : " To talk about a success only makes the next success more difficult."

His greatness in foreign policy came from this possession of both the basic qualities and the technical skill required in the most difficult of the political arts. When he died Sir Edmund Monson, the ambassador who had been his closest diplomatic collaborator during recent years, wrote to Lord Lansdowne a tribute to Lord Salisbury's " profound sagacity, tact and dexterity "—he possessed " a very exceptional mastery of details, as well as the highest instinct of statecraft ". Instinct and skilled craftsmanship were combined in him in the highest and rarest degree—the flash of inspiration, followed by immersion in detail ; an instinct that could survive prolonged calculations ; a policy swiftly visioned and steadily elaborated.

There are no absolute rules in diplomacy, and Lord Salisbury knew that every problem in international affairs had its own complex of special circumstances and different personalities, and that their relative significance and importance often took time to become apparent. That was another reason why at the outset of negotiations he often found it wise not to reveal too clearly the whole of his mind and intention. He knew the importance of timing. The most acceptable solution might be deemed unacceptable if it were proffered too early or too late.

But the overruling intention of his policies was always to maintain, at home, his country's good health and solvency ; and abroad to nourish the comity of nations—to establish neighbourly relationships and to keep the international atmosphere as wholesome as possible. If the fundamentals were sound, sound results would flow from them. In home politics, in particular, it brought no permanent cure to tinker with effects if the cause of the trouble were left unremedied. The principle was all-important. And so also in foreign affairs. If good relations were sincerely fostered—Lord Salisbury did not talk of " friendship " with other nations—and if—no less important—evil designs were firmly and instantly countered, the chances were good that peace would be maintained. It may be noted parenthetically that Lord Salisbury by a long while anticipated the late President Roosevelt in advocating a " good neighbour " policy. " A nation like ours ", he said at Carnarvon in 1888, " should behave to other nations just as a man should behave to neighbours. . . . There is all the difference in the world between good-natured, good-humoured effort to keep well with your neighbours, and that spirit of haughty and sullen isolation. . . ." We have seen how indefatigably he exerted himself to sustain the Concert of Europe ; and, equally, to obtain by peaceful methods the legitimate advantages for his country for which he might have been justified by his contemporaries in making war. The incalculables of his greatness are the disasters he averted from Britain and the whole human race by wise statesmanship. Disasters have come in plenty after his guiding hand had been removed.

Yet at the end of his long career, crowded with achievement and singularly free from failures, there remained a sense of disappointment and dissatisfaction. To most people Lord Salisbury appeared the very opposite of an idealist. But his intimates—which is to say his family circle, for he had no intimates outside Hatfield—knew that he had a passion, and an ideal. His political passion was for liberty—liberty of the individual, liberty of action, liberty of speech. His ideal was the highest possible Christian standard between man and man and between nation and nation. And he saw that standards of conduct were slipping. He was aware, sadly aware, that he himself, like Cavour, had had recourse to expedients which he disliked in the interests, as he saw them, of his country. He had been the temporary trustee of those interests ; and whatever his personal feelings it had been his plain duty to serve them in the best way which he deemed effective. He had put the finishing of the task entrusted to him above every other consideration. In his old age he seems to have been obsessed by the conviction that he had fallen short of his own moral standard.

Nor was he the man to console himself with the good he had done ; his nature was to think of what he had left undone. He might have reflected on the large territories in East and West and Central Africa to which his policies had carried civilization, on the vast lands of the Sudan which had been liberated on his initiative, on the enlargement of British dominion and British influence in the world, on the manifold increase of prosperity at home and the apparent contentment of the masses. Not only had the Empire grown more powerful and closer knit, but the parliamentary system was undoubtedly healthier and more stable than when he had entered politics in the early 'fifties ; and his own exertions and example had counted for as much in the one case as in the other. But any self-gratulation of this kind was totally alien to his character. Nothing was due to him. There was his startling aphorism : " With the result I have nothing to do." It was axiomatic for the statesman whose rule was that " action should go along with words ", who had been supreme in getting things done, in obtaining results, it was axiomatic for him that he deserved no credit for these results. He sought divine guidance, did what he believed to be right, and left the event to God. Nor did he ever claim to " be doing good ". Lady Gwendolen Cecil tells the story of a young man who had been discussing which profession he ought to choose for the sake of " the good he might do ". Lord Salisbury was troubled. Somebody expostulated that surely it was a noble wish to get good done in the world ; to which he answered with " intensity of expression " : " Yes, but not by you—never by you—never allow yourself to believe that for an instant." It was this constant sense of an overruling direction which gave him his monumental calm in time of personal affliction or political crisis. Presumption was the deadly peril for men and nations. Lord Salisbury was perhaps the last great statesman of Europe—there had been many before him—who believed in an overruling Providence ; and he held that where belief in God no longer provided the source of authority a false idol would inevitably be set up and worshipped in His stead. Only trust in God could make a man both lowly and authoritative, which was one of Lord Salisbury's salient characteristics and an essential feature of his statesmanship.

This combined lowliness and authority was one more example of his remarkable capacity for uniting opposites in his own personality—caution with boldness, cynicism with sincerity, extreme personal shyness with amplitude of public life, circumvention with directness, readiness to take international risks with utter detestation of war, sharp antagonism in an unavoidable quarrel with benevolence at home, love of seclusion with ability to hold the largest popular audience, a scholar's mind with a craving for action. He could be as subterranean as any Forsyte, and was famous for his public indiscretions ; immovably stubborn, and on occasions gracefully compliant. The list could be prolonged. But the important point about the opposites of his character is that these contrary impulses were never allowed to clash. He had them all at command. Caprice never inspired his action, private or public. The stern self-control engendered by his religious belief was the unifying and integrating force which placed the most diversified faculties at his service according to the immediate need. One last paradox of this least dogmatic of men was his firm belief that, without dogma, religion, which he regarded as the most powerfully beneficent influence on the actions of men in the mass, must inevitably wither and decay. The purity of Christian morality, on which the national health depended, could not be reached or maintained without " its stubborn and inflexible creed ". A passage in his *Quarterly Review* article which expounds this, his profound conviction, has been quoted in Chapter II ; it is perhaps that one of his utterances which he would most have wished to be impressed on the minds of his countrymen. For two or three generations the standards of Christian conduct may continue to be maintained by men who have renounced the faith. They have been brought up in the Christian ethos, in a believing community. But if they have no dogma the later generation, children of unbelieving parents, will not learn the self-restraint of which religion alone explains the need. " The dream of undogmatic religion is too baseless to impose long upon educated minds. . . . We shall either cling to our articles of faith in spite of rationalist and unsectarian teaching, or we shall learn, by a cruel experience, that men will not be moral without a motive, and that a motive can only be furnished by religious belief."

Lord Acton generalized that great men are almost always bad men ; and Tolstoy has a passage in *War and Peace* in which he dwells on the difficulty which any man of strict principles must experience in attaining greatness in the world of action.

Lord Salisbury stands in history as an example of a man animated by the highest principles who successfully occupied the highest offices of State. And had he possessed a talent for histrionics, like Chatham or Lloyd George, he would have been popularly acclaimed a great man. But his nature was the opposite of theirs. He so intensely disliked political flamboyancy. In terms of modern speech he was a " back-room " Prime Minister. He would have been glad enough, if such self-effacement were possible, to be an anonymous Prime Minister.

His whole life, private and public, had been one long response to the will of God, as he understood His will. There is the evidence of Lady Gwendolen Cecil that he always regarded political action as being " of infinitely small importance " compared with " maintaining the Christianity of our civilization ". Perhaps therefore the verdict which posterity will pass on him may be best expressed in those words which were spoken by himself when he paid his last tribute to Gladstone : " He will leave behind him the memory of a great Christian statesman."

[private]

Feb. 17. 88

Dear Mr. Kennedy

I have been pressed by Lord Bridport to invoke Signor Crispi's aid in respect of a lawsuit in which the former is engaged, & in which he fears that he may be deprived of a fair trial by illegitimate influences.

You will be best judge how

FACSIMILE OF LETTER WRITTEN BY LORD SALISBURY TO MR. J. G. KENNEDY, CHARGÉ D'AFFAIRES IN ROME, ON FEBRUARY 17, 1888

N.B. Lord Bridport was also Duke of Brontë (in Sicily)

far the fear is well-founded
- & what assistance can
be properly given to him. But
I should be very much
obliged for any protection
which
against injustice, can be
given to Lord Bradford, both
as a friend of my own, &
still more as a valued servant
of the Queen.

My impression of what is going
on in Abyssinia is not favourable

to the Italians. It looks 3

of as if - after a good deal of
blustering - they would have to
withdraw their troops before
anything was done on account
of the climate. I am afraid
such a result will not be
helpful to Crispi.

France, from all I hear, is
much more angry with Italy
than with Germany. The
share taken by Italy is what makes
the Triple Alliance so bitter to
her: & we have been receiving
constant hints that it is there

which is driving her into the
arms of Russia. Whether this
indignation is real, or produced
by a recollection of 1859: or whether
it is stimulated to justify an
attempt to annex Genoa - I do
not know.

The papers are full of suggestions
that we have undertaken
to protect the courts of Italy &
Austria in case of a war with France.
It is needless to say no such
covenant exists.

Yours very truly
Salisbury

NOTES

CHAPTER I

P. 3. The first Earl of Salisbury, before he gained his title, spelt his name Cecyll (as may be seen in one of the show-cases in the Library at Hatfield).

P. 4. *Lord Salisbury in the Library.* Among the books which were to be found in the Hatfield library and which may be presumed to have appealed to Lord Salisbury's special tastes were : Sir John Lubbock's *Prehistoric Times*, Tylor's *Primitive Culture*, Alison's *History of Europe* (20 vols.) ; *Journal of the Statistical Society* ; Gordon's *Khartum Journal* ; Metternich's *Memoirs* ; Whewell's *Philosophy of the Inductive Sciences* ; Bentham's Works ; Justin Martyr's *St. John* ; Salmon's *The Infallibility of the Church* (on the fly-leaf of which Lord Salisbury inscribed his name).

He must also, no doubt, have perused the first edition of Bacon's *Essays*—

Essays or Counsels : Civill & Morall : Francis Lo Verulam : Viscount St Albans : 1625.

P. 8. *Lady Salisbury, friend of the Duke of Wellington.* The 2nd Marquess of Salisbury (father of the Prime Minister) was a cousin of the Duke. He was twice married, and each wife in turn became a close friend of her cousin-by-marriage. His first wife was Frances Gascoyne, sprung from a rich Liverpool family. One of her ancestors had been Lord Mayor of London— a lineage which the future Prime Minister was fond of laying stress on. It was perhaps on the distaff side that he inherited his keen business ability and financial carefulness. His mother died when Robert was 9 years old. According to Sir Herbert Maxwell the Duke of Wellington " felt the shock [of her death] very severely ".

The second wife of the 2nd Marquess was Lady Mary Sackville-West. She married him in 1847, and when he died she married the 15th Earl of Derby. She had included " Arthur " among the names of each of her three children.

P. 10. For the story of Lord Salisbury's days in the Australian Gold Fields I have relied on the late Sir Ernest Scott's little book *Lord Robert Cecil's Gold Fields Diary*, published in Australia and now out of print. It was kindly lent to me by Mr. W. W. Hadley, former editor of the *Sunday Times*. Scott was for many years Professor of History in Melbourne University.

CHAPTER II

P. 17. For the close similarity of certain aspects of Lord Salisbury's spiritual outlook with that of Cardinal Newman see *Apologia pro Vita Sua*, p. 238 (1893 ed.) : " From the time I became a Catholic I have no further history of my religious opinions to relate. In saying this, I do not mean to say that my mind has been idle, or that I have given up thinking on theological subjects ; but that I have had no variations to record, and have had no anxiety of heart whatever." And again : " I am far of course from denying that every article of the Christian Creed, whether as held by Catholics or by Protestants, is beset with intellectual difficulties ; and it is simple fact that, for myself, I cannot answer those difficulties . . . but I have never been able to see a connection between apprehending those difficulties . . . and on the other hand doubting the doctrines to which they are attached."

P. 18. While the Rev. Joseph Butler, as he then was, lived in his quiet parish of Stanhope (in Co. Durham), writing his *Analogy*, the Archbishop of Canterbury (Secker) recommended him to Queen Charlotte for promotion. " I thought he was dead," exclaimed the Queen. " No, Madam," replied the Archbishop. " He is not dead, but he is buried."

P. 18. Before Salisbury and Gladstone, William Pitt the younger had been a great reader of Bishop Butler.

P. 20. " *The creature is finite, the Creator infinite.*" Lord Salisbury would, I think, have approved the words used by the eminent zoologist, Professor A. C. Hardy, at the meeting of the British Association held at Newcastle in September, 1949 : " We fool ourselves if we imagine that our present ideas about life and evolution are more than a tiny fraction of the truth yet to be discovered in the almost endless years ahead."

Works Consulted

Butler's Works, edited by W. E. Gladstone.
Dean Church : *The Oxford Movement.*
Cardinal Newman : *Apologia pro Vita Sua.*
Algernon Cecil : *British Foreign Secretaries.*
D. C. Somervell : *English Thought in the Nineteenth Century.*

CHAPTER III

P. 35. " *Democracy* " *as it appeared in 1848–9.* The following extracts from *The Times* of 1848–9 exemplify the attitude of Britain's leading newspaper to the " democratic " and revolutionary movements on the Continent —an attitude to which Lord Robert Cecil closely conformed.

Monday, February 7, 1848.

It cannot be repeated too often that the French Revolution, or rather the revolution in the affairs of Europe produced mainly by the dissemination of French principles, is not an event terminated, concluded, and accomplished, but that it is still and continually in progress. It is still fomenting the same hatred of religious and aristocratical institutions and privileges ; it is still subverting the principles of authority to which men yielded in former ages a loyal or unconscious obedience ; and though it cares but little for the evils of anarchy or the benefits of genuine liberty, no sacrifice is too great to throw off and extirpate the natural checks to democratic licence.

Wednesday, March 15, 1848.

We believe there is not a single branch of employment, or of idleness, in Paris that has not marched *en masse* to the Hotel de Ville to demand more wages, less work, certainty of employment, and a release from all the rules and restrictions which the experience of their masters had found to be necessary. It is unwise to damp the expectations of five thousand men. In some cases, therefore, the Government capitulated on rather hard terms. By and by it . . . requested the trade to nominate their several deputies. . . . Then there came deputations of women, of students, of pawnbrokers' tickets, of bankers, of bread-eaters, of bread-makers, of cabmen, of 'busmen, of sailors, of porters, of everything that had, or had not, an office and a name. . . . By the side of the universal procession to the Hotel de Ville behold another in a contrary direction—thousands of English artisans, nay, even domestic servants, proscribed, banished, and flying from the ungrateful soil they had done so much to adorn and enrich ; flying in terror and haste, without their wages or their property, and only just rescued in time by their own country's benevolence from starvation on the shores of Republican France.

Wednesday, October 11, 1848.

Anything is better than the licence of a mob and the wholesale murder and pillage that must take place if the extreme party become triumphant.

Wednesday, January 17, 1849.

Mr. Macaulay has recently informed us that the words " mob " and " sham " both came into use in England in one year. Whatever may be the philological merit of this discovery, we are at no loss to detect the political connection of the two substantives, and if ever these nouns are to migrate across the channel, they cannot find a more favourable moment than the present to take their rank in the principal dialects of continental Europe. From the day that the mobs of Paris, Berlin, and Vienna succeeded in vesting themselves with the principal attributes of government, government itself became for the time a sham, a sleight, and a counterfeit. In France, a pretended banquet led in a few hours to all the realities of a social revolution. Instantly everything was designated by its furthest opposite. The conspiracy which had ruined the country, and all but dissolved society was a glorious achievement ; M. Garnier-Pagès, whilst he plundered the savings-banks, saved France from bankruptcy ; M. Lamartine by his grandiloquent language encouraged insurrection throughout the world and, by his acts, abandoned them to their fate ; fraternity expelled the foreign workmen from France ; and the hideous sore of pauperism was inflamed by the pledges of the Government and dignified by the title of National Labour. It is no exaggeration to assert that from first to last, every act of the Provisional Government was a make-believe—their own existence being the greatest imposition of all ; since they affected to derive their power from the people, whilst the people desired nothing so much as to consign them to perdition. . . . The French nation have been conquered and are still enslaved by phrases.

Monday, October 15, 1849.

The proceedings now going on at Versailles will complete the contempt into which the " great men of February " have already fallen. The disclosures of some of the witnesses, and the bold avowals, so far as they have yet gone of the man now on his trial, form an additional chapter to the narrative of imbecility, treachery, and selfishness, of certain of the actors in that drama. What is not the least remarkable in the conduct of these men, whose plots and crimes have almost rendered the term " patriotism " one of shame and scorn, is the merciless, the ignoble war they now wage against each other. Every expression that hatred can suggest—liar, traitor, perjurer, coward, &c.—is now freely and mutually flung at each other by those who were accomplices in bringing society to the brink of ruin.

The names of Raspail, Blanqui, Barbes, Huber, &c., have become ominous and ridiculous ; ominous from the moment there is not courage enough to resist them ; contemptible the instant that society dares to look them in the face, and defy them. Several of these heroes of liberty are now found to be an equal admixture of the conspirator and the informer—the spy and the revolutionist. Hesitating between punishment and reward, they have one foot in the dungeon and the other in the cabinet of the secret police. One night sees them brooding, with pallid and ferocious faces over plots of insurrection, pillage, and massacre ; and the next beholds them disgorging for lucre the mass of iniquity they have thus acquired, and in which they are still more than half disposed to participate.

CHAPTER IV

P. 54. *" Reform of the Franchise " in the Queen's Speech.* In the Queen's Speech of February 5, 1867, Reform was referred to in the following terms : " Attention will again be called to the state of the representation of the people in Parliament."

P. 60. *Acceptance of the opposite Party's legal enactments.* Cranborne had expressed the same conviction in an earlier article in the *Quarterly* (January, 1863) : " So long as the great institutions which are essential to our form of government are preserved, Conservatives are bound by their own principles to uphold as laws alterations which, as projects, they opposed."

P. 63. *Lady Cranborne on her husband's resignation.* Lady Cranborne, who was heart and soul with her husband in the matter of his resignation, had a sharp wit of her own. Lord George Hamilton tells the story of how Lord Derby, the Prime Minister, gave a " reconciliation " dinner to the Cranbornes directly afterwards and remarked good-humouredly to Lady Cranborne : " So I hear, Lady Cranborne, you devote your Sundays to arithmetic." " Yes," came that lady's reply, " and we did a very odd sum : we deducted three from sixteen, and we found nothing left "—there being 16 members in Lord Derby's Cabinet, from which Carnarvon, Peel and Cranborne himself had resigned (Lord George Hamilton : *Parliamentary Reminiscences and Reflections, 1886–1906*, p. 315).

CHAPTER V

P. 64. The " Liberal friend " to whom Lord Salisbury wrote the letter here referred to was Mr. John Coleridge, afterwards Lord Coleridge and Lord Chief Justice. Coleridge forwarded the letter to his father with the comment : " It is very manly and touching, I think, and shows the fine and tender side of Cranborne's nature which I have always found he had, but which he is so chary of showing in public " (Lord Cranborne had spoken feelingly about the possibility of losing the friendship of Coleridge). *Life and Correspondence of Lord Coleridge*, Vol. II, p. 156.

Five years later (December 15, 1872) Coleridge writes from Hatfield : " We are here in miserable weather, but it is a noble house, and they are kindness itself in the perfect liberty they leave us. It is pleasant to see such fine natures as the lord and lady of this place in such a position, and discharging all its duties so well and worthily "—*Coleridge*, Vol. II, p. 216.

The children of Lord Salisbury were :

James, 4th Marquess, 1861–1947.

He held several Ministerial offices and was Leader of the House of Lords for many years.

William, 1863–1936.

Rector of Hatfield and Bishop of Exeter.

Robert, 1864– , created Viscount Cecil of Chelwood (1923).

Under-Secretary for Foreign Affairs, 1915–18 ; Minister of Blockade, 1916–18 ; Lord Privy Seal, 1923–4 ; Chancellor of the Duchy of Lancaster, 1924–7 ; a prime mover in the foundation of the League of Nations and a leading figure of it.

Edward, 1867–1918, K.C.M.G., D.S.O.

Col. Grenadier Guards. Under-Secretary for War in Egypt, Under-Secretary for Finance, Agent General for the Sudan ; and Financial Adviser to the Egyptian Government.

Hugh, 1869– , created Baron Quickswood (1941).

M.P. for Greenwich, 1895–1906, and for Oxford University, 1910–37 ; Provost of Eton, 1936–44

Beatrix, Lady Selborne, 1858–1950.

As wife of the High Commissioner for South Africa and Governor and C-in-C. of the Orange River Colony and the Transvaal, 1905–10, Lady Selborne played her part in the resettlement of South Africa after the Boer War.

Gwendolen, 1860–1945.

Biographer of her father.

Fanny Georgina died in infancy in 1867.

CHAPTER VI

P. 87. " *Niggers*." Lord Salisbury regretted himself having once carelessly referred to a native of Hindustan as a " black man "—especially as he was a Parsee with a complexion probably no darker than his own.

P. 88. For the relations between Lord Salisbury and Florence Nightingale see *Florence Nightingale*, by Cecil Woodham Smith, pp. 540–3 and 561.

P. 91. In considering the events of this period it has to be remembered that Turkey was still a great empire, which included not only Albania, reaching to the Aegean Sea, and Macedonia up to the frontier of the Austro-Hungarian Monarchy, but also Epirus, Thessaly, Thrace, Crete, Tripoli, Syria, Palestine, Arabia and Mesopotamia.

P. 92. *Disraeli's peerage.* When Disraeli wrote to some of his Cabinet colleagues asking them what they felt about Queen Victoria's proposal to him that, on account of his failing health, he should be transferred to the House of Lords, Lord Salisbury's sympathetic reply included the following typical observation : " You would be very heartily welcomed by the House of Lords : and you would give life to the dullest assembly in the world " (Buckle, Vol. V, p. 494).

P. 92. *Gladstone's " missionary zeal ".* The vindictiveness felt by Beaconsfield for Gladstone at this time (October, 1876) is shown in one of his letters to Lord Derby : " Posterity will do justice to that unprincipled maniac Gladstone—extraordinary mixture of envy, vindictiveness, hypocrisy, and superstition ; and with one commanding characteristic—whether Prime Minister, or Leader of the Opposition, whether preaching, praying, speechifying or scribbling—never a gentleman ! " No feelings of this sort were entertained for Gladstone by Lord Salisbury, caustically though he criticized his policy. Lord Salisbury did much by his example to assuage the personal bitterness between Party politicians which was usual in the 'sixties and 'seventies.

As a pendent to Disraeli's opinion of Gladstone it seems appropriate to recall Lord Clarendon's opinion of Disraeli expressed in a letter to Lord Lyons ten years earlier : " *He* really would have been, (as Foreign Secretary), a personal offence to every foreign Power, for although the various For. Secretaries in England have been of every variety of intellect and fitness they have always been *Gentlemen*, and the most enthusiastic admirers of Dizzy, (if such parties exist), would not think of saying that of him " (June 28, 1866). From Lord Clarendon's papers.

P. 96. Pera was the European quarter of Constantinople, Stambul the official ; and Galata was its port.

P. 96. Difference between western and eastern European mentality.

Those who have travelled—or better, have lived—all over Europe will agree with me, I believe, that a sharp difference, unmistakable though difficult to define, is observable after one has passed eastward and south-eastward of the Baltic States, Poland, Hungary and Austria. The same kind of invisible but potent barrier divides Ulster from the rest of Ireland, and in the past divided the Highlands from the Lowlands of Scotland. As Bailie Nicol Jarvie of Glasgow said to Frank Osbaldistone : " Ye ken nothing about our hill country, or Hielands, as we ca' them. They are clean another set frae the like o' huz."

P. 98. Sir Henry Austen Layard, who succeeded Elliot as ambassador to the Porte, considered that Lord Salisbury was duped by Ignatieff, whose unscrupulous intrigues, aided by his wife, drove a wedge between the special envoy and the old diplomatist (Layard's private Memoirs, Section I, p. 5). Later in the same section Layard writes : " My experience of Russian Diplomatists has led me to believe that they are so trained to habits of deception and dissimulation that their word can be rarely, if ever depended upon."

P. 100. Lord Salisbury used to tell the story of how Lady Salisbury had been honoured by the Sultan at the end of the Conference by the bestowal of the " Order of Chastity 3rd Class " ! This was strictly according to the protocol of the Ottoman Court. Only the wives of crowned heads were entitled to receive the First Class of the Order ; other Royal ladies were worthy of the Second Class ; and diplomatists' wives received the Third Class.

CHAPTER VII

P. 103. A sketch of Lord Salisbury at work in the India Office is provided by Lord George Hamilton (*Parliamentary Reminiscences, 1868–1885*, p. 73) :

" Lord Salisbury was then Secretary of State for India. He was in the zenith of his vigour. Those only who served under him and whom he liked can have any idea of his charm as a Chief. . . . His extraordinary quickness of apprehension spoiled one, for you rarely had to finish a sentence before he intervened with a remark anticipating your conclusion. He was a wonderfully concise draftsman. Over and over again, when I brought him an answer to an embarrassing question which, with the aid of heads of departments, we had contrived to boil down to, say, two pages, he would reply, taking up his pen : A good answer ; still it might be put thus ; and reducing our long statement to two or three sentences, he would cover the ground more effectively than we had done with the long answer.

" He could transact an enormous amount of business quickly and thoroughly, and he maintained an extraordinarily high literary level in all his writings, despatches and speeches. Of all the political speakers and writers of his generation, he will in the future be regarded as the greatest master of crisp, compact and epigrammatic English. Most courteous and considerate to his subordinates, he exacted from them in return full measure. Never ruffled or perturbed, he would give equally close attention to the most meticulous [*sic*] matter as to a big question of policy. . . . By his death I lost not only a noble Chief, but an old and proved friend. On thinking over his career, let us hope that he is not the last *grand seigneur* to hold the post of Prime Minister of England."

P. 103. *The ageing Beaconsfield.* There seems to be little doubt that Disraeli would not have had the physical strength to stand the strain of his last Ministry if he had not been able to rely on the sustaining vitality and the loyalty of Lord Salisbury. When they returned a year later from the Berlin Congress one who was present at the Guildhall banquet (Boyd-Carpenter, afterwards Bishop of Ripon) wrote : " To me it was most painful. Lord Beaconsfield looked like a corpse. . . . The face was like a mask, ghastly and expressionless."

P. 109. Highclere and Hatfield were two of the big houses where the custom of week-end parties was first introduced.

P. 110. *Sir Andrew Buchanan.* Ambassadors were often colourful figures in those days. One of Sir Andrew's foibles was to take members of his staff for rides across country in their evening clothes during the long daylight of a Russian summer night (Col. Wellesley, p. 111).

P. 113. *Proposed occupation of Cyprus and/or Alexandretta.* As far back as in December, 1877, Beaconsfield had addressed a " most secret " letter to Layard suggesting that Britain might afford " substantial assistance " to the Porte if " we could contrive to purchase some territorial station conducive to British interests ". He mentioned Batoum, or " a commanding position in the Persian Gulf ", or " a British Army Corps at Gallipoli ", and invited Layard's opinion in the matter (Buckle, Vol. VI, p. 252, and Layard's private Memoirs, Section VII, p. 1).

CHAPTER VIII

P. 114. *The Salisbury Circular.* Although Lord Salisbury's Circular Despatch was written outside the Foreign Office, all relevant papers had, of course, been circulated to him as a Cabinet Minister, and he had had the advantage of studying Layard's ample and effective criticisms of the Russian terms. The document is approximately 3,000 words in length—a good night's work, as my fellow-journalists will readily agree. For those not accustomed to measure documents in terms of the number of words, I may mention that a full first leader in *The Times* averages 1,000 to 1,200 words.

The Circular is dated " Foreign Office, April 1st ", and must, I suppose, be the only despatch ever sent out so headed by a Minister who was not in name or by proxy the Foreign Secretary of the day. It opens with the words : " I have received the Queen's commands to request Your Excellency to explain to the Government to which you are accredited. . . ."

P. 114. Beaconsfield claimed, and of course deserved, some share of the credit for the Salisbury Circular which he whole-heartedly approved. He wrote to Queen Victoria : " Lord Beaconsfield thinks it does Lord Salisbury great credit, and that it will produce a considerable and beneficial effect. It is an attempt also to take the composition of important despatches out of the manufactury of the Hammonds and the Tenterdens, who have written everything in their Foreign Office jargon, during the last ten years. Mr. Canning wrote his own despatches on great occasions, and also Lord Palmerston " (Buckle, Vol. VI, p. 282).

Lord Tenterden, who succeeded Lord Hammond as Permanent Under-Secretary of State for Foreign Affairs at the Foreign Office, must have spent quite an appreciable time each day on the elaborate flourishes with which he decorated his signature. Lord Salisbury's, by contrast, is never so much as underlined.

It is perhaps an illustration of Lord Salisbury's predisposition to the task of a Foreign Secretary that from the moment he took it over he instituted the habit of initialing or commenting on in red ink the documents submitted to him. Thus the Chief's remarks, or mark, could always be distinguished at once. This custom has, I understand, since been generally observed.

P. 117. Lord Odo Russell, later created Lord Ampthill, possessed in high degree the inborn Russell liking for wild animals. This once induced him, when he was on a visit to Marseilles, to buy a boa-constrictor, which he unfortunately allowed to escape from its wooden case in his hotel bedroom. Being totally unwilling, of course, to summon either housemaid or manager to help him, he tackled the brute alone and succeeded in forcing him back into the box. The manifest courage of his outlook gained the respect of Bismarck, just as his charm of manner won the affection of the whole diplomatic corps in Berlin.

P. 118. *Marvin's disclosure.* Lord Salisbury himself was inclined to believe that Schouvaloff may have had a hand in the Marvin leakage.

P. 119. Describing the effect of Lord Salisbury's two secret Conventions on the British public Lord Morley writes (in his *Life of Gladstone*, Vol. II, p. 575) : " The country received a shock that made men stagger."

P. 119. In addition to Cyprus, various other harbours and islands of the Eastern Mediterranean had been considered by the British Cabinet as bases from which to oppose further Russian advances in Asia Minor. They included Batoum, St. Jean d'Acre, " a post on the Persian Gulf ", Alexandretta, Crete, Lemnos and Mitylene, and a " port on the Persian Gulf " (Buckle, VI, pp. 252–3, Lady Gwendolen Cecil, Vol. II, p. 270, and Layard, Memoirs, Sections VII and XII).

In June, 1951, the Parachute Regiment was sent to Cyprus for just the same purpose as that for which the Beaconsfield Government obtained the use of the island in 1878—to defend British interests in South-West Asia.

P. 120. Lord Salisbury's personal messages to Layard. The three cipher telegrams are referred to by the ambassador in Constantinople as " your three personal telegrams " in the archives of the Public Record Office, but there is no record there of the text of the messages composed by the Foreign Secretary. Lady Gwendolen Cecil shows acquaintance with them, and I can only suppose that on this occasion, as on many others, Lord Salisbury carried his personal policy to the point of leaving no trace of the transaction in the Foreign Office.

Lord Salisbury's political wisdom can often best be studied in his private letters to ambassadors. In his private and secret letter of May 2, 1878, to Layard he reveals succinctly his opinions about Turkish rule in Asia, Russia's designs there and the need for Britain to occupy Cyprus. He writes : " As a Governor of European Christians the Porte has failed. . . . If we desire to avoid new ' atrocities ' and recurring interventions its jurisdiction for administrative purposes over the Christians in Europe must be subject to considerable limitation. In Asia it is otherwise. Its Government there has been as good as that of any other Power except England's. . . . If we can protect the Asiatic Empire from disintegration, and procure a more reasonable frontier in Europe, there will be a fair chance of the Ottoman Government retaining Constantinople for a considerable period.

" The mere presence of the Russians at Kars will cause Persia, Mesopotamia, Syria to turn their faces northward. There a Russian party will arise, and consequent disorder and the languid administrative powers of the Porte will be taxed, and chaos will follow, of which, in some form or other, the Russians will take advantage to reduce the Porte to impotence and to turn its provinces into Russian Satrapies. The presence of England is the only remedy which can prevent this process of destruction. . . . But it would be ridiculous to attempt to exercise any such protective office from such a distance as Malta. . . . It will probably be the last time that any English Ministry will offer it [the Porte] a hand."

And on May 9 he writes : " Sooner or later the greater part of his [the Turk's] European Empire *must* go."

It will be noted that he correctly foretold Turkey's retention of Constantinople and the loss of the greater part of her European possessions.

P. 124. *Ready acceptance of the Cyprus Convention by Turkey.*

I have followed closely Layard's own account of the proceedings in Constantinople during the crucial days May 24 to June 4, and I am surprised that Mr. B. H. Sumner, in his monumental work *Russia and the Balkans (1870–1880)*, should write in a footnote (p. 491) : "Layard had the utmost difficulty in extracting the consent of the Turks and keeping them to it." The Sultan was, according to Layard, delighted to get the pledged word of Britain to support him, and seems to have raised no protest against the counter-pledge of the island of Cyprus. Layard had to use no threats of any kind, and the Turkish Sovereign immediately offered him the first-class of the Order of the Osmanayeh, with his portrait set in diamonds. It is true that intrigues, changes of Ministers, and the Sultan's own recurring habit of vacillation delayed the actual issue of the *firman* which was required to authorize the Turkish officials in Cyprus to admit British administrators and troops. Above all, the Turks had in the meantime, to their amazement and disgust, learned of Lord Salisbury's surprising secret pact with Schouvaloff. All Layard's skill in the art of diplomacy had no doubt then to be deployed in order to get the *firman* issued—which was done on July 7. We occupied the island on July 10.

P. 124. Bessarabia is one of the classic border provinces of Europe whose unlucky inhabitants are continually transferred from one sovereignty to another. Russia took it from Turkey after her 1812 campaign against Napoleon. The Treaty of Paris (1856) gave its southern strip to the newly-formed semi-independent principality of Moldavia. In 1878 Russia regained that strip, which brought her back to the Danube again. After the 1914–18 War the whole province was awarded to Rumania. During the 1939–45 World War Russia took the whole province back again.

P. 124. For Beaconsfield's journey to Berlin see J. M. M'Carthy, *Short History of Our Own Times.*

P. 125. According to Prince Hohenlohe, who was a junior member of the German delegation, the original proposal had been that Bismarck should have his two aides, Hohenlohe himself and Bülow, on each side of him ; to which the Chancellor had objected : "I do not think Hohenlohe or Bülow will have any difficulty in agreeing with me, but I am less certain of Andrassy and Waddington. I therefore prefer these latter beside me and Bülow and Hohenlohe further off."

P. 125. *Beaconsfield dissuaded from speaking in French.* Lord Rowton (the former Monty Corry) told Eckardstein that he and Ampthill had dissuaded Beaconsfield from addressing the Congress in French by getting a leading newspaper correspondent in Berlin to get the paragraph about " the greatest master of English prose " published in London and they then drew Beaconsfield's attention to it. Eckardstein, *Ten Years at the Court of St. James's,* p. 19.

P. 126. According to Eckardstein it was when the fortification of Batoum came before the Congress that Beaconsfield began to mutter, " *Casus belli, casus belli.*" Owing to the difference between British and Continental pronunciation of Latin, nobody realized what he meant except Bismarck—whom it suited, however, not to understand (Eckardstein, p. 26).

P. 127. The dictum that at Berlin Lord Salisbury was " a lath painted to look like iron " is traditionally attributed to Bismarck, but according to Arthur Mee (in *Lord Salisbury*, p. 40), it was Count Corti who said it. On the other hand Mr. Lowe, who was Correspondent of *The Times* in Berlin between 1878 and 1891, describes the epigram as apocryphal (*Nineteenth Century and After*, February, 1922).

P. 129. " *Peace with honour.*" The eye-witnesses who both at different times recorded in letters to *The Times* their impressions at Dover and 10 Downing Street respectively were Mr. John Rooker, of Tunbridge Wells, and Sir Reginald Antrobus who in 1878 was an official in the Colonial Office. The scene in Downing Street has also been described by Sir Henry Ponsonby, the Queen's Secretary, and by F. S. Pulling.

In regard to Mr. Neville Chamberlain's use of the phrase on his return from Munich in 1938, I have been told by Mrs. Chamberlain that it was not in the Prime Minister's mind to use that language, but an eager crowd were shouting for him outside, and as he mounted the stairs to show himself from the window somebody reminded him that that was the very window from which Beaconsfield had spoken in 1878. Mr. Chamberlain was both elated and fatigued after his strenuous visit to Germany and the tumultuous welcome he had received on his return, at the airport and in London, and repeated almost mechanically the words that had just been recalled to his memory. He afterwards much regretted his mistake.

P. 132. It was no doubt incorrect for Lord Derby to imply that a firm decision had been taken to seize Cyprus, if necessary by force and without the consent of the Sultan ; but that a suggestion to that effect was put forward seems to be proved by a Memorandum drawn up by the Lord Chancellor for Queen Victoria on March 8, 1878, after a Cabinet meeting : " A new naval station in the East of the Mediterranean must be obtained, and if necessary by force." The Cabinet agreed to this in certain circumstances which did not occur (Buckle, Vol. VI, p. 256).

P. 137. *Lord Salisbury's " Secret Department ".*

This information is supplied by Layard in his unpublished Memoirs. As already indicated in the text of this Chapter, Lord Salisbury also insisted on " one-man " treatment of despatches at the Constantinople end. The ambassador was directed to regard all these communications as strictly " personal and secret ", and Layard's own despatches had to be directed to Lord Salisbury personally—nothing was to pass through the hands of the Foreign Office in the ordinary way, not even through the head of the Turkish Department (Layard's Memoirs, Section XIV, p. 11).

CHAPTER IX

P. 139. *Life at Hatfield.* Beaconsfield on a visit to Hatfield in March, 1880, writes to Lady Bradford : " I am here quite alone. The eldest son of the house, an agreeable youth, is assisting his brother-in-law [Mr. Arthur

Balfour, actually the first cousin of Lord Cranborne] in canvassing Hertford.
. . . He sometimes gets home for dinner. Then another son comes for a day
with his tutor, and one evening two ladies arrived (an aunt and a cousin)
and so on. Everybody seems to do what they like—an extraordinarily free
and easy house " (Buckle, Vol. VI, p. 522).

P. 140. *Death of Beaconsfield.* The contrast of characters between Lord
Salisbury and Beaconsfield having been so marked in later life, it is interesting
to compare the autobiographical picture of himself in youth painted by Disraeli
—most of which might have been applied to the young Lord Robert Cecil.

" What narrative by a third person could sufficiently paint the melancholy
and brooding childhood, the first indications of the predisposition, the growing consciousness of power, the reveries, the loneliness, the doubts, the moody
misery, the ignorance of art, the failures, the despair ? " of the young man
whose " thought and passion were so much cherished in loneliness and
revealed often only in solitude " (Preface to *Contarini Fleming*).

P. 141. *Lord Salisbury's method of preparing his speeches.* I am indebted
to Lord Cecil of Chelwood for a personal account of how Lord Salisbury
used to prepare his speeches. As Lord Robert Cecil, Lord Cecil acted as
Private Secretary to his father for a time.

P. 152. *Gladstone's weakness in foreign policy.* In his *Life of Lord Lyons*
Lord Newton writes (p. 440) : " The interest of the year 1881 lies in the fact
that it makes a fresh departure in French foreign policy and the abandonment
of the retiring and timorous attitude which had prevailed ever since the war
with Germany " (1870–71).

P. 152. *Bombardment of Alexandria.* Italy, as well as France, was invited
to send warships to Alexandria, but she also declined.

P. 153. *Gladstone on Britain in Africa.* That Gladstone had seen the
Egyptian problem clearly when he was in Opposition was proved by his
article contributed to the *Nineteenth Century* in August, 1877. He then wrote :
" We cannot enjoy the luxury of taking Egypt by pinches. . . . Our first
site in Egypt . . . will be the almost certain egg of a North African Empire,
that will grow and grow, until another Victoria and another Albert, titles
of the lake-sources of the White Nile, come within our borders ; and till we
finally join hands across the Equator with Natal and Cape Town, to say
nothing of the Transvaal and the Orange River on the south, or of Abyssinia
or Zanzibar." It is one of the ironies of history that the mission was declined
by the man who stated it, and carried out by his opponent—who never spoke
of it beforehand.

P. 154. The cartoon " Purse, Pussy, Piety and Prevarication " shows Lord
Salisbury admonishing the Liberal peers, Lords Northbrook, Granville and
Selborne. The accompanying letterpress is so typical of the blunt political
taunts of those days that it is here reproduced :

" Such dignity and statesmanship as are still left in Parliament have
visibly taken refuge in the House of Lords. . . . In proportion as the reputation
of this House has increased, so they have been increased who would trouble
it. Insolent threats of speedy abolition fill the air whenever the Lords exercise
their invaluable function of defeating, delaying, or diminishing any revolutionary measure pressed upon them from below. Yet the House of Lords still

exists, for it is built on foundations which the English people, of whatever degree, do all admire, respect, venerate, and believe to be the only sure foundation on which a permanent system of government can be fixed.

Among the Peers there are four prominent men who have attained to pre-eminence among their fellows precisely because they represent in a marked and special manner the principles and methods by which Englishmen love to be governed ; and in them these principles and methods may well be contemplated.

Lord Northbrook, the descendant of a Lutheran banker from Bremen, is the son of the first Baring who was promoted from banking to the Peerage. He is not a man of genius or even of transcendent ability, yet he is honest as men go, modest, painstaking, and full of the business-like habits which he has inherited. He did not himself make his wealth ; had he done so his wealth would hardly have made him. But he has a great sense of his own importance, and having inherited vast possessions and the traditions of the Whigs, he has allied himself with the Radicals to so much purpose that he has been a Governor-General of India and has survived it to return to his country and to be in the present Cabinet the representative of the power of the purse in English political life.

Lord Granville on the other hand is an idle, self-indulgent, dinner-loving Whig, who took up public affairs when they were still a decent and not too engrossing pastime for a gentleman. He has a considerable experience but an inconsiderable knowledge of such foreign affairs as extend beyond the making of a French speech or the instructions of a French cook, and the sincerity of his convictions and his dealings is not such as will ever bring him to the stake for the sake of a principle. He is timid, vacillating, wavering, and incapable of conceiving, much less of carrying out, any systematic policy that does not promise to satisfy everybody at every moment. He is therefore a time-serving and temporizing Foreign Minister, intent only upon avoiding difficulties out of the House and questions in it, and upon meandering through expedients which may relieve him from the awful necessity of coming to resolutions.

But if he lacks courage, he is fertile in expedients. He abounds in pre-cautions which have for their only defect that they never produce safety. Never clear and determined as to what should be done, he is always per-suaded that the doing of nothing is a master-stroke of policy, that dawdling is a fine art, and that procrastination is the whole secret of statesmanship. With his fellow-idlers this method of handling affairs seems to be a triumph of skill. His soft answers turn away questions ; his pleasing, well-bred, amiable demeanour conciliates men to whom politics is as a pastime whereof the prize is applause. And so it is that he is approvingly called " Pussy ", and is treated as though he were a man fitted to be trusted with the destinies of an Empire.

Lord Selborne, who from a fair advocate, an excellent Sunday-school teacher and a compiler of hymnbooks, has become Lord Chancellor, keeps the Queen's conscience and represents Piety in the Cabinet. He once refused the woolsack because he would not at that time associate himself with Mr. Gladstone in the disestablishment of the Irish Church ; but this having become an accomplished fact, he has remembered that he is nothing if not a foremost partisan, and has joined in the crusade against the Irish landlords. He has moreover appeared as a supporter of the claims to sit in the House of Commons of Mr. Bradlaugh, the atheist—a fact which shows how far a man may go even towards the desertion of his Piety, when that becomes a necessary condition to the support of his Party. Yet there is no reason to believe that Lord Selborne is otherwise than a sincere man ; but his sincerity has become muddled between his Piety and his Party, so that he sees a divided allegiance which it is his present object to conciliate. He has never given any promise of statesmanship.

Lord Salisbury, from the time when, as a poor man, he wrote for obscure journals, has aspired to be not merely the avowed, but the brilliant chief of the Conservatives. He is a fine debater, a speaker of a bold and effective kind, an eager and intrepid leader, and a man of great acuteness and ability. But he lacks that without which the Conservative Party can never be held together before the world. He lacks Honesty, and he believes in Prevarication. He is the man who wrote the famous First of April Circular and then buried it in the Treaty of Berlin. He is the man who made the secret agreement with Russia, and then before the House of Lords denied its authenticity in terms which led the Peers to disbelieve its existence. He is the man who suggested to the French to take Carthage, and then denied that he advised them to take Tunis. And yet he is the man to whom the Conservatives now look to lead them to victory and to power.

Thus it is that this people love to have their rulers. The Purse they really respect, Pussy they admire, Piety they trust and Prevarication they accept without question. They have therefore now, and always will have, the Government they deserve."

JEHU JUNIOR.

CHAPTER X

Pp. 155 and 170. For the story of the piece of wire I am indebted to Mr. Edward Salmon, who was told it by a member of the Cecil family.

P. 155. *Lord Salisbury at Balmoral.* Lord Salisbury disliked Balmoral. On an earlier visit there, Sir Henry Ponsonby, the Queen's Private Secretary, noted : " He refused to walk out and did not conceal his entire abhorrence of the place and the life here. He positively refused to admire the prospect or the deer which Lady Ely pointed out to him " (*Henry Ponsonby*, by his son, Arthur Ponsonby, p. 273).

P. 157. *The premiership and the Foreign Office in the same hands.* Mr. Ramsay Macdonald in 1927 said to my friend, Sir Walford Selby, then Private Secretary to the Secretary of State for Foreign Affairs : " The Foreign Secretaryship should never be separated from the post of Prime Minister." Mr. Ramsay Macdonald, it will be remembered, had combined the two posts during his first premiership ; but the burden was too much for him and when he became Prime Minister for the second time—in spite of what he said to Selby—he confined himself to the premiership, though he continued to give much attention to foreign policy.

P. 159. *Sir William White.* Lord Hardinge of Penshurst, who, as a young Secretary in the Diplomatic Service, served under White in Constantinople, writes of him as follows in *Old Diplomacy* : " He was indeed a very remarkable man. His father, a Scotsman, managed the estates of Prince Sartoriski in Poland. He spoke English with a Scotch and foreign accent. . . . By sheer ability he made his way into the Diplomatic Service. . . . He greatly impressed Lord Salisbury (during the Constantinople Conference of 1877), by his extraordinary knowledge of Near-Eastern politics and by his acquaintance with all the scoundrels and worst political characters in Europe. He was a man after Lord Salisbury's own heart, bluff, very capable and not too scrupulous ! . . . I learnt a lot from him."

In support of Lord Hardinge's estimate of Lord Salisbury's confidence in White is the fact that in 1885 when White, who was only *locum tenens* in Constantinople during the absence of the ambassador, proposed to ask the ambassador to return for the Conference, Lord Salisbury told him not to do so.

P. 160.   An interesting impression of Lord Salisbury's private view of the Berlin Congress is given by Monsieur Chedo Mijatovitch in the *Fortnightly Review* of December, 1907.   M. Mijatovitch had been Servian Minister in London in 1885, and in a conversation with the Foreign Secretary had then complained that the Treaty of Berlin " created artificial conditions ".   Lord Salisbury replied : " Yes, you are quite right.   The Berlin Treaty is altogether artificial.   It created artificial conditions which probably, as you say, cannot last very long.   But what human work, and more especially diplomatic work, is not artificial ?   Not only diplomacy, but history also creates artificial conditions."   Turkey in Europe, he said, was not only an artificial, but an unnatural creation in itself.   " If you wish to know my personal opinion," he added, " I will tell you that the only natural, logical and healthy Balkan policy for Great Britain would be that one formulated by Mr. Gladstone : the Turks ought to be driven out of Europe with all their bag and baggage."

P. 163.   See also *New Chapters of Bismarck's Autobiography*, p. 286.

P. 164.   The bearer of Bismarck's message to Lord Salisbury was the British military attaché in Berlin.   See Lord George Hamilton's *Parliamentary Reminiscences, 1868–85*, p. 274.

P. 164.   For an interesting and amusing account of the conversation between Lord Dufferin and the Ameer of Afghanistan which settled " the Penjdeh incident ", and for the conquest of Burma, see Harold Nicolson's *Helen's Tower*, pp. 196–205.

P. 167.   *The Parnell interview*.   For the text of the Memorandum which Carnarvon wrote for Lord Salisbury immediately after his hour-and-a-quarter meeting with Parnell at 15, Hill Street, see Sir Arthur Hardinge, *The Fourth Earl of Carnarvon*, Vol. III, pp. 178–81.   The Memorandum was written at Hatfield and shown to nobody else.

A personal account of Carnarvon's Viceroyalty can be read in Lord Howard of Penrith's *Theatre of Life, 1863–1905*, pp. 53 et seq.   Howard was one of his Private Secretaries.

Other Works Consulted

Sutherland Edwards, *Sir William White—His Life and Correspondence*.
R. W. Seton-Watson, *Britain in Europe*.

CHAPTER XI

P. 172. *Home Rule.* For the Liberal view of the Home Rule question I have relied mainly on J. L. Hammond, who provides a full, detailed, scrupulous study in *Gladstone and the Irish Nation*, a book of 768 pages. A good short account is given in Herbert Paul's *Life of Gladstone*. And Morley of course wrote of it with the exceptional authority of one who was engaged in the negotiations of 1886 as Chief Secretary for Ireland in Gladstone's Ministry. Further, the story of the Home Rule struggle is told in all standard histories of modern England. In re-telling it from Lord Salisbury's point of view I have borne in mind the opinion of the great Liberal historian, G. M. Trevelyan : " It is difficult to say whether the cause of Irish conciliation was retarded or advanced by Gladstone's proceedings " (*History of England,* p. 688).

P. 172. *Character of Parnell.* John Morley, who as Secretary for Ireland was brought into the closest contact with Parnell, thus describes him : " Of constructive faculty he never showed a trace. He was a man of temperament, of will, of authority, of power ; not of ideas or ideals, or knowledge, or political maxims ; or even of the practical reason in any of its higher senses, as Hamilton, Madison and Jefferson had practical reason. But he knew what he wanted " (*Life of Gladstone,* Vol. III, p. 304).

P. 175. *The use of force by Orangemen.* In private conversation Lord Salisbury used to criticize the boycotted landowners for not combining together for the purpose of forcible self-defence (Lady Gwendolen Cecil, Private Memoranda).

P. 176. The news of Mr. Gladstone's defeat by 30 votes evoked a typical exclamation from Lord Salisbury : " Too good ! The old sinner will resign " (Lord Cecil of Chelwood, *All the Way,* p. 38).

P. 177. An excellent account of Rosebery's Foreign Secretaryship is given in E. T. Cook's *The Foreign Policy of Lord Rosebery.*

P. 178. *Greece.* See Sir Horace Rumbold, *Final Recollections of a Diplomatist,* pp. 77–80, for an account of the Powers' restraint of Greece. Sir Horace was the British minister in Athens at the time. He was the father of the Sir Horace Rumbold who ended his career as ambassador in Berlin in 1933.

P. 180. *Lord Hartington* (1833–1908). Lord Hartington had held several Cabinet posts in Gladstone's Ministries, but from the first opposed the idea of Home Rule for Ireland. It was his brother (Lord Frederick Cavendish) who was murdered in Phœnix Park. He was a man of singularly upright character and decided views, but his manner was so lethargic that it used to be said of him that he yawned during his own speeches. He became Duke of Devonshire in 1891.

CHAPTER XII

P. 184. The Minister whom Lord Salisbury failed to recognize at the man's breakfast party was W. H. Smith, one of his closest Cabinet colleagues (Lady Gwendolen Cecil, Vol. II, p. 7). Lord Salisbury was very short-sighted ; but he and Smith were on the right and left hand side respectively of their host. He sometimes failed to recognize his own sons until they began to speak—then he knew at once which one it was of them.

P. 184. *Lord Salisbury and Lord Randolph Churchill.* The fullest accounts of Lord Randolph's resignation are, of course, to be found in Lady Gwendolen Cecil and in Mr. Winston Churchill's *Life of Lord Randolph Churchill.* Laay Gwendolen writes as usual with remarkable detachment ; Mr. Churchill with rather more filial bias. But he has lately confided to one of his Cabinet colleagues that since he became Prime Minister he understood better Lord Salisbury's refusal to retain or reinstate Randolph Churchill ; and in the preface to the 1952 edition of his Life of his father he writes : " Everyone can see now what a mistake he [Lord Randolph] made in breaking with Lord Salisbury."

From Sir Henry Drummond Wolff's account, published for the first time in this new edition of Mr. Churchill's Life, it appears that Lord Salisbury, while determined not to have Randolph Churchill in his Cabinet, would have been ready to serve in the same Cabinet as he, if Hartington could have been persuaded to assume the premiership.

Lord Rosebery, who knew very well both protagonists, wrote brilliantly of Lord Randolph's resignation in his review of Winston Churchill's biography in 1906. He attributed it largely to " physical causes . . . Randolph's nervous system was always tense and highly strung ". And in Rosebery's opinion Lord Randolph did not intend his resignation to be definite.

Lord George Hamilton was another personal friend of Randolph Churchill and had been with him at Windsor Castle when he wrote his first letter of resignation. Hamilton gives a graphic account of this episode in *Parliamentary Reminiscences, 1886–1906.* He and Churchill had been summoned together to Windsor Castle on a routine ministerial visit.

Lady Gwendolen Cecil tells in detail the story of her father's reception of Lord Randolph's second and final letter of resignation. It reached Hatfield just after midnight. A county ball was being held there, and one of the guests was the Duchess of Marlborough, Lord Randolph's mother. Another guest was the Duchess of Teck, the mother of Queen Mary, with whom Lord Salisbury was conversing when the Red Box was brought to him. He glanced at the contents and continued the conversation. Next morning when he and Lady Salisbury were called, she reminded him that they had better get up early to say good-bye to the departing guests, including the Duchess of Marlborough. " Send for *The Times* first," was his sleepy response. " Randolph resigned in the middle of the night, and if I know my man it will be in *The Times* this morning." The copy of the paper which was brought to them proved his guess to be right, and Lord Randolph's mother was allowed to depart without a leave-taking which might have been embarrassing to all concerned.

The following contemporary opinion of a political opponent and personal friend of Lord Salisbury may be worth quoting, though events proved it to be very wide of the mark : " With such a man as Salisbury at the head of affairs, dominated (he was always dominated by someone), by such a Flibbertigibbet as Randolph Churchill, we may wake up some morning at war with half the world " (Lord Coleridge to Sir Mountstuart Grant Duff, July 13, 1885).

P. 188. " *A cursed profession.*" Such sentiments about politics as a profession were often expressed by Lord Salisbury in private. At about this same time he wrote to a peer who was a keen scientist and an applicant for political office : " If it is only a question of the employment of time—are you well advised in taking to politics ? I know very little of science, and a good deal of politics : and I never would advise anybody to travel along the intolerably tiresome road on which I have travelled myself—who has the other open to him " (February 15, 1887).

P. 189. " *The Foreign Secretary alone can know.*" The arguments I have advanced to show the unique position of a Foreign Secretary for judging foreign events correctly are a paraphrase of a passage in the address delivered by Lord Grey of Fallodon at the annual Chatham House dinner in 1930 ; and what was true in Lord Grey's time was certainly still more applicable to the experience of Lord Salisbury. See also Winston Churchill, *The Gathering Storm*, p. 107.

P. 190. For Balfour's administration of the Irish Office see *Arthur James Balfour, 1st Earl Balfour* by his niece Mrs. Blanche Dugdale, and *Gladstone and the Irish Nation* by J. L. Hammond.

CHAPTER XIII

P. 192. I am indebted to the present Lord Salisbury for placing at my disposal the memorandum " Home Policy " left behind by Lady Gwendolen Cecil, on which my estimate of Prime Minister Lord Salisbury's Conservative standpoint is based.

It seems appropriate also to quote in this connexion a definition of the Tory's faith contributed to *The Common Problem* in 1943 by Lord Selborne, grandson of the Prime Minister, for it would, I think, have been approved by Lord Salisbury even if he could not endorse every sentence : " The Tory looks at the State as a whole. To him it is the quasi-mystical body politic composed of legion individuals of infinite variety, worth, capacity and function ; existing as much in the past and the future as in the present. To him it is signified in the word England and all that England has ever stood for. English tradition, English institutions, English Christianity, English liberty, English justice, English valour, English power. The British Empire is the geographical extension and the witness of all these."

P. 193. " *Distinguishing man from animals.*" That the right to possess property is " one of the chief points of distinction between man and the animal creation " is a basic argument in the remarkable Papal Encyclical of 1891, with which Lord Salisbury must have been familiar. Other points of Pope Leo XIII were : that the family has rights and duties peculiar to itself which are quite independent of the State : that undue State interference is mischievous : that inequalities are inevitable : that class war is wrong : that the poor have a special claim upon the State : that justice is sacred and that if any injustice oppressed any section of society the law should be invoked to remedy the evil or remove the mischief, but should not undertake more than is required for that purpose.

P. 199. *The L.C.C.* It was another instance of the ready co-operation between Lord Salisbury and Lord Rosebery that the latter became the first Chairman of the London County Council, which the former had brought into existence.

P. 203. *The Right Honble. Edward Stanhope.* In the general post caused by the resignation of Randolph Churchill, Edward Stanhope, against his wishes, was hustled across from the Colonial to the War Office, vacated by W. H. Smith. Stanhope had been very happy at the Colonial Office and· had himself written the invitations to his first Colonial Conference. He was the first Colonial Secretary to give due importance to the representatives of the overseas countries, and when he wrote out in his own hand the invitations to them to confer together when they came to London for the Jubilee he said : " There is on all sides a growing desire to draw closer in every practicable way the bonds which unite the various parts of the Empire." The words seem commonplace today, but when they are contrasted with the language Lord Granville was using to Canada a few years before and the general Little England attitude of the Liberal rank and file they are seen in perspective to be the words of a pioneer.

CHAPTER XIV

P. 208. " An imperial people—it is a word of service, not of seizure," says one of Mr. Charles Morgan's characters in his novel *The River Line*, and I have adapted the phrase to Lord Salisbury, because I believe it exactly fits his outlook.

P. 208. *Benefits brought to Africa by white civilization.* Harold Evans, in *Men in the Tropics*, has interesting extracts from the earlier travellers in West and East Africa (and other parts of the tropics).

P. 210. *Reluctance of British Governments to take over more African territory.* *The Times* had written on November 24, 1849 : " There is a growing opinion that our colonies are useless encumbrances and idle boasts ; that they contribute little to our trade, and less than nothing to our power ; that they are chiefly useful to Government as a source of patronage and of official as well as military employment. Already the figures of bankrupt speculation are before the world. . . . The tie of affection and of force is all that remains."

Most Liberal leaders shared this view in greater or smaller degree. The most notable exception was Joseph Chamberlain. " Chamberlain raged against the disastrous foreign policy and Colonial policy of Granville and Derby " (J. L. Garvin, *Life of Joseph Chamberlain*, Vol. I, p. 491).

P. 211. *Sokotra.* See Lord Crewe, *Life of Lord Rosebery*, Vol. I, p. 284.

P. 213. The texts of these exchanges of notes and Lord Sanderson's minute, as well as Lord Salisbury's letter to Alfred Austin, are given in Gooch and Temperley, *British Documents on the Origins of the War*, Vol. VIII.

The chargé d'affaires in Rome, Mr. J. G. (afterwards Sir John) Kennedy, was the author's father. Lord Salisbury's letter is not only written throughout in his own hand but is also addressed by himself. It is reproduced in facsimile on pp. 360–3.

P. 220. The Anglo-German Agreement of 1890 also contained a cession of territory in South-West Africa. It came to be known as the " Caprivi Strip ", after the name of Bismarck's successor in the Chancellorship. Holland Rose calls the 1890 settlement " one of the most solid gains peacefully achieved for the cause of civilization throughout the nineteenth century ". The naval arguments for and against the retention of Heligoland are set out in his *Parliamentary Reminiscences and Reflections, 1886–1906* by Lord George Hamilton, who was First Lord of the Admiralty at the time.

P. 221. *The Times* was one of the earliest champions of " responsible self-government for the colonies ".

P. 221. *The Liberal Cabinet and Uganda.* Cecil Rhodes related that the Liberal Cabinet had had to choose between retaining Uganda or losing Rosebery. Mr. Gladstone had said to Rhodes, " Fancy being dragged into the middle of Africa ; and, do you know, it is all due to these wretched missionaries. Our burden is too great ; as it is, I cannot find the people to govern all our dependencies. We have too much, Mr. Rhodes, to do " (Speech by Rhodes on October 25, 1898).

See E. T. Cook, *The Foreign Policy of Lord Rosebery,* p. 8.

P. 224. *The 1890 Anglo-French Agreement.* It was formally agreed between Lord Salisbury and the French ambassador that the east and west boundaries of the Saharan hinterland allotted to France should run north and south and not bulge outwards so as to include territory in the rear of the Italian colony to the east or Spanish territory to the west. This understanding has since, perhaps inevitably, been disregarded.

P. 230. *Major Pinto.* By a curious coincidence the name of this adventurous Portuguese officer was the same as that of one of the earliest pioneers of Portugal, Fernao Mendez Pinto, who in the sixteenth century won fame in India and South-East Asia and penetrated to the Far East. This circumstance tended to increase his countrymen's enthusiasm for the exploits of his modern namesake.

P. 231. *Portugal's " archæological arguments ".* The King of Portugal at this time (1890) still preserved among his titles that of " Lord of Guinea, Persia, Ethiopia and Arabia ". Monomotapa appears on the Map of Africa in Emanuel Bowen's *Complete Atlas* of 1752. It forms part of Cafreria (or Kaffir Land) and nothing indicates that it was under Portuguese Sovereignty. See *Geographical Magazine* of May, 1950.

P. 231. Some thirty years before this time Kirk had described the degraded life of white settlers in the region now known as Nyasaland. They seemed to have lost all sense of European standards. " I believe," he recorded, " that there is not one white man or one who may call himself white in the whole district without venereal disease." Nor had he any doubts as to their utter incapacity to govern or develop " their great dependency ". " Let the Portuguese go on as they are doing and they will soon be extinct or arise as a race of bastards to do the drudgery of some active race. The Slave Trade has brought about this miserable state of things " (R. Coupland, *Kirk on the Zambesi*).

Dr. Holland Rose, in the chapter on " The Partition of Africa " in *The Development of the European Nations*, describes Portuguese administration of the Zambesi region as " notoriously inefficient and generally corrupt ", and states that slave-hunting was still going on in the upper basin of the river (pp. 540 and 547). No doubt reports to this effect were reaching Lord Salisbury during his negotiations and contributed to stiffen his attitude.

P. 235. Matabeleland was only finally secured to the British Empire after the Matabele Campaign of 1893.

P. 236. *The special vocation of Englishmen for the work of colonization.* One of the most recent travellers, the American author Negley Farson, writes in his introduction to *Behind God's Back* : " I believe that it is under the Englishman that the native will have the best chance to progress in Africa."

Works Consulted

With an almost immeasurable amount of material available, I have relied mainly on the following sources :

W. L. Langer : *The Diplomacy of Imperialism*, Vol. I. Amply documented and covers much more than is usually implied by the term " imperialism ". It is a continuation of the same author's *European Alliance and Alignments 1871–1890*.

A. J. P. Taylor : *Germany's First Bid for Colonies 1884–5.* Particularly enlightening on Bismarck's attitude to colonization.

Sir Charles Lucas : *The Partition and Colonization of Africa.* A valuable series of lectures.

J. A. Williamson : *A Notebook of Empire History.* A concise handbook of facts and dates.

Harold Evans : *Men in the Tropics.*

Miss Margery Perham's biography of Lord Lugard has been published since this chapter was written. It gives vivid and valuable information on the part played by Lugard in Central and West Africa in the 'nineties and 1900's.

CHAPTER XV

P. 237. Lord Rosebery unveiled the memorial bust of Lord Salisbury in the Oxford University Union (Debating) Society on November 14, 1904.

P. 240. *The Vineyard.* The vine may have been grown on the slopes of the river Lea in Roman times. In any case a vineyard was planted here by the first Lord Salisbury in the time of King James I. According to Edward Hyams (*The Grape Vine in England*, p. 49), " Sir Robert Cecil, first Earl of Salisbury, planted a large vineyard on the banks of the River Lea, at Hatfield, the vines for which were obtained from France by Madame de la Boderie, wife of the French Ambassador."

Roman remains were found on the Hatfield estate in Lord Salisbury's day, among them a marble bath (or sarcophagus !), which Lady Salisbury had placed in her bedroom.

P. 246. *Lord Salisbury's refusal to receive Lord Rosebery on handing over the*

Foreign Office to him. See *Henry Ponsonby, His Life from his Letters,* by his son, Arthur Ponsonby, p. 276.

P. 246. *The extension of British rule.* The conviction that the best thing that could happen to the world would be to be governed by Britain was quite common in the 'nineties. Lord Curzon, then Mr. George Nathaniel Curzon and recently Lord Salisbury's Private Secretary, dedicated his book *The Problems of the Far East* "To those who believe that the British Empire is, under Providence, the greatest instrument for good that the world has seen ", and declared that " the best hope of salvation for the old and moribund in Asia, the wisest lessons for the emancipated and new, are still to be derived from the ascendancy of British character, and under the shelter, where so required, of British dominion " (*History of the Times,* Vol. III, p. 186).

Cecil Rhodes, in his first will (September 19, 1877), bequeathed the fortune which was still to be made to " the establishment, promotion and development of a Secret Society the aim and object whereof shall be the extension of British rule throughout the world. . . ."

P. 247. The two Houses of Parliament of those days live again in the pages of Sir Henry Lucy's *Peeps at Parliament* and his *Later Peeps at Parliament.*

P. 250. These opinions of Queen Victoria are based upon her own words. She wrote of Lord Salisbury's peculiarities in one of her letters (second series, II, p. 322) ; and Bishop Boyd-Carpenter (of Ripon) has left (in *Some Pages of my Life*) a full account of a conversation with the Queen in which he questioned her about her Prime Ministers. She was obviously somewhat unprepared to say much impromptu on the subject of their respective merits ; but she said decidedly that Disraeli was " not so great as the present Prime Minister " (Lord Salisbury) ; and the Bishop left her presence with the impression that " she gave him [Lord Salisbury], if not the highest, an equal place with the highest among her Prime Ministers ".

Bishop Boyd-Carpenter later—when Queen Victoria was dead and Lord Salisbury had retired—wrote an account of this conversation to Lord Salisbury at Hatfield. Lord Salisbury acknowledged it as " a most interesting letter to me ", and, without making any allusion to the Queen's estimate of himself, paid his own tribute to Her Majesty. " The late Queen ", he wrote, " was always most indulgent to me, both in hours of political difficulty—which in my long service under her were not infrequent—and also in the more trying periods of personal sorrow. [Lord Salisbury lost his wife in 1899.] She always displayed a sympathy, a consideration, and a wisdom which, if my life ran to ten times its probable span, I never could forget " (Bishop Boyd-Carpenter, *Some Pages of my Life,* pp. 235–7).

CHAPTER XVI

P. 251. *The premier statesman of Europe.* Eight years later, when the news of Lord Salisbury's death reached Paris, M. Hanotaux, French Foreign Minister and distinguished historian, who was by no means prejudiced in Lord Salisbury's favour, in conversation with the British ambassador, Sir Edmund Monson, called him " La tête dominante de l'Europe " (Monson to Lansdowne, August 23, 1903).

P. 252. " *A tremendous air about this wise old Statesman.*" Readers of

Mr. Churchill's books will recollect the vivid description, in *My Early Life*, of his meeting with Lord Salisbury when he was a young man of 24. The Prime Minister had read his book *The Malakand Field Force* and expressed a wish " to discuss some parts of it " with the author, the son of his erstwhile colleague, Lord Randolph. " I remember well ", writes Mr. Churchill, " the old world courtesy with which he met me at the door and with a charming gesture of welcome and salute conducted me to a seat on a small sofa in the midst of his vast room " (at the Foreign Office). At the end of their talk Lord Salisbury offered to " do anything which might be of assistance " to Churchill, saying that he " reminded him so much of his father ". There is no doubt, I think, that Lord Salisbury, though he never repented his dismissal of Lord Randolph, was sorry that he had brought so promising a career to a fatal conclusion, and he may have wished to show particular friendliness to his son, who moreover might be expected to be a valuable recruit to the Conservative Party.

P. 256. *The mood of imperialism in 1895.* It was symptomatic of the mood of the country that Keir Hardie, who had been elected the first Labour member of Parliament in 1892, was rejected at the General Election of 1895.

P. 258. In justice to the U.S Government it should be mentioned that the British minister's mode of life had given rise to much expostulation in American official society. Lord Salisbury eventually sent to take his place Sir Julian Pauncefote, who had worked under him at the Foreign Office and in whom he had the utmost confidence. In 1893 Lord Rosebery raised the Washington post to the rank of an embassy.

P. 261. *Mr. Pulitzer.* An account of Mr. Pulitzer's approach to the Prince of Wales, later King Edward VII, was given by Sir Sydney Lee in an article published in *The Times* of July 20, 1921.

P. 263. *The Anglo-American Draft Arbitration Treaty.* The origination of this treaty is claimed by both parties. See Woodrow Wilson, *History of the American People*, p. 248.

P. 265. *No record of Lord Salisbury's conversation.* The difficulty of following Lord Salisbury's dealings with Germany was stated by Sir Eyre Crowe as follows : " For the whole of Lord Salisbury's two [sic] Administrations our official records are sadly incomplete, all the most important business having been transacted under the cover of 'private' correspondence. . . . A methodical study of our relations with Germany during that interesting period is likely to remain for ever impossible."

The note was attached by Crowe to his masterly Memorandum of January 1, 1907, on " British Relations with France and Germany " (Gooch and Temperley, III, 409).

P. 268. *Splendid Isolation.* The phrase may have been used before this by Mr. Goschen, speaking from the Treasury Bench (see Lord Grey, *Twenty-Five Years*, Vol. I, p. 4). But Grey gives no date.

P. 270. *Cession of Wei-hai-wei.* About the same time as Britain was offered Wei-hai-wei the Chinese population of Formosa seem to have proposed that Britain should also take their island over.

P. 273. *Crete.* Crete remained titularly Turkish in 1897, but it was largely owing to the leadership of Lord Salisbury in the Concert of Europe that the island was placed first under the control of a board of European admirals and then under a Christian administrator, Prince George of Greece.

P. 274. *Lord Salisbury's proposal to Russia for a " partition of preponderance "*. The draft of the despatch of January 25, 1898, which is written throughout in Lord Salisbury's own hand, and marked across the top in red ink " Tel. copy of this to the Queen before it goes. S.", is as follows :

Sir N. O'Conor. Tel. No. 22, Jan. 25, 2 p.m.

Our idea was this. The two Empires of China and Turkey are so weak that in all important matters they are constantly guided by the advice of foreign powers. In giving this advice Russia and England are constantly exposed, neutralizing each other's efforts, much more frequently than the real antagonism of their interests would justify : and this condition of things is not likely to diminish, but to increase. It is to remove or lessen this evil that we have thought that an understanding with Russia might benefit both nations.

We contemplate no infraction of existing rights. We would not admit the violation of any existing treaties or impair the integrity of the present empires of either China or Turkey. These two conditions are vital. We aim at no partition of territory ; but only a partition of preponderance. It is evident that both in respect to Turkey and China there are portions [?—paper torn], which interest Russia much more than England and *vice versa*. Merely as an illustration, and binding myself to nothing, I would say that the portion of Turkey which drains into the Black Sea, or the sea as far as the beginning of the Egean sea, together with the drainage [of the] valley of the Euphrates as far as Bagdad, interest Russia much more than England : whereas Turkish Africa, Arabia and the valley of the Euphrates below Bagdad interest England much more than Russia. A similar distinction exists in China between the valley of the Hoangho with the territory north of it, and the valley of the Yangtse.

Would it be possible to arrange that where in regard to these territories our counsels differ, the Power least interested should give way to and assist the other. I do not disguise from myself that the difficulty would be great : is it insuperable ?

I have designedly omitted to deal with large tracts in each empire : because neither Power has shown any keen interest in them.

S.

This telegram was paraphrased, but without in any degree altering its meaning, and sent in cipher to Sir N. O'Conor.

Soon after he returned to office in 1895 Lord Salisbury had told Hatzfeldt that Britain had been wrong in refusing Tsar Nicholas's proposal for " partition " of the Turkish Empire in 1853. Constantinople (according to the Tsar) was not to belong to any great Power ; but the Balkan States would be under Russian protection, and " England could take Egypt and Crete ". These proposals however were not explicit and were never committed to paper by the Russian Government. See Seton Watson, *Britain in Europe*, pp. 305-7.

P. 276. *The deputation of Cabinet colleagues to Lord Salisbury*. During Lord Salisbury's illness Mr. Balfour was acting as Foreign Secretary, and George

Curzon, a regular fire-eater, was frequently attending Cabinet meetings in his capacity of Under-Secretary for Foreign Affairs.

Works Consulted

For a fuller account of Mr. Joseph Chamberlain's part in the events of this chapter J. L. Garvin's *Life of Joseph Chamberlain* should, of course, be consulted. Chamberlain had a hand in every large event, imperial, foreign and domestic, between 1895 and 1900.

Langer has a detailed account of the Jameson raid and its foreign implications in *The Diplomacy of Imperialism*, Vol. I, 1890–1902, and of the clash of European interests in the Far East in Vols. I and II. For the much disputed interview of the German Emperor and Lord Salisbury at Cowes in August, 1895, I have followed Langer and also Sir Valentine Chirol, who was as well-informed as anybody official or unofficial (see *Fifty Years in a Changing World*, pp. 289–91).

Lord Ronaldshay's *Life of Lord Curzon* (Vol. I) affords much interesting material on Lord Salisbury's management of foreign affairs from the point of view of his Parliamentary Under-Secretary.

CHAPTER XVII

Pp. 280–2. *The Paris Conversations*. I am indebted to the Quai d'Orsay for the official, and hitherto secret, accounts of Lord Salisbury's three conversations in Paris on March 26, 1897, which they have kindly made available to me. They will shortly be published among the official documents covering the events leading up to the First World War.

At the time *Le Temps* made the conversations the occasion for an impressive tribute to the British Prime Minister : " His mind is one of the most masculine, his understanding one of the broadest, his reason one of the clearest and most luminous of his country and his age." Written after meetings held when Lord Salisbury was in such poor health this appreciation of *Le Temps* deserves to be recorded.

Among the several topics that came up for discussion with MM. Hanotaux and de Courcel was the policy of Germany under the Kaiser. M. Hanotaux notes : " The Germans seem greatly to pre-occupy the Marquis of Salisbury. . . . The brusque moves of William II cause him an anxiety which he did not hide from me. ' There is the dark cloud,' he said to me." And later when Baron de Courcel spoke reassuringly of the personal charm and intelligence of the young emperor Lord Salisbury only said, " He is very dangerous."

P. 282. It is curious that in the two conversations between Lord Salisbury and M. Hanotaux no mention was made of possible complications on the Upper Nile. How vividly that possibility was in the mind of the French Foreign Minister was proved by his conversation in Paris one month earlier with Mr. Wickham Steed, then Correspondent of *The Times* in Rome (and later its Editor). M. Hanotaux " descanted threateningly upon the dangers of any further British advance against the Mahdists. He assured me that French influence in Abyssinia was supreme . . . and that Colonel Marchand would assuredly link up with the Abyssinians, and so strengthen the position of France on the Upper Nile as to enable her to throttle Egypt should England continue to ignore French remonstrances " (*Through Thirty Years*, Vol. I, p. 106).

P. 284. *Lord Salisbury's secret instructions to Generals Kitchener, Hunter and Rundle*. The mysterious precautions of Lord Salisbury were related to me by General Sir Archibald Hunter during the last weekend of July, 1927, when we were both the guests of Mr. Mark Fenwick in Gloucestershire, and written down by me immediately afterwards. The General concluded his narrative by exclaiming : " I don't know why the old boy did it in that way."

By the time he wrote these secret instructions Lord Salisbury can have had no doubt about Marchand's objective. During the discussion of the French Africa vote in the French Parliament in March, 1897, a well-informed Senator, M. Richard Waddington (brother of the former ambassador in London), said in one part of his speech, " Captain Marchand and M. Gentil are engaged in travelling through the region " (of Upper Ubanghi) ; and in another " our national flag is flying, so to speak, and perhaps at the present moment in actual fact, on the banks of the Nile ". Monson reported these passages at once. (Monson to Secretary of State, March 19, 1897.) This was just before Lord Salisbury's visit to Hanotaux, and may have been his reason for making it.

P. 288. *Lord Salisbury's return from Schlucht*. Sir Harry Luke (who had a distinguished career in the Colonial Service) told me how well he remembered the one occasion on which he saw Lord Salisbury—just about this time (late summer 1898) when he (Sir Harry, then still a schoolboy) returned from France on the same Channel steamer as the Prime Minister. The weather was bad, windy and wet, the sea rough—but Lord Salisbury was standing forward, aloof, a monolith on a deserted deck, gazing towards the English coast. Sir Harry described him as " a very Tennysonian figure wearing a cloak and a floppy hat ".

P. 288. " *By right of conquest.*" Discussing in 1863 motives and circumstances of the partitions of Poland (*Quarterly Review*, April, 1863) Lord Robert Cecil, as he then was, wrote : " Whatever they may think as to the abstract morality of conquest in general, mankind have agreed to admit that its guilt differs widely in degree according to the motive by which it has been urged, or, rather, according to the secondary motives by which the one prevailing impulse—the greed of empire—has been qualified. Lowest in the ethical scale stand the conquests which have been undertaken for mere conquest's sake. Such enterprises, for instance, as the seizure of Silesia by Frederick, or of Alsace by Louis XIV, without a vestige of a claim, or a pretence of sympathy, or of resentment, or of necessity, to cloak the wrong, must be held to consign the culprit to the lowest gulf in the Conqueror's circle of the Inferno. A somewhat paler tinge of guilt may be assigned to those who, like Napoleon, were forced to aggression by the imperious ambition of their subjects, and, in effect, conquered that they themselves might exist. . . . Lighter still is the responsibility of Powers who have conquered large territories in the course of efforts to repel unjust and unprovoked aggression. Some such plea may be advanced in extenuation of most—we wish we could say of all—of the acquisitions that England has made in India. But the motives which are the least guilty of all . . . are those which rest either upon an ancient claim to the territory attacked, or a sympathy, dictated by a community of race or of religion, for the suffering of its inhabitants. Of such a character were the conquests of Calais by the French, of Granada by the Spaniards, and in our own times of Milan by the Italians."

P. 289. *The promise to evacuate Egypt.* Lord Salisbury's case was that actual circumstances did not allow Great Britain to fulfil undertakings given in wholly different circumstances. The promised evacuation therefore was " postponed to an undetermined date, if indeed evacuation was foreseen as possible at all ".

P. 293. " *Lord Salisbury had his ultimatum ready.*" Wilfrid Blunt records (*My Diaries*, Vol. II, pp. 127–8) that a friend of Sir E. Monson confirmed to him that Lord Salisbury had drawn up an ultimatum, and instructed Monson to deliver it. Monson gave Delcassé warning of it confidentially through a mutual friend, and indicated a signal that he would give to Delcassé (" hand in breast pocket "), when he was due to present it. Delcassé took the hint, and gave way before the ultimatum was actually delivered.

I find no record of this ultimatum, but that does not disprove the story. Lord Salisbury always preferred to let the other party know when his limit had been reached. To hint at an ultimatum—no bluff, for he was prepared to have it presented—was one of his methods of gaining his ends without a war and without humiliation for the other party. Compare his treatment of Portugal in 1890 (Chapter XIV).

P. 295. *Fashoda renamed Kodok.* A curious commentary on this act of courtesy to France was the attitude of Marchand himself. He much re-gretted the suppression of the original name. The hero of Fashoda—for so he was always regarded by the French—lived to fight by the side of British troops in the 1914–18 War. Afterwards he used on occasions to be one of the French representatives at League of Nations meetings in Geneva ; and on a return journey to Paris from one of these he expressed to my friend Mr. Tracy Phillips his keen regret at the " disappearance " of Fashoda. " The bitter-ness is past," he said. " It was a historic episode *which should not be forgotten.*" That this is also the view of the municipalities of Paris is proved by the naming of a street in the 16th arrondissement " Rue de la Mission Marchand " ; and the suburb of Courbevoie has its " Boulevard de la Mission Marchand ".

Works Consulted and Not Mentioned in the Text

Lord Grey of Fallodon, *Twenty-Five Years*, Vol. I.
Sir J. Rennell Rodd, *Social and Diplomatic Memories*, Vol. II.
Lord Cromer, *Modern Egypt.*
Lemonon, *L'Europe et la politique Britannique, 1882–1911.*
Seton-Watson, *Britain in Europe.*
British Official Bluebooks.

CHAPTER XVIII

P. 301. *Old Age Pensions.* Mr. Lloyd George described Joseph Chamber-lain as " the statesman who on the whole has done more to popularize the question of Old Age Pensions in this country than anyone else " (House of Commons, June 15, 1908).

Between 1892 and 1904 the Liberal-Unionists and Conservatives tabled many Bills dealing with " Old Age Provident Pensions " which never reached the Statute Book.

P. 302. *" Preferments in the Church."* " When Lord Salisbury offered the Rev. Cosmo Gordon Lang, then Vicar of Portsea, the Suffragan Bishopric of Stepney, he as usual wrote and addressed the letter in his own hand. He made a mistake in the address, so the letter was never delivered ; and Lang was surprised to receive, a few days after the letter had been written, a telegram from Lord Salisbury's Private Secretary : ' Announcement of your appointment will be in the Press on Monday '. " (Lockhart, *Cosmo Gordon Lang*, p. 127).

P. 302. *Alfred Austin as Poet Laureate.* According to Sir Algernon West, Mr. Gladstone's personal adviser and erstwhile Private Secretary, Lord Salisbury, when asked why he had given the post to Austin, replied : " For the best possible reason, because he wanted it."

Among the names considered and rejected by Mr. Gladstone had been Swinburne, Bridges, Lewis Morris, Frederick Locker and Ruskin (West, *Private Diaries*, p. 65).

CHAPTER XIX

P. 312. *Mafeking relieved.* The excitement in the country over the relief of Mafeking was so great that even Lord Salisbury had to take part in the rejoicing. When the news was announced the people of Hatfield made so imposing a demonstration before Hatfield House that he felt constrained to go out to them and make a short speech from the North steps. He had to repeat the performance some months later when his soldier son, Lord Edward Cecil, returned from the front. Lord Edward had been through the siege and when he returned from Africa he was escorted from the station to the house by a large, enthusiastic crowd.

Works Consulted

Mrs. Dugdale, *(Life of) Arthur James Balfour.*
Lord Grey of Fallodon, *Twenty-Five Years.*
Lord Hardinge of Penshurst, *Old Diplomacy.*
Lord Newton, *Lord Lansdowne.*
Langer, *The Diplomacy of Imperialism*, Vol. II.
H. Wickham Steed, *Through Thirty Years.*
G. P. Gooch, *Studies in German History.*
H. M. Hyndman, *The Record of an Adventurous Life.*
Jack Jones, *The Man David* (Lloyd George).

CHAPTER XX

P. 329. *Mutual devotion of Lord Salisbury and Queen Victoria.* In a private letter to me Lord Cecil of Chelwood wrote (January, 1951) : " I suppose the chief interests of his [Lord Salisbury's] life ended with the deaths of his wife and the Queen."

But his devotion did not prevent Lord Salisbury from taking a line against her wishes on occasions. For instance, in September, 1900, Queen Victoria very much wanted her son the Duke of Connaught to succeed Wolseley as Commander-in-Chief. Lord Salisbury, backed by Lansdowne, insisted on Roberts having the post. Queen Victoria then opposed Lord Salisbury's proposal that Kitchener should be Commander-in-Chief for India, upon which Lord Salisbury wrote to Lansdowne : " This is her *riposte* to my objection to Connaught ! " Kitchener was still in South Africa and it was only two years later that he had finished his job there. That the question of his appointment to India should have been raised in 1900 shows how little those in authority expected the Boer resistance to be continued until 1902.

P. 329. *The " Hotel Cecil "*. Lord Salisbury's eldest son, Lord Cranborne, was Under-Secretary for Foreign Affairs, his nephew Arthur Balfour, First Lord of the Treasury, his other nephew Gerald Balfour, President of the Board 'of Trade, his son-in-law, Lord Selborne, First Lord of the Admiralty.

P. 335. *Lord Salisbury understood better than Chamberlain the underlying hostility of Germans to England's great position in the world.* In his famous speech at Leicester on December 1, 1899, Chamberlain had said : " The natural alliance is between ourselves and the Great German Empire (*loud cheers*). I may point out to you that at bottom the character of the Teutonic race differs very slightly indeed from the character of the Anglo-Saxon (*cheers*). "

" He [Joseph Chamberlain] was singularly unsuspicious," is Mr. Garvin's comment.

P. 336. *Lord Lansdowne's doubts of German good faith.* I had several conversations with Lord Lansdowne in his last years, and in the course of one of them I asked him why he had finally given up trying to reach agreement with Germany. He answered me :

" It was something to do with Manchuria. I found I couldn't trust them." An explanation of this unexpected reply can be found in Bertie's Memorandum of November 9, 1901 ; and there are references to it in Lansdowne's own despatch of April 7 and Memorandum of November 11.

P. 340. *Lord Salisbury's preference for " natural development " rather than " legislative action "* : We may compare the preference of a later British statesman for the " natural development " of a European Parliament. At Strasbourg on August 11, 1950, Mr. Churchill argued that the Consultative Assembly was not a machine but a " living plant " ; and in another passage he said : " I have always thought that the progress of building up a European Parliament must be gradual, and roll forward on a tide of facts, rather than by elaborate constitution-making."

P. 343. *The immediate cause of Lord Salisbury's resignation.* Legge's evidence points to Sir Thomas Lipton as the man whose name Lord Salisbury would on no account include in the list of new peerages. His refusal to comply with his Sovereign's command—for that is what it amounted to—would itself appear to Lord Salisbury to be a reason for retiring from King Edward's service.

P. 346. *The finite could not comprehend the infinite.* Lord Cecil of Chelwood wrote to me (in January, 1951) : " I am sure you are right in treating as fundamental my father's conviction that in dealing with the Infinite the Finite minds of men are powerless and I can recall sayings and opinions of his which are only consistent with this view."

NOTES: CHAPTER XX–EPILOGUE

Works Consulted

G. P. Gooch, in *British Documents* (Gooch and Temperley) and *Studies in German History.*

J. A. Spender, *Fifty Years of Europe.*

Langer, *The Diplomacy of Imperialism,* Vol. II.

Lord Newton, *Lord Lansdowne.*

Lord Hardinge of Penshurst, *Old Diplomacy.*

Sir Sidney Lee, *King Edward VII,* Vol. II.

Baron von Eckardstein, *Ten Years at the Court of St. James's.*

Lady Victoria Hicks-Beach, *Life of Sir Michael Hicks-Beach,* Vol. II.

Julian Amery, *The Life of Joseph Chamberlain,* Vol. IV.

EPILOGUE

P. 352. *" Honour " as the guide in international affairs.* In connexion with Lord Salisbury's use of the word " honour " in international affairs, the reflexions of a modern master of statecraft may be read in comparison. Mr. Winston Churchill writes in the first volume of his *Second World War,* pp. 250–1 : " There is however one helpful guide, namely, for a nation to keep its word and to act in accordance with its treaty obligations. This guide is called honour." He then goes on to admit that it is baffling that what men call honour does not always correspond to Christian ethics. Some of this passage has already been quoted on pp. 81–2 ; but the whole of the four paragraphs should be read consecutively.

P. 358. *Lord Salisbury's greatness.* When Lord Salisbury died, Wilfrid Scawen Blunt, who was anti-Imperialist, an opponent of Lord Salisbury's policies, and by nature more disposed to belittle than to praise, made the following entry in his Diary :

" August 31, 1903. He [Lord Salisbury] has been certainly in his way a great man, and without much pomp or parade one who has achieved great things. People only half recognize these things as yet because he has never talked much about them, but they are very real and will some day be recognized for what they are ; not that I am in sympathy with his doings, only in the manner of their doing. By far the largest of his achievements has been the partition of Africa. This was imagined in secret and developed silently . . . The reconquest of the Sudan was a policy wholly Lord Salisbury's. . . . At the Foreign Office he re-established in large measure England's influence on the Continent.

"He rehabilitated the Monarchy and resurrected the House of Lords. He was head and shoulders taller as a statesman than the other statesmen of his day, including Gladstone and Disraeli ; I mean judged by results."

(*My Diaries :* Vol. II, p. 69.)

BIBLIOGRAPHY

Existing biographies of Lord Salisbury are :

Lady Gwendolen Cecil : *Life of Robert Marquis of Salisbury (1830–1892)*.

H. D. Traill : *The Marquis of Salisbury* in the series " The Queen's Prime Ministers ", 1891.

F. S. Pulling : *Life and Speeches of the Marquis of Salisbury*, 2 vols., 1885.

F. D. How : *The Marquis of Salisbury 1902*. (Notable for contemporary illustrations and cartoons.)

S. H. Jeyes : *The Life and Times of the Marquis of Salisbury*, 4 vols., 1895. (Very discursive and profusely illustrated.)

Arthur Mee : *Lord Salisbury 1901*. (Very eulogistic.)

Edward Salmon : *Lord Salisbury 1901*. (A brief study designed to show that Lord Salisbury was more progressive in home politics than he was generally reputed to be.)

All works dealing in detail with English and European events during the second half of last century contain allusions to Lord Salisbury, as do almost all the political Memoirs written of the same period. For the books on Europe a useful list has been complied by Alan Bullock and A. J. P. Taylor under the title, " Select List of Books on European History 1815–1914 ". The Memoirs I have used are noted chapter by chapter.

Of the general works on Britain's diplomatic relations with European countries I have relied mainly on :

Seton-Watson : *Britain in Europe*.

Langer : *The Diplomacy of Imperialism*, 2 vols. (First Edition).

R. C. K. Ensor : *Oxford History of England*, Vol. XIV.

I have had the advantage of not having to begin the writing of this book until the Foreign Office documents of 1887 to 1902 were made available for public research.

If complete biographies of Lord Salisbury are singularly lacking, the articles, essays and studies are without number, beginning with the contribution to the now extinct *Monthly Review* which his son, then Lord Robert Cecil (Lord Cecil of Chelwood), made anonymously soon after his father's death, and the excellent sketch by G. W. E. Russell in *Prime Ministers and Some Others*, down to the quite recent chapter " Lord Salisbury " in A. J. P. Taylor's *From Napoleon to Stalin* and the thoughtful short study by A. P. Ryan in *History Today* for April, 1951. Studies of the archivist-historian type are those of

Professor Lilian Penson in " The Principles and Methods of Lord Salisbury's Foreign Policy " and " The New Course in British Foreign Policy (1892–1902) ", being addresses published respectively in the *Cambridge Historical Journal*, Vol. 5 (1935), and in *Transactions of the Royal Historical Society*, Series IV, Vol. XXV (1943). Brilliant as these studies are, I would venture the criticism that no analysis of Lord Salisbury's policies can have full value which does not assess the man as well as the statesman. Sir John Tilley and Sir Stephen Gaselee's *History of the Foreign Office* contains some information about Lord Salisbury's methods—or lack of method—in the Foreign Office and recounts some amusing anecdotes. Much that is interesting about his uncle will be found in Lord (A. J.) Balfour's fragment of Autobiography.

I have tried as far as possible to base my judgment of Lord Salisbury's actions on contemporary evidence and views rather than on the wisdom of those who judged him after the event. I have for that reason delved deep into contemporary accounts of his doings, especially into the back numbers of that day-by-day history of the world, *The Times*. In that way one is able to see the problem much as it must have appeared to Lord Salisbury at the time and not as it appears to those who know what has happened since.

In conclusion I have had to bear in mind that Lord Salisbury did much of his business orally both in home and foreign affairs, and that of the greater number of these conversations no record whatever remains.* His refusal to set down on paper the gist of talks even with foreign ambassadors was partly deliberate, partly due to press of business, and partly, so I have been assured by one who started his career at the Foreign Office under him, the result of " pure idleness ". In any case this habit gives special importance to such conversations as have been authentically handed down. An instance is that of his remarks to his daughter Lady Gwendolen, recorded in one of her private memoranda (and related near the end of Chapter XVI of this book), which throws more light on her father's attitude to France and Russia in 1898 than any official despatch or memorandum which I have been able to discover.

P.S. Mr. Algernon Cecil's *Queen Victoria and her Prime Ministers* was published after my book was in the hands of the printers.

* See particularly Sir Eyre Crowe's note already quoted on p. 387.

INDEX

INDEX

INDEX